Digital Image Processing

with Application to Digital Cinema

By

K. S. Thyagarajan

160201

ELSEVIER

AMSTERDAM • BOSTON • HEIDELBERG • LONDON
NEW YORK • OXFORD • PARIS • SAN DIEGO
SAN FRANCISCO • SINGAPORE • SYDNEY • TOKYO

Focal Press is an imprint of Elsevier

Focal Press

Acquisitions Editor Angelina Ward
Project Manager Paul Gottehrer
Assistant Editor Rachel Epstein
Marketing Manager Christine Veroulis
Cover Design Cate Barr
Interior Design Julio Esperas

Focal Press is an imprint of Elsevier
30 Corporate Drive, Suite 400, Burlington, MA 01803, USA
Linacre House, Jordan Hill, Oxford OX2 8DP, UK

Recognizing the importance of preserving what has been written, Elsevier prints its books on acid-free paper whenever possible.

Library of Congress Cataloging-in-Publication Data
Application submitted

British Library Cataloguing-in-Publication Data
A catalogue record for this book is available from the British Library.

ISBN 13: 978-0-240-80729-4
ISBN 10: 0-240-80729-4

For information on all Focal Press publications visit our website at www.books.elsevier.com

05   06   07   08   09   10   10 9 8 7 6 5 4 3 2 1

Printed in Canada

In memory of my beloved parents.

"Because when there is duality, as it were, then one smells something, one **sees** something, one hears something, one speaks something, one thinks something, one knows something. (But) when to the knower of Brahman everything has become the Self, then what should one smell and through what, what should one **see** and through what, what should one hear and through what, what should one speak and through what, what should one think and through what, what should one know and through what? Through what should one know That owing to which all this is known—through what, O Maitreyī, should one know the Knower?"

Verse II.iv.14 from the Bṛhadāraṇyaka Upanishad

Contents

Foreword   xv

Preface   xvii

Acknowledgments   xxi

1   Introduction   1

1.1   **Background** 1

1.2   **Enhancement** 1

1.3   **Compression** 4

1.4   **Restoration** 6

1.5   **Computed Tomography** 8

1.6   **Image Analysis** 8

1.7   **Summary** 11

       References 11

2   Two-Dimensional Signals, Systems, and Discrete Fourier Transform   13

2.1   **Two-Dimensional Discrete Signals** 13

2.2   **Two-Dimensional Discrete Systems** 15

     2.2.1   Linear Systems 15

     2.2.2   Space Invarient Systems 16

     2.2.3   System Response via 2-D Convolution 16

     2.2.4   Causal and Stable Systems 17

2.3   **Two-Dimensional Discrete Fourier Transform**   17

2.4   **Frequency Response**   19

2.5   **Two-Dimensional Filtering**   23

2.6   **FIR Filter Design**   27

    2.6.1   Separable FIR Filters   27
        2.6.1.1   Window-Based Methods   27
        2.6.1.2   Frequency Sampling Technique   39
        2.6.1.3   Optimal Design Techniques   40
    2.6.2   Nonseparable FIR Filters   41

2.7   **Summary**   44
    References   44

3   Human Visual Perception   47

3.1   **Introduction**   47

3.2   **Brightness Perception**   47

    3.2.1   Intensity, Luminance, and Brightness   47
    3.2.2   Simultaneous Contrast   50
    3.2.3   Mach Bands   52
    3.2.4   Transfer Function of the HVS   54
    3.2.5   Monochrome Vision Model   55
    3.2.6   Visual Masking and an Improved HVS Model   57

3.3   **Color Perception**   59

    3.3.1   Color-Matching Functions   61
    3.3.2   Color Coordinate Systems   63
        3.3.2.1   CIE XYZ Primaries   64
        3.3.2.2   NTSC Receiver and Transmission Primaries   66
    3.3.3   HVS Model for Color Vision   69
    3.3.4   Opponent Color Model   70

3.4   **Summary**   70
    References   71

4   Image Acquisition   73

4.1   **Introduction**   73

4.2   **Image Sensors**   73

    4.2.1   CCD Sensors   74

4.2.1.1 Full-Frame Architecture   76
4.2.1.2 Interline Architecture   76
4.2.1.3 Frame-Transfer CCD   77
4.2.2 CMOS Sensors   79
4.2.3 Color Sensors   79

4.3 **Image Sampling**   82

4.4 **Image Quantization**   87
4.4.1 Uniform Quantization   87
4.4.2 Optimal Quantization   88

4.5 **Image Scanning**   90
4.5.1 Interlaced and Progressive Scanning   90
4.5.2 Color Image Scanning   91
4.5.3 Color Encoding in Digital Video   91

4.6 **Film-to-Digital Conversion**   93

4.7 **Summary**   94
References   95

5   Image Inhancement   97

5.1 **Background**   97

5.2 **Point Processing**   97
5.2.1 Logarithmic Transformation   98
5.2.2 Contrast Stretching   98
5.2.3 Histogram Modification   101
5.2.3.1 Histogram Equalization   101
5.2.3.2 Adaptive Histogram Modification   104

5.3 **Neighborhood Processing**   104
5.3.1 Simple Mask Operations   106
5.3.2 Two-Dimensional Filters Satisfying Specified Frequency
Responses   109
5.3.3 Median Filtering   111

5.4 **Color Image Enhancement**   117

5.5 **Summary**   120
References   121

6   Discrete Transforms for Image Processing   **123**

6.1   **Introduction**   123

6.2   **Unitary Transforms**   123

    6.2.1   One-Dimensional Unitary Transforms   123
       6.2.1.1   One-Dimensional DFT   124
       6.2.1.2   One-Dimensional Discrete Cosine Transform (DCT)   125
       6.2.1.3   One-Dimensional Discrete Sine Transform (DST)   126
       6.2.1.4   One-Dimensional Discrete Hartley Transform   127
       6.2.1.5   Hadamard, Haar, and Slant Transforms   128
    6.2.2   Two-Dimensional Discrete Transforms   133
    6.2.3   Some Properties of Unitary Transform   137

6.3   **Karhunen-Loeve Transform**   140

6.4   **Choice of a Transform**   144

6.5   **Summary**   144

    References   144

7   Wavelet Transform   **147**

7.1   **Introduction**   147

7.2   **Continuous Wavelet Transform**   149

7.3   **The Wavelet Series**   151

7.4   **Discrete Wavelet Transform**   160

7.5   **Implementation of the Discrete Wavelet Transform**   160

7.6   **Relationship of Scaling and Wavelet Filters to Wavelets**   164

    7.6.1   Orthogonal Discrete Wavelet Transform   166
    7.6.2   Biorthogonal Discrete Wavelet Transform   168
    7.6.3   Construction of Wavelets   171

7.7   **Two-Dimensional Discrete Wavelet Transform**   171

7.8   **Summary**   189

    References   189

8   Image Compression   **193**

8.1   **Introduction**   193

    8.1.1   Image Fidelity Criterion   197

8.1.1.1   Quantitative Measures   197

8.1.1.2   Subjective Measures   198

8.2   **Lossless Compression**   199

8.2.1   Elements of Information Theory   199

8.2.2   Huffman Coding   202

8.2.3   Run-Length Coding   205

8.2.4   Arithmetic Coding   206

8.2.5   Golomb–Rice (GR) Coding   208

8.3   **Predictive Coding**   212

8.3.1   One-Dimensional DPCM   212

8.3.2   Adaptive DPCM   215

8.3.3   Two-Dimensional DPCM   218

8.4   **Transform Coding**   218

8.4.1   Choice of a Transform   220

8.4.2   Optimal Bit Allocation   220

8.4.3   Quantizer Design   222

8.4.4   Entropy Coder   226

8.4.5   Variable Block Size DCT Coder   230

8.5   **Compression in the Wavelet Domain**   231

8.5.1   Choice of Wavelets   232

8.5.2   Quantization   234

8.5.3   Zero-Tree Wavelet Coding   234

8.5.4   JPEG2000 Standard   244

8.6   **Video Coding Principles**   255

8.6.1   Temporal Prediction in the Pixel Domain   256

8.6.1.1   Motion Estimation   256

8.6.2   Wavelet-Based Interframe Coding   259

8.6.3   Interframe Coding Using Three-Dimensional DCT   260

8.6.3.1   Temporal Depth   261

8.6.3.2   Three-Dimensional DCT   261

8.6.3.3   Quantization   262

8.6.3.4   Zigzag Scanning   263

8.6.3.5   Entropy Coding   263

8.6.4   Role of Human Visual Perception in Image and Video Coding   263

8.6.4.1   Quantization Matrix for DCT Domain Coding   263

8.6.4.2   Quantization Matrix for Wavelet Domain Coding   265

8.6.4.3   Use of Spatial and Temporal Masking Models   266

8.6.5   MPEG Standard   270

8.7 **Summary** 278

References 280

9 **Application of Image Compression to Digital Cinema** **285**

9.1 **Introduction** 285

9.2 **Digital Cinema Technology Requirements** 285

9.2.1 Image Resolution and Format 285

9.2.2 Digital Projector 286

9.2.3 Image Compression System 287

9.3 **Case Study** 289

9.3.1 QUALCOMM's Digital Cinema System 289

9.3.1.1 Adaptive Block-Size DCT Encoder 290

9.3.1.2 ABSDCT Decoder 292

9.3.1.3 QUALCOMM's Decoder ASIC 292

9.3.2 Digital Cinema Using Motion JPEG2000 Standard 295

9.3.2.1 MJ2K Image Resolution and Format 295

9.3.2.2 Compression in the Wavelet Domain 295

9.3.2.3 MJ2K File Format 295

9.3.2.4 Error Resilience 296

9.4 **Concluding Remarks** 297

References 298

Appendices

A **Continuous and Discrete Fourier Transforms** **301**

A.1 **Continuous Fourier Transform** 301

A.1.1 Properties of Continuous Fourier Transform 302

A.2 **Discrete Fourier Transform** 303

B **Radiometric and Photometric Quantities** **305**

B.1 Radiometric Quantities 305

B.1.1 Radiant Energy 305

B.1.2 Radiant Flux 305

B.1.3 Radiant Exitance 305
B.1.4 Irradiance 305
B.1.5 Radiant Intensity 306
B.1.6 Radiance 306

B.2 **Photometric Quantities** 306

B.2.1 Luminous Flux 306
B.2.2 Lumens 307
B.2.3 Luminous Intensity 307
B2.4. Luminance 307
B2.5 Illumanation 308

C   MATLAB M Files for Selected Chapters   309

C.1 **M Files from Chapter 2** 309

C.2 **M Files from Chapter 3** 313

C.3 **M Files from Chapter 4** 317

C.4 **M Files from Chapter 5** 318

C.5 **M Files from Chapter 6** 331

C.6 **M Files from Chapter 7** 340

C.7 **M Files from Chapter 8** 346

D   Suggested MATLAB-Oriented Projects   367

D.1 **Projects in Chapter 2** 367

D.1.1 Effect of Filtering an Image 367
D.1.2 Nonlinear Filtering 367
D.1.3 Phase Distortion 367

D.2 **Projects in Chapter 3** 368

D.2.1 Contrast Sensitivity 368
D.2.2 Spatial Masking Effect 368
D.2.3 Color Sensitivity 368

D.3 **Projects in Chapter 5** 368

D.3.1 Adaptive Histogram Equalization 368
D.3.2 Noise Cleaning 369
D.3.3 Color Image Enhancement 369

D.4   **Projects in Chapter 8**   369

   D.4.1   DPCM   369
   D.4.2   DPCM Using GR Coding   369
   D.4.3   Transform Coder   369
   D.4.4   Transform Coder for Color Images   370
   D.4.5   Encoder Using Discrete Wavelet Transform   370
   D.4.6   DWT Encoder for Color Image Compression   370
   D.4.7   Motion Estimation   370

Index   371

Foreword

K.S. Thyagarajan has produced a comprehensive treatment of digital image processing of considerable value for most of the current applications of interest involving both still and video acquisition, storage, and transmission. He presents and elucidates the principal algorithms and techniques, many of which have developed and evolved considerably since the publication of previous texts on this subject well over a decade ago.

After an introductory chapter followed by a tutorial chapter on two-dimensional digital filtering, three more chapters are devoted successively to the physiology of visual perception, image acquisition, and image enhancement. The rest of the book deals with the main topic of processing for compression and transmission. This includes chapters on spectral transforms as well as wavelets, and lossy and lossless compression coding, including JPEG and MPEG standards. The final chapter gives important details of particular digital cinema systems, partly drawn from the author's own experience.

As a leader in digital image processing research and development at Qualcomm, Incorporated, Dr. Thyagarajan brings a unique perspective based on extensive involvement in a highly complex field which has gone through a recent major evolution and has reached a level of maturity which warrants a thorough exposition. Consequently, this book is certain to become a standard reference for a wide population of technologists and scientists who depend on digital images in the exercise of their professions.

Andrew J. Viterbi
November 2005

Preface

Digital image processing is a matured field but continues to advance due to the availability of super fast PCs and fairly inexpensive memory devices. The rapid growth in the use of multimedia over wireless and Internet highways has paved the way for highly efficient image and video compression systems. Medical imaging is another field that prompts the use of scientific image sensors of high dynamic range along with innovative processing algorithms. With the advancement of both sensor and display technologies and other transmission media, time has come to deploy high quality, efficient, compression and distribution techniques for the digital delivery of movies to theaters.

This book grew out of the author's class notes on digital signal and image processing courses taught at San Diego State University as well as his industrial experience. The book aims predominantly at the working professionals in the field of digital imaging. However, the book is also suitable for senior undergraduate and first year graduate students in electrical engineering, supplemented with some additional materials. Derivations are kept to a minimum so as not to lose sight of the main theme. Numerous examples are provided to illustrate various digital processes as well as their effects on the processes. MATLAB tools are used throughout to generate all the figures, tables, and images. Two chapters receive greater emphasis, which are hard to find in standard textbooks. The chapter on human visual perception emphasizes the importance of not only the familiar spatial and temporal visual phenomena such as contrast sensitivity but also the spatial and temporal masking effects through the use of a more refined nonlinear model. These models are useful in image and video compression. The chapter on image compression is fairly extensive though not exhaustive and includes spatial, transform, and wavelet domain algorithms in greater detail. Compression based on wavelet transform includes zero-tree embedded coding, which is fairly a recent concept. A separate section is devoted to the use of human vision model in the compression process.

Though there are numerous applications of digital image processing techniques, this book aims at one particular but recent application, namely the digital cinema. Currently digital projectors with very high contrast ratios are available in the market and are highly suitable for projecting feature movies in theaters. Image and video compression techniques have advanced to such a level wherein near lossless visual quality is practical. Thus it is appropriate to put together various compression, security, and projection technologies to design a digital cinema system. Case studies include Qualcomm's adaptive block size DCT-based digital cinema system and a system based on Motion JPEG2000 with MPEG4-based file format.

As the field of digital image processing is vast, the author decided not to include topics related to computer vision. Computer vision in itself is worth a whole book to cover. However, basic edge detection methods are included in the introductory chapter, which is hoped to motivate earnest readers to go further into computer vision.

BOOK ORGANIZATION

Salient features of some of the chapters are as follows:

Chapter 1 introduces the readers to a plethora of digital processing techniques by way of examples and brief descriptions. Chapter 2 is more of a review of two-dimensional discrete signals and systems. Keeping in mind the target audience, mathematical derivations are omitted. But it is unavoidable to introduce some mathematical preliminaries at the earlier part of the book. However, impatient readers may skip Chapter 2 without losing sight of the various processing techniques to be introduced later.

Chapter 3 describes the human visual perception from a system's point of view. Human vision plays a key role in the design of image and video compression and display systems. Therefore, the chapter describes vision models in detail, in particular the model that predicts masking effects in digital imaging.

Discrete wavelet transform is introduced in Chapter 7. Without derivations and proof, the computation of the DWT using the familiar subband coding scheme is described and illustrated with examples. The chapter also explains the connection between wavelets and quadrature mirror filters and shows how to compute a wavelet function from the analysis and synthesis filters with examples.

Chapter 8 is devoted to the discussion on image and video compression techniques. This rather lengthy chapter develops various ideas involved in both transform- and wavelet-based methods. Under wavelet-based compression, new compression tools such as zero-tree embedded coder are described. It also describes the basic ideas used in JPEG2000 and MPEG2 standards. MPEG2 standard is not discussed in length since the case studies considered don't require MPEG2.

Chapter 9 pertains to the case study of digital cinema system. More specifically, two case studies are covered. One is Qualcomm's ABSDCT-based digital cinema system and the other based on Motion JPEG2000 standard. These two systems are very interesting because the former uses DCT as the compression vehicle while the latter uses DWT for compression. This chapter also includes some characteristics of digital projectors.

NOTE TO THE PROFESSIONALS

Those who find Chapter 2 to be hard to grasp can skip it and continue with the rest of the book without losing sight of the main concepts. The intent to include this chapter was to make the book more complete. For those serious-minded readers, it may be beneficial to brush up on basic digital signal processing definitions and terminologies to get a good grasp of the subject matter. As an incentive to an apt reader, some possible projects are listed in one of the appendices. They may, in fact, be more suitable to students. All these projects are solvable through MATLAB tools. Another appendix lists MATLAB M files that generate the various figures and tables in the book. Perhaps, these M files could be used as templates to carry out the listed projects.

NOTE TO THE INSTRUCTORS

The book is suitable for one semester senior undergraduate and first-year graduate students or selected topics for one quarter. No exercises are given at the end of the chapters. Therefore the instructor should supplement lectures with some problems to be solved. The MATLAB projects could serve as term projects.

K.S. Thyagarajan
October 2005

Acknowledgments

I would like to thank the following people who have influenced the writing of this book.

My sincere and special thanks to Dr. Andrew J. Viterbi for writing the Foreword for this book. This book would not have been possible without the experience I gained under his guidance, support and encouragement at QUALCOMM.

My sincere thanks to Steve A. Morley of QUALCOMM with whom I had the opportunity to work in developing video compression technology for digital cinema. His initial review of the book and his feedback on Chapter 9 were extremely helpful. His support throughout the writing of this book is deeply appreciated.

I have collaborated with Dr. Kesh Bakhru of Cubic Corp. on many projects and proposal writings in the area of digital signal and image processing. He has been my mentor and a great friend throughout my career in San Diego. I wish to offer my heartfelt thanks to him for his initial review of the book and his encouragement.

I also wish to thank my former colleagues at San Diego State University: Dr. Leonard Marino who was always willing to be the co-chair for my graduate students' theses, Fred Harris for his continued support towards my professional growth, and Dr. Huseyin Abut with whom I have worked in many research projects, including the one where I got introduced to image processing. I also wish to thank all my students, whose feedback helped me improve my knowledge.

My very special thanks to Arjun Jain, VP, Micro USA for giving me encouragement and support throughout the course of writing this book.

I am very grateful to Rick Patterson, my distinguished colleague at Micro USA, who has helped me enormously by constantly engaging me in fruitful discussions on DSP, image sensors and optics and also for his constant caring about the outcome of this book.

My thanks to Steve Wicks, my other respected colleague at Micro USA, for helping me prepare some of the diagrams.

I wish to thank Barry Sandrew, Ph.D. of Legend Films, for reviewing the manuscript in the midst of his hectic work.

I would like to sincerely thank Focal Press, an imprint of Elsevier Inc., for publishing my book. My special thanks to Lothlorien Homet, Angelina Ward, Becky Golden-Harrell, Rachel Epstein, and Paul Gottehrer of Focal Press for overseeing the book project, and all others at Focal Press who helped me towards the manuscript.

I greatly appreciate the generous grant from MathWorks, Inc. in the form of MATLAB software tools.

My very special thanks to my son, Vikram Rajan, M.D., who encouraged me tremendously by giving me constructive comments and suggestions to improve the contents of the book.

Most of all, I owe my gratitude to my wonderful and talented wife Vasu who said to me one day, "Thyag, why don't you write a book on image processing?" Without her love, sacrifices, constant encouragement, cooperation, patience, and editing assistance, I would not have been able to write this book in a million years.

1 | Introduction

CHAPTER

1.1 BACKGROUND

With the advent of digital computers in the 1960s dawned the era of digital signal processing and digital image processing. Processing in the early days was off line since the computers were not powerful enough. With the introduction of PCs in the 1980s, the field of digital image processing started to mature. Now that ultrahigh-speed PCs with almost unlimited internal memory are in the market at affordable price ranges, digital image processing is a household name.

Digital image processing refers to any computer method—software or hardware—by which the properties of an image are altered to satisfy certain objectives. Obviously, the original image must be in digital format so that it can be manipulated using a computer. Only software-oriented approaches are dealt with in this book. Depending on the properties altered, digital image processing techniques fall under different categories. A broad classification of the field of digital image processing is exemplified in Figure 1-1. These classes of processing methods are outlined briefly in the following.

1.2 ENHANCEMENT

Image enhancement refers to any process by which the visual quality of an image is improved. Because there could be significant variations in the acquired images due to varying lighting conditions, camera types, and so on, there are no set procedures to be adopted in image enhancement. Generally speaking, enhancement techniques are ad hoc in nature. For example, if the original image lacks sharpness, a suitable algorithm called unsharp masking can be designed so that the subjective quality of the original image is improved by increasing its sharpness without altering its other qualities. Figure 1-2a shows an original image, and a sharpened version of it is shown in Figure 1-2b. Clearly, the enhanced image looks much sharper, although a bit grainy. Another application of image enhancement may arise when the original image is acquired under poor lighting conditions. The image in this case may appear to lack details. Again, by

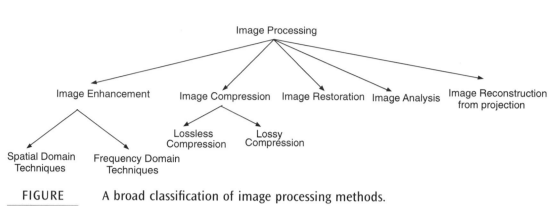

FIGURE   A broad classification of image processing methods.

1-1

a   b

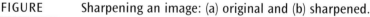

FIGURE   Sharpening an image: (a) original and (b) sharpened.

1-2

applying a suitable enhancement procedure, the details can be restored. This type of enhancement is termed histogram equalization. An example of such a process is shown in Figure 1-3b. The original image appears in Figure 1-3a. Note that the processed image brings out much more details that are not seen in the original image. Moreover, the overall contrast has also been improved.

Enhancing medical images requires techniques somewhat different from those used in Figures 1-2 and 1-3. Medical images usually lack contrast and the delineating boundaries are not sharp. Figure 1-4a shows an original MRI image and an enhanced version of it in Figure 1-4b. Note how the edges are well preserved and how details are visible that are not clear in the original image.

a   b

FIGURE

1-3

Enhancing an image by histogram equalization: (a) original image and (b) enhanced image. Original image courtesy of the Center for Image Processing Research, Rensselaer Polytechnic Institute.

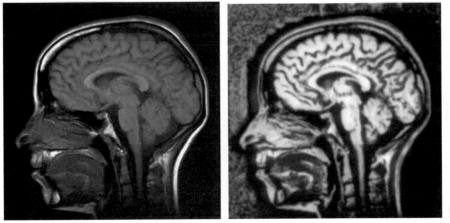

a   b

FIGURE

1-4

Enhancement of a medical image: (a) original MRI image and (b) enhanced image. The original image is courtesy of Signal Compression and Classification Group of the Information Systems Laboratory, Stanford University, California.

There are situations where the captured image may be corrupted by noise. Noise is always present either due to very low lighting conditions, which affect the sensors, or due to the noise generated by the electronic circuitry of the imaging hardware. This situation is depicted in Figure 1-5a where the image is contaminated by impulse noise. The noise-cleaned image is shown in Figure 1-5b. Impulse noise is also commonly referred to as salt and pepper noise. This

a   b

An example of noise cleaning: (a) image corrupted by impulse noise with a
    density of 0.05 and (b) noise-cleaned image. Original image is courtesy of the
1-5   Center for Image Processing Research, Rensselaer Polytechnic Institute.

type of noise is characterized by isolated pixels having values very different from
their neighboring pixels. A parameter characterizing such a noise is its density,
i.e., the fraction of the number of pixels that are noisy. The denser the impulse
noise, the harder it is to clean it.

1.3   COMPRESSION

Enhancement is not the only type of digital processing available. Many a time it
is necessary to reduce the amount of data contained in an image for efficient
storage or transmission. The corresponding image processing is known as image
compression. In one such method the original image can be restored completely,
resulting in no loss of data. This class of algorithms falls under what is known as
a lossless compression. Alternatively, one can compress an image in such a
manner that some amount of information is irrecoverably lost in the restored or
reconstructed image, resulting in what is called a lossy compression. Compres-

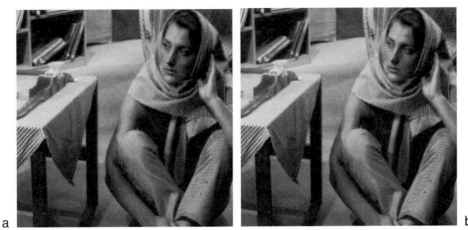

 FIGURE

1-6

An example of lossy image compression using discrete cosine transform: (a) original image and (b) compressed/decompressed image.

sion techniques are rooted in classical information theory. As a rule of thumb, lossy compression results in a larger reduction of data compared to the lossless case. Of course, when we refer to an image compressed using a lossy compression method, it is implied that the decompressed image is quite useful. Otherwise, one can obtain an unlimited amount of compression at the expense of image quality. A typical example of a compressed image is shown in Figure 1-6b. The uncompressed original appears in Figure 1-6a for comparison. Because it is a lossy compression, artifacts are clearly seen in the reconstructed image. If we allow a larger compression the artifacts will be even more visible. Thus, we can trade quality for higher compression when using a lossy compression method.

What we have just described applies to a still image or a single frame of image. More dynamic and interesting images are the so-called sequence images or video images. A sequence of images, as in a TV or movie, consists of a number of consecutive frames that contain smooth motion or live action. Therefore, we have an additional dimension, namely temporal dimension, to exploit in reducing the amount of data. Since the change in consecutive frames in a scene is small, it is not necessary to store or send all the pixels in each and every frame. Instead, only pixels that are different from a previous frame, for instance, are stored or transmitted. Hence a large amount of compression is achieved in compressing a video or movie. As an example, consider two consecutive frames of a sequence image as shown in Figures 1-7a and 1-7b. These two frames correspond to the fifth and sixth frames in the sequence. The difference image obtained by subtracting frame 5 from frame 6 is shown in Figure 1-7c. The difference image

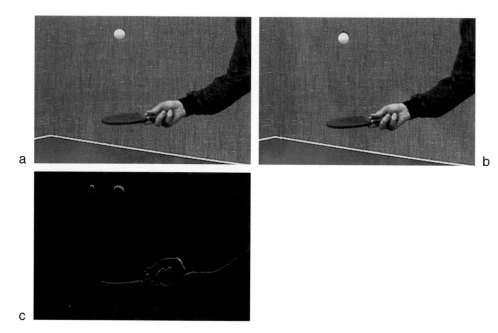

a

b

c

FIGURE

1-7

Sequence image: (a) fifth frame, (b) sixth frame, and (c) difference of frames 5 and 6. Original image is courtesy of the Center for Image Processing Research, Rensselaer Polytechnic Institute.

shows that part of the image in frame 5 that has moved. Compared to the image in frame 6, the amount of data contained in the difference image is much smaller and therefore will result in a reduction of data to be stored or transmitted. This is the motivating factor behind various compression schemes. More will be explained in later chapters.

1.4   RESTORATION

Image restoration refers to a process by which one removes the ill effect imposed on the image during its acquisition. An image may be degraded either due to blurring caused by a relative motion between camera and object or out of focusing or due to corruption by noise. Blurring is typically modeled as a linear operation on the image. Hence if we know a priori the exact linear operation due to camera motion, then we can undo it by its inverse operation. Hence restoration is also known as inverse filtering or deconvolution. To illustrate this idea, con-

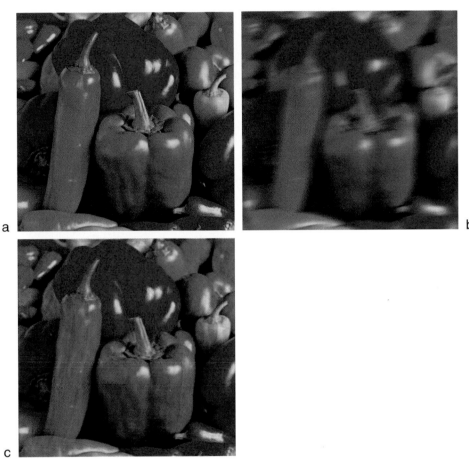

FIGURE

1-8

Image restoration: (a) original clean image, (b) camera motion-induced blurred image, and (c) deblurred image.

sider the image shown in Figure 1-8b, which is a blurred version of the image in Figure 1-8a. In this example the original clean image is deliberately blurred by linearly filtering the image by a filter that models the camera motion. Image restoration is generally ill conditioned. It means that the degraded image may not always be restored to its original condition. From Figure 1-8c we see that some artifacts are introduced by the restoration process. Since the degrading process is not always known a priori, one might have to devise a procedure that is iterative in nature. In this procedure, one starts with the given degraded image and iteratively improves the quality of the image. This procedure is referred to as blind deconvolution.

1.5   COMPUTED TOMOGRAPHY

A fourth type of digital image processing arises in the field of medical imaging. Noninvasive techniques are used to view the trans-axial cross section of a human body. X-rays are used for this purpose. However, a single beam of X-ray can only project a line along its transmission path on to a single point. Hence, multiple projections are obtained at different orientations of the body part. The cross-sectional view is then constructed by processing the whole set of projection data. This type of processing is known as computed tomography (CT). As an example, a phantom head and its reconstructions from projections are shown in Figure 1-9. Two types of projections are shown in Figure 1-9. Figures 1-9b through 1-9d correspond to reconstruction of the phantom head using parallel projection with the number of projections equal to 18, 36, and 90, respectively. Similarly, reconstructed images from the projections using the fan beam method are shown in Figures 1-9e through 1-9g, for sensor spacing of 2, 1, and 0,25, respectively. As can be seen from Figure 1-9, the quality of the reconstructed image gets better as the number of projections increase or the sensor spacing decreases corresponding to the two cases.

1.6   IMAGE ANALYSIS

The categories of image processing just described belong to the traditional discipline of electrical engineering. There is yet another category called image understanding or image analysis that typically falls under the discipline of computer science. Image understanding, as the name implies, is concerned with the recognition and enumeration of objects in an image using computer methods. This requires that an image be first segmented into homogeneous regions followed by identification of each region with an object. A simple segmentation procedure involves detecting object boundaries or edges. An example of detecting edges in an image, using a method known as Canny's method, is shown in Figure 1-10b. The original image can be seen in Figure 1-10a. Such tasks are used routinely in automatic inspection of assembly line products for quality control. More involved tasks are encountered in biomedical imaging, e.g., counting blood cells. Complex algorithms are needed in human activity recognition in such applications as forensic medicine.

This book deals with the basic principles involved in processing images for different end results. In particular, it describes in detail image enhancement and image compression. The topic on image compression includes the popular JPEG

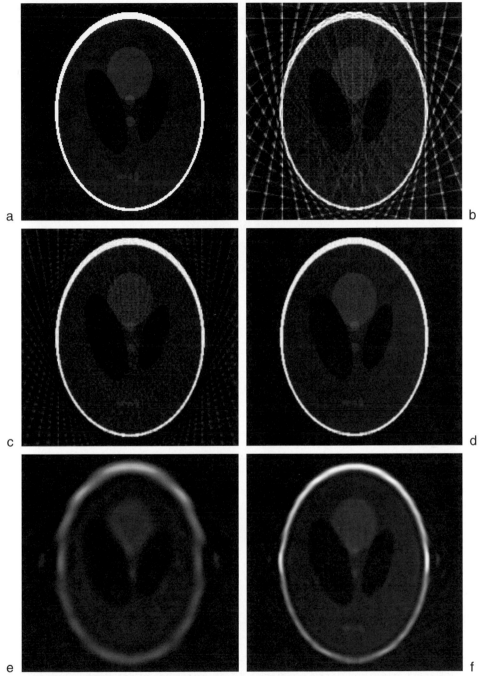

FIGURE 1-9   An example of computed tomography: (a) original phantom head, (b) reconstruction with 18 projections, (c) reconstruction with 36 projections, (d) reconstruction with 90 projections, (e) reconstruction with a sensor spacing of 2, (f) reconstruction with a sensor spacing of 1, and (g) reconstruction with a sensor spacing of 0.25.

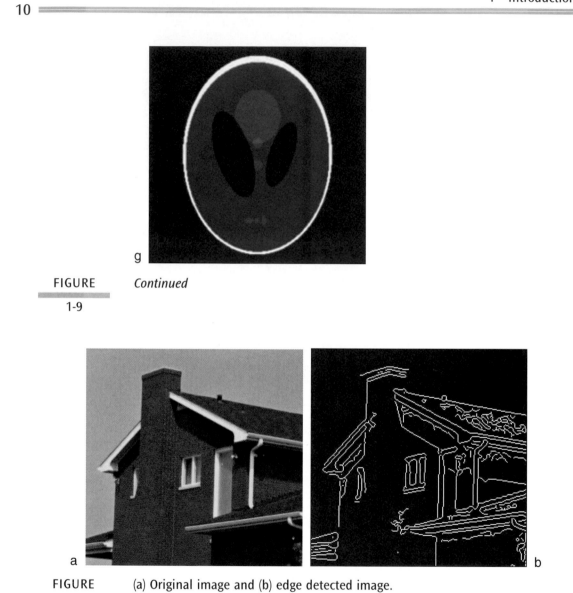

g

FIGURE   *Continued*

1-9

a   b

FIGURE   (a) Original image and (b) edge detected image.

1-10

and MPEG standards based on both transform and wavelet domains. It further includes an exciting application of image compression to digital cinema.

1.7   SUMMARY

This chapter has briefly described different digital image processing methods, which are specific to different applications. Image enhancement techniques are very important in improving image quality. They are also used routinely as pre-processing in machine vision and so on to enhance the detection process. Image compression is another important aspect of digital image processing that enables us to store and transmit an enormous of amount image and video data efficiently. As the demand for image and video transmission increases in this Internet age, more research is needed to develop efficient compression algorithms to keep up with the demand. Although we have mentioned image restoration, CT, and image analysis as other areas of digital image processing, this book does not deal with these topics in any detail. Rather the intent here is to introduce to the reader various aspects of digital image processing so as to give enough motivation for further reading. The following chapters describe in detail the topics of digital image enhancement and compression along with various topics that are relevant.

REFERENCES

There are excellent textbooks available in the area of digital image processing and its applications. A list of titles in this category follows.

A.N. Netravali and B.G. Haskell, Digital Picture: Representation and Compression, Plenum Press: New York, 1988

A.K. Jain, Fundamentals of Digital Image Processing, Prentice Hall: Englewood Cliffs, NJ, 1989

W.K. Pratt, Digital Image Processing, 2nd Ed., John Wiley & Sons: New York, 1991

Two-Dimensional Signals, Systems, and Discrete Fourier Transform

Mathematical preliminaries are unavoidable in any system theory discipline, especially image processing. However, this chapter introduces some basic ideas concerning two-dimensional (2-D) signals and systems, which are useful in the analysis and design of image processing systems, and defers detailed derivations to an appendix. If you are familiar with 2-D signals and systems, you may skip this chapter.

2.1   TWO-DIMENSIONAL DISCRETE SIGNALS

There are a few basic signals that are very useful in the analysis of 2-D discrete systems. Some of these signals parallel those used in one-dimensional (1-D) systems. This section defines a few basic 2-D discrete signals. A 2-D unit impulse $\delta[m,n]$ is defined as

$$\delta[m,n] = \begin{cases} 1, & m = n = 0 \\ 0, & \textit{otherwise} \end{cases} \tag{2-1}$$

and is shown in Figure 2-1. The impulse function is very useful in the analysis of 2-D systems, as shown in this chapter. Another useful 2-D signal is unit step function $u[m,n]$, which is defined as

$$u[m,n] = \begin{cases} 1, & m,n \geq 0 \\ 0, & \textit{otherwise} \end{cases} \tag{2-2}$$

The 2-D unit step is shown in Figure 2-2. An often used 2-D signal is the complex exponential, defined as

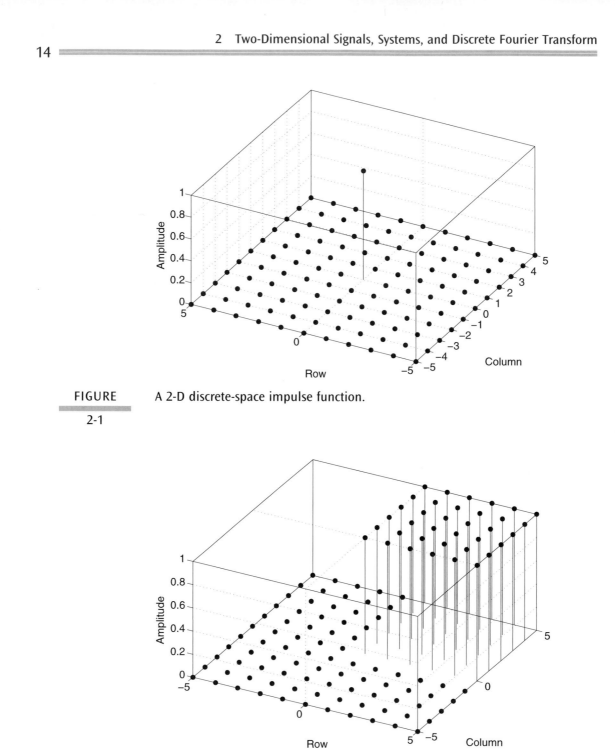

FIGURE   A 2-D discrete-space impulse function.

2-1

FIGURE   A 2-D discrete-space unit step function.

2-2

$$x[m,n] = e^{j(m\Omega_{10} + n\Omega_{20})}, \tag{2-3}$$

where Ω_{10} and Ω_{20} are the given normalized sinusoidal frequencies in the two spatial frequency variables Ω_1 and Ω_2, respectively. As seen later, sinusoidal signals play an important role in linear system analysis.

2.2   TWO-DIMENSIONAL DISCRETE SYSTEMS

In order to be able to process images, we need a mathematical description of a system that characterizes the effect of processing an image. Such a description not only gives us a tool to analyze the performance of a particular processing algorithm, but also enables us to design efficient systems for a particular application. The most practical of all systems is the linear system, as it gives us the power to obtain closed-form solution to the analysis and design of useful 2-D systems.

2.2.1   Linear Systems

A general 2-D discrete system accepts a 2-D discrete signal and produces a corresponding output signal. Since this book deals with images, we will interchangeably use the words images and 2-D discrete signals. This can be stated formally as

$$y[m,n] = T(x[m,n]). \tag{2-4}$$

In order to be able to analyze a 2-D system, the system operator T must be explicitly stated. A 2-D discrete system can be either linear or nonlinear depending on whether the following holds:

$$y[m,n] = T(\alpha x_1[m,n] + \beta x_2[m,n]) = \alpha T(x_1[m,n]) + \beta T(x_2[m,n]). \tag{2-5}$$

In Eq. (2-5), α and β are real or complex constants. If Eq. (2-5) does not hold, the system is said to be nonlinear. Another way to interpret Eq. (2-5) is that the output of the system to a linear sum of scaled input signals or images is a superposition of scaled outputs. Just as a 1-D discrete-time signal is decomposed as a sum of orthogonal signal components, a 2-D discrete signal can also be represented as a sum of orthogonal 2-D component signals. Now we can appreciate the advantages of a linear 2-D system: the output signal is the sum of output signals, as the input is a linear sum of signals.

Example 2-1

a. Consider a 2-D discrete system described by $T(x[m,n]) = x[m - m_0,n]$, where m_0 is a positive integer. Is the system linear? b. What about the system $T(x[m,n]) = x^2[m,n]$?

Solution

a. Let the input to this system be a linear combination of scaled inputs: $x[m,n] = ax_1[m,n] + bx_2[m,n]$, where a and b are any constants. Then, $y[m,n] = T(x[m,n]) = T(ax_1[m,n] + bx_2[m,n]) = ax_1[m - m_0,n] + bx_2[m - m_0,n]$. Hence the system is linear. The system merely shifts the input image to the right by m_0 pixels.

b. If $x[m,n] = ax_1[m,n] + bx_2[m,n]$, then the system output is found to be $y[m,n] = T(ax_1[m,n] + bx_2[m,n]) = (ax_1[m,n] + bx_2[m,n])^2 \neq ax_1^2[m,n] + bx_2^2[m,n]$. Hence the system in b is nonlinear.

2.2.2   Space Invariant Systems

A 2-D discrete system is said to be *space invariant* if a shifted input results in a shifted output. That is, if the system response to $x[m,n]$ is $y[m,n]$, then $y[m - m_0,n - n_0]$ is the response when the input to the system is $x[m - m_0,n - n_0]$. Otherwise, the system is *space variant.*

2.2.3   System Response via 2-D Convolution

In addition to linearity, a 2-D discrete system can be space invariant, causal and stable. We usually define stability in the sense that a bounded input results in a bounded output. In order to be able to determine the response of a 2-D linear discrete system to any given input, a useful tool is its *impulse* response, which is the response of the system to a 2-D unit impulse and is commonly denoted $h[m,n]$. In terms of the impulse response, we can compute the response of a 2-D LSI system to any input $x[m,n]$, as given by Eq. (2-6) or:

$$y[m,n] = \sum_{k=-\infty}^{\infty} \sum_{l=-\infty}^{\infty} x[k,l]h[m-k,n-l] \qquad (2\text{-}6)$$

$$y[m,n] = \sum_{k=-\infty}^{\infty} \sum_{l=-\infty}^{\infty} h[k,l]x[m-k,n-l]. \qquad (2\text{-}7)$$

The right-hand side of Eq. (2-6) or Eq. (2-7) is known as the 2-D discrete con-volution and is often expressed in symbolic equation:

$$y[m,n] = x[m,n] * h[m,n]. \qquad (2\text{-}8)$$

When interpreted graphically, the 2-D convolution consists of the following: Given the input $x[m,n]$ and the impulse response $h[m,n]$, flip the impulse response array first about the vertical axis and then flip the resultant array about the horizontal axis. Next, slide the flipped impulse response array from left to right one pixel at a time and compute the sum of products over the region the two arrays overlap. The system output at the current location equals the sum of products. Continue this procedure for every m and n value.

2.2.4   Causal and Stable Systems

A 2-D discrete system is causal if it is nonanticipatory. In terms of the system impulse response $h[m,n]$, it can be shown that a 2-D discrete system is causal if and only if the following is satisfied:

$$h[m,n] = 0, \quad for \; m,n < 0. \qquad (2\text{-}9)$$

Otherwise it is noncausal. A 2-D discrete system is stable in the *bounded-input bounded-output* sense if its impulse response array $h[m,n]$ is absolutely summable:

$$\sum_{m=-\infty}^{\infty} \sum_{n=-\infty}^{\infty} |h[m,n]| < \infty. \qquad (2\text{-}10)$$

If the condition in Eq. (2-10) is not satisfied, the 2-D system is said to be unsta-ble. We desire a stable 2-D system for processing images to produce meaningful images, otherwise, we will get saturated images, which are of no use to us.

2.3   TWO-DIMENSIONAL DISCRETE FOURIER TRANSFORM

Fourier transform is a very useful tool in the analysis and design of linear systems. Just as periodic signals are represented as an infinite sum of sinusoids of harmonic frequencies, an a-periodic signal can be decomposed into an integral sum of sinusoids of continuous frequencies. If a 2-D signal is discrete space, then it can be represented in a Fourier transform known as the discrete-space Fourier transform. Let $x[m,n]$ be a 2-D discrete-space a-periodic signal. Then its discrete-space Fourier transform $X(\Omega_1,\Omega_2)$ is defined by

$$X(\Omega_1,\Omega_2) = \sum_{m=-\infty}^{\infty} \sum_{n=-\infty}^{\infty} x[m,n]e^{j(m\Omega_1 + n\Omega_2)}, \tag{2-11}$$

where Ω_1 and Ω_2 are the continuous, spatial frequencies in the vertical and horizontal directions, respectively. Note that $X(\Omega_1,\Omega_2)$ is periodic in both Ω_1 and Ω_2 (doubly periodic) with periods 2π and that it is a complex function. Hence, $X(\Omega_1,\Omega_2)$ has magnitude $|X(\Omega_1,\Omega_2)|$ and phase function $\theta(\Omega_1,\Omega_2)$. The magnitude function is an even function and the phase is an odd function of the spatial frequencies. Because $X(\Omega_1,\Omega_2)$ is doubly periodic, it has a Fourier series expansion and Eq. (2-11) is indeed its Fourier series expansion. Therefore, the 2-D array $x[m,n]$ can be recovered from $X(\Omega_1,\Omega_2)$ through the inverse discrete-space Fourier transform as

$$x[m,n] = \frac{1}{4\pi^2} \int_{-\pi}^{\pi} \int_{-\pi}^{\pi} X(\Omega_1,\Omega_2)e^{j(m\Omega_1 + n\Omega_2)}d\Omega_1\Omega_2. \tag{2-12}$$

When a 2-D signal $x[m,n]$ is of finite extent or support, i.e., if

$$x[m,n] \neq 0, 0 \leq m \leq M-1, 0 \leq n \leq N-1, \tag{2-13}$$

then it can be expressed as

$$X(k,l) = X\left(\frac{2\pi}{M}k, \frac{2\pi}{N}l\right) = \sum_{m=0}^{M-1} \sum_{n=0}^{N-1} x[m,n]W_M^{mk}W_N^{nl}, \quad 0 \leq k \leq M-1, 0 \leq l \leq N-1, \tag{2-14}$$

where we have used the fact that $W_M^{mk} \equiv e^{-j\frac{2\pi}{M}mk}$ and $W_N^{nl} \equiv e^{-j\frac{2\pi}{N}nl}$. $X(k,l)$ in Eq. (2-14) is known as the 2-D *discrete Fourier transform* (DFT) of $x[m,n]$. Comparing Eq. (2-11), we notice that the 2-D DFT equals the discrete-space Fourier transform evaluated at equispaced points:

$$X(k,l) = X(\Omega_{1k},\Omega_{2l}) = X(\Omega_1,\Omega_2)\big|_{\Omega_{1k}=\frac{2\pi}{M}k, \Omega_{2l}=\frac{2\pi}{N}l}. \tag{2-15}$$

Conversely, given the 2-D DFT $X(k,l)$ of the finite extent array $x[m,n]$, inverse DFT (IDFT) yields the original array. Thus,

$$x[m,n] = \frac{1}{MN} \sum_{k=0}^{M-1} \sum_{l=0}^{N-1} X(k,l) W_M^{-mk} W_N^{-nl}, \quad 0 \le m \le M-1, 0 \le n \le N-1 \quad (2\text{-}16)$$

The 2-D DFT in Eq. (2-14) is separable [see Eq. (2-28)] and can therefore be effected in a row–column fashion. That is, the 2-D DFT can be computed as a sequence of 1-D DFTs, once along the rows of the image and then along the columns of the row-processed image. As in 1-D signals, the 2-D DFT can be computed efficiently with the aid of the *fast Fourier transform* (FFT). Because the 2-D DFT and its inverse are similar except for a scale factor, FFT can be used to perform the 2-D IDFT as well. It should be pointed out that FFT can be used to compute the 2-D DFT even if it is nonseparable.

Example 2-2

Read a black and white image, calculate its 2-D DFT, and display the magnitude of the 2-D DFT as an image.

Solution

We will use MATLAB to solve this problem. For the sake of illustration, we use a black and white image called the *cameraman*. This image is one of the many images available in the MATLAB tools. It is in TIF format of size 256×256 pixels with 8 bits of gray level per pixel. Figure 2-3a is the input image. Figure 2-3b is the log magnitude of the 2-D DFT of the image in Fig. 2-3a. The 2-D DFT is of the same size as the image as long as no padding is done, as the rows and columns of the image are powers of 2. The first coefficient $X(0,0)$ corresponds to a scaled average of the image and is placed at the top left corner of the DFT array. For visualizing purposes, we can shift the origin to the center. This is shown in Fig. 2-3c.

2.4   FREQUENCY RESPONSE

Sinusoidal signals play an important role in linear system analysis, as a linear system responds to a sinusoid in a sinusoidal fashion. Consider, for instance, a spatially rectangular sinusoid in complex form given by

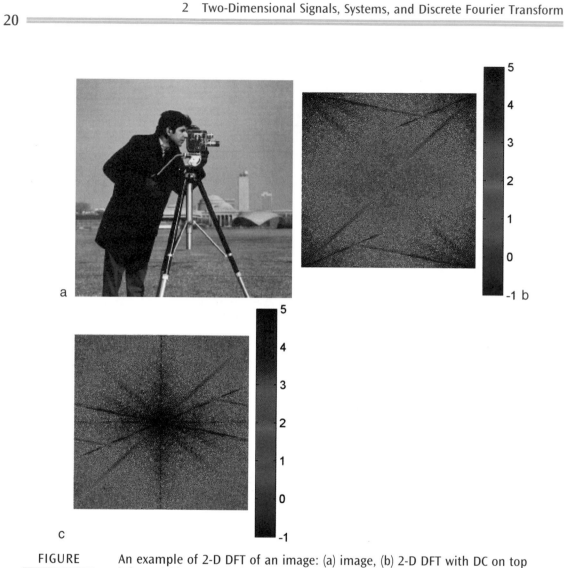

FIGURE

2-3
An example of 2-D DFT of an image: (a) image, (b) 2-D DFT with DC on top left, and (c) 2-D DFT with DC at the center.

$$x[m,n] = e^{jm\Omega_1} e^{jn\Omega_2}. \tag{2-17}$$

In Eq. (2-17), Ω_1 and Ω_2 are the normalized frequencies of the applied sinusoids in the horizontal and vertical directions, respectively. The response of a 2-D discrete LSI system can be found from Eq. (2-7) after a little algebraic manipulation as

$$y[m,n] = e^{j(m\Omega_1 + n\Omega_2)} \sum_{k=-\infty}^{\infty} \sum_{l=-\infty}^{\infty} h[m,n] \exp(-j(k\Omega_1 + l\Omega_2)). \tag{2-18}$$

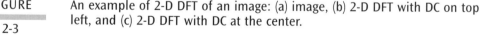

Because the double summation on the right-hand side of Eq. (2-18) is independent of the input location, we have

$$y[m,n] = H(\Omega_1,\Omega_2)\exp(j(m\Omega_1 + n\Omega_2)) = H(\Omega_1,\Omega_2)x[m,n], \qquad (2\text{-}19)$$

where

$$H(\Omega_1,\Omega_2) = \sum_{k=-\infty}^{\infty} \sum_{l=-\infty}^{\infty} h[k,l]\exp(-j(k\Omega_1 + l\Omega_2)). \qquad (2\text{-}20)$$

Thus, we find that the 2-D discrete LSI system responds sinusoidally to an applied 2-D sinusoid with a possible change in amplitude and phase. This scale factor, $H(\Omega_1,\Omega_2)$, is a complex function of the applied sinusoidal frequencies and is known as the *frequency response* or *transfer function* of the 2-D LSI system. It can be expressed in polar form as

$$H(\Omega_1,\Omega_2) = |H(\Omega_1,\Omega_2)| \angle \theta(\Omega_1,\Omega_2) \qquad (2\text{-}21)$$

where $|H(\Omega_1,\Omega_2)|$ is the magnitude response and $\angle\theta(\Omega_1,\Omega_2)$ is the phase response.

Example 2-3

A 2-D discrete LSI system produces a signal $2.5\cos\left(m\Omega_{1x} - \dfrac{\pi}{4}\right)$ when the input signal is $\cos(m\Omega_{1x})$. Determine its frequency response.

Solution

Expressing the input and output signals in complex exponential form, we can write

$$\cos(m\Omega_{1x}) = \frac{e^{jm\Omega_{1x}} + e^{-jm\Omega_{1x}}}{2}$$

and

$$2.5\cos\left(m\Omega_{1x} - \frac{\pi}{4}\right) = 2.5\frac{e^{j\left(m\Omega_{1x} - \frac{\pi}{4}\right)} + e^{-j\left(m\Omega_{1x} - \frac{\pi}{4}\right)}}{2}.$$

The response to each sinusoid can then be written as

$$y_1[m,n] = T\left(\frac{e^{jm\Omega_{1x}}}{2}\right) = 2.5^{-j\frac{\pi}{4}}\frac{e^{jm\Omega_{1x}}}{2}.$$

Therefore,

$$H(j\Omega_{1x}, j\Omega_2) = 2.5\exp\left(-j\frac{\pi}{4}\right).$$

Similarly, we find that the frequency response corresponding to $\exp(-jm\Omega_{1x})$ as

$$H(j\Omega_{1x}, j\Omega_2) = 2.5\exp\left(j\frac{\pi}{4}\right).$$

Thus,

$$|H(\Omega_{1x}, \Omega_2)| = 2.5$$

and

$$\theta(\Omega_{1x}, \Omega_2) = \begin{cases} \dfrac{\pi}{4}, & \Omega_1 = -\Omega_{1x} \\ -\dfrac{\pi}{4}, & \Omega_1 = \Omega_{1x} \end{cases}.$$

Example 2-4

Find the magnitude and phase responses of a 2-D discrete LSI system whose transfer function is given by

$$H(\Omega_1, \Omega_2) = e^{j\Omega_1} + e^{j\Omega_2} - e^{j(\Omega_1 + \Omega_2)} + e^{j2\Omega_1} + e^{j2\Omega_2}.$$

Solution

Using trigonometric identity, we can write $H(\Omega_1,\Omega_2)$ as

$$H(\Omega_1,\Omega_2) = \frac{1}{2}(\cos(\Omega_1) + \cos(\Omega_2) + \cos(2\Omega_1) + \cos(2\Omega_2) - \cos(\Omega_1 + \Omega_2)) +$$

$$j\frac{1}{2}(\sin(\Omega_1) + \sin(\Omega_2) + \sin(2\Omega_1) + \sin(2\Omega_2) - \sin(\Omega_1 + \Omega_2))$$

The magnitude and phase responses can then be found as

$$|H(\Omega_1,\Omega_2)| = \frac{1}{2}\left\{5 + 2\begin{bmatrix}\cos(\Omega_1) + \cos(\Omega_2) + \cos(\Omega_1 - \Omega_2) + \cos(\Omega_1 - 2\Omega_2)\\ +\cos(\Omega_2 - 2\Omega_1) + \cos(\Omega_1 + \Omega_2) + \cos(\Omega_2 + 2\Omega_1)\end{bmatrix}\right.$$

$$\theta(\Omega_1,\Omega_2) = \tan^{-1}\left(\frac{\sin(\Omega_1) + \sin(\Omega_2) + \sin(2\Omega_1) + \sin(2\Omega_2) - \sin(\Omega_1 + \Omega_2)}{\cos(\Omega_1) + \cos(\Omega_2) + \cos(2\Omega_1) + \cos(2\Omega_2) + \cos(\Omega_1 + \Omega_2)}\right)$$

Figures 2-4a and 2-4b show the magnitude and phase responses, respectively. It should be noted that the magnitude function is even and doubly periodic in Ω_1 and Ω_2, with periods 2π while the phase function is odd.

2.5   TWO-DIMENSIONAL FILTERING

$H(\Omega_1,\Omega_2)$ in Eq. (2-20) is also known as the 2-D discrete-space Fourier transform of the array $h[m,n]$. In general, the 2-D discrete-space Fourier transform $X(\Omega_1,\Omega_2)$ of an array $x[m,n]$ is defined as

$$X(\Omega_1,\Omega_2) = \sum_{k=-\infty}^{\infty}\sum_{l=-\infty}^{\infty} x[k,l]\exp(-j(k\Omega_1 + l\Omega_2)). \qquad (2\text{-}22)$$

Note that $X(\Omega_1,\Omega_2)$ is a continuous, periodic function of the two spatial frequency variables Ω_1 and Ω_2, with period 2π in both variables.

Filtering of an image can be understood from the 2-D discrete convolution operation. Using Eq. (2-6), we can show that the system output is related to the input in the frequency domain via

$$Y(\Omega_1,\Omega_2) = X(\Omega_1,\Omega_2)H(\Omega_1,\Omega_2). \qquad (2\text{-}23)$$

Eq. (2-23) implies that the Fourier transform of the output image equals the product of the Fourier transforms of its input image and the system transfer

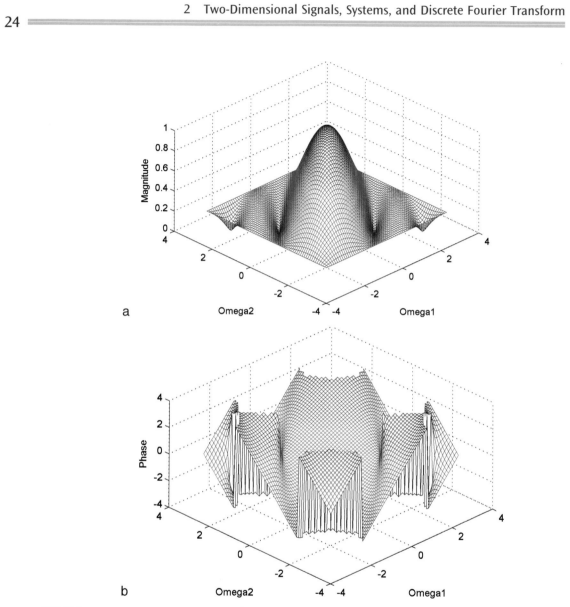

Frequency response of the 2-D LSI system of Example 2-4: (a) magnitude response and (b) phase response.

function. Thus we obtain a frequency domain representation of the output image. Its frequency response is a shaped or *filtered* version of the input image, and the frequency shaping function corresponds to $H(\Omega_1,\Omega_2)$. This processing is known as 2-D linear filtering. In order to filter an image, one needs to specify a suitable filtering function either in the spatial domain as the impulse response array $h[m,n]$ or in the frequency domain as the transfer function $H(\Omega_1,\Omega_2)$. In practice it is advantageous to describe a linear filter in terms of its transfer function, as the visual effects of the processed image can be associated more with the spatial frequencies than with a spatial function. Besides, a wealth of analytical, filter design procedures are available in the frequency domain. The following, therefore, describes the design of 2-D digital filters in the frequency domain.

The transfer function of a 2-D discrete LSI system is, in general, a rational polynomial in the two spatial frequencies. Therefore, it can be represented by

$$H(\Omega_1,\Omega_2) = \frac{N(\Omega_1,\Omega_2)}{D(\Omega_1,\Omega_2)}, \tag{2-24}$$

where $N(\Omega_1,\Omega_2)$ and $D(\Omega_1,\Omega_2)$ are polynomials in the spatial frequency variables Ω_1 and Ω_2, of order n and m, respectively, with $n < m$. If the denominator $D(\Omega_1,\Omega_2)$ is a zero degree polynomial, i.e., $D(\Omega_1,\Omega_2)$ is a constant and $N(\Omega_1,\Omega_2)$ is a polynomial of order n, then the filter is called a 2-D *finite impulse response* (FIR) filter. Otherwise the filter is known as an *infinite impulse response* (IIR) filter. For example, the filter in Eq. (2-25) is a 2-D FIR filter of order 2:

$$H(\Omega_1,\Omega_2) = a_{00} + a_{10}e^{j\Omega_1} + a_{01}e^{j\Omega_2} + a_{11}e^{j(\Omega_1+\Omega_2)} + a_{20}e^{j2\Omega_1} + a_{02}e^{j2\Omega_2}, \tag{2-25}$$

whereas Eq. (2-26) corresponds to a 2-D IIR filter of order 2:

$$H(\Omega_1,\Omega_2) = \frac{a_{00} + a_{10}e^{j\Omega_1} + a_{01}e^{j\Omega_2}}{b_{00} + b_{10}e^{j\Omega_1} + b_{01}e^{j\Omega_2} + b_{11}e^{j(\Omega_1+\Omega_2)} + b_{20}e^{j2\Omega_1} + b_{02}e^{j2\Omega_2}}. \tag{2-26}$$

Design of a 2-D filter amounts to the specification of the coefficients of the two polynomials in Eq. (2-24) such that the filter frequency and/or the phase response meets the design objective. Of course, it is, in general, not feasible to satisfy the magnitude and phase response specifications simultaneously. Thus, the goal is to determine the filter coefficients so as to meet either one of the requirements. Typically, filters are specified in terms of their magnitude response. Filters can then be designed to meet the user requirements. For the same set of specifications it is possible to obtain a number of filters depending on the design criteria used. Filter design is discussed in the next section.

Of the two types of filters mentioned earlier, FIR filters are the most preferred in practice due to (1) they are unconditionally stable and (2) they can have exact linear phase characteristics. It is important that a 2-D filter has linear phase characteristics, as image distortions due to nonlinear phase response are easily noticeable to the naked eye. An example is shown later in this section. The main difficulty with IIR filters arises due to the fact that there is no known procedure to factorize polynomials of two variables, except in trivial cases. Therefore, IIR filters cannot guarantee unconditional stability. Moreover, IIR filters do not have, in general, linear phase characteristics. Hence, discussion in this book is limited to the design of linear phase FIR filters.

A 2-D FIR filter, $H(\Omega_1, \Omega_2)$, is said to be *separable* if it can be written as a product of two 1-D functions as

$$H(\Omega_1, \Omega_2) = H_1(\Omega_1) H_2(\Omega_2). \tag{2-27}$$

Conversely, the impulse response of a 2-D separable filter can be written as the product of two 1-D impulse response functions, i.e.,

$$h[m, n] = h_1[m] h_2[n]. \tag{2-28}$$

Otherwise $H(\Omega_1, \Omega_2)$ is said to be *nonseparable*. Generally, the two 1-D functions in Eq. (2-28) are identical. The advantages in using separable FIR filters are (1) the 2-D filtering can be implemented as a row–column operation, namely an image can be filtered first along its rows and then along the columns of the row-filtered image, and (2) the implementation can be more efficient. The row–column operation can be shown as follows. Using the 2-D convolution in Eq. (2-6) and the condition for separability in Eq. (2-28), we have

$$y[m, n] = \sum_{k=-\infty}^{\infty} \sum_{l=-\infty}^{\infty} x[k, l] h_1[m - k] h_2[n - l] = \sum_k h_1[m - k] \sum_l x[k, l] h_2[n - l]. \tag{2-29}$$

In Eq. (2-29) the second summation on the right-hand side can be considered as running the filtering along the kth row of the image $x[m, n]$. Thus, we can filter each row using the filter $h_2[n]$ and store the result. Denoting the row-filtered image by $y'[k, n]$, we can write Eq. (2-29) as

$$y[m, n] = \sum_k y'[k, n] h_1[m - k], \tag{2-30}$$

where

$$y'[k, n] = \sum_l x[k, l] h_2[n - 1]. \tag{2-31}$$

From Eq. (2-31) we see that the row-filtered image $y'[k,n]$ is now filtered along its columns. This proves the fact. It can be seen that the row–column operation can be performed *in place*, requiring only one image store plus an additional storage equal to a row of pixels.

2.6   FIR FILTER DESIGN

2.6.1   Separable FIR Filters

Since the impulse response of a separable 2-D FIR filter is a product of two 1-D filters, we need to focus only on designing 1-D FIR filters. A number of techniques are available for the design of FIR filters. This section describes these design techniques.

2.6.1.1   *Window-Based Methods*

In this approach we begin with the specification of an ideal low-pass digital filter as shown in Figure 2-5. It is expressed as

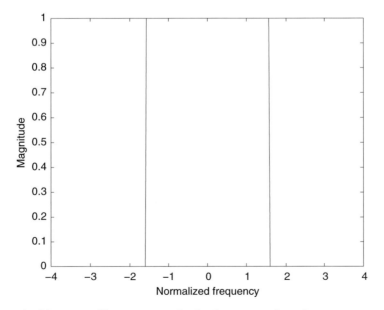

FIGURE   Ideal low-pass filter response in the frequency domain.

2-5

$$H_I(\Omega) = \begin{cases} 1, & |\Omega| \le \Omega_c \\ 0, & \Omega_c < |\Omega| \le \pi \end{cases}. \tag{2-32}$$

Because the phase is not specified, we will assume that it is zero for all frequencies. However, a physically realizable filter will introduce a finite amount of delay or spatial shift, which will correspond to a phase shift. This can be accounted for in our design by simply shifting the impulse response of the ideal filter by a finite number of pixels.

Because we seek the impulse response rather than the magnitude response, the impulse response of the ideal filter in Eq. (2-32) can be obtained from

$$h_I[n] = \frac{1}{2\pi}\int_0^{2\pi} H_I(\Omega)e^{-jn\Omega}d\Omega = \frac{1}{2\pi}\int_{-\Omega_c}^{\Omega} e^{-jn\Omega}d\Omega. \tag{2-33}$$

Performing the integration in Eq. (2-33), we obtain the impulse response of the ideal filter as

$$h_I[n] = \frac{\sin(n\Omega_c)}{n\pi}, \quad -\infty < n < \infty. \tag{2-34}$$

From Eq. (2-34) we find that the impulse response of the ideal filter is of infinite duration! Because we require an FIR filter, we need to limit the impulse response to a finite duration or length, say, N. This will necessarily result in an approximation to the desired *brick wall* characteristics of the ideal low-pass filter. The desired FIR filter with N even is then given by

$$h_D[n] = \begin{cases} h_I[n], & -\dfrac{N-1}{2} \le n \le \dfrac{N-1}{2} \\ 0, & otherwise \end{cases}. \tag{2-35}$$

Note that the desired filter is noncausal, as its impulse response is not zero for $n < 0$. However, as pointed out earlier, the desired filter can be made causal by shifting its impulse response by $(N-1)/2$ samples to the right, as given by

$$h_D[n] = h_I\left[n - \frac{N-1}{2}\right] = \frac{\sin\left(\left(n - \dfrac{N-1}{2}\right)\Omega_c\right)}{\left(n - \dfrac{N-1}{2}\right)\pi}, \quad 0 \le n \le N-1. \tag{2-36}$$

Example 2-5. Low-Pass Filter Design

Design a FIR filter of order 9 to approximate an ideal low-pass filter with a cutoff frequency of $\dfrac{\pi}{4}$.

Solution

From Eq. (2-36) the impulse response of the desired FIR filter is found to be

$$h_D[n] = \frac{\sin\left(\dfrac{(n-4)\pi}{4}\right)}{(n-4)\pi}, \quad 0 \le n \le 8.$$

The impulse response of the desired filter is shown in Figure 2-6a. The corresponding magnitude and phase responses are shown in Figures 2-6b and 2-6c, respectively. Observe from Figure 2-6b that the magnitude has ripples in the passband and stop band. This oscillation in the passband and stop band is known as the Gibbs phenomenon and is due to truncating the ideal impulse response abruptly. This is in direct agreement with the principle of time–frequency resolution, which says that one cannot achieve arbitrary resolution in both time and frequency simultaneously. Finally, Figure 2-6c depicts the phase response of the filter, which has an exact linear phase versus frequency. In fact, with some algebraic manipulation, we can show that the phase function is given by the following:

$$\theta(\Omega) = -4\Omega, \quad -\pi \le \Omega \le \pi.$$

Another observation on the magnitude response is the fact that increasing the filter length N does not reduce the ripple heights and that the transition width decreases. This is shown in Figure 2-6d.

In the aforementioned design procedure we can consider the abrupt truncation of the ideal infinite duration impulse response to be equivalent to multiplying the ideal impulse response by a rectangular window of finite length. Thus the desired impulse response $h_d[n]$ can be written as

$$h_d[n] = h_I[n]w_R[n], \quad -\frac{N-1}{2} \le n \le \frac{N-1}{2}. \tag{2-37}$$

In Eq. (2-37), $h_I[n]$ is of infinite length and the rectangular window $w_d[n]$ is symmetric and of finite length, N. Using the theorem that the Fourier transform of

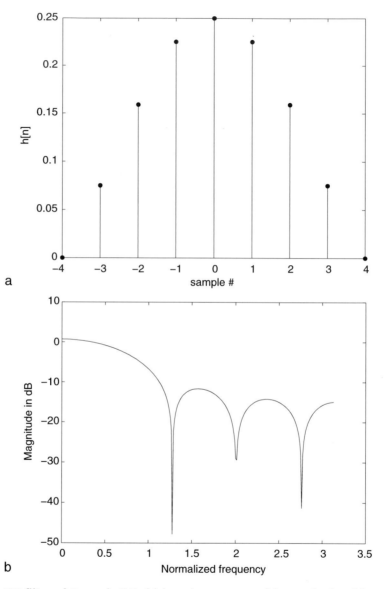

a

b

FIGURE 2-6

FIR filter of Example 2-5: (a) impulse response, (b) magnitude of frequency response, and (c) phase response.

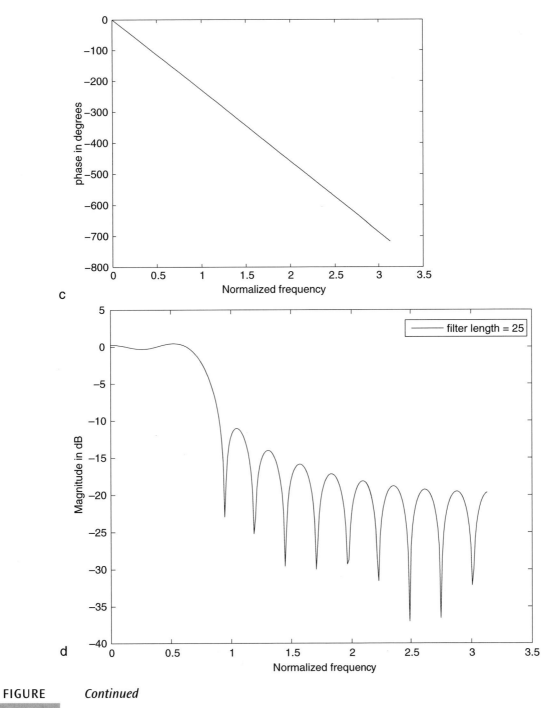

a product of two functions in the time or spatial domain equals the convolution of the corresponding Fourier transforms, we can write the Fourier transform of Eq. (2-37) as

$$H_d(\Omega) = H_I(\Omega) \otimes W_R(\Omega) \qquad (2\text{-}38)$$

Because $H_I(\Omega)$ is a rectangular function of width $2\Omega_c$ and $W_R(\Omega)$ is a sinc function of infinite support, the convolution of the two functions has ripples in both the passband and the stop band. Thus the ripple height depends on the window function. By choosing a proper window function it is possible to control the ripple heights in the two bands. A number of windows have been proposed in the literature. A few of them are described along with design examples.

Hanning Window

The Hanning window function of length $2M + 1$ is described by

$$w_H[n] = \frac{1}{2}\left[1 + \cos\left(\frac{2n\pi}{2M+1}\right)\right], \quad -M \le n \le M. \qquad (2\text{-}39)$$

Hamming Window

The Hamming window of length $2M + 1$ is given by

$$w_{ham}[n] = 0.54 + 0.46\cos\left(\frac{2n\pi}{2M+1}\right), \quad -M \le n \le M. \qquad (2\text{-}40)$$

Blackman Window

The Blackman window function is given in Eq. (2-41):

$$w_B(n) = 0.42 + 0.5\cos\left(\frac{2n\pi}{2M+1}\right) + 0.08\cos\left(\frac{4n\pi}{2M+1}\right), \quad -M \le n \le M. \qquad (2\text{-}41)$$

All of these windows have fixed parameters and the user can only choose the window length. Therefore, we will find that FIR filters based on these windows for a given filter length will have fixed ripple and stop band attenuation. Figure 2-7a depicts the three window functions with length equal to 9. The magnitude of the discrete-space Fourier transform of these windows is shown in Figure 2-7b. From Figure 2-7 we note that the Blackman window has the largest minimum

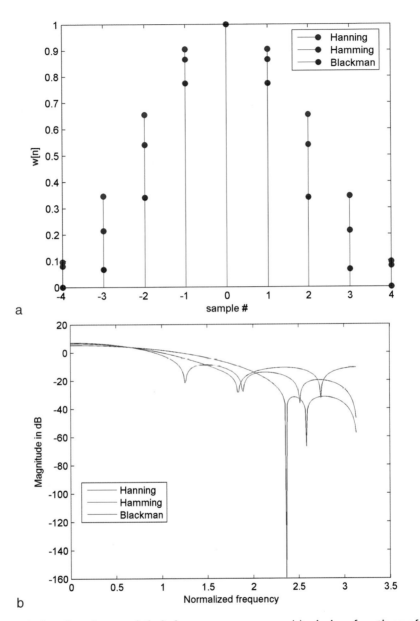

FIGURE

2-7

Window functions and their frequency responses: (a) window functions of length 9 and (b) magnitude of the DFTs of window functions.

stop band attenuation of about $-60\,$dB. We also note from Figure 2-7 that each window function has a *main lobe* centered at $\Omega = 0$ and a series of *side lobes*. The main lobe width is the largest for the Blackman window. Thus there is a trade-off between the minimum stop band attenuation and the transition width. The rectangular window achieves the smallest transition width at the expense of minimum stop band attenuation, whereas the Blackman window achieves the largest minimum stop band attenuation at the expense of the transition width for a fixed length. Thus, the choice of a particular window depends on the required minimum stop band attenuation and transition band width for a given application.

Windows with Adjustable Parameters

Note that there is no trade-off between transition width and minimum stop band attenuation possible in the aforementioned fixed windows. There are window functions that have adjustable parameters, which enable one to trade-off transition width for minimum stop band attenuation. We describe one such window, called the Kaiser window. It is given by

$$w_K[n] = \frac{I_0\left(\alpha\sqrt{1-\left(\frac{n}{M}\right)^2}\right)}{I_0(\alpha)}, \quad -M \le n \le M. \tag{2-42}$$

where α is an adjustable parameter and $I_0(x)$ is the modified zeroth-order Bessel function, which has a power series expansion of the type

$$I_0(x) = 1 + \sum_{k=1}^{\infty}\left[\frac{\left(\frac{x}{2}\right)^k}{k!}\right]. \tag{2-43}$$

The parameter α controls the minimum stop band attenuation of the windowed filter. A typical frequency response specification is shown in Figure 2-8. The passband ripple width is $2\delta_p$ and the corresponding quantity in the stop band is $2\delta_s$. Empirical formulas used to determine the filter length and α for specified δ_s in dB and transition band width $\Delta\Omega$ have been developed by Kaiser and are given by

$$\alpha = \begin{cases} 0.1102(\delta_s - 8.7), & \text{for } \delta_s > 50 \\ 0.5842(\delta_s - 21)^{0.4} + 0.07886(\delta_s - 21), & \text{for } 21 \le \delta_s \le 50 \\ 0, & \text{for } \delta_s < 21 \end{cases} \tag{2-44}$$

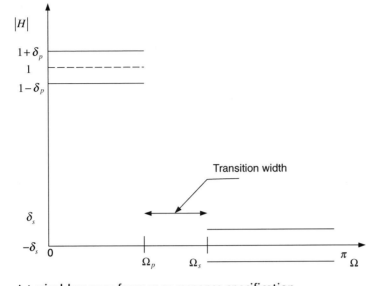

FIGURE
2-8

A typical low-pass frequency response specification.

$$N \approx \begin{cases} \dfrac{\delta_s - 7.95}{14.36\dfrac{\Delta\Omega}{2\pi}} + 1, & \text{for } \delta_s > 21 \\[4mm] \dfrac{0.9222}{\Delta\Omega\big/2\pi} + 1, & \text{for } \delta_s \leq 21 \end{cases} \tag{2-45}$$

Example 2-6

Let it be required to design a low-pass FIR filter satisfying the magnitude response specifications given in Figure 2-9. Use a Kaiser window of suitable length. It is typical to specify a magnitude response in terms of a *tolerance* scheme as in Figure 2-9. Because practical filters cannot have discontinuities in their frequency response, a suitably designed realizable filter is supposed to have its magnitude response characteristic fall within the tolerance specifications.

Solution

The stop band attenuation is expressed in dB as $\delta_{s\,dB} = -20\log_{10}\delta_s = 40$. Therefore, $\delta_s = 10^{-2} = 0.01$. The parameter α is determined from Eq. (2-44) to be 3.3953. Next, to determine the filter length, obtain the transition width

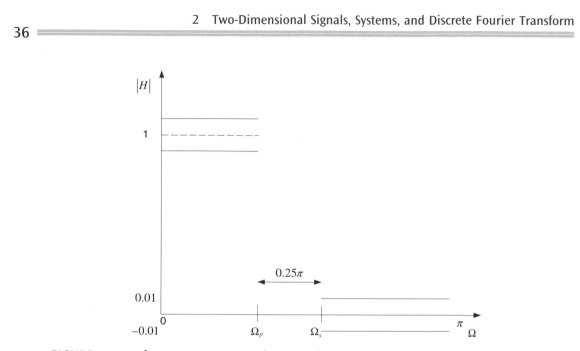

FIGURE

2-9

A frequency response tolerance scheme.

$$\Delta f = \frac{\Delta\Omega}{2\pi} = \frac{\Omega_s - \Omega_p}{2\pi} = \frac{0.5\pi - 0.25\pi}{2\pi} = 0.125 \text{ and then } N \text{ from Eq. (2-45). Thus}$$

$$N = \frac{40 - 7.95}{14.36 \times 0.125} + 1 = 18.855. \text{ Choose the next odd integer value of 19 as}$$

the filter length and so M = 9. Note that the filter cutoff frequency is

$\Omega_c = \dfrac{\Omega_p + \Omega_s}{2} = 0.375\pi$. Using the Kaiser window parameters just found, we now

obtain the window function $w_k[n]$, $-9 \le n \le 9$. Finally, the desired filter impulse response is determined from

$$h_d[n] = w_K[n] \cdot \frac{\sin(n\Omega_c)}{n\pi}, \quad -9 \le n \le 9.$$

Figure 2-10a shows a plot of the Kaiser-windowed FIR filter impulse response. The corresponding magnitude response is shown in Fig. 2-10b. For the same value of the filter length N, Figure 2-10c also shows the Hanning, Hamming, and Blackman windows. The magnitude responses of these filters are shown in Figure 2-10d. As expected, the filter using the Kaiser window has the smallest transition width.

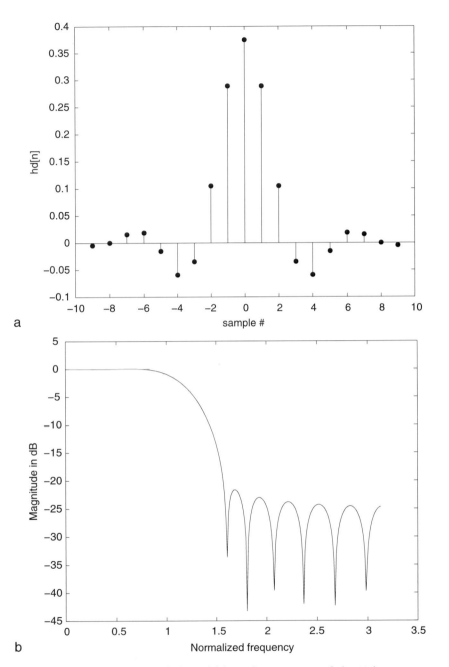

FIGURE

2-10

A FIR filter using a Kaiser window: (a) impulse response of the Kaiser-windowed FIR filter, (b) its frequency response, (c) other window functions having the same length as the Kaiser window, and (d) magnitude responses of the windowed filters as a comparison.

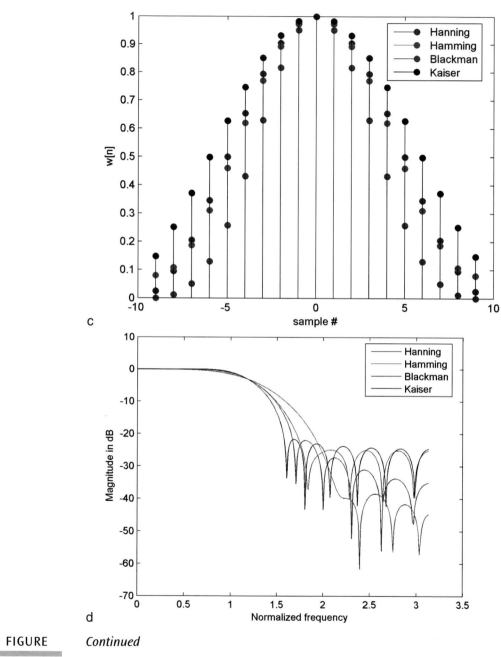

c

d

FIGURE   *Continued*

2-10

2.6.1.2   *Frequency Sampling Technique*

In this approach, the specified frequency response $H_d(\Omega)$ of the FIR filter is first sampled uniformly at N equally spaced points $\Omega_k = \dfrac{2\pi k}{N}, 0 \le k \le N-1$. From these N samples Ω_k, the impulse response $h[n]$ of the FIR filter is then obtained using the N-point inverse discrete Fourier transform (DFT) as

$$h[n] = \frac{1}{N} \sum_{k=0}^{N-1} H(k) e^{j\frac{2\pi nk}{N}}, \quad 0 \le n \le N-1. \tag{2-46}$$

Note that we have obtained the impulse response $h[n]$ corresponding to a sampled frequency response. However, we know that the frequency response of the FIR filter $h[n]$ is a continuous function of Ω. So what is the fallacy here? We now show that the impulse response $h[n]$ is an aliased version of the impulse response $h_d[n]$, where the frequency response of $h_d[n]$ is the specified function of the continuous frequency variable Ω. From the definition of the Fourier transform, we have

$$H_d(\Omega) = \sum_{k=-\infty}^{\infty} h_d[n] e^{-jk\Omega}. \tag{2-47}$$

Sampling $H_d(\Omega)$ at N equally spaced points, the sampled frequency response can be written as

$$H_d(k) = H_d\left(\frac{2\pi k}{N}\right) = \sum_{k=-\infty}^{\infty} h_d[n] e^{-j\frac{2\pi nk}{N}}, \quad 0 \le k \le N-1 \tag{2-48}$$

However, the impulse response corresponding to $H_d(k)$ is found from the inverse DFT as

$$h[n] = \frac{1}{N} \sum_{k=0}^{N-1} H_d[k] e^{j\frac{2\pi nk}{N}}, \quad 0 \le n \le N-1. \tag{2-49}$$

Substituting for $H_d(k)$ in the aforementioned equation, we get

$$\begin{aligned} h[n] &= \frac{1}{N} \sum_{k=0}^{N-1} \left\{ \sum_{l=-\infty}^{\infty} h_d[l] e^{-j\frac{2\pi lk}{N}} \right\} e^{j\frac{2\pi nk}{N}} \\ &= \sum_{l=-\infty}^{\infty} h_d[l] \left\{ \frac{1}{N} \sum_{k=0}^{N-1} \exp\left(j\frac{2\pi k(n-l)}{N} \right) \right\}, \quad 0 \le n \le N-1 \end{aligned} \tag{2-50}$$

Because

$$\frac{1}{N}\sum_{k=0}^{N-1}\exp\left(j\frac{2\pi k(n-l)}{N}\right) = \begin{cases}1, & \text{if } l = n + mN \\ 0, & \text{otherwise}\end{cases}, \qquad (2\text{-}51)$$

we arrive at the expression for $h[n]$:

$$h[n] = \sum_{m=-\infty}^{\infty} h_d[n + mN], \quad 0 \leq n \leq N - 1. \qquad (2\text{-}52)$$

The impulse response of the FIR filter derived from samples of a continuous function $H_d(\Omega)$ is the infinite sum of shifted impulse response $h_d[n]$. Due to the infinite sum, the impulse response $h[n]$ is, in general, an aliased version of $h_d[n]$.

2.6.1.3   Optimal Design Techniques

The design techniques described so far are analytical in nature. There are situations when filters need to satisfy arbitrary magnitude response specifications for which there are no analytical solutions possible. In such cases, we resort to computer-aided design. MATLAB has some neat functions that can be used to design optimal linear phase FIR filters.

We start with a specified magnitude response $H_D(\Omega)$ of a FIR filter. Let $|H(\Omega)|$ be the magnitude response of the FIR filter to be designed to approximate $H_D(\Omega)$ in some sense. Since the filter function in terms of its impulse response that generates $|H(\Omega)|$ is known, the design procedure iteratively adjusts $h[n]$ in such a way as to minimize an objective function. Define the error function

$$E(\Omega) = w(\Omega)[|H(\Omega)| - H_D(\Omega)], \qquad (2\text{-}53)$$

where $w(\Omega)$ is some weighting function. The design procedure then iteratively adjusts $h[n]$ such that the objective function

$$\varepsilon = \max_{0 \leq \Omega \leq \pi} |E(\Omega)| \qquad (2\text{-}54)$$

is minimized. The criterion in Eq. (2-54) is known as the *Chebyshev* or *minimax* criterion.

2.6.2   Nonseparable FIR Filters

Again, we will confine ourselves to FIR filters. In particular, we will look at 2-D filters that have circular symmetry. Here the 2-D window function with approximate circular symmetry can be obtained by sampling a circularly rotated, 1-D continuous function as

$$w_c[m,n] = w\left(\sqrt{m^2 + n^2}\right). \tag{2-55}$$

Similar to the 1-D case, we multiply the ideal 2-D filter impulse response array by the appropriate 2-D window function as in Eq. (2-55). We show a design example here.

Example 2-7

Consider the design of a [9 × 9]-point 2-D FIR filter to approximate the ideal frequency response

$$H_I(\Omega_1, \Omega_2) = \begin{cases} 1, & \text{for } \Omega_1^2 + \Omega_2^2 \leq (0.3\pi)^2 \\ 0, & \text{otherwise}, -\pi \leq \Omega_1, \Omega_2 \leq \pi \end{cases}$$

using a Kaiser window. Assume a Δ of 30 dB.

Solution

The impulse response corresponding to the ideal frequency response is found as follows:

$$h_I[m,n] = \frac{1}{4\pi^2} \int\limits_{-\pi}^{\pi} \int\limits_{-\pi}^{\pi} H_I(\Omega_1, \Omega_2) e^{j(m\Omega_1 + n\Omega_2)} d\Omega_1 d\Omega_2 = \frac{1}{4\pi^2} \iint\limits_{A} e^{j(m\Omega_1 + n\Omega_2)} d\Omega_1 d\Omega_2,$$

where A is the region such that $A: \Omega_1^2 + \Omega_2^2 \leq (0.3\pi)^2$. It is easier to evaluate the integral in the aforementioned equation if we use the polar coordinates. Define $\Omega = \sqrt{\Omega_1^2 + \Omega_2^2}$, $\phi = \tan^{-1}\dfrac{\Omega_2}{\Omega_1}$, and $\theta = \tan^{-1}\dfrac{n}{m}$. Using these definitions in the aforementioned equation for $h_I[m,n]$, we get

$$h_I[m,n] = \frac{1}{4\pi^2} \int\limits_{0}^{0.3\pi} \int\limits_{0}^{2\pi} \Omega e^{j\Omega\sqrt{m^2+n^2}\cos(\theta-\phi)} d\phi d\Omega = \frac{1}{2\pi} \int\limits_{0}^{0.3\pi} \Omega J_0\left(\Omega\sqrt{m^2+n^2}\right) d\Omega$$

$$= 0.15 \frac{J_1\left(0.3\pi\sqrt{m^2+n^2}\right)}{\sqrt{m^2+n^2}}$$

where $J_0(x)$ and $J_1(x)$ are the Bessel functions of the first kind of orders 0 and 1, respectively. The circularly symmetric Kaiser window is obtained from its 1-D counterpart by a circular rotation with $m^2 + n^2 \le 16$ and is given by

$$w_C[m,n] = \begin{cases} \dfrac{I_0\left(\alpha\sqrt{1-[(m^2-n^2)/16]}\right)}{I_0(\alpha)}, & m^2 + n^2 \le 16 \\ 0, & \text{otherwise} \end{cases}$$

The parameter α is given by

$$\alpha = \begin{cases} 0.56(\Delta - 20.2)^{0.4} + 0.083(\Delta - 20.2), & 20 < \Delta < 60 \\ 0, & \Delta < 20 \end{cases}, \qquad (2\text{-}56)$$

where

$$\Delta = -20 \log \sqrt{\delta_p \delta_s} \qquad (2\text{-}57)$$

and δ_p and δ_s are the passband and stop band ripples, respectively, as shown in Figure 2-11. Finally, the windowed FIR filter corresponding to $H_I(\Omega_1, \Omega_2)$ is

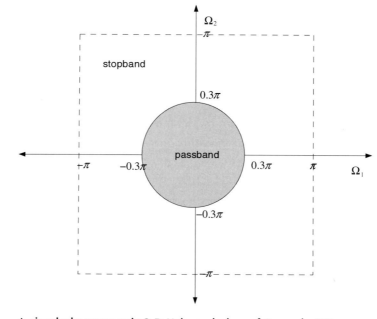

FIGURE 2-11   A circularly symmetric 2-D Kaiser window of Example 2-7.

obtained as $h[m,n] = h_I[m,n]\,w_c[m,n]$, $|m| \le 4$, $|n| \le 4$. Figure 2-12a shows the magnitude response of the filter, and the contour plot is shown in Figure 2-12b. As expected, the contours are approximately circular. It should be pointed out that we can only achieve approximate circular symmetry due to the fact that we are using a rectangular grid.

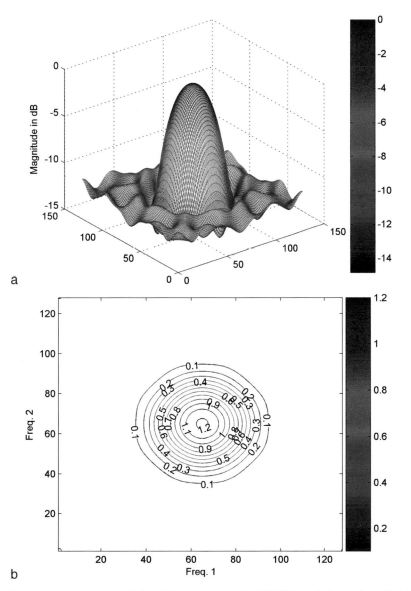

a

b

FIGURE
2-12

Frequency response of the 2-D nonseparable FIR filter of Example 2-7: (a) magnitude response and (b) contours of the magnitude response.

2.7   SUMMARY

This chapter described 2-D discrete-space signals and systems, which are used in later chapters for the design of image processing algorithms, such as enhancement and compression. Specifically, we have developed 2-D discrete convolution to determine the response of 2-D LSI systems through the system impulse response. Using the definition of the 2-D discrete-space Fourier transform, we introduced the idea of image filtering. Finally, we briefly described procedures for the design of 2-D FIR filters. Because 2-D IIR filters are generally not unconditionally stable, even though they are more efficient to implement, we have not discussed their design.

The next chapter looks at modeling the human visual perception, exploiting which efficient storage of images can be achieved.

REFERENCES

Because this text is about two or higher dimensional signal processing, we have assumed that the reader is familiar with 1-D digital signal processing (DSP). To review the basic concepts in 1-D DSP, refer to Oppenheim and Schafer, 1975; Rabiner and Gold 1975; Oppenheim and Schafer, 1989; and Jackson, 1996. For further reading on 2-D discrete systems, see Dudgeon and Mersereau, 1984; and Jain, 1989.

For details on 1-D FIR filter design, refer to Oppenheim and Schafer, 1989; and Mitra, 1998. For further details on window functions, the reader is referred to Blackman, 1965; Hamming 1989; Kaiser 1974; and Harris, 1978.

For further reading on the design of 2-D FIR filters, see Dudgeon and Mersereau, 1984; Huang, 1972; McClellan, 1973; Meresereau, 1976; Rajan and Swamy, 1983; and Yu and Mitra, 1985. Although 2-D IIR filter design techniques have not been dealt with in this text, inquisitive readers may refer to Aly and Fahmy, 1978; Costa and Venetsanopoulos, 1974; Ramamoorthy and Bruton, 1979; Swamy, Thyagarajan, and Ramachandran, 1977; and Thyagarajan, 1978, 1980, and 1981.

A.V. Oppenheim and R.W. Schafer, *Digital Signal Processing*, Englewood Cliffs, NJ: Prentice Hall, 1975.

A.V. Oppenheim and R.W. Schafer, *Discrete-Time Signal Processing*, Englewood Cliffs, NJ: Prentice Hall, 1989.

L.R. Rabiner and B. Gold, *Theory and Application of Digital Signal Processing*, Englewood Cliffs, NJ: Prentice Hall, 1975.

L.B. Jackson, *Digital Filters and Signal Processing*, third edition, Boston MA: Kluwer, 1996.

D.E. Dudgeon and R.M. Mersereau, *Multidimensional Digital Signal Processing*, Englewood Cliffs, NJ: Prentice Hall, 1984.

A.K. Jain, *Fundamentals of Digital Image Processing*, Englewood Cliffs, NJ: Prentice Hall, 1989.

S.K. Mitra, *Digital Signal Processing: A Computer-Based Approach*, McGraw-Hill, 1998.

R.B. Blackman, *Linear Data Smoothing and Prediction in Theory and Practice*, Reading MA: Addison-Wesley, 1965.

R.W. Hamming, *Digital Filters*, third edition, Englewood Cliffs, NJ: Prentice Hall, 1989.

J.F. Kaiser, "Nonrecursive digital filter design using the I_0-sinh window function," in Proc. 1974 IEEE International Symposium on Circuits & Systems, pages 20–23, San Francisco CA, April 1974.

F.J. Harris, "On the use of windows for harmonic analysis with the discrete Fourier transform," Proc. IEEE, Vol. 66, pp. 51–83, January 178.

T.S. Huang, "Two-dimensional Windows," IEEE Trans. Audio Electroacoust., Vol. AU-20, pages 88–90, March 1972.

J.H. McClellan, "The design of two-dimensional digital filters by transformation," in Proc. 7th Annu. Princeton Conf. Inform. Sci. Syst., pages 247–251, 1973.

R.M. Mersereau, W.F.G. Mecklenbrauker, and T.F. Quatieri, Jr., "McClellan transformations for two-dimensional digital filtering. I. Design," IEEE Trans. Circuits Syst., Vol. CAS-23, pages 405–414, July 1976.

P.K. Rajan and M.N.S. Swamy, "Design of circularly symmetric two-dimensional FIR digital filters employing transformations with variable parameters," IEEE Trans. Acoust., Speech and Sig. Proc., Vol. ASSP-31, pages 637–642, June 1983.

T.H. Yu and S.K. Mitra, "A new two-dimensional window," IEEE Trans. Acoust., Speech and Sig. Proc., Vol. ASSP-33, pages 1058–1061, August 1985.

S.A.H. Aly and M.N. Fahmy, "Design of two-dimensional recursive digital filters with specified magnitude and group delay characteristics," IEEE Trans. Circuits Syst., Vol. CAS-25, pages 908–916, November 1978.

J.M. Costa and A.N. Venetsanopoulos, "Design of circularly symmetric two-dimensional recursive filters," IEEE Trans. Acoust., Speech and Sig. Proc., Vol. ASSP-22, pages 432–442, December 1974.

P.A. Ramamoorthy and L.T. Bruton, "Design of stable two-dimensional analog and digital filters with applications in image processing," Int. J. Circuit Theory Appl., Vol. 7, pages 229–245, April 1979.

M.N.S. Swamy, K.S. Thyagarajan, and V. Ramachandran, "Two-dimensional wave digital filters using doubly terminated 2-variable LC ladder configurations," Journal of the Franklin Institute, Vol. 304, No. 4/5, Oct./Nov. 1977.

K.S. Thyagarajan, "Circularly symmetric 2-d recursive digital filters," Proc. European Conf. Ckt. Theory & Design, Sept. 1978.

K.S. Thyagarajan, "Equiripple stopband characteristic for circularly symmetric 2-d recursive filters," Proc. IEEE, Vol. 68, February 1980.

K.S. Thyagarajan, "Design of 2-d IIR digital filters with circular symmetry by transformation of the variable," Proc. IEEE ICASSP, March 1981.

3 | Human Visual Perception

3.1   INTRODUCTION

In most image processing systems, a human observer is the final destination to
view the processed images. As shown in this chapter, the human visual system
(HVS) is more receptive to a certain frequency band than others. Moreover, the
human vision is sensitive to objects against certain backgrounds. In a like fashion,
the HVS favors certain colors over others. It is, therefore, imperative that an
image processing system exploits the characteristics of the HVS so as to deliver
images of the best quality in color and detail. Another objective in mimicking
the HVS is to be able to reduce or compress the amount of data in the original
image to a maximum without being able to notice any degradation in the image
quality. As shown later in this book, efficient compression algorithms exploit not
only the spatial but also the temporal aspect of the HVS in achieving a large
amount of data compression at visually lossless quality. This chapter describes
the human visual perception from a system standpoint to explain such phenomenon as *spatial masking*, etc.

A large body of work exists in the area of human vision. It is not the
intent here to describe such works in detail. Rather we would like to focus
attention on the systems approach to the HVS, sidelining lengthy discussions to
the references. The overall objective here is to explain how the human vision
works in terms of linear/nonlinear systems as briefly as possible so that these
ideas may be incorporated in the design of visually lossless video compression
systems.

3.2   BRIGHTNESS PERCEPTION

3.2.1   Intensity, Luminance, and Brightness

Our common experience tells us that we perceive both stationary and moving
objects in color or in black and white (B/W). Brightness perception refers
to achromatic or B/W perception. The human vision is sensitive to the visible

portion of the electromagnetic spectrum, called light. Light is an electromagnetic radiation and is characterized by a spectral energy distribution, $L(\lambda)$, where λ is the wavelength of the electromagnetic radiation ranging between 350 and 780 nm. When a light source with spectral energy distribution (SED) $L(x,y,\lambda)$ at wavelength λ and spatial coordinate (x,y) illumines an object, the object reflects light depending on its surface reflection characteristics, $\rho(x,y,\lambda)$. Therefore the SED of light emitted by the object at a particular wavelength λ can be written as

$$I(x,y,\lambda) = \rho(x,y,\lambda)L(x,y,\lambda), \quad 0 \le \rho(x,y,\lambda) \le 1. \tag{3-1}$$

An opaque object has a reflection coefficient $\rho(x,y,\lambda) = 0$, while a perfect reflector has $\rho(x,y,\lambda) = 1$. The intensity in Eq. (3-1) is the *stimulus* to the visual system. At this time we consider stationary stimulus fields.

A cross section of the human eye is shown in Figure 3-1. The incident light is focused on to the retina by the lens. The retina contains photoreceptors called

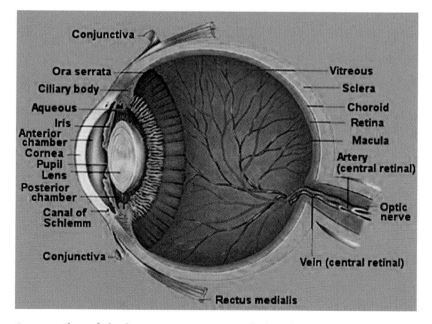

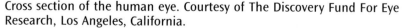

FIGURE   Cross section of the human eye. Courtesy of The Discovery Fund For Eye Research, Los Angeles, California.

3-1

rods and *cones.* The rods are thin and elongated and have a population numbering about 100 million and are concentrated away from the fovea. The rods are responsible for *scotopic* vision, which is our ability to see at very low light levels. At relatively higher light levels, cones are responsible for *photopic* vision. Cones are also the reason why we are able to perceive colors. Cones, however, are fewer in number than rods and are more abundant near the fovea. This may explain why the HVS can only discern fewer colors than it can discern a larger number of shades of gray. Between scotopic and photopic vision, both receptors function at intermediate light levels to provide *mesopic* vision.

Photoreceptors convert the optical signal into electrical impulses and transmit them to the central nervous system through the optic nerves. From a systems point of view, we would like to model the HVS in terms of a functional block. To this end, first the spectral energy of light from an object is converted into a spatial distribution of light intensity, called *luminance* $f(x,y)$, and is related to the intensity through

$$f(x,y) = \int_0^\infty I(x,y,\lambda)V(\lambda)d\lambda, \tag{3-2}$$

where $V(\lambda)$ is called the *relative luminous efficiency function* of the HVS. It is the ratio of the energy of a spectral light of the wavelength, λ_{max}, to which the eye is most sensitive, to the energy of a spectral light of wavelength, λ at which the two lights produce equivalent luminous sensations. This is so because the eye is not equally sensitive to lights of all wavelengths. For example, if the maximum sensitivity of the eye occurs at $\lambda_{max} = 555\,nm$, then a monochromatic light of wavelength $500\,nm$ must have three times the energy of the light at a wavelength of $555\,nm$ to give the same luminous sensation. The luminous efficiency function, which has been determined experimentally for the standard photopic observer by the CIE (Commission Internationale de l'Eclairage) in 1924, is a dimensionless, bell-shaped function as shown in Figure 3-2 and its characteristics depend on whether the vision takes place in dark or bright light. Figure 3-2 also shows the relative luminous efficiency function for the standard scotopic observer, also determined by the CIE in 1951. Each of these functions is normalized to have a peak value of unity. It is seen from Figure 3-2 that the visual response peaks at about 555 nm under photopic vision, corresponding to the yellow–green light. One can infer from $V(\lambda)$ that the human vision has the highest sensitivity to yellow–green light, the lowest sensitivity to blue light, and an intermediate sensitivity to red. Note that the luminance in Eq. (3-2) is proportional to the light intensity and has the unit $cd.m^{-2}$ ("nits").

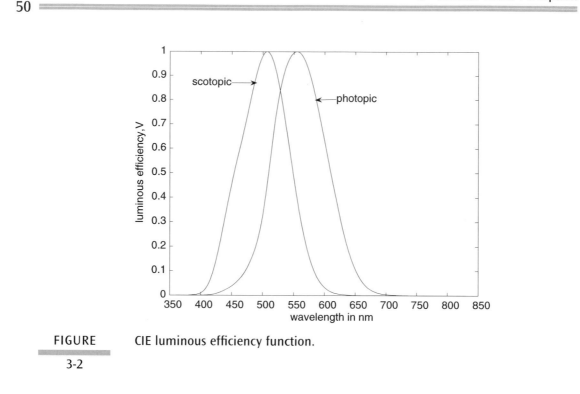

FIGURE   CIE luminous efficiency function.

3-2

3.2.2   Simultaneous Contrast

Observe that even though the luminance in Eq. (3-2) takes into account the relative luminous efficiency function of the HVS, it is not what is perceived because (1) what we perceive is a sensation and we cannot measure our brightness perception in the same unit as the luminance and (2) the luminance in Eq. (3-2) is independent of any background. Human vision does not take place in isolation, rather it is influenced by the background. In this context, we define *contrast ratio* as the ratio of luminances of the brightest and darkest areas in an image. If we are viewing a video or motion picture, the contrast ratio changes with time. So the term *simultaneous contrast ratio* is used to signify the contrast ratio at one instant. A cinema viewed in a movie theater has a typical value of 100 : 1 for simultaneous contrast ratio, while watching television in a living room has 20 : 1. We therefore have to express our ability to discriminate between two luminance values in terms of the contrast ratio. More specifically, our ability to discriminate between luminance values is expressed in terms of *contrast sensitivity*, which is the ratio of luminance values between two adjacent areas of nearly equal luminance.

Weber was the first one to quantify contrast sensitivity in human vision. In fact, Weber's law states that the ratio of just noticeable difference (JND) in luminance between an object and its surround to the luminance of the object is constant over a wide range of the object luminance. That is, if f_s and f_0 denote the background and object luminance, respectively, then

$$\frac{|f_s - f_0|}{f_0} = \text{constant} \qquad (3\text{-}3)$$

The constant in Eq. (3-3) is called the Weber fraction and is equal to about 0.02. Figure 3-3 shows two examples of simultaneous contrast. The term *just noticeable* is used to indicate the threshold of vision, i.e., the condition where the object is visible 50% of the time when the background luminance is adjusted accordingly. To account for the large spread in the human visual characteristics, the term *just noticeable* is applied to the HVS with average vision. If we let $f_0 = f$ and the surround luminance $f_s = f + \Delta f$, where Δf is small for just noticeable difference in luminance, Weber's law in Eq. (3-3) can be written as

$$\frac{\Delta f}{f} = d(\log f) = \Delta c = \text{constant}. \qquad (3\text{-}4)$$

Δc in Eq. (3-4) is the change in contrast. The implication of Weber's law is that the JND in luminance is proportional to the object luminance. In other words, equal increments of the luminance on a logarithmic scale should be perceived to be equally different. The Weber fraction, however, increases at both lower and upper values of the luminance. It has been found that the human vision can discriminate 1% of the object luminance over 2 decades of luminance, which is indeed quite remarkable! The solution to Eq. (3-4) is found to be

$$c = a_0 + a_1 \log f, \qquad (3\text{-}5)$$

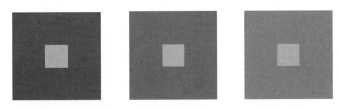

FIGURE   Simultaneous contrast.

3-3

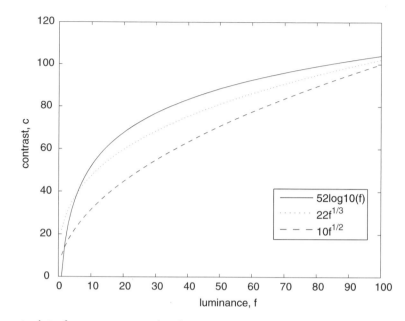

FIGURE   A plot of contrast versus luminance.

3-4

where c is the contrast and a_0 and a_1 are constants. Figure 3-4 shows a plot of the contrast function in Eq. (3-5). It also shows the power law equations of contrast that are commonly used in practice. Thus, we find from Weber's law that what is perceived is not the absolute luminance in Eq. (3-2), which is linearly related to the incident light intensity, but contrast as in Eq. (3-5), which is nonlinearly related to the luminance. This nonlinearity is a point operation, meaning that no spatial interaction exists between intensities.

3.2.3   Mach Bands

When spatial interaction between an object and its surround takes place, a phenomenon called the *Mach band effect* results. Consider the gray pattern shown in Figure 3-5a, where the intensity of each band is constant. When this is viewed carefully, notice that the left side appears to be less bright than the right side at the boundaries. An intensity profile of the bar chart and what is perceived are shown in Figure 3-5b. Notice undershoots and overshoots in the luminance at the boundaries. This is typical of a linear system where a step function produces a system response with under- and overshoots. The step response of the visual system is shown in Figure 3-5c.

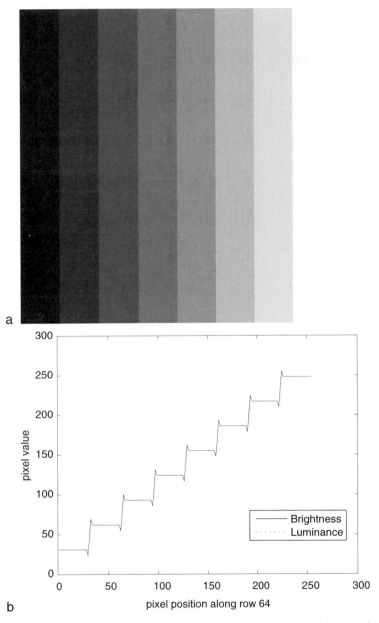

a

b

FIGURE

3-5

Mach band effect in human vision: (a) intensity pattern, (b) intensity profile, and (c) step response.

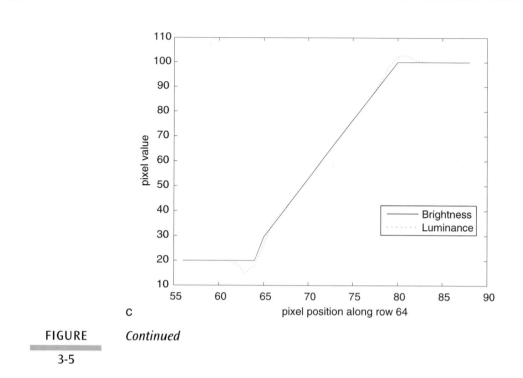

C

FIGURE   *Continued*

3-5

3.2.4   Transfer Function of the HVS

What was described in Section 3.2.3 was the spatial response of the HVS to step functions in intensities. It is possible to determine the impulse response of the HVS from the Mach band effect. Alternatively, we can describe the HVS in the frequency domain directly, which is called the *contrast sensitivity function* (CSF). A direct measurement of the CSF is obtained by considering a sinusoidal grating function of varying contrast and spatial frequency, as shown in Figure 3-6. When this intensity grating is viewed directly in front at a distance of about 1 m, thresholds of visibility or the inverse, contrast sensitivity, at the different frequencies are obtained. The curve representing the various thresholds is the CSF of the HVS. Of course, it depends on the viewer as well as the viewing conditions, such as lighting and viewing angle. One of the curve-fitted formulae is given by

$$H(f) = k\left(\alpha + \frac{f}{f_0}\right)e^{-\left(\frac{f}{f_0}\right)^\beta}, \tag{3-6}$$

where $f = \sqrt{f_1^2 + f_2^2}$ cycles/degree, f_1 and f_2 are the two spatial frequencies in cycles/unit length, and k, α, β, and f_0 are constants. For $\alpha = 0$ and $\beta = 1$, f_0 is the

FIGURE   A sinusoidal grating function of varying intensity and frequency.

3-6

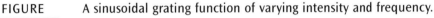

frequency at which the CSF peaks. The CSF curve corresponding to Eq. (3-6) is shown in Fig. 3-7a, which is seen to be a band-pass filter. The impulse response of the HVS whose frequency response is given in Eq. (3-6), with $\alpha = 1$ and $\beta = 1$, can be obtained from the inverse Fourier transform as

$$h(x) = 2Af_0 \frac{\left(1 - 4\pi^2 f_0^2 x^2\right)}{\left(1 + 4\pi^2 f_0^2 x^2\right)}, \tag{3-7}$$

where x is the distance in minutes of arc from the fovea. Figure 3-7b illustrates Eq. (3-7).

3.2.5   Monochrome Vision Model

Putting together the different visual effects described so far, we can model the HVS for brightness perception as follows. Light intensity enters the eye, whose optical characteristic is represented by a low-pass filter, $H_0(f_1, f_2)$. The spatial response of the eye to light intensity, represented by the relative luminous efficiency function $V(\lambda)$, results in the luminance function $f(x,y)$ as in Eq. (3-1). The inherent nonlinearity of the rods and cones transforms the luminance into a contrast function $c(x,y)$ in Eq. (3-5). Next, the lateral inhibition phenomenon of the photoreceptors is represented by a spatially invariant, isotropic, linear

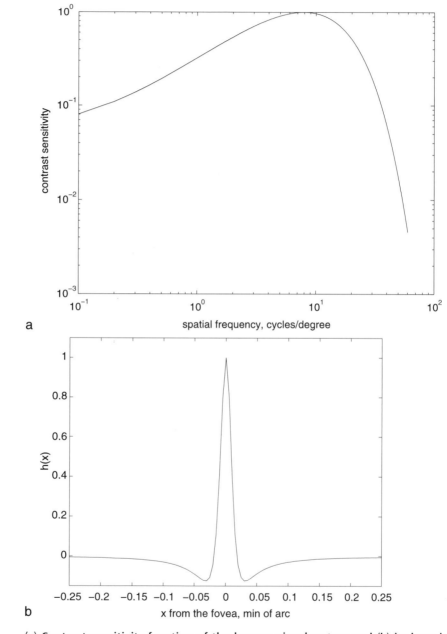

FIGURE

3-7

(a) Contrast sensitivity function of the human visual system and (b) its impulse response.

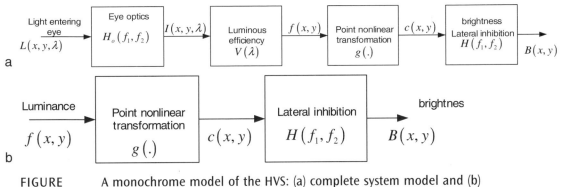

FIGURE   A monochrome model of the HVS: (a) complete system model and (b)
simplified model.

3-8

system whose frequency response is $H(f_1,f_2) = H(\sqrt{f_1^2 + f_2^2})$. The output of this filter is the perceived brightness $B(x,y)$, which is then transported to the central nervous system through the optic nerves.

So far no temporal dimension has been added to the visual perception. It is found that the HVS performs temporal integration, which is equivalent to low-pass filtering. The temporal frequency response of the HVS has been found to be of similar shape to that of the CSF. Therefore, the temporal filter is cascaded to the spatial filter and the output is now a function of space and time, $B(x,y,t)$. Because our understanding of the cerebral function as far as vision is concerned is limited, we stop at the filter response $B(x,y,t)$, which is the perceived brightness. Figure 3-8a shows a block diagram of the HVS. A simplified form of the HVS is shown in Figure 3-8b where the optic filter $H_0(f_1,f_2)$ is omitted, as the eye is assumed to have focused on the object of interest.

When we deal with a single frame of image, we can ignore the temporal dimension. This reduces the temporal filter impulse response to an impulse and so we can simply replace the temporal filter in Figure 3-8b by a line.

3.2.6   Visual Masking and an Improved HVS Model

The HVS model in the previous section was concerned with basic brightness perception when objects and backgrounds are assumed simple and constant. However, real world images seldom have simple objects and backgrounds. As pointed out at the beginning of this chapter, it is advantageous to exploit the HVS to achieve high image compression with visually lossless quality. As shown later, lossy image and video compression produce degradations that may or may not be visible to the naked eye. These degradations are usually noisy in nature,

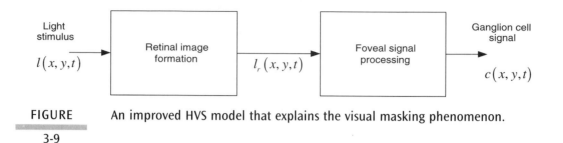

FIGURE

3-9
An improved HVS model that explains the visual masking phenomenon.

and the threshold of their visibility depends not only on the type and amount of compression, but also on the image structure. For example, degradation introduced by the compression process may be less visible in *busy* areas of the image, while it may be more visible in *flat* areas. Thus, the image structure has a tendency to *mask* the compression artifacts, which are the *targets*. This type of visual masking is known as *spatial masking*. In video compression where motion is present, *temporal masking* may also be present, whereby certain image structure present over a period of time may influence the visibility of compression artifacts more than certain other temporal masks. Efficient compression techniques exploit spatial and temporal visual masking effects to hide the compression artifacts to deliver high-quality images at as low a data rate as possible.

Girod has proposed a visual model that explains both spatial and temporal masking in the HVS and is shown in Figure 3-9. The model in Figure 3-9 is essentially nonlinear. The spatiotemporal luminance signal $l(x,y,t)$ undergoes a coordinate transformation, which depends on the direction of the optical axis, $(x_0(t),y_0(t))$. It is then filtered spatially by the optical PSF $h_0(x,y,t)$ to form the retinal signal $l_r(x,y,t)$, as given by

$$l_r(x,y,t) = h_0(x,y,t) * l(x - x_0(t), y - y_0(t)). \qquad (3\text{-}8)$$

The convolution in Eq. (3-8) is three-dimensional, involving the two spatial coordinates and time. The PSF $h_0(x,y,t)$ is assumed to be an isotropic Gaussian function with a spread $\sigma_0 \approx 1\,\text{arc min}$ and is purely spatial, i.e., it is an impulse in the temporal dimension. When the eye focuses on the object of interest, we ignore any eye movements and assume $(x_0(t),y_0(t)) = (0,0)$.

After this early processing, the retina converts the luminance signal $l_r(x,y,t)$ into a train of nerve impulses, which are transmitted to the central nervous system through the optic nerve. Because the receptors are highly concentrated around the fovea, Girod's model describes the hypothetical ganglion cell signal $g(x,y,t)$ in the fovea as output of the visual system. Thus, Figure 3-10 shows the nonlinear signal processing that takes place in the fovea. The first part corresponds to temporal low-pass filtering due to the photoreceptors in the retina and is modeled as a leaky integrator with a time constant $\tau_1 = 18\,\text{ms}$. Next, the joint action by the photochemical processes and neural interconnections in the retina are modeled by a spatiotemporally adaptive gain control operation and may be described by

$$g_i(x,y,t) = \frac{l_t(x,y,t)}{l_t(x,y,t) * h_i(x,y,t) + L_a}. \qquad (3\text{-}9)$$

The adaptive gain control mechanism in Eq. (3-9) allows the HVS to operate over a large range of brightness levels. The spatiotemporal inhibition spread $h_i(x,y,t)$ in Eq. (3-9) is an isotropic Gaussian PSF of spatial spread $\sigma_i = 8\,\text{arc min}$ and a second-order exponential of time constant $\tau_i = 35\,\text{ms}$ in the temporal dimension. The HVS adapts to the ambient luminance level L_a and then operates incrementally around this value. A CCIR recommended value is $L_a = 7\,cd/\text{m}^2$. Because the ganglion cells have a limited dynamic range, saturation occurs and is modeled by

$$g_s(x,y,t) = \begin{cases} g_i(x,y,t), & \text{for } g_i(x,y,t) \le 1 \\ 1 + \dfrac{1}{k_s}\ln(k_s \cdot [g_i(x,y,t)-1]+1), & \text{for } g_i(x,y,t) > 1. \end{cases} \qquad (3\text{-}10)$$

Saturation in the fovea as per Eq. (3-10) leads to spatial and temporal masking effects. Psychophysical tests suggest a value of 8 for k_s. Finally, conversion of the continuous amplitude signal $g_i(x,y,t)$ into an impulse train by the ganglion cells might be represented by another leaky integrator in the time domain with a time constant of $\tau_g = 18\,\text{ms}$. The final output is the ganglion cell output $g(x,y,t)$, as shown in Figure 3-10.

We will show later how the visual masking model of the HVS just described can be used to design a visually lossless compression algorithm. The following sections describe color perception in the HVS, as all natural images and video are in color.

3.3   COLOR PERCEPTION

In the previous sections we learned how brightness or black and white is perceived. Because color images are more realistic and pleasing to the eye, they are widely used in still images, video, and cinema. We should therefore know how to represent colors numerically and how the human eye perceives color. A color

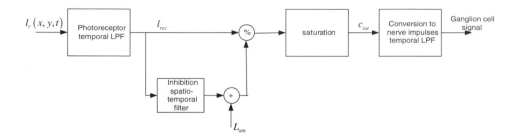

FIGURE   Signal processing in the fovea.

3-10

stimulus is specified in terms of a SED $C(\lambda)$ similar to the light intensity. This stimulus evokes a color sensation in the human vision. Colors are identified by their names, as red, yellow, green, and so on. It has been found that stimuli with differing spectral power distributions can evoke the same color sensation. Thus, color is that aspect of visible light by which a human distinguishes between different spectral energy distributions of light. Unlike luminance, color cannot be specified by a single quantity. In fact, it has three attributes, namely brightness, hue, and saturation. As shown earlier, brightness refers to the perceived luminance of an object. The hue of a color is an attribute associated with the dominant wavelength in a mixture of light waves and refers to the dominant color as perceived by an observer, as in a "red," "yellow," or "pink" object. Saturation refers to the relative purity or the amount of white light mixed with a hue. Thus we see that three independent attributes or parameters are needed to describe colors.

A stimulus $C(\lambda)$ in terms of a SED may be continuous in λ or it may be specified at a set of discrete values of λ. Because $C(\lambda)$ is not unique in terms of color perception, it would be practical to specify color in terms of a few independent parameters so that colors as perceived can be identified uniquely by these few parameters. Evidence shows that the human retina contains three types of cones with overlapping spectral sensitivities, centered around 445 (corresponding to blue), 535 (corresponding to green), and 570 (corresponding to red) nm in wavelength. In response to incident light, each type of cone integrates the incident intensity weighted by the respective sensitivity and produces a number, so to speak, at each pixel location. These three numbers then are mainly responsible for the color sensation. This has given rise to the so-called *tristimulus* theory of color vision. According to this theory, the color of light entering the HVS may be specified by only three numbers rather than specifying a complete spectral energy distribution. Thus a color stimulus can be expressed as a linearly weighted sum of three independent color sources, called the *primaries*. The color source depends on the application. In optical systems the color sources are the red, green, and blue lights of specified dominant wavelengths, and color mixing is known as *additive color mixing*, whereas in color printing, the sources are yellow, magenta, and cyan pigments and the resulting color mixing is called *color subtraction*. A color is, therefore, uniquely specified by the three coefficients that adjust the amounts of primaries mixed in producing a particular color sensation. It is understood that the three primaries are also specified in order to synthesize colors.

3.3.1   Color-Matching Functions

The trichromacy of color vision can be called the analysis of a color stimulus, whereas the trichromacy of color mixture is the synthesis of a color stimulus, and it states that light of any color can be synthesized by an appropriate additive mixture of three properly chosen primary light sources. This topic has developed into the science of *colorimetry* or *color matching*. In order to be able to synthesize a color, which will evoke the same color sensation as a given SED, we need to determine tristimulus values of the color stimulus. This is aided by *color matching functions* (CMFs), which are determined experimentally as follows. Three appropriate, monochromatic primary sources of known SED are chosen. A 10° bipartite field is projected against a dark, neutral surround, as shown in Figure 3-11. The test color of a monochromatic source at a particular wavelength

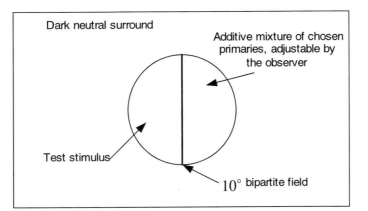

FIGURE   A setup to determine 10° color-matching functions.

3-11

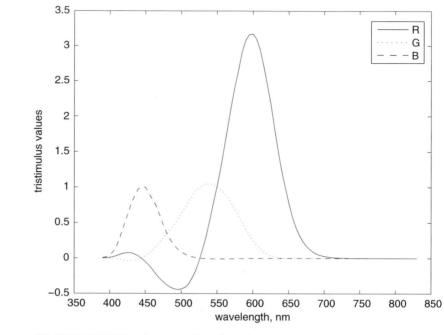

λ is projected onto the left field and a standard observer tries to match the left field by adjusting the amounts of the three primaries at wavelengths 645.2 (red), 525.3 (green), and 444.4 (blue) nm until a match is obtained. The tristimulus values of the color being matched at λ are then the amounts of the three primaries just found. The experiment is repeated for every λ in the visible portion of the spectrum. It is evident that at some wavelengths there are no matches to the test field by positive linear combination of the primaries, as the primaries are independent sources. In such cases, a known amount of red is added to the test field and the resulting field is matched by an appropriate combination of the other two primaries. Hence the negative values for the CMFs, as shown in Figure 3-12.

With the aid of CMFs, the tristimulus values of any color stimulus $C(\lambda)$ can be determined by

$$R = \int_{\lambda_{\min}}^{\lambda_{\max}} C(\lambda)r(\lambda)d\lambda,\, G = \int_{\lambda_{\min}}^{\lambda_{\max}} C(\lambda)g(\lambda)d\lambda,\, B = \int_{\lambda_{\min}}^{\lambda_{\max}} C(\lambda)b(\lambda)d\lambda, \qquad (3\text{-}11)$$

where $r(\lambda)$, $g(\lambda)$, and $b(\lambda)$ are the CMFs as shown in Figure 3-12. If the CMFs and the SED of a color stimulus are specified at k discrete values of λ, the tristimulus values in Eq. (3-11) can be written in matrix form as

$$\begin{bmatrix} R \\ G \\ B \end{bmatrix} = \begin{bmatrix} r(\lambda_1)....r(\lambda_k) \\ g(\lambda_1)....g(\lambda_k) \\ b(\lambda_1)....b(\lambda_k) \end{bmatrix} \begin{bmatrix} c(\lambda_1) \\ : \\ c(\lambda_k) \end{bmatrix}, \tag{3-12}$$

where $\lambda_1 = \lambda_{\min}$ and $\lambda_k = \lambda_{\max}$. Two color stimuli, $C_1(\lambda)$ and $C_2(\lambda)$, will evoke the same color sensation if the corresponding tristimuli are equal, i.e.,

$$R_1 = \int_{\lambda_{\min}}^{\lambda_{\max}} C_1(\lambda)r(\lambda)d\lambda = \int_{\lambda_{\min}}^{\lambda_{\max}} C_2(\lambda)r(\lambda)d\lambda = R_2$$

$$G_1 = \int_{\lambda_{\min}}^{\lambda_{\max}} C_1(\lambda)g(\lambda)d\lambda = \int_{\lambda_{\min}}^{\lambda_{\max}} C_2(\lambda)g(\lambda)d\lambda = G_2$$

$$B_1 = \int_{\lambda_{\min}}^{\lambda_{\max}} C_1(\lambda)b(\lambda)d\lambda = \int_{\lambda_{\min}}^{\lambda_{\max}} C_2(\lambda)b(\lambda)d\lambda = B_2 \tag{3-13}$$

In such a case, $C_1(\lambda)$ and $C_2(\lambda)$ are called *metamers*.

3.3.2   Color Coordinate Systems

Instead of specifying a color in terms of its tristimulus values R, G, and B, it is customary to use normalized tristimuli called *chromaticites*. These are defined, respectively, by

$$r = \frac{R}{R+G+B}, \; g = \frac{G}{R+G+B}, \; b = \frac{B}{R+G+B}. \tag{3-14}$$

Of course, because $r + g + b = 1$, two of the three chromaticities are sufficient to locate any color in this RGB color coordinate system. However, a third dimension is necessary, which is the brightness Y, to specify any color. Thus, a color is specified by the two chromaticities r and g, along with the brightness value Y. Note that brightness corresponds to equal values of R, G, and B. Therefore, given r, g, and Y of a color, its tristimuli can be obtained from Eq. (3-14) as

$$R = rY, \; G = gY, \; B = (1 - r - g)Y. \tag{3-15}$$

The CMFs $r(\lambda)$, $g(\lambda)$, and $b(\lambda)$ in Figure 3-12 were developed by the CIE in 1931 for a standard observer, and the corresponding primaries are known as CIE *spectral primaries*. Using these spectral curves, one can obtain the tristimulus values required to match a given SED of a color through the use of Eq. (3-11) or Eq. (3-12) depending on whether continuous or discrete SEDs are specified.

3.3.2.1   CIE XYZ Primaries

One drawback of the CIE spectral primary system is that CMFs have negative values. To avoid this defect, CIE introduced a new color coordinate system called the CIE XYZ primary system. In this system, all the CMFs are positive, as shown in Figure 3-13. However, the XYZ primaries are not physically realizable. The XYZ values are defined by the CIE in terms of the RGB tristimulus values and are given by

$$\begin{bmatrix} X \\ Y \\ Z \end{bmatrix} = \begin{bmatrix} 0.490 & 0.310 & 0.200 \\ 0.177 & 0.813 & 0.011 \\ 0.000 & 0.010 & 0.990 \end{bmatrix} \begin{bmatrix} R \\ G \\ B \end{bmatrix} \tag{3-16}$$

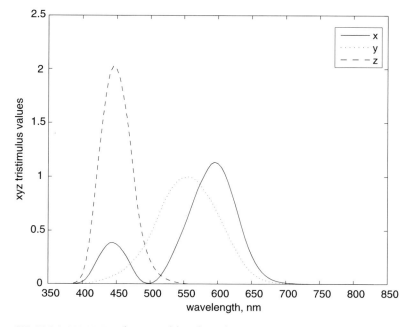

FIGURE   CIE 1964 10° XYZ color-matching functions.

3-13

The primaries used in describing Eq. (3-16) have wavelengths of 700, 546.1, and 435.8 nm for red, green, and blue, respectively. In Eq. (3-16), Y corresponds to the luminance.

The RGB values corresponding to the XYZ tristimulus values of a color can be obtained by matrix inversion of Eq. (3-16) and are given by

$$
\begin{bmatrix} R \\ G \\ B \end{bmatrix} = \begin{bmatrix} 2.364 & -0.896 & -0.468 \\ -0.515 & 1.425 & 0.088 \\ 0.005 & -0.014 & 1.009 \end{bmatrix} \begin{bmatrix} X \\ Y \\ Z \end{bmatrix}
\tag{3-17}
$$

The chromaticites in the CIE XYZ system are defined by

$$
x = \frac{X}{X+Y+Z}, \ y = \frac{Y}{X+Y+Z}, \ z = \frac{Z}{X+Y+Z}.
\tag{3-18}
$$

Of course, $x + y + z = 1$. In the CIE standard, color perception is measured by viewing mixtures of the three standard primary color sources: red, green, and blue with wavelengths of 700, 546.1, and 435.8 nm, respectively. Figure 3-14 shows

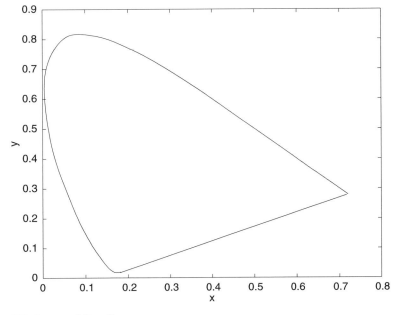

FIGURE   CIE chromaticity diagram.

3-14

the CIE chromaticity diagram in which the primary colors and other spectrally pure colors obtained by mixing the primary colors are shown as points along the boundary of the *horseshoe*-shaped figure. Each point on the diagram represents a unique color and can be located by the chromaticity (x,y). White light falls in the middle of the figure with chromaticity $\left(\dfrac{1}{3},\dfrac{1}{3}\right)$. Colors within the boundary are perceived as becoming more pastel toward white. Given the chromaticity x, y and the brightness Y of a color, its XYZ values can be obtained from

$$X = \frac{x}{y}Y, \ Y = Y, \ Z = \frac{1-x-y}{y}Y. \tag{3-19}$$

3.3.2.2   NTSC Receiver and Transmission Primaries

The CIE XYZ system is not the only color coordinate system in use to represent the tristimulus values of colors. A variety of color coordinate systems have been proposed for different applications. Table 3-1 lists various color coordinate systems.

The National Television Systems Committee (NTSC) developed two color coordinate systems, one for the TV receivers and one for the TV transmission. The NTSC receiver primary system uses three phosphor primaries that emit light in the red, green, and blue regions of the visible portion of the electromagnetic spectrum. The reference white in this system corresponds to equal tristimulus values of R_N, G_N, and B_N. Note that we have used a subscript N for the three NTSC receiver primaries to distinguish them from the corresponding CIE spectral primaries. The NTSC receiver tristimuli of a color can be converted to the CIE RGB tristimuli to match the same color, using the following equation:

$$\begin{bmatrix} R \\ G \\ B \end{bmatrix} = \begin{bmatrix} 1.167 & -0.146 & -0.151 \\ 0.114 & 0.753 & 0.159 \\ -0.001 & 0.059 & 1.128 \end{bmatrix} \begin{bmatrix} R_N \\ G_N \\ B_N \end{bmatrix} \tag{3-20}$$

Similarly, the formula for converting tristimuli in the NTSC receiver primary system into CIE XYZ values is

$$\begin{bmatrix} X \\ Y \\ Z \end{bmatrix} = \begin{bmatrix} 0.607 & 0.174 & 0.201 \\ 0.299 & 0.587 & 0.114 \\ 0.000 & 0.066 & 1.117 \end{bmatrix} \begin{bmatrix} R_N \\ G_N \\ B_N \end{bmatrix} \tag{3-21}$$

Table 3-1. List of Color Coordinate Transformations

Color Coordinate System	Remarks
C.I.E. spectral primary system: Coordinates are R, G, and B.	Primaries are monochromatic light sources whose wavelengths for Red, Green, and Blues are 700 nm, 546.1 nm, and 435.8 nm, respectively. Reference white corresponds to $R = G = B = 1$. The color matching curves and chromaticity diagrams are shown in Fig. 3-12 and 3-14, respectively.
C.I.E. XYZ system in which, Y represents luminance.	X, Y, and Z are expressed in terms of R, G, and B by $$\begin{bmatrix} X \\ Y \\ Z \end{bmatrix} = \begin{bmatrix} 0.490 & 0.310 & 0.200 \\ 0.177 & 0.813 & 0.011 \\ 0.000 & 0.010 & 0.990 \end{bmatrix} \begin{bmatrix} R \\ G \\ B \end{bmatrix}$$
NTSC Receiver primary system with coordinates R_N, G_N, B_N	XYZ values are obtained by linear transformation and is based on TV phosphor primaries. Reference white corresponds to $$R_N = G_N = B_N = 1$$ $$\begin{bmatrix} R_N \\ G_N \\ B_N \end{bmatrix} = \begin{bmatrix} 1.910 & -0.533 & -0.288 \\ -0.985 & 2.000 & -0.028 \\ 0.058 & -0.118 & 0.896 \end{bmatrix} \begin{bmatrix} X \\ Y \\ Z \end{bmatrix}$$
YUV of Rec. 601 with luminance Y and chrominance U and V R, G, and B are gamma corrected values.	$$\begin{bmatrix} Y \\ U \\ V \end{bmatrix} = \begin{bmatrix} 0.299 & 0.587 & 0.114 \\ -0.147 & -0.289 & 0.436 \\ 0.615 & -0.515 & -0.100 \end{bmatrix} \begin{bmatrix} R \\ G \\ B \end{bmatrix}$$ $$\begin{bmatrix} R \\ G \\ B \end{bmatrix} = \begin{bmatrix} 1 & 0 & 1.140 \\ 1 & -0.395 & -0.581 \\ 1 & 2.032 & 0 \end{bmatrix} \begin{bmatrix} Y \\ U \\ V \end{bmatrix}$$
Y, C_B, C_R of Rec. 601 for 8-bit RGB. C_B, C_R in the range ± 128	$$\begin{bmatrix} Y \\ C_B \\ C_R \end{bmatrix} = \begin{bmatrix} 0.299 & 0.587 & 0.114 \\ -0.168 & -0.330 & 0.498 \\ 0.498 & -0.417 & -0.081 \end{bmatrix} \begin{bmatrix} R \\ G \\ B \end{bmatrix}$$

Table 3-1. *Continued*

Color Coordinate System	Remarks
RGB values from Y, C_B, C_R of Rec. 601 for SDTV RGB values in the range 0 to 255	$\begin{bmatrix} R \\ G \\ B \end{bmatrix} = \begin{bmatrix} 1 & 0 & 1.397 \\ 1 & -0.343 & -0.711 \\ 1 & 1.765 & 0 \end{bmatrix} \begin{bmatrix} Y \\ C_B \\ C_R \end{bmatrix}$
Y, C_B, C_R of Rec. 709 for HDTV for 8-bit RGB. The luminance value has an excusion of 219	$\begin{bmatrix} Y \\ C_B \\ C_R \end{bmatrix} = \begin{bmatrix} 16 \\ 128 \\ 128 \end{bmatrix} + \begin{bmatrix} 0.213 & 0.715 & 0.722 \\ -0.117 & -0.394 & 0.511 \\ 0.511 & -0.465 & -0.047 \end{bmatrix} \begin{bmatrix} R \\ G \\ B \end{bmatrix}$
RGB from Y, C_B, C_R of Rec. 709	$\begin{bmatrix} R \\ G \\ B \end{bmatrix} = \begin{bmatrix} 0.0046 & 0 & 0.007 \\ 0.0046 & -0.001 & -0.002 \\ 0.0046 & 0.008 & 0 \end{bmatrix} \begin{bmatrix} Y \\ C_B \\ C_R \end{bmatrix} - \begin{bmatrix} 16 \\ 128 \\ 128 \end{bmatrix}$

In the NTSC transmission system, luminance is represented by Y and the chrominance by I and Q, respectively. I and Q are called the color difference signals. Because black and white TV was commissioned first, color transmission, which came later, was to be achieved in the same bandwidth requirement as black and white TV. The I and Q channels modulate the carrier in quadrature amplitude. Tristimulus values in the NTSC transmission system can be expressed in terms of those in the NTSC receiver primary system and vice versa by the following equations:

$$\begin{bmatrix} Y \\ I \\ Q \end{bmatrix} = \begin{bmatrix} 2.999 & 0.587 & 0.114 \\ 0.596 & -0.274 & -0.322 \\ 0.211 & -0.523 & 0.312 \end{bmatrix} \begin{bmatrix} R_N \\ G_N \\ B_N \end{bmatrix} \tag{3-22}$$

$$\begin{bmatrix} R_N \\ G_N \\ B_N \end{bmatrix} = \begin{bmatrix} 1.0000 & 0.9562 & -0.6214 \\ 1.0000 & -0.2727 & -0.6468 \\ 1.0000 & -1.1037 & 1.7006 \end{bmatrix} \begin{bmatrix} Y \\ I \\ Q \end{bmatrix} \tag{3-23}$$

In addition to these color coordinates, other coordinate systems are also used in applications, such as digital cinema. These are discussed in a later chapter.

3.3.3   HVS Model for Color Vision

Discussions from the previous sections lead us to a system model of the HVS for color vision. There are now three channels instead of one in the color vision. First the spectral responses of the three types of cones to a color stimulus are coded into the tristimulus values, as given by

$$\alpha_R(C) = \int_{\lambda_{\min}}^{\lambda_{\max}} S_L(\lambda)C(\lambda)d\lambda, \, \alpha_G(C) = \int_{\lambda_{\min}}^{\lambda_{\max}} S_M(\lambda)C(\lambda)d\lambda,$$

$$\alpha_B(C) = \int_{\lambda_{\min}}^{\lambda_{\max}} S_S(\lambda)C(\lambda)d\lambda.$$

(3-24)

In Eq. (3-24), $S_L(\lambda)$, $S_M(\lambda)$ and $S_S(\lambda)$ are the spectral absorption characteristics of the cone pigments corresponding to the long (red), medium (green), and short (blue) wavelengths, respectively, as shown in Figure 3-15. In the next stage of visual processing, the tristimulus values undergo a nonlinear point transformation, as discussed in the context of brightness perception. Note that the tristimulus values in Eq. (3-24) correspond to the RGB coordinates. However, these

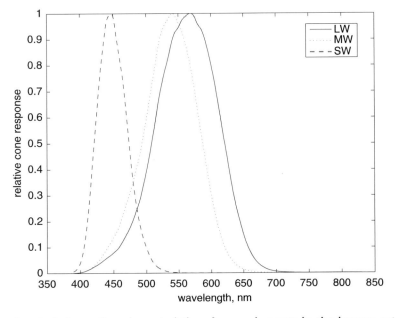

FIGURE   Spectral absorption characteristics of cone pigments in the human retina.

3-15

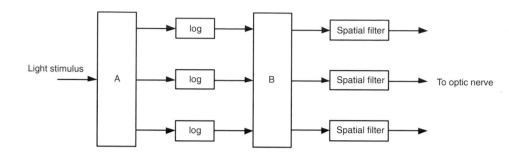

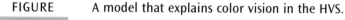

FIGURE   A model that explains color vision in the HVS.

3-16

cone signals have a very high redundancy. The visual system removes the redundancy by converting the RGB tristimuli into brightness and chrominance signals. For our purpose, we can accomplish this by a 3×3 matrix transformation. Finally, the three signals are spatially processed by the three filters, which correspond to the brightness and chrominance components. The overall model of the HVS for color vision is shown in Figure 3-16.

3.3.4   Opponent Color Model

From our day-to-day experience, we know that there is no such color as reddish green or yellowish blue. This suggests the possibility that the HVS encodes a color stimulus into three components: yellow, red–green, and yellow–blue. This is known as the *opponent color* model. Figure 3-17 is a schematic diagram that shows how the initial cone responses are encoded into luminance and two opponent-color channels. It should be noted that the luminance channel of the opponent-color model is not the same as in, say, television in that the B cones have no contribution to the luminance. If this indeed is how the HVS operates, it may perhaps be of value in using this color coordinate system in video compression schemes.

3.4   SUMMARY

This chapter showed how the photoreceptors in the eye perceive monochromatic or black and white objects—relationship between monochromatic light stimulus and perceived brightness. These are governed by contrast threshold

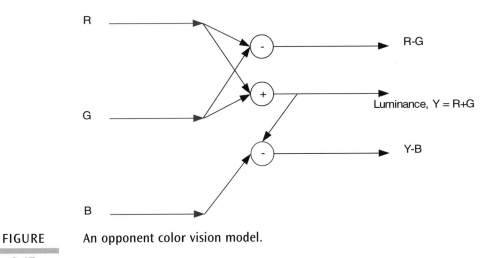

FIGURE   An opponent color vision model.

3-17

vision and spatial frequency selectivity of the eye. We also learned how certain spatial stimuli have the ability to mask targets and explained this visual masking phenomenon in terms of a nonlinear system model.

Human visual perception of colors was introduced by beginning with trichromatic theory of light, followed by cone spectral responses. We also described various color coordinate systems that are commonly used in different applications. Finally, we described a system model for color vision as well as an opponent-color model, which may be more suitable for video compression.

REFERENCES

As mentioned at the outset of this chapter, a large body of works in both eye anatomy and color science is available in the literature. It is therefore not feasible to exhaustively list all references here. The listed references should be taken as a representative of the research works done in these fields.

Refer to Cornsweet (1971), Carterette and Friedman (1975), and Hecht (1924) for detailed information on fundamental topics in visual perception.

For information on measurement and applications of the visibility function, refer to Netravali and Haskell (1988).

For further details on the monochrome vision model, refer to the following: Hall and Hall (1977), Mannos and Sakrison (1974), Sakrison (1977), Leeuwenberg and Buffart (1978), and Girod (1989).

For introduction to color perception, color representation, and general reading in color, refer to Young (1802), Maxwell (1861), MacAdam (1970), Wyszecki and Stiles (1982), and Grassman (1954).

For color vision model, their applications, and so on, as well as temporal visual perception, refer to Frei and Baxter (1977), Limb and Rubinstein (1977), Boynton (1979), and Kelly (1961).

T.N. Cornsweet, *Visual Perception*, New York: Academic Press, 1971.

E.C. Carterette and M.P. Friedman, eds., *Handbook of Perception*, Vol. 5, New York: Academic Press, 1975.

S. Hecht, "The visual discrimination of intensity and the Weber-Fechner law," J. Gen. Physiol., 7, 1924.

A.N. Netravali and B.G. Haskell, *Digital Pictures: Representation and Compression*, New York: Plenum Press, 1988.

C.F. Hall and E.L. Hall, "A nonlinear model for the spatial characteristics of the human visual system," IEEE Trans. Syst. Man. Cybern., SMC-7, 3, pages 161–170, 1977.

J.L. Mannos and D.J. Sakrison, "The effects of a visual fidelity criterion on the encoding of images," IEEE Trans. Info. Theory IT-20, no. 4, pages 525–536, July 1974.

D.J. Sakrison, "On the role of observer and a distortion measure in image transmission," IEEE Trans. Communication COM-25, pages 1251–1267, Nov. 1977.

T. Young, "On the theory of light and colors," Philosophical Transactions of the Royal Society of London, 92, pages 20–71, 1802.

J.C. Maxwell, "On the theory of three primary colours," Lectures delivered in 1861. W.D. Nevin (ed.), Sci. Papers 1, Cambridge Univ. Press, London, pages 445–450, 1890.

D.L. MacAdam, *Sources of Color Science*, Cambridge, MA: MIT Press, 1970.

G.W. Wyszecki and W.S. Stiles, *Color Science: Concepts and Methods, Quantitative Data and Formulae*, New York: John Wiley, 1982.

H.G. Grassman, "Theory of compound colours," Philosophic Magazine 4, no. 7, pages 254–264, 1954.

W. Frei and B. Baxter, "Rate distortion coding simulation for color images," IEEE Trans. Coom. COM-25, pages 1385–1392, Nov. 1977.

J.O. Limb, C.B. Rubinstein, and J.E. Thompson, "Digital coding of color video signals," IEEE Trans. Comm. COM-25, pages 1349–1384, Nov. 1977.

R.M. Boynton, *Human Color Vision*, Holt, Rinehart and Winston, 1979.

D.H. Kelly, "Visual responses to time dependent stimuli. I. Amplitude sensitivity measurements," J. Opt. Soc. America, 51, pages 422–429, 1961. Also see pages 917–918 of this issue, and Vol. 59, 1969.

4 Image Acquisition

4.1 INTRODUCTION

In order to be able to process images by computers, images must first be made available in digital format. In a conventional camera, objects in a scene are focused by the optical elements on to a film, which is placed at the focal plane of the lens. The object is imaged onto the film when it is exposed to light from the object. In a digital camera, an array of photosensitive electronic sensors takes the place of the film. When the sensors are exposed to light, each sensor element develops an electrical charge that is proportional to the number of photons falling on the sensor. This electrical charge is then converted to a decimal number represented in a binary format. Figure 4-1 illustrates the principle of imaging an object. The process of image acquisition consists of focusing the object onto the sensor array by optical means, exposing the sensors to the focused object, scanning the sensor array, and converting the analog electrical signal to digital format. This chapter discusses the methods used in the acquisition process. Current technology uses sensors made out of semiconductor materials, called charge-coupled devices (CCD). So, we will describe CCD sensors. We will also describe briefly the mathematics behind the sampling process and its implications. Finally we will introduce the equipments used in converting film into video format for digital cinema application.

Still images are stored in computers as 2-D arrays or matrices of integers consisting of a number of rows, with each row having a number of picture elements or pixels or pels. Each still image is also called a frame of image. A moving picture consists of a sequence of image frames. When the sequence of frames is displayed at a certain rate, we get the illusion of continuous motion. A movie film is projected at a rate of 24 frames/s (fps) whereas the TV rate is 30 fps in North America.

4.2 IMAGE SENSORS

Semiconductor or solid-state image detectors operate on the principle of internal photoelectric effect, whereby the charge carriers generated as a result

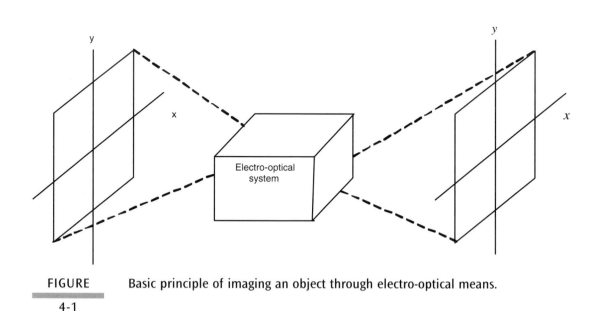

FIGURE 4-1   Basic principle of imaging an object through electro-optical means.

of photon absorption produce electrical conduction internal to the device. The absorption of photons by the device causes the generation of charge carriers, which drift across the depletion layer due to an applied electric field to cause a current to flow. Since the current flow in the depletion layer is only due to the generated charge carriers, we have the conversion of light intensity into an electrical signal.

Solid-state photo detectors fall into the categories of photo emissive devices, photovoltaic cells, photoconductors, and silicon sensors. Because digital cameras use photo sensors made out of highly purified silicon crystals, we are only concerned with them here. The advantages of solid-state photo detectors are compact size, low bias voltage and power consumption, high peak quantum efficiency, ruggedness, wide operating temperature, and low cost.

4.2.1   CCD Sensors

The charge-coupled device was invented at Bell Labs in the late 1960s and was used as a computer memory circuit. Subsequently it was used as an image detector due to the light sensitivity property of silicon. A CCD, which is essentially a metal-oxide semiconductor (MOS) or a metal-insulator semiconductor (MIS) with multiple gates, consists of an array of sensors built into a silicon substrate.

Each sensor corresponds to a pixel (picture element) in the digital image. Each silicon sensor creates an electron-hole pair when excited by a photon. A silicon device with a thin metal layer deposited on the surface and biased with positive voltage will create a potential well, which can collect and hold the photoelectrons generated by impinging light intensity. Each sensor element in the array has a potential well that can hold about 1000 electrons per square micrometer of silicon area, which translate to about 100,000 electrons per pixel of size 9×9 square micrometer. The photoelectrons that are collected in each potential well due to the incident light are shifted out as a charge packet, converted to a voltage, and subsequently digitized.

CCDs have some important parameters, which characterize their performance and are as follows.

Saturation or well fill refers to the maximum electron density of each potential well, which is a function of the thickness and area of each sensor element. A good design criterion is that the residual charge in the oxide be small and not approach the saturation value.

Quantum efficiency refers to the ratio of the rate of photoelectrons generated to the rate of photons absorbed by the sensor. Values of 30 to 40% over the visible portion of the electromagnetic spectrum for the quantum efficiency are not uncommon in back-illuminated CCDs.

Dark current is the result of thermal shot noise in the device, and its effect is significant at low light levels, where the photoelectrons generated are small in number. A typical value for dark current is around 10 pA per square centimeter. To calibrate the sensor, the dark current image, which is obtained with the shutter closed, is subtracted from the captured image.

Maximum integration time corresponds to the maximum time interval over which the sensor is exposed. Because dark current is always present as a result of thermal shot noise, it integrates during exposure and may saturate the sensor potential well. The maximum integration time is therefore related to the dark current and saturation value of the CCD.

Dynamic range is defined as the ratio of the electrons corresponding to saturation to that corresponding to dark current. The dynamic range can be very large in a well-designed CCD. Similarly, the shot noise can be very low.

Blooming occurs as a result of overflow of a potential well into adjacent wells when a sensor element is overexposed.

Selection of a CCD chip should therefore be made on the basis of the aforementioned parameters. For example, a CCD with a very large potential well is suitable for scientific applications, whereas a CCD with a moderate well fill value may be used for professional photography. The sensor arrays can be built in different ways depending on how the charges are read out, yielding different CCD architectures. The following section describes these architectures briefly.

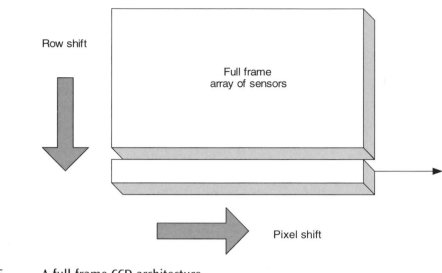

Row shift

Full frame
array of sensors

Pixel shift

FIGURE   A full-frame CCD architecture.

4-2

4.2.1.1   Full-Frame Architecture

In this architecture (Figure 4-2) the shutter is closed after the array has been exposed to light. Once the shutter is closed, the charge packets in the bottommost row are shifted out one pixel at a time. Next the charge packets in the array are shifted down one row and again the bottommost row is shifted out one pixel at a time. This process of shifting the array of charges down one row and shifting the bottommost row out is carried out until the entire array has been read. The array is now ready to capture another frame of image. Figure 4-3 shows a full-frame CCD chip from Kodak.

4.2.1.2   Interline Architecture

In this architecture, as shown in Figure 4-4, alternating columns of sensors are covered by opaque masks. These masked columns are used only in the readout process. Unlike the full-frame CCD, the array in interline CCD is exposed continuously. After exposure, charge packets are shifted into the adjacent masked wells almost instantaneously. The charges in the masked columns are shifted down and out in a manner similar to the full-frame CCD, while the exposed array elements are integrating charges in the respective potential wells. As a result of the architecture, interline CCD has only half the spatial resolution of the full-frame CCD. An interline CCD chip from Kodak is shown in Figure 4-5.

FIGURE   Kodak's KAF-4202 full-frame CCD (reproduced with permission from Kodak).

4-3

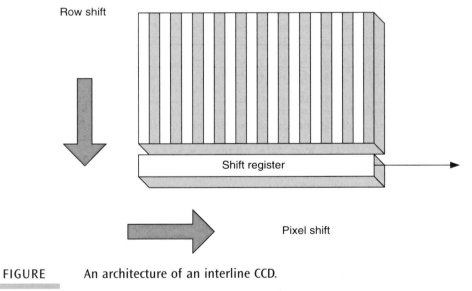

Row shift

Shift register

Pixel shift

FIGURE   An architecture of an interline CCD.

4-4

4.2.1.3   *Frame-Transfer CCD*

As shown in Figure 4-6, there are two arrays in frame-transfer CCDs. The upper array, called the image array, is the actual detector array. The lower array, which

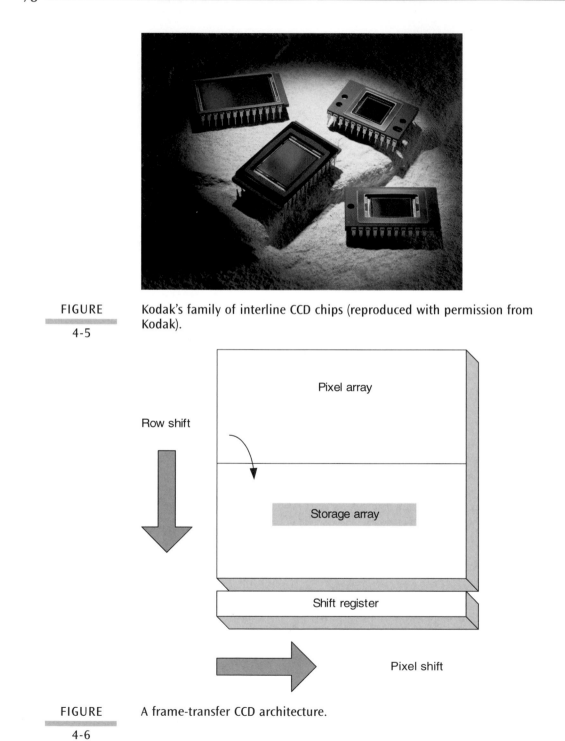

FIGURE
4-5

Kodak's family of interline CCD chips (reproduced with permission from Kodak).

FIGURE
4-6

A frame-transfer CCD architecture.

is masked, is called the storage array. At the end of the integration period, the charge packets in the entire image array are shifted to the storage array one row at a time in almost a negligible time interval. The charges from the storage array are then read out in the same manner as in the full-frame CCD. The integration begins as soon as the charge packets are shifted out to the storage array. In essence, both interline and frame-transfer CCDs are exposed to light continuously. As a result, image capturing is possible at or greater than the video rates with these CCD devices.

4.2.2   CMOS Sensors

Another type of a solid-state image pickup is the CMOS sensor. The light-sensing aspect of the CMOS sensor is the same as that of the CCD sensor. However, the difference lies in the fact that the CMOS device has an amplifier associated with each pixel, whereas the CCD device does the amplification after the scanning process. While this improves the speed of operation of the CMOS device, it also consumes more real estate due to more transistors involved and hence reduced sensitivity to light as a consequence of reduced electron capacity. A second difference between these two devices is that the CMOS fabrication process for the image pickup is the same as that used in fabricating the microprocessors. This, therefore, lowers the cost of digital cameras using CMOS technology. CMOS devices also consume much less power than their CCD counterparts. While these are the advantages that CMOS devices offer, CCD devices have much higher sensitivity than CMOS devices and therefore are used more in scientific instruments. Figure 4-7 shows Kodak's CMOS chips. As a comparison, CCD and CMOS chips from Rad-Icon are shown in Figure 4-8.

4.2.3   Color Sensors

The image pickup devices discussed so far convert light energy into gray-scale values. That is, these devices as such deliver black and white images. In order to obtain true color digital images we could use one of the following: We can use three CCD or CMOS chips with each chip being exposed to light in the red, green, and blue portions of the visible light spectrum through the use of appropriate color filters or we can use a single chip and exploit the light-penetrating property of the silicon to capture the three primary colors of the objects being imaged. An example of the latter is shown in Figure 4-9, which illustrates a single chip that captures true color images. These two methods are used in high-end cameras, which are expensive. A third possibility is to use a color filter array

FIGURE

4-7

Kodak's CMOS sensor chips (reproduced with permission from Kodak).

FIGURE

4-8

CCD (left) and CMOS (right) sensor devices from Rad-Icon (reproduced with permission from Rad-Icon Imaging Corp.).

(CFA) that is overlaid on the sensor array such that each color is occupied by a single pixel. Even though different CFAs are possible, the most common CFA is known as the Bayer color pattern and is shown in Figure 4-10. As can be seen from Figure 4-10, 50% of the image array is made up of green and 25% each of red and blue. Green occupies twice as much as red or blue due to the higher

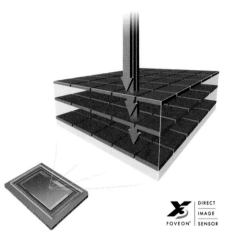

FIGURE   A single chip CCD color sensor from Foveon (reproduced with permission from
           Foveon, Inc.).
4-9

G	R	G	R	G	R	G	R
B	G	B	G	B	G	B	G
G	R	G	R	G	R	G	R
B	G	B	G	B	G	B	G
G	R	G	R	G	R	G	R
B	G	B	G	B	G	B	G
G	R	G	R	G	R	G	R
B	G	B	G	B	G	B	G

FIGURE   A CFA using the Bayer pattern.

4-10

sensitivity of the HVS to green light. This arrangement of the CFA is most common in lower-end digital cameras. However, in order to get full color resolution, pixels must be interpolated, which is done by digital image processing.

4.3   IMAGE SAMPLING

Image sampling refers to a process of converting the continuous spatial distribution of light intensity of an object into a discrete array of samples of the light intensity distribution. The CCDs described earlier perform image sampling by the very construction of the sensor elements arranged in a rectangular array. Conversely, the continuous image can be obtained from its sample values when the number of samples obtained is greater than a certain value. Consider the rectangular array of sensors shown in Figure 4-11. Each element senses the

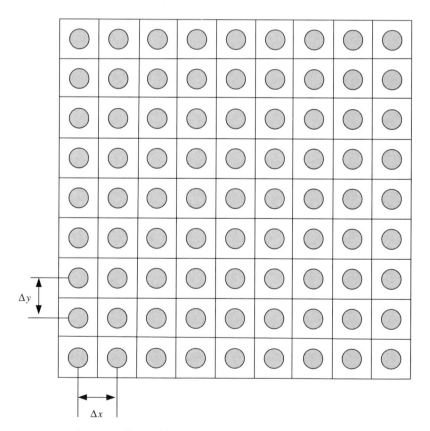

FIGURE   A rectangular sampling grid.

4-11

distribution of light intensity of the object being imaged at a discrete spatial location. The question then is what should be the maximum spacing between the elements in the horizontal and vertical directions or what should be the minimum number of samples required in order to exactly represent the continuous image by these samples? The answer to this question is given by the sampling theory. Before stating the sampling theory formally, let us analyze the situation a bit more carefully.

Let us suppose that $f(x,y)$, $-\infty < x,y < \infty$ is the continuous image intensity and that $f_s(x,y)$ is the sampled image. The continuous Fourier transform $F_s(\omega_x,\omega_y)$ of the sampled image can be written in terms of $F(\omega_x,\omega_y)$, the Fourier transform of the continuous image as

$$F_s(\omega_x,\omega_y) = \omega_{xs}\omega_{ys} \sum_{m=-\infty}^{\infty} \sum_{n=-\infty}^{\infty} F(\omega_x - m\omega_{xs},\omega_y - n\omega_{ys}), \qquad (4\text{-}1)$$

where ω_x and ω_y are the radian frequencies in the horizontal and vertical directions, respectively, and ω_{xs} and ω_{ys} are the corresponding sampling frequencies. Eq. (4-1) says that the Fourier transform of the sampled image is obtained by first replicating the Fourier transform of the continuous image at every integer multiple of the sampling frequency in the horizontal and vertical directions, adding all the transforms, and finally scaling the sum by the product of the sampling frequencies. It is clear from Eq. (4-1) (see Figure 4-12) that the Fourier transform of the sampled image will be identical to that of the continuous image to within a scalefactor in the low-pass region $-\dfrac{\omega_{xs}}{2} \leq \omega_x \leq \dfrac{\omega_{xs}}{2}, -\dfrac{\omega_{ys}}{2} \leq \omega_y \leq \dfrac{\omega_{ys}}{2}$ only if the Fourier transform is band limited, as given by

$$F(\omega_x,\omega_y) = 0, |\omega_x| > \omega_{xc}, |\omega_y| > \omega_{yc}. \qquad (4\text{-}2)$$

If this condition does not hold good, then the replicated transforms will overlap, giving rise to a spectrum that has no resemblance, in the worst case, to that of the continuous image. This overlapping gives rise to frequency aliasing distortion in the image that is reconstructed from the samples. It is important to mention that this type of sampling is called impulse sampling, as each sample occupies zero width. In practice, impulse sampling is not feasible and, as a consequence, there will be some distortion in the reconstructed image due to the finite width of the samples.

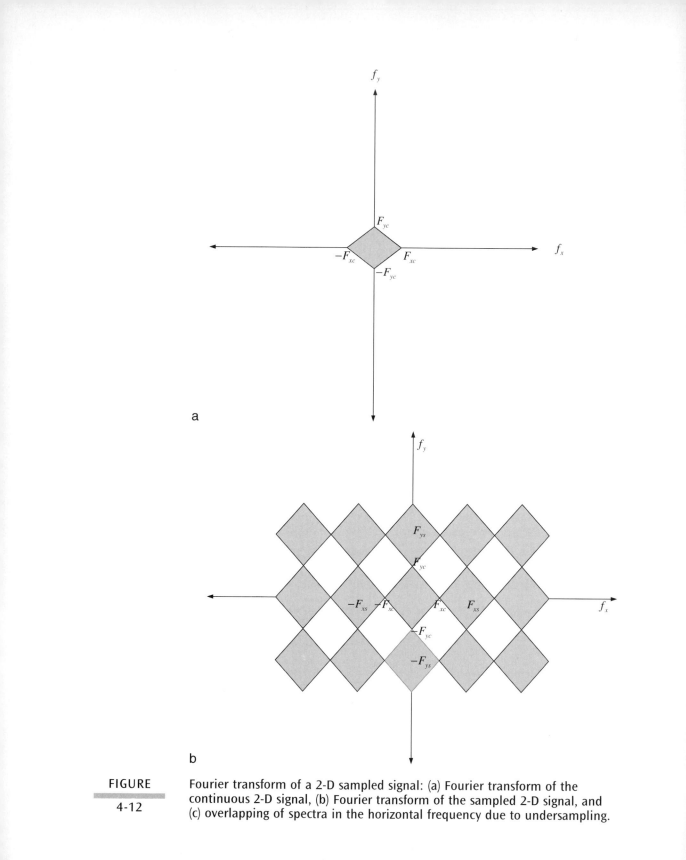

FIGURE
4-12

Fourier transform of a 2-D sampled signal: (a) Fourier transform of the continuous 2-D signal, (b) Fourier transform of the sampled 2-D signal, and (c) overlapping of spectra in the horizontal frequency due to undersampling.

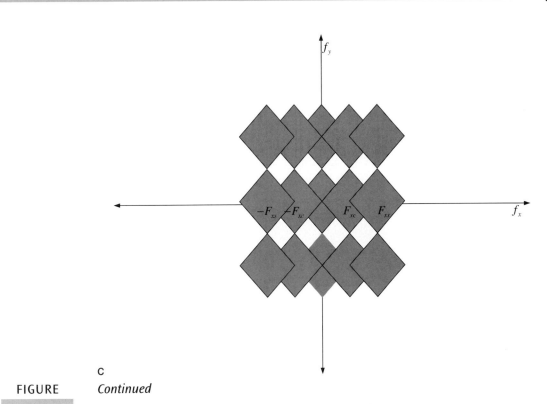

c

FIGURE   *Continued*

4-12

Sampling Theorem

A continuous image $f(x,y)$ that is band limited as in Eq. (4-2) can be represented exactly by its samples $f(m\Delta x, n\Delta y) = f(x,y)|_{x = m\Delta x, y = n\Delta y}$, spaced uniformly on a rectangular grid with spacing Δx and Δy in the horizontal and vertical dimensions, respectively, provided that the sampling frequency is greater than or equal to twice the highest frequency of the image along both directions. That is, $f_{xs} \geq 2f_{xc}$ and $f_{ys} \geq 2f_{yc}$ or, equivalently, $\Delta x \leq \dfrac{\Delta x_c}{2}$ and $\Delta y \leq \dfrac{\Delta y_c}{2}$. This condition implies that we should have at least two samples over the finest detail to be preserved in each direction. Thus, $f(x,y)$ can be written as

$$f(x,y) = \sum_{m=-\infty}^{\infty} \sum_{n=-\infty}^{\infty} f(m\Delta x, m\Delta y)\mathrm{sinc}(xf_{xs} - m)\mathrm{sinc}(yf_{ys} - n) \qquad (4\text{-}3)$$

In Eq. (4-3), $f_{xs} = \dfrac{\omega_{xs}}{2\pi}$ and $f_{ys} = \dfrac{\omega_{ys}}{2\pi}$. ω_{xs} and ω_{ys} are called the Nyquist frequencies. From Eq. (4-3) it can be ascertained that the right-hand side exactly equals the continuous image at the sampling points and at other spatial locations the samples are interpolated by the sinc functions. Another point of view is that the continuous image is recovered from its samples by passing the samples through a 2-D linear filter whose point spread function is the product of the two sinc functions.

The effect of sampling an image below the Nyquist rate is illustrated by the following example. The original girl image is an intensity (black and white) image of size 512×512 pixels with 8 bits per pixel. This image is reduced to a size of 128×128 pixels simply by dropping every other row and column. The image in Figure 4-13b shows the subsampled image with a magnification factor

a

b

c

FIGURE

4-13

An example illustrating sampling effect on an image: (a) original image cropped, (b) subsampled image with no low-pass prefiltering, and (c) subsampled image with low-pass prefiltering. All images were magnified by a factor of 2.

of 2. Next, the same original image is resized to 128×128 pixels by low-pass filtering the image first and then dropping every other row and column. The magnified version of it is shown in Figure 4-13c. Figure 4-13a is the original image cropped to correspond approximately to the subsampled images. The aliasing effect is clearly seen in the image that is subsampled without initially low-pass filtering. Even with initial low-pass filtering, we can see some aliasing effect in Figure 4-13c, which asserts the fact that low-pass filtering of the original image still has some spectral frequencies left over beyond the fold-over frequency.

Instead of taking the samples at uniformly spaced intervals, nonuniform sampling can be used. For example, dense sampling can be used in areas where the image details are very fine, whereas coarse sampling can be used in areas with coarse or little details. This procedure may result in a fewer number of total samples than that using uniform sampling while preserving the finest details in the image. However, practical sampling systems employ the uniform sampling procedure, which simplifies the system design.

In addition to the use of rectangular sampling grids, circular and hexagonal grids are also used where the number of samples generated must be as small as possible.

4.4 IMAGE QUANTIZATION

4.4.1 Uniform Quantization

So far we have considered the steps of camera exposure and sampling of the image signal in the image acquisition process. Sampling has discretized the continuous image into pixels that form a 2-D matrix. It should be pointed out that the charge packets shifted out of the CCD array generate analog voltage samples. The next step in the image acquisition process is to convert this analog voltage into a digital value that can be represented in a suitable binary format. A simple way to quantize an image sample is as follows. Divide the input range of analog values uniformly into a given number of decision intervals and determine the corresponding output levels as lying midway between consecutive input decision boundaries. Number the output levels sequentially starting from the lowest to the highest and represent them in binary format. Then map the given analog value to the nearest output level and read out its binary number. This type of quantization is known as uniform quantization.

Example 4.1

As an example, consider an image sensor whose output signal voltage ranges between 0 and 300 mV. If the number of bits of quantization of the analog-to-digital converter (ADC) is 10, then the decision boundaries and output levels of a uniform quantizer are given by

$$d_i = \frac{300(i-1)}{1024}, \quad 1 \leq i \leq 1025$$
$$r_i = d_i + \frac{150}{1024}, \quad 1 \leq i \leq 1024 \tag{4-4}$$

For this uniform quantizer the quantization step or interval is found to be

$$q = d_i - d_{i-1} = r_i - r_{i-1} = \frac{300}{1024} \, mV. \tag{4-5}$$

The maximum error due to quantization is one-half of the step size and is equal to 150/1024 mV. The decision boundaries and output levels for this example are shown in Figure 4-14. As can be seen from Figure 4-14, the output levels fall midway between two consecutive input decision boundaries. A quantitative measure of performance of a quantizer is commonly expressed in terms of its signal-to-noise ratio (SNR), which is defined as

$$SNR = 10 \log_{10} \left(\frac{\sigma_s^2}{MSE} \right) dB, \tag{4-6}$$

where σ_s^2 is the signal power. The MSE for the uniform quantizer equals $\frac{q^2}{12}$. For this quantizer the signal-to-noise ratio from Eq. (4-6) can be found to be about 60 dB. A rule of thumb is that every bit increase of the uniform quantizer adds 6 dB to the SNR.

4.4.2   Optimal Quantization

The optimal way to quantize an analog sample for a given number of bits is to determine the decision intervals and output levels by minimizing a cost function. Typical cost functions include mean square error, maximum of absolute error, and so on. However, the cost function used often is the mean square error (MSE) between the input analog sample and the quantized value, as it is mathematically tractable. The cost function is dependent not only on the number of bits of quantization, but also on the probability density function of the input image. Therefore, the minimization in general requires the solution to a

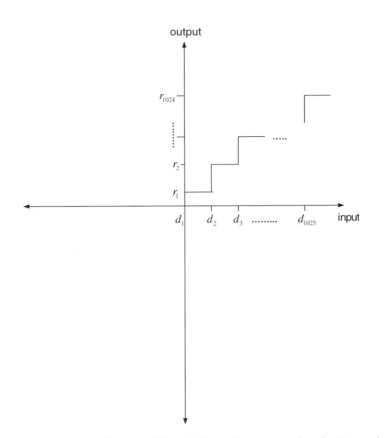

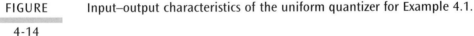

FIGURE   Input–output characteristics of the uniform quantizer for Example 4.1.

4-14

transcendental equation. Hence it results in an iterative solution to the minimization problem. The quantizer that minimizes the mean square error is called the Lloyd–Max quantizer. A uniform quantizer is optimal for an image with uniform distribution and the corresponding Lloyd–Max quantizer simplifies to

$$
\begin{aligned}
d_i &= \frac{f_{max}(i-1)}{L}, \quad 1 \le i \le L+1, \\
r_i &= d_i + \frac{f_{max}}{2L}, \quad 1 \le i \le L
\end{aligned}
\tag{4-7}
$$

where L is the number of levels of quantization. It is implicit in Eq. (4-7) that the minimum value of the analog samples is zero.

When an image has a nonuniform distribution, the Lloyd–Max quantizer assigns nonuniformly spaced decision boundaries and output levels, which are optimal for that distribution and given number of quantization levels.

4.5   IMAGE SCANNING

4.5.1   Interlaced and Progressive Scanning

Image scanning is a mechanism to either read out or display an image, which is a 2-D signal. Suppose that an image has 512×512 pixels. In order to display this image in one shot, we need an array of 512×512 parallel lines through which to feed the pixel values. A similar situation exists in reading the pixel values in a single shot. This is certainly not an efficient engineering practice. In image acquisition systems utilizing CCDs, the image of the object is already in spatially discrete form, as the sensor elements are placed in a 2-D rectangular array. The signals in the array are then read out in a predetermined pattern—usually in a raster-scanning fashion of left to right and top to bottom. The CCD chip contains all of the circuitry necessary to read out the signals. This type of scanning is truly a 2-D sampling and is called a self-scanning mechanism. Other devices use raster scanning with different external control circuitry. However, CRT-based image display devices such as TV utilize a type of scanning mechanism called raster scanning, whereby an image frame is read out or displayed sequentially in time. Because later chapters deal with video compression techniques, it is necessary to understand some basic scanning standards that are in vogue in the television field.

The intensity or black and white image is scanned in the United States using a scanning standard adopted by the Radio Electronics Television Manufacturers Association (RETMA). A complete scan of the image is called a *frame*. In standard definition TV (SDTV), each frame contains 525 lines and the image is scanned at a rate of 30 fps, actually 29.97 fps to be exact. Each frame is scanned twice successively and each such scan is called a *field*, denoted first field and second field, giving a field rate of 59.94 per second, or simply 59.94 Hz. Each field consists of 262.5 lines, but the second field is displaced in time by half the frame period. Thus the fields are interlaced (see Figure 4-15). At the end of the

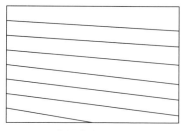

1st field @ time t

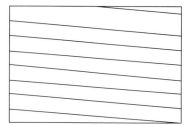

2nd field @ time t + 1/59.94s

FIGURE   Interlaced scanning in the NTSC system.

4-15

scanning of each line, the scanning beam returns to the left. Similarly, at the end of each field, the scanning beam returns to the top center. During these intervals, the beam is blanked so that it is not visible. Synchronization pulses are inserted at the end of each scanning line and at the end of each scanning field. When digitizing an image, as in a video camcorder, the synchronization pulses are removed and the digitized image is stored as an array.

In Europe, Asia, and Australia, the field rate is 50 Hz, and each field consists of 312.5 lines, giving a total of 625 lines per frame.

Noninterlaced or *progressive* scanning is used in desktop computers, digital TV, and high-definition TV (HDTV), as well as in digital video camcorders. In progressive scanning, an image frame is scanned sequentially from left to right, top to bottom, once per frame.

The interlaced and progressive scanning systems are denoted by the format, which consists of number of lines followed by the letter i or p followed by the frame rate. For example, the SDTV scanning system is denoted $480i29.97$. Similarly, the PAL system is denoted by $625i50$.

4.5.2   Color Image Scanning

In NTSC and PAL, color video consists of three components, luminance Y and chrominance U and V. U and V are actually color differences; U is obtained by subtracting Y from blue followed by low-pass filtering, and V is obtained by subtracting Y from red followed by low-pass filtering. A composite TV signal consists of the sum of Y and modulated U and V components.

4.5.3   Color Encoding in Digital Video

Component digital video uses three components denoted Y, C_B, and C_R. Y is the luminance, C_B is B-Y, and C_R is R-Y, both followed by subsampling. Subsampling has different formats and are as follows.

4:4:4 Subsampling

This scheme is shown in Figure 4-16a. All the three components have the same number of pixels and the video has the largest data rate. The term $4:4:4$ indicates that for every 4 Y pixels, there are 4 pixels of each C_B and C_R.

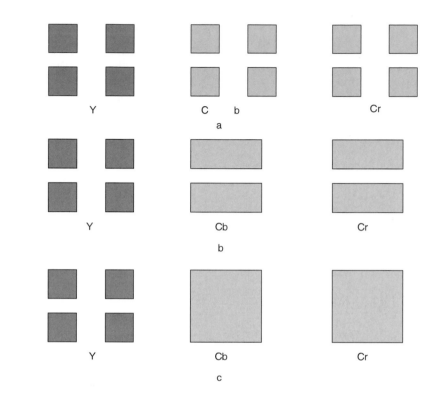

FIGURE

4-16

Sampling formats of luminance and chrominance signals: (a) 4:4:4 subsampling, (b) 4:2:2 subsampling, and (c) 4:2:0 subsampling.

4:2:2 Subsampling

Because the HVS is less sensitive to color than brightness, the chrominance components are subsampled to reduce the bandwidth. In this scheme, the Y component has the full resolution, but the chrominance components are subsampled horizontally by a factor of 2, as shown in Figure 4-16b. Thus, for every 4 Y pixels there are 2 pixels of each C_B and C_R. Hence the notation 4:2:2.

4:2:0 Subsampling

In this scheme (Figure 4-16c), each chrominance component is subsampled in both horizontal and vertical directions. Therefore, for every 4 Y pixels there is one pixel of each C_B and C_R. In this notation the digit 0 indicates that C_B and C_R are subsampled by a factor of 2 in the vertical direction as well.

4.6   FILM-TO-DIGITAL CONVERSION

Movies on film are produced at 24 fps. Because many TV programs, especially prime-time programs, are shot on films, there arises the need to convert materials in film format into TV format. This process of film-to-video conversion is known as *telecine*. Telecine equipment from Cintel is shown in Figure 4-17.

Because the video in TV is field interlaced at 60 fields per second rate, while the film when converted into fields produces only 48 fields per second, 12 extra fields must be introduced to conform to the 60 fields per second rate. A process known as 3:2 pull down is used to convert 48 fields per second rate to 60 fields per second rate. Film frames are scanned at approximately 60 fields per second rate. A pattern of 2 and 3 fields is repeated every second to generate the required TV field rate, as shown in Figure 4-18. Observe that the first two fields of film

FIGURE   Telecine equipment for converting film into digital format (reproduced with
            permission from Cintel, Inc.).
4-17

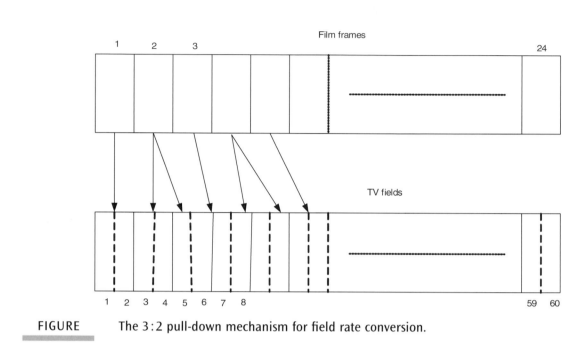

FIGURE   The 3:2 pull-down mechanism for field rate conversion.

4-18

frame 1 get transferred to the first two video fields, the next two fields of film map to the corresponding video fields, and the second filed of film frame 2 is repeated in the video fields. This pattern is repeated.

With the advancement of camera and solid-state device technologies, professional digital video camcorders for HDTV using progressive scanning are currently available. As a consequence, there is impetus for movie producers to directly use digital video camcorders instead of film cameras. This saves time and money and has the added advantage of easy editing and creation of special effects. Figure 4-19 shows a high-end digital video camcorder suitable for movie making.

4.7   SUMMARY

This chapter discussed the process of acquiring digital images from continuous images. Solid-state CCD and CMOS image detectors were described. Next we described image sampling using rectangular and nonrectangular grids followed by optimal quantization. We also introduced scanning systems used in TV broadcasting, wherein we touched upon chrominance subsampling methods. Finally, we introduced the telecine process of converting movie films into video format.

FIGURE
4-19

A high-end digital video camera suitable for shooting movies (reproduced with permission from Panasonic TV and Broadcast Systems).

REFERENCES

A large volume of references can be cited for details on image sensors and their applications. However, only a few of them are listed here as representatives of the works in this field. Interested readers should consult textbooks on solid-state physics to gain more in-depth knowledge. An excellent source of information on imaging sensors and optical systems is the International Society for Optical Engineering (SPIE). The following articles refer to CCD sensors: Janesic et al. (1987), Blouke et al. (1987), Hiraoka et al. (1987), Williams and Carta (1989), Hoover and Dotty (1996), Freeman (1987) and Blouke et al. (2001). A good practical source on scientific CCDs can be found in Janesick (2001). Some of the concepts of sensors and their design can be found in textbooks by Castleman (1996) and Donati (2000).

For details regarding image sampling and quantization, refer to Jain (1989) and Dudgeon (1984).

For further reading on image scanning and color subsampling, refer to Poynton (2003).

J.R. Jenesic, S.T. Elliot, A.S. Collins, H.H. Marsh, M.M. Blouke, and J. Freeman, "Scientific charge-coupled devices," Optical Engineering, 26(8): 692–714, 1987.

M.M. Blouke et al., "Large format, high resolution image sensors," Optical Engineering, 26(9): 837–843, 1987.

Y. Hiraoka, J.W. Sedat, and D.A. Agard, "The use of a charge-coupled device for quantitative optical microscopy of biological structures," Science, 238: 36–41, 1987.

B. Williams and D. Carta, "CID cameras: More than an alternative to CCDs," Advanced Imaging, 2–13, January 1989.

R.B. Hoover and F. Dotty, *Hard X-ray/gamma-ray and neutron optics, sensors, and applications*, ISBN 0-8194-2247-9, SPIE Press, Bellingham, WA.

C. Freeman, *Imaging sensors and displays*, ISBN 0-89252-800-1, SPIE Press, Bellingham, WA.

M.M. Blouke, N. Sampat, and J. Canosa, *Sensors and camera systems for scientific, industrial, and digital photography applications-II*, ISBN 0-8194-3583-X, SPIE Press, Bellingham, WA.

J.R. Janesick, *Scientific charge-coupled devices*, SPIE Press, Bellingham, WA, 2001.

K. Castleman, *Digital Image Processing*, Prentice Hall, Englewood Cliffs, NJ, 1996.

S. Donati, *Photodetectors: Devices, Circuits, and Applications*, Prentice Hall PTR, Upper Saddle River, NJ, 2000.

A.K. Jain, *Fundamentals of Digital Image Processing*, Prentice Hall, Englewood Cliffs, NJ, 1989.

D. Dudgeon and R.M. Mersereau, *Multidimensional Digital Signal Processing*, Prentice Hall, Englewood Cliffs, NJ, 1984.

C. Poynton, *Digital Video and HDTV*, Morgan Kaufmann Publishers, 2003.

5 | Image Enhancement

5.1   BACKGROUND

As mentioned in Chapter 1, image enhancement refers to any digital processing by which the image quality is improved. By image quality we mean such image features as contrast, sharpness, edges, boundaries, etc. There are situations where the originally acquired images lack contrast due to poor lighting conditions. In such cases, simple contrast stretching could rectify the problem. Lack of sharpness in images is another instance that could be corrected by linear filtering. When images are acquired through optical means, nonlinear filtering might be required in order to increase the contrast or image sharpness. Since enhancement is aimed at improving the visual quality of images, it is rather difficult to quantify the performance of the different enhancement techniques. Any technique that results in improving the visual quality of an image is acceptable. The only factor that influences the choice of an enhancement algorithm is the complexity of the algorithm. Table 5-1 lists various processing options available for the enhancement of images. Depending on which aspect of the original image is to be improved, we could choose any one of the class of algorithms from the list as the candidate.

Most of the enhancement procedures listed in Table 5-1 are suitable for black and white or simply luminance images. In enhancing color images, care must be exercised to avoid false coloring that could result in the processed image. This chapter describes some of the commonly used enhancement techniques for luminance and color images and illustrates them with several examples. Some of these techniques could be used in reducing the compression artifacts in digital cinema as postprocessing procedures.

5.2   POINT PROCESSING

In this type of enhancement, each pixel in the input image is mapped to a new value in the output image independent of other pixels in the input image. The kind of mapping used determines the enhancement procedure.

Table 5-1. Image Enhancement Procedures

Image enhancement techniques		
Point processing	Spatial processing	Frequency domain processing
Contrast stretching	Neighborhood processing	Linear filtering
Gray level transform	Averaging	Low pass
Clipping	Directional smoothing	High-pass nonlinear filtering
Level slicing	Median filtering	Homomorphic filtering
Histogram techniques	Unsharp masking	
Equalization		
Histogram modification		
Histogram specification		

5.2.1   Logarithmic Transformation

The image display device maps the intensity level zero to black and the maximum allowed value to white. The maximum allowed value depends on the bit width of the display device. When the dynamic range of the image to be displayed is very large and a large proportion of the pixels occupy low values, the displayed image will be poorly visible. This is especially true in displaying, for example, an image spectrum. In such cases if we compress the intensity values using a non-linear transformation, the rendering will be enhanced greatly. One such transformation is the logarithmic transformation, which is described by the equation

$$g[m,n] = k \log_{10}(1 + f[m,n]), \qquad (5\text{-}1)$$

where f is the input image at location $[m,n]$, g is the output image at the same location, and k is a suitable constant. Since the logarithmic curve is steeper at low values compared to high input values, larger pixel values all map to nearly the same output value while the low pixel values are stretched, thus improving the visibility of low pixel intensities. An example of the logarithmic transformation is shown in Figure 5-1.

5.2.2   Contrast Stretching

Even when the dynamic range of an image is within that of the display device, the image may still have low contrast. This may be due to poor lighting conditions under which the image was captured or due to a smaller dynamic range of

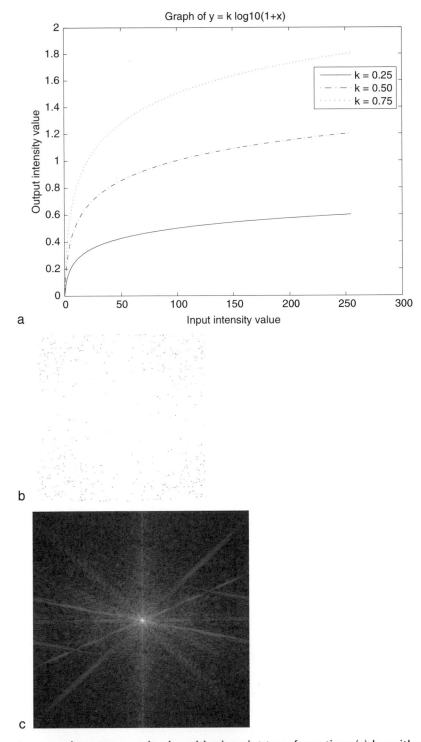

FIGURE

5-1

Image enhancement using logarithmic point transformation: (a) logarithmic plot, (b) magnitude of 2-D FFT of an intensity image, (c) image in b using logarithmic transformation with $k = 0.25$.

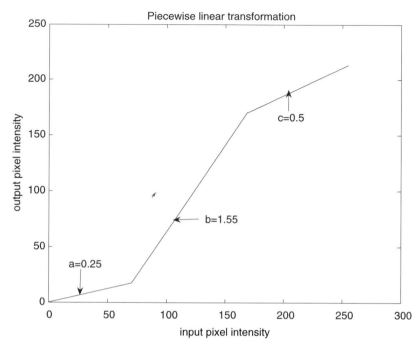

FIGURE

5-2

Piecewise linear transformation of pixel intensity for contrast stretching.

the capturing device. In such cases a simple rescaling of the pixel intensities might be adequate to improve the visibility. This involves a piecewise linear transformation of the input pixel intensities, as shown in Figure 5-2. Such a transformation can be expressed by the following equation:

$$y = \begin{cases} ax, 0 \le x < x_1 \\ b(x - x_1) + y_{x_1}, x_1 \le x < x_2 \\ c(x - x_2) + y_{x_2}, x_2 \le x < B \end{cases} \tag{5-2}$$

In Eq. (5-2), a, b, and c are appropriate constants, which are the slopes in the respective regions, and B is the maximum intensity value. The intent here is to enlarge low values and reduce high values of the pixel intensities while keeping the intermediate values approximately intact. However, there should be continuity in the output pixel intensities, which requires that the output pixel intensities be nondecreasing, otherwisethe mapping will be incorrect and will result in a wrong interpretation of the image. Figure 5-3 shows the original image and the enhanced image using contrast stretching.

a   b

FIGURE   Contrast stretching: (a) original image and (b) enhanced image.

5-3

5.2.3   Histogram Modification

A histogram of an intensity image refers to the distribution of pixel intensities. Since the pixel intensities are discrete, the histogram is also discrete. One can infer a few things from the histogram of an image. If the histogram is narrow and confined mainly to low-intensity values, the image will appear very dark with no details visible. On the other hand if the histogram is narrow and centered mainly at high pixel values, the image may look bright but will still lack in details. The reason is that the image contrast in both cases is low. This section describes procedures whereby the enhanced image has a histogram different from that of the original image, which has low contrast.

5.2.3.1   *Histogram Equalization*

Histogram equalization is an enhancement procedure by which the histogram of the processed image is made uniform irrespective of the histogram of the original image. A uniform histogram implies that all the image intensities are occupied with an equal number of pixels. For instance, if an intensity image is of size 256×256 pixels with 8 bits/pixel, then a uniform histogram will imply that there are 256 pixels in each intensity level. Since all intensity levels are equally occupied, the resulting image will have the largest contrast.

We now describe a procedure used to enhance an image by histogram equalization. Let us assume without loss of generality that an image $f[m,n]$ has a continuum of intensity values f in the interval (f_{min}, f_{max}) with a probability density function $p_f(f)$. We want to determine a mapping of the intensity f to g such that the processed image $g[m,n]$ has a uniform probability density function $p_g(g)$ with intensity values g in the interval (g_{min}, g_{max}). From the probability theory we can write

$$\int_{g_{min}}^{g} p_g(x)dx = \int_{f_{min}}^{f} p_f(y)dy.$$
(5-3)

Because $p_g(x) = \dfrac{1}{g_{max} - g_{min}}$, we find that the output intensity value g is given by

$$g = g_{min} + (g_{max} - g_{min})CDF_f(f),$$
(5-4)

where $CDF_f(f) = \displaystyle\int_{f_{min}}^{f} p_f(x)dx$ is the cumulative distribution of the input image $f[m,n]$. Since the actual image has discrete intensity values, the corresponding transformation involves the summation as given by

$$g(k) = g_{min} + (g_{max} - g_{min}) \sum_{j=f_{min}}^{k} p_f(j).$$
(5-5)

Once the pixel intensity mapping is determined as given by Eq. (5-5), the histogram equalization procedure is to scan each pixel in the input image $f[m,n]$ and assign a corresponding value as given by Eq. (5-5) in the output image $g[m,n]$. An example of image enhancement using histogram equalization is illustrated in Figure 5-4. Figure 5-4a shows the histogram of the original image, which reveals the fact that the pixels have high values but low contrast and hence appears to be washed out. The histogram of the equalized image is seen in Figure 5-4b, which appears to be much broader than that of the original image. Figures 5-4c and 5-4d show original and enhanced images. It is important to point out that the histogram of the equalized image may not be exactly uniform because of the discrete nature of the pixel intensities.

In addition to histogram equalization, it is also possible to modify the histogram of the original image to any specified histogram in the output image. Some useful histograms for image enhancement are listed in Table 5-2 with corresponding transformation of the input intensity values, which can be obtained via Eq. (5-3). It is interesting to note that when the output histogram is negative cube root, the image actually visualized has a uniform histogram, as the HVS has a one-third power law relationship as noted in Chapter 3. An important point

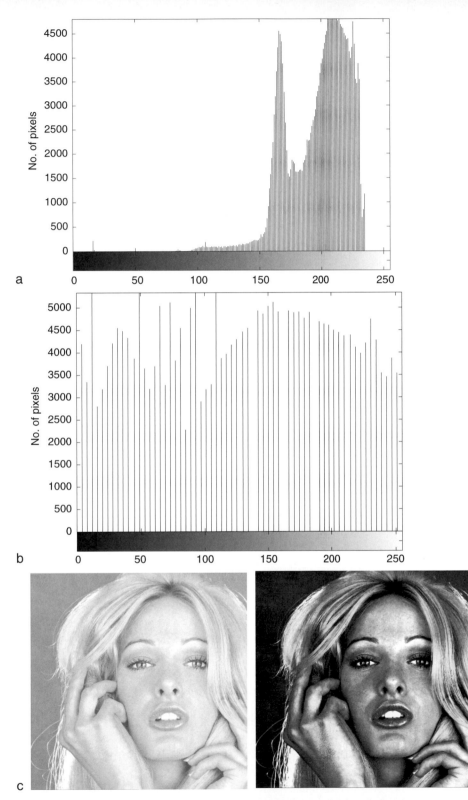

FIGURE

5-4

Image enhancement by histogram equalization: (a) histogram of the original image, (b) histogram of the equalized image, (c) original image, and (d) histogram-equalized image. The original image is courtesy of The Center for Image Processing Research, Rensselaer Polytechnic Institute.

Table 5-2. Intensity Mapping for Nonadaptive Histogram Modification

Name of pdf	pdf	Intensity mapping
Uniform	$p_g(g) = \dfrac{1}{g_{max} - g_{min}},\ g_{min} \leq g \leq g_{max}$	$g = g_{min} + (g_{max} - g_{min})\,CDF_f(f)$
Rayleigh	$p_g(g) = \dfrac{g - g_{min}}{\beta^2}\, e^{\frac{(g-g_{min})^2}{2\beta^2}},\ g \geq g_{max}$	$g = g_{min} + \left\{ 2\beta^2 \ln\left(\dfrac{1}{1 - CDF_f(f)}\right) \right\}^{\frac{1}{2}}$
Exponential	$p_g(g) = \alpha e^{-\alpha(g - g_{min})},\ g \geq g_{min}$	$g = g_{min} + \dfrac{1}{\alpha} \ln\left(\dfrac{1}{1 - CDF_f(f)} \right)$
Hyperbolic (cube root)	$p_g(g) = \dfrac{1}{3}\, \dfrac{g^{-\frac{2}{3}}}{g_{max}^{\frac{1}{3}} - g_{min}^{\frac{1}{3}}}$	$g = \left\{ g_{min}^{\frac{1}{3}} + \left(g_{max}^{\frac{1}{3}} - g_{min}^{\frac{1}{3}} \right) CDF_f(f) \right\}^3$
Hyperbolic (logarithmic)	$p_g(g) = \dfrac{1}{g \ln\left(\dfrac{g_{max}}{g_{min}} \right)}$	$g = g_{min} \left(\dfrac{g_{max}}{g_{min}} \right)^{CDF_f(f)}$

to remember is that histogram equalization is effective only when the original image has poor contrast to start with, otherwise histogram equalization may degrade the image quality.

5.2.3.2   Adaptive Histogram Modification

The previous section considered modifying the global histogram of an intensity image. Although the overall contrast is improved, the image may still lack in contrast locally. We therefore need to apply histogram modification to each pixel based on the histogram of pixels that are neighbors to a given pixel. This will probably result in maximum contrast enhancement. According to this method, we partition the given image into blocks of suitable size and equalize the histogram of each subblock. In order to eliminate artificial boundaries created by the process, the intensities are interpolated across the block regions using bicubic interpolating functions. This is illustrated in Figure 5-5.

5.3   NEIGHBORHOOD PROCESSING

So far we have discussed several procedures whereby each intensity value in the input image is mapped to an output value such that the image contrast is

a

c

Histogram of original intensity image

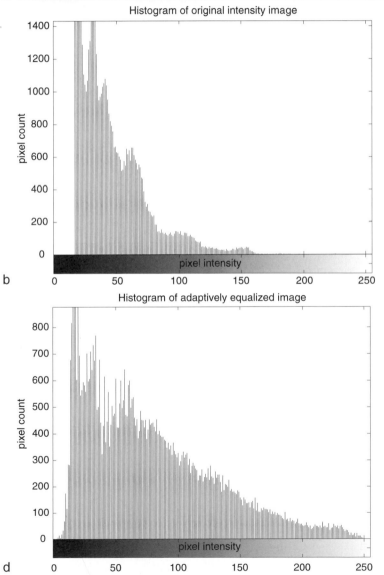

b

Histogram of adaptively equalized image

d

FIGURE

5-5

Image enhancement by adaptive histogram equalization: a) Original image,
b) Histogram of the original image, c) Equalized image, d) Histogram of the
equalized image.

improved. This procedure entails each input pixel to be assigned to an output pixel without regard to the neighboring pixel values. However, there are situations where the processing has to consider a neighborhood of pixels centered on the current pixel being processed for a particular type of processing. Hence the name *neighborhood processing* or *spatial processing*. This section describes several such procedures to enhance images. Each such procedure will modify a certain aspect of the image in enhancing it.

5.3.1   Simple Mask Operations

Smoothing Operation

A mask is a small square window of values by which a current pixel and its immediate neighbors are weighted to produce an output pixel. Mask weights, or simply masks, are ad hoc in nature. Depending on the mask values, the enhancement will amount to either low-pass or high-pass filtering. Consider the mask shown in Figure 5-6. When the mask w is centered on the pixel at location $[m,n]$, the corresponding output pixel can be written as

$$g[m,n] = \sum_{[i,j] \in W} w[i,j] f[m-i, n-j]. \tag{5-6}$$

In Eq. (5-6), f, w, and g are, respectively, the input pixel centered on $[m,n]$, mask, and the output pixel at location $[m,n]$ and W is the mask region. Figure 5-7 shows a few masks that correspond to spatial averaging. Note that the weights in Figure 5-7 add up to unity. The mask in Figure 5-7c has unequal weights with the center

W[i-1,j-1]	W[i-1,j]	W[i-1,j+1]
W[I,j-1]	W[i,j]	W[I,j+1]
W[i+1,j-1]	W[i+1,j]	W[i+1,j+1]

FIGURE   A general 3×3 spatial mask with weights $w[i,j]$.

5-6

1/4	1/4
1/4	1/4

a

1/9	1/9	1/9
1/9	1/9	1/9
1/9	1/9	1/9

b

0	1/8	0
1/8	1/2	1/8
0	1/8	0

c

FIGURE
5-7

Ad hoc masks for spatial averaging: (a) 2×2 mask, (b) 3×3 mask, and (c) 3×3 weighted averaging mask.

value equal to four times that of off-center values, indicating that the center pixel is given more weight than off-center pixels.

These masks are applied to an image and the results are shown in Figure 5-8. The original image of a baboon appears a bit rough. Hence smoothing enhances the appearance of the image. The mask in Figure 5-8e is obtained by discretizing a Gaussian function over a window of size 7×7 with zero mean and a given variance. Even though it is not an ad hoc mask, it is used here as a comparison against the other ad hoc masks.

Edge Sharpening

It is our common experience that an image appears to be more pleasing to the eye when the edges are sharp. Edges in an image can be sharpened by a mask that performs differencing of, instead of averaging pixels. Some useful edge-sharpening masks are listed in Figure 5-9. Of course, the mask weights should sum up to unity, otherwise the output image will be amplified. The effects of using edge sharpening by the masks in Figure 5-9 are illustrated in Figure 5-10. Since the sharpened images are too crispy, we can soften them without losing

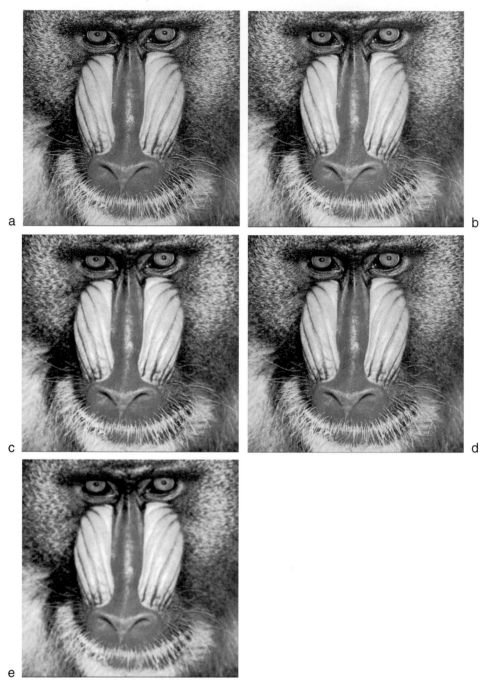

FIGURE
5-8

Results of applying spatially averaging masks to an image: (a) original,
(b) original image filtered by a 2 × 2 mask, (c) original image filtered by a
3 × 3 mask, (d) original image filtered by a 3 × 3 mask with nonzero weights
only in the vertical and horizontal directions, and (e) original image filtered
by a Gaussian mask of size 7 × 7.

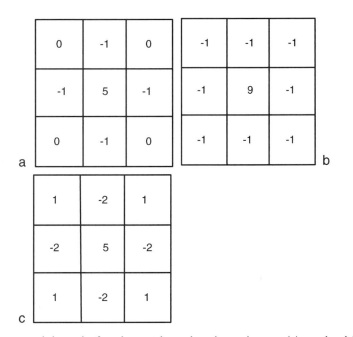

FIGURE

5-9

Spatial masks for sharpening edges in an image: (a) mask with weights in north–south–east–west directions, (b) mask with equal weights in all four directions, and (c) mask with weights emphasizing horizontal and vertical directions more than diagonal directions.

sharpness of the edges by adding a fraction of the edge-sharpened image to the original image and rescaling its intensity to that of the input image. This is shown in Figure 5-10e, where we see that the stripes in the pants are crisper while the face is as smooth as the original. This process is also referred to as unsharp masking.

5.3.2   Two-Dimensional Filters Satisfying Specified Frequency Responses

The simple masks considered in the previous section all have fixed spatial frequency response characteristics. When sharp transitions in the frequency response are required, we need to design the appropriate filters. However, such filters do not have simple masks. Instead, we have the choice of linear-phase FIR filters or IIR filters with nonlinear phase response characteristics. The design of separable and nonseparable FIR filters with linear phase was described in Chapter 2. Here we illustrate image enhancement using such filters.

FIGURE

5-10

An example of edge sharpening using the masks in Figure 5-9: (a) original image, (b) result of using mask in Figure 5-9a, (c) result of using mask in Figure 5-9b, (d) result of using mask in Figure 5-9c, and (e) result of original image + 0.75* image in d and rescaled.

Example 5.1

Design a 2-D low-pass FIR filter with circular symmetry in the frequency domain and a passband edge at $R = 0.5$, where $R = \sqrt{f_x^2 + f_y^2}$, f_x and f_y are the horizontal and vertical spatial frequencies, respectively. Process an intensity image with this filter. Also, design a 2-D band-stop FIR filter with stop-band edges at $R = 0.5$ and $R = 0.75$ and process the same image with this filter. Compare the results. Use a Hamming window for both filters.

Solution

Use the MATLAB function *freqspace(13,'meshgrid')* from the image processing toolbox to specify the frequency points in the 2-D frequency domain. Define the desired filter response as

$$H_1(R) = \begin{cases} 1, & R \le 0.5 \\ 0, & otherwise \end{cases}, \qquad R = \sqrt{f_x^2 + f_y^2}.$$

Next, design a Hamming windowed 2-D FIR filter of size 13×13 satisfying the just-given specification using the function *fwind1(H$_1$ hamming(13))*. Then filter the image using the MATLAB function *imfilter(I,H$_1$,'symmetric','same')*. The parameter *symmetric* is used to pad the borders of the image by mirror imaging, and the parameter *same* keeps the size of the filtered image the same as the input image. Repeat the procedure for the band-stop filter. Results are shown in Figure 5-11. Observe that the low-pass filter smudges the stripes in the pants whereas the band-stop filter retains them.

5.3.3   Median Filtering

Often times, images may be corrupted by noise. Noise is present as a result of the electronic circuitry or in the image transmission process. Image noise may be categorized as additive or multiplicative. Noise power is usually present uniformly in all the spatial frequencies and so it is called white noise. Thus, when noise is additive, all we can hope to do is to minimize its presence in the output image by a suitable linear process. However, noise may also multiply an image, in which case it is called multiplicative noise. One has to use some kind of a nonlinear process, which is discussed in the next section, to reduce multiplicative noise.

Noise is a random signal characterized by having a probability density function (PDF) for its amplitude. Typical PDFs of noise encountered in imaging are uniform, Gaussian, Rayleigh, and impulse, which are expressed by the following equations:

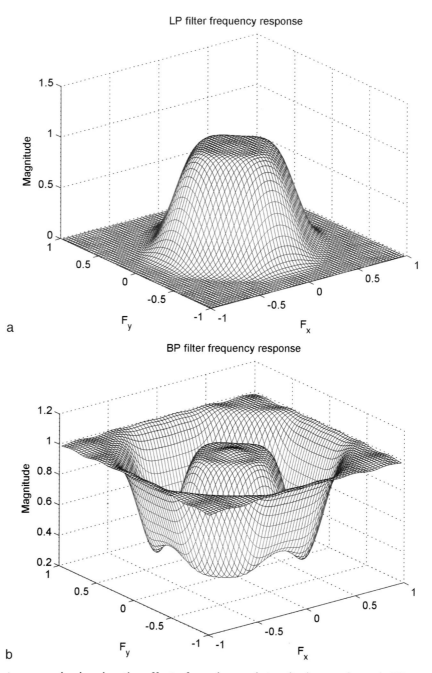

a

b

FIGURE

5-11

An example showing the effect of passing an intensity image through FIR filters satisfying specified frequency response characteristics: (a) low-pass filter frequency response, (b) band-pass filter frequency response, (c) original image, (d) result of low-pass filtering, and (e) result of band-stop filtering.

c

d

e

FIGURE   *Continued*

5-11

Uniform Distribution

Here we assume a continuum of amplitude of the additive noise in the interval between zero and one, as given by

$$p(x) = \begin{cases} 1, & 0 \leq x \leq 1 \\ 0, & otherwise \end{cases}. \tag{5-7}$$

Gaussian Distribution

$$p(x) = \frac{1}{\sigma\sqrt{2\pi}} e^{-\frac{(x-\mu)^2}{2\sigma^2}}, \quad -\infty < x < \infty, \tag{5-8}$$

where μ and σ are the mean and standard deviation, respectively, of the noise.

Rayleigh Distribution

$$p(x) = \frac{x}{\alpha^2} e^{-\frac{x^2}{\alpha^2}}, \quad x \geq 0. \tag{5-9}$$

PDF of Impulse Noise

Impulse noise is also known as *salt and pepper* noise due to its appearance. It is on or off at each pixel with a PDF expressed by

$$p(x) = \begin{cases} P_1, & x = A \\ P_2, & x = B \\ 0, & \text{otherwise} \end{cases} \tag{5-10}$$

If the probabilities P_1 and P_2 are equal, the impulse noise will appear as salt and pepper.

In median filtering an image, the current pixel value is replaced by the median of pixel values over a rectangular window centered on the current pixel. More specifically, median filtering can be written as

$$g[m,n] = Median\{f[m-i, n-j], \quad [i,j] \in W\}, \tag{5-11}$$

where f and g are, respectively, the input and output images, $[m,n]$ is the location of the current pixel being processed, and W is a window of size $M \times N$ pixels. Typically, M and N are equal and odd integers. Pixels over the $M \times N$ window are arranged in an increasing or decreasing order in a vector and the middle value represents the median of the pixels. If the window size is even, then the median is the average of the two elements in the middle. Since a noisy pixel will probably have a value that is too different from its neighbors (an outlier), the median value will most probably belong to the image. Therefore, a median filter works best when the image is corrupted by impulse noise. Observe that the median of sum of two arrays A and B is not equal to the sum of median values of the individual array and so median filtering is nonlinear. The median filter is a subclass of nonlinear filters called *order statistics filters*. It can be shown that the number of comparisons, required to determine the median, is proportional to the square of the size of the window. To be computationally efficient, typical window sizes used in median filtering are 3×3 and 5×5. An example of median filtering an image corrupted by impulse noise is shown in Figure 5-12. It also shows the effect of median filtering the same image when corrupted by uniform and Gaussian noise. It is clear that median filtering is very effective in removing

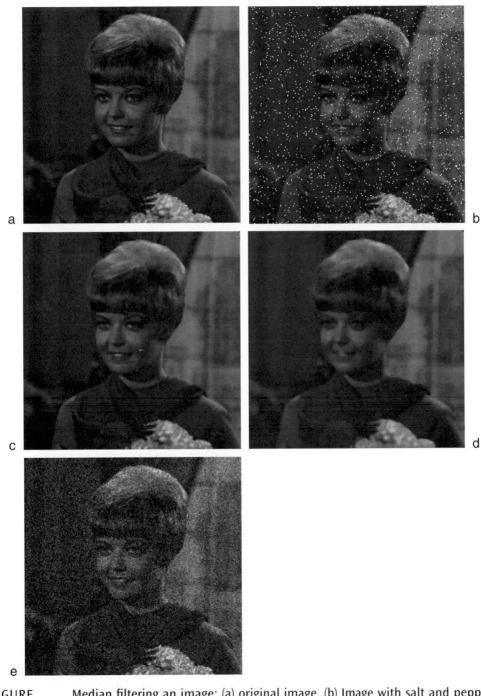

FIGURE

5-12

Median filtering an image: (a) original image, (b) Image with salt and pepper noise of density 0.05, (c) 3 × 3 median-filtered image, (d) 5 × 5 median-filtered image, (e) image with Gaussian noise of variance 0.01, (f) 3 × 3 median-filtered version of image in e, and (g) 5 × 5 median-filtered version of image in e.

f   g

FIGURE   *Continued*

5-12

salt and pepper noise. In contrast, median filtering is ineffective in removing additive Gaussian noise. In fact, it destroys the edges, as can be seen from Figure 5-12.

5.3.4   Homomorphic Filtering

When images are acquired by optical means, the image of the object is a product of the illuminating light source and the reflectance of the object, as described by

$$f(x, y) = I(x, y)\rho(x, y), \tag{5-12}$$

where I is the intensity of the illuminating light source, f is the image, and $0 \leq \rho \leq 1$ is the reflectance of the object. Reflectance of an opaque object is zero, whereas a perfect reflector has a reflectance equal to one. Since the light source has a constant intensity, it can essentially be considered a slowly varying 2-D signal. The reflectance, however, depends on the object surface properties and so can be considered a high-pass signal. Thus we have an image with multiplicative components, which are approximately disjoint in the frequency domain. If noise is present, then it is also multiplicative. In order to enhance an image with poor contrast, we can use the model in Eq. (5-12) and selectively filter out the light source while boosting the reflectance component. The result will be an enhancement of the image. In order to separate the two components, they must be additive. We therefore transform the image into the log domain, whereby the multiplicative components become additive, as

$$\ln(f) = \ln(I) + \ln(\rho). \qquad (5\text{-}13)$$

Since the natural logarithm is monotonic, $\ln(I)$ is low pass and $\ln(\rho)$ is high pass. Now we have an image $f' = \ln(f)$, which has additive components and can therefore be selectively filtered by a linear filter. In order to enhance an image, the homomorphic filter must have a higher response in the high-frequency region than in the low-frequency region so that the details, which fall in the high-frequency region, can be accentuated while lowering the illumination component. We can therefore specify a response of α in the low-pass region and one in the high-frequency region with a cutoff frequency of Ω_c. These are user-specified parameters. Typical values for α and Ω_c are 0.5 and 0.5, respectively. The block diagram in Figure 5-13 describes homomorphic processing. The natural logarithm is applied to the image plus one rather than just the image to ensure that the zero pixel value in the input image is mapped to zero in the log domain. Similarly, the filtered image is exponentiated and a value of one is subtracted.

The idea of homomorphic filtering as an image enhancement technique is illustrated in Figure 5-14. The 2-D filter frequency response is shown in Figure 5-14a. This is a FIR filter with circular symmetry, a size of 13×13, and a value of 0.5 for α and a cutoff frequency of 0.5. An image with poor contrast (Figure 5-14b) is filtered homomorphically by the filter in Figure 5-14a, and the processed image is shown in Figure 5-14c. One can note the improvement in contrast—the scarf has more details and the leaf and the dark flower are clearly visible, as is the face.

5.4   COLOR IMAGE ENHANCEMENT

Because a true color image has R, G, B components, we can process the image in this color space. However, in histogram equalizing a color image, it is

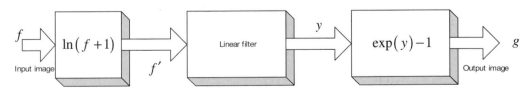

FIGURE   A block diagram depicting homomorphic filtering.

5-13

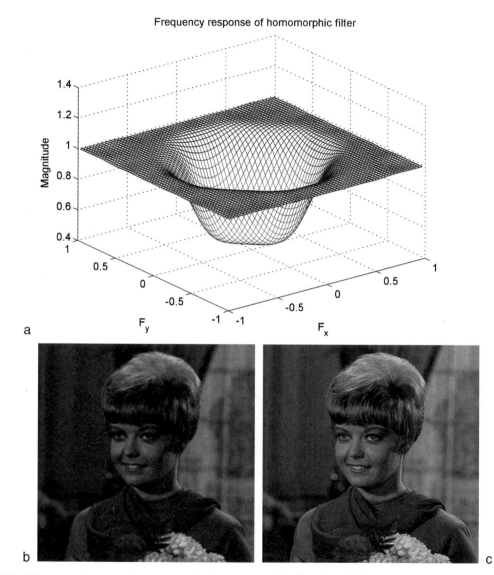

a

b

c

FIGURE

5-14

Image enhancement by homomorphic filtering: (a) frequency response of the filter, (b) original image, and (c) enhanced image.

advisable to process it in a perceptually based color space, such as hue, saturation, and intensity (HSI). As pointed out in Chapter 3, saturation refers to the purity or the amount of white light present and hue refers to the perceived color. Thus depending on the saturation level of a color image, it can be scaled up or down. Since hue is an angle, one can add or subtract a certain amount to shift the color up or down the color space. As the HVS is more sensitive to brightness than to color, we should perform histogram equalization of the intensity component only. The overall procedure for color contrast enhancement, therefore, is to (a) convert the RGB image to an HSI image, (b) histogram equalize the I component, (c) modify H, S, or both—scale S up or down, add or subtract a constant to H, and (d) convert the HSI image back to an RGB image.

The conversion of RGB to HSI is achieved by the following equations:

$$I = \frac{R + G + B}{3}, \tag{5-14a}$$

$$S = 1 - \frac{3 \times \min(R, G, B)}{R + G + B}, \tag{5-14b}$$

$$H = \begin{cases} \theta, & \text{if } B \leq G \\ 360 - \theta, & \text{if } B > G \end{cases} \tag{5-14c}$$

with

$$\theta = \cos^{-1}\left(\frac{R - \frac{1}{2}[G + B]}{\sqrt{(R - G)^2 + (R - B)(G - B)}} \right). \tag{5-14d}$$

Similarly, the RGB components can be obtained from the HSI components via the equations

$$B = I(1 - S), \tag{5-15a}$$

$$R = I\left(1 + \frac{S \cos(H)}{\cos(60° - H)} \right), \tag{5-15b}$$

$$G = 1 - (R + B). \tag{5-15c}$$

The aforementioned procedure is applied to an image (Figure 5-15a), which appears to be dim and a bit reddish. The result of enhancing the image in the HSI space is shown in Figure 5-15b. Figure 5-15c is the result of histogram equal-

FIGURE

5-15
Color image enhancement: (a) original image, (b) enhanced in the HSI space, and (c) enhanced in the RGB space.

ization of the RGB components. Notice a bluish tinge in Figure 5-15c due to the histogram equalization in the RGB color space.

5.5   SUMMARY

This chapter demonstrated a few techniques used to enhance an image that has poor contrast. First we described techniques to enhance intensity images. These techniques fall into the categories of point operation and spatial or neighborhood operation. Under point processing we discussed techniques such as logarithmic transformation, simple amplitude scaling, piecewise linear transformation, and histogram equalization. Next, adaptive histogram equalization was introduced, which takes into account the local intensity distributions in equalizing the histogram. It was found that adaptive histogram equalization yields better contrast enhancement than its nonadaptive counterpart. Under spatial processing we first described ad hoc mask operations, which included averaging as well as edge-sharpening masks. Next, spatial processing using FIR filters satisfying a specified frequency response was introduced. Another aspect of image enhancement is noise cleaning. In this context, median filtering was described as a mask operation and its effectiveness in removing impulse noise in images. Homomorphic filtering was discussed as an effective method in improving image contrast by utilizing the optical imaging model, which consists of the product of illumination and reflectance components. By selectively filtering out the illumination and boosting the object reflectance in the log domain, we showed an improvement in the image contrast. Finally, the idea of color enhancement was discussed, where it was found that processing in the HSI domain was beneficial.

REFERENCES

For topics in all the sections, the reader is referred to the following.

W.K. Pratt, *Digital Image Processing*, John Wiley & Sons, New York, 1991.

A.K. Jain, *Fundamentals of Digital Image Processing*, Prentice Hall, Englewood Cliffs, NJ, 1989.

K.R. Castleman, *Digital Image Processing, Image Processing*, Prentice Hall, Englewood Cliffs, NJ, 1996.

R.C. Gonzalez and R.E. Woods, *Digital Image Processing*, Addison-Wesley, Reading, MA, 1992.

6 | Discrete Transforms for Image Processing

6.1   INTRODUCTION

We know from time-domain signal analysis that Fourier series gives an alternative representation of a periodic signal in terms of sinusoids whose frequencies are integer multiples of the fundamental frequency of the signal and whose amplitude and phase can be determined from the signal itself. These sinusoids are so-called *basis functions* and form a complete orthogonal set for the signal expansion. Thus one can use these sinusoids in representing the signal at each instant of time. Similarly, we use the Fourier transform for the representation of aperiodic time-domain signals. Digital images, which are 2-D discrete-space signals, can be described alternatively by discrete orthogonal transforms. These transform-domain representations are useful in image compression, image analysis, and image understanding. This chapter describes some of the most popular sinusoidal and nonsinusoidal 2-D discrete transforms, also known as *block transforms*, which will be used in image compression.

6.2   UNITARY TRANSFORMS

6.2.1   One-Dimensional Unitary Transforms

Let us first consider 1-D linear transforms. Let $\mathbf{x}$ be an $N \times 1$ vector and $\mathbf{T}$ an $N \times N$ matrix. A linear transformation of $\mathbf{x}$ by $\mathbf{T}$, denoted $\mathbf{y}$, can be written as

$$\mathbf{y} = \mathbf{Tx} \quad \text{or} \quad y_i = \sum_{j=0}^{N-1} x_j t_{i,j}, \quad 0 \le i \le N-1. \tag{6-1}$$

In Eq. (6-1), the *kernel* matrix $\mathbf{T}$ may be real or complex. The elements of $\mathbf{y}$ are called the transform coefficients, and the vector $\mathbf{y}$ is called the transformed vector. We can interpret Eq. (6-1) as follows. If the indices i and j in $\mathbf{T}$

correspond to the frequency and time instant, respectively, then each element of **y** is determined by the corresponding frequency component over the whole time period. We can recover **x** from **y** by the inverse transform

$$\mathbf{x} = \mathbf{T}^{-1}\mathbf{y} = \mathbf{G}\mathbf{y} \quad \text{or} \quad x_i = \sum_{j=0}^{N-1} y_j g_{i,j}, \quad 0 \le i \le N-1, \tag{6-2}$$

provided the inverse matrix $\mathbf{T}^{-1}$ exists. We can interpret Eq. (6-2) in the same way as we did in Eq. (6-1), except that now **x** at each time instant gets contribution from all the frequency components at that instant of time.

Unitary Transform

A matrix **T** is called unitary if its inverse is its own conjugate transpose. That is, **T** is unitary if

$$\mathbf{T}^{-1} = \mathbf{T}^{*\prime} \quad \text{and} \quad \mathbf{T}\mathbf{T}^{*\prime} = \mathbf{T}\mathbf{T}^{-1} = \mathbf{I}, \tag{6-3}$$

where the asterisk stands for complex conjugate and the prime for matrix transpose, and **I** is the identity matrix. The corresponding transform is known as the *unitary transform*. Therefore, the signal **x** can be expressed as

$$x_i = \sum_{j=0}^{N-1} y_j t_{j,i}^*, \quad 0 \le i \le N-1. \tag{6-4}$$

Note that in Eq. (6-4), each element of **x** is represented by a weighted sum of **y**, where the weights correspond to the column of the unitary matrix **T**. The columns of **T** are called *basis vectors*.

Orthogonal Transform

If the elements of a unitary matrix **T** are real, then **T** is called an orthogonal transform and its inverse is its own transpose, i.e.,

$$\mathbf{T}^{-1} = \mathbf{T}'. \tag{6-5}$$

6.2.1.1   One-Dimensional DFT

The 1-D DFT of an N-point sequence **x** is defined by

$$y[k] = \frac{1}{\sqrt{N}} \sum_{n=0}^{N-1} x[n] w_N^{nk}, \quad 0 \le k \le N-1, \tag{6-6}$$

where we have used the familiar notation $w_N \equiv \exp\left(-j\dfrac{2\pi}{N}\right)$. The inverse DFT (IDFT) gives the signal x:

$$x[n] = \frac{1}{\sqrt{N}} \sum_{k=0}^{N-1} y[k] w_N^{-nk}, \quad 0 \le n \le N-1. \tag{6-7}$$

For computational efficiency, the 1-D DFT is often implemented with a scaling factor of $1/N$ in the forward transform and 1 in the inverse transform. As an example, the DFT kernel matrix for $N = 4$ is given by

$$T_{DFT} = \frac{1}{2}\begin{bmatrix} 1 & 1 & 1 & 1 \\ 1 & -j & -1 & j \\ 1 & -1 & 1 & -1 \\ 1 & j & -1 & -j \end{bmatrix}, \quad \text{where } j = \sqrt{-1}.$$

Observe that the 1-D DFT uses sinusoidal basis functions, which are the conjugates of the columns of T. Since the inverse of the 1-D DFT matrix is its own transpose, the 1-D DFT is a unitary transform. Figure 6-1 shows the rows of the DFT unitary matrix for $N = 8$.

6.2.1.2   *One-Dimensional Discrete Cosine Transform (DCT)*

The DCT of an N-point sequence **x** is defined as

$$X[k] = \alpha(k) \sum_{n=0}^{N-1} x[n] \cos\left(\frac{(2n+1)\pi k}{2N}\right), \quad 0 \le k \le N-1, \tag{6-8}$$

where

$$\alpha(k) = \begin{cases} \dfrac{1}{\sqrt{N}}, & k = 0 \\[2ex] \sqrt{\dfrac{2}{N}}, & 1 \le k \le N-1 \end{cases} \tag{6-9}$$

The elements of the 1-D DCT matrix are given by

$$C(k,n) = \begin{cases} \dfrac{1}{\sqrt{N}}, & k = 0, 0 \le n \le N-1 \\[2ex] \sqrt{\dfrac{2}{N}} \cos\left(\dfrac{(2n+1)\pi k}{2N}\right), & 1 \le k \le N-1, 0 \le n \le N-1 \end{cases} \tag{6-10}$$

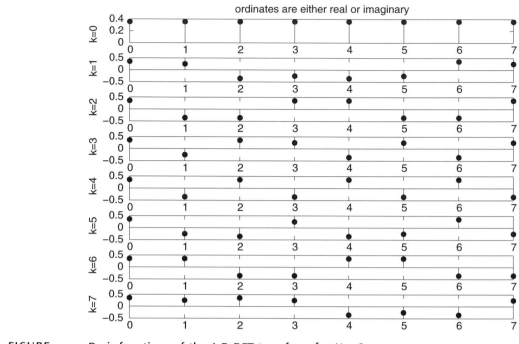

FIGURE

6-1

Basis functions of the 1-D DFT transform for $N = 8$.

Because the 1-D DCT is orthogonal, the sequence **x** can be recovered by

$$x[n] = \sum_{k=0}^{N-1} \alpha[k]X[k]\cos\left(\frac{(2n+1)\pi k}{2N}\right), \quad 0 \le n \le N-1. \tag{6-11}$$

See Figure 6-2 for functions of 1-D DCT.

6.2.1.3   One-Dimensional Discrete Sine Transform (DST)

The DST of an N-point sequence **x** is defined as

$$X[k] = \sqrt{\frac{2}{N+1}}\sum_{n=0}^{N-1} x[n]\sin\left(\frac{(n+1)(k+1)\pi}{N+1}\right), \quad 0 \le k \le N-1. \tag{6-12}$$

The inverse DST is expressed as

$$x[n] = \sqrt{\frac{2}{N+1}}\sum_{k=0}^{N-1} X[k]\sin\left(\frac{(n+1)(k+1)\pi}{N+1}\right), \quad 0 \le n \le N-1. \tag{6-13}$$

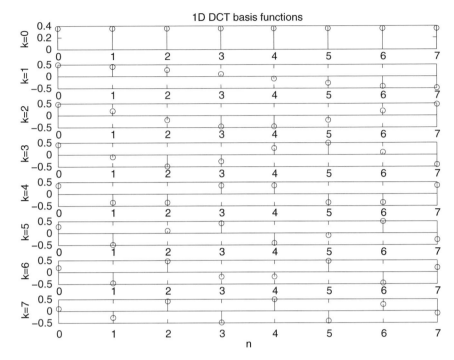

FIGURE

6-2

Basis functions of 1-D DCT for $N = 8$.

The elements of the kernel matrix of the DST are written as

$$T(k,n) = \sqrt{\frac{2}{N+1}} \sin\left(\frac{(n+1)(k+1)\pi}{N+1}\right), \quad 0 \leq k, n \leq N-1. \qquad (6\text{-}14)$$

See Figure 6-3 for functions of 1-D DST.

6.2.1.4   *One-Dimensional Discrete Hartley Transform*

Bracewell defined a discrete unitary transform by modifying a continuous integral transform, which was introduced by Hartley. This discrete transform came to be known as discrete Hartley transform and it uses both sine and cosine functions. The discrete Hartley transform has the kernel matrix whose elements are given by

$$T(k,n) = \frac{1}{\sqrt{N}} cas\left(\frac{2\pi nk}{N}\right), \quad 0 \leq k, n \leq N-1, \qquad (6\text{-}15)$$

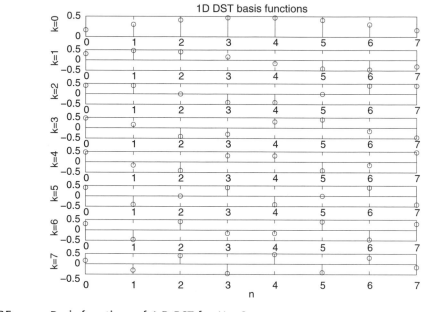

FIGURE

6-3

Basis functions of 1-D DST for $N = 8$.

where $cas(\theta) = \cos(\theta) + \sin(\theta)$. Note that the discrete Hartley transform is also real, similar to DCT and DST. The corresponding transform pair is defined by

$$X[k] = \frac{1}{\sqrt{N}} \sum_{n=0}^{N-1} x[n] cas\left(\frac{2\pi nk}{N}\right), \quad 0 \le k \le N-1 \tag{6-16}$$

$$x[n] = \frac{1}{\sqrt{N}} \sum_{k=0}^{N-1} X[k] cas\left(\frac{2\pi nk}{N}\right), \quad 0 \le n \le N-1 \tag{6-17}$$

See Figure 6-4 for functions of 1-D discrete Hartley transform.

6.2.1.5   Hadamard, Haar, and Slant Transforms

The unitary transforms discussed in the previous sections are sinusoidal, i.e., they use sinusoidal basis functions, whereas the Hadamard, Haar, and Slant transforms use rectangular basis functions.

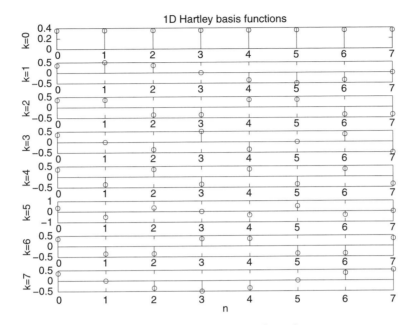

1D Hartley basis functions

FIGURE

6-4

Basis functions of 1-D discrete Hartley transform for $N = 8$.

6.2.1.5.1 Hadamard Transform

The Hadamard transform is real and orthogonal. A 2×2 Hadamard matrix is given by

$$\mathbf{H}_2 = \frac{1}{\sqrt{2}}\begin{bmatrix} 1 & 1 \\ 1 & -1 \end{bmatrix}. \tag{6-18}$$

Hadamard matrices of higher order can be constructed using the following recursion formula for $N \geq 2$:

$$\mathbf{H}_{2N} = \begin{bmatrix} \mathbf{H}_N & \mathbf{H}_N \\ \mathbf{H}_N & -\mathbf{H}_N \end{bmatrix} \tag{6-19}$$

With the definition of the Hadamard matrix given earlier, the forward and inverse Hadamard transforms of an N-point sequence (Figure 6-5) are obtained from

$$\mathbf{y} = \mathbf{H}\mathbf{x}\mathbf{H}' \tag{6-20}$$

$$\mathbf{x} = \mathbf{H}'\mathbf{y}\mathbf{H} \tag{6-21}$$

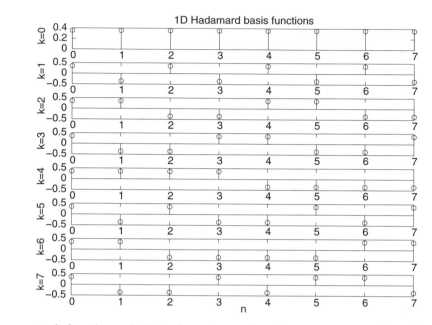

1D Hadamard basis functions

FIGURE 6-5

Basis functions of 1-D Hadamard transform for $N = 8$. For nonsinusoidal transforms, the term sequency is used instead of frequency and is a measure of the number of zero crossings.

For example, the Hadamard matrices of order 4 and 8 are given by

$$\mathbf{H}_4 = \frac{1}{2} \begin{bmatrix} 1 & 1 & 1 & 1 \\ 1 & -1 & 1 & -1 \\ 1 & 1 & -1 & -1 \\ 1 & -1 & -1 & 1 \end{bmatrix} \tag{6-22a}$$

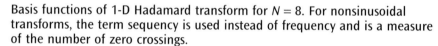

$$\mathbf{H}_8 = \frac{1}{\sqrt{8}} \left[\begin{array}{cccc|cccc} 1 & 1 & 1 & 1 & 1 & 1 & 1 & 1 \\ 1 & -1 & 1 & -1 & 1 & -1 & 1 & -1 \\ 1 & 1 & -1 & -1 & 1 & 1 & -1 & -1 \\ 1 & -1 & -1 & 1 & 1 & -1 & -1 & 1 \\ \hline 1 & 1 & 1 & 1 & -1 & -1 & -1 & -1 \\ 1 & -1 & 1 & -1 & -1 & 1 & -1 & 1 \\ 1 & 1 & -1 & -1 & -1 & -1 & 1 & 1 \\ 1 & -1 & -1 & 1 & -1 & 1 & 1 & -1 \end{array} \right] \tag{6-22b}$$

6.2.1.5.2 Haar Transform

The Haar matrix of size 8×8 is given by

$$\mathbf{H}_8 = \frac{1}{\sqrt{8}} \begin{bmatrix} 1 & 1 & 1 & 1 & 1 & 1 & 1 & 1 \\ 1 & 1 & 1 & 1 & -1 & -1 & -1 & -1 \\ \sqrt{2} & \sqrt{2} & -\sqrt{2} & -\sqrt{2} & 0 & 0 & 0 & 0 \\ 0 & 0 & 0 & 0 & \sqrt{2} & \sqrt{2} & -\sqrt{2} & -\sqrt{2} \\ 2 & -2 & 0 & 0 & 0 & 0 & 0 & 0 \\ 0 & 0 & 2 & -2 & 0 & 0 & 0 & 0 \\ 0 & 0 & 0 & 0 & 2 & -2 & 0 & 0 \\ 0 & 0 & 0 & 0 & 0 & 0 & 2 & -2 \end{bmatrix} \qquad (6\text{-}23)$$

See Figure 6-6 for functions of 1-D Haar transform.

6.2.1.5.3 Slant Transform

The slant transform matrix of order 2 is identical to that of the Hadamard transform. For N = 4, the slant matrix is described by

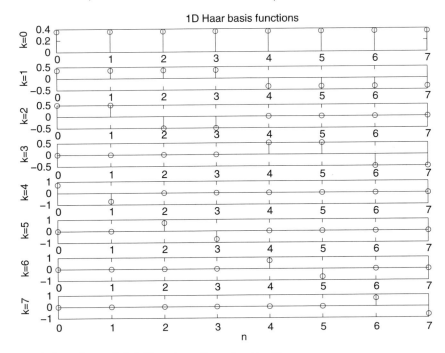

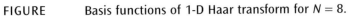

FIGURE   Basis functions of 1-D Haar transform for $N = 8$.

6-6

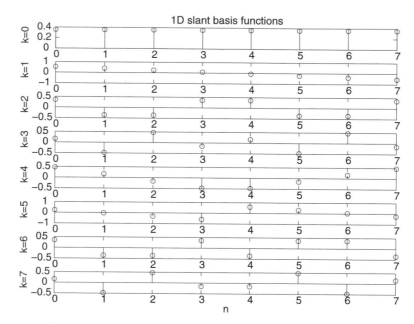

$$\mathbf{S}_4 = \frac{1}{\sqrt{4}} \begin{bmatrix} 1 & 1 & 1 & 1 \\ \dfrac{3}{\sqrt{5}} & \dfrac{1}{\sqrt{5}} & \dfrac{-1}{\sqrt{5}} & \dfrac{-3}{\sqrt{5}} \\ 1 & -1 & -1 & 1 \\ \dfrac{1}{\sqrt{5}} & \dfrac{-3}{\sqrt{5}} & \dfrac{3}{\sqrt{5}} & \dfrac{-1}{\sqrt{5}} \end{bmatrix} \tag{6-24}$$

See Figure 6-7 for functions of 1-D slant transform.

Higher order slant matrices can be generated using the recursive relation

$$\mathbf{S}_N = \frac{1}{\sqrt{2}} \left[\begin{array}{cc|c|cc|c} 1 & 0 & \mathbf{0} & 1 & 0 & \mathbf{0} \\ a_N & b_N & & -a_N & b_N & \\ \hline \mathbf{0} & & \mathbf{I}_{\frac{N-4}{2}} & \mathbf{0} & & \mathbf{I}_{\frac{N-4}{2}} \\ \hline 0 & 1 & \mathbf{0} & 0 & -1 & \mathbf{0} \\ -b_N & a_N & & b_N & a_N & \\ \hline \mathbf{0} & & \mathbf{I}_{\frac{N-4}{2}} & \mathbf{0} & & -\mathbf{I}_{\frac{N-4}{2}} \end{array} \right] \left[\begin{array}{c|c} \mathbf{S}_{\frac{N}{2}} & 0 \\ \hline 0 & \mathbf{S}_{\frac{N}{2}} \end{array} \right], \tag{6-25}$$

where $\mathbf{I}_L$ is an $L \times L$ identity matrix. The constants a_N and b_N are defined by

$$a_{2N} = \sqrt{\frac{3N^2}{4N^2 - 1}} \tag{6-26a}$$

$$b_{2N} = \sqrt{\frac{N^2 - 1}{4N^2 - 1}} \tag{6-26b}$$

6.2.2   Two-Dimensional Discrete Transforms

Similar to the 1-D transform, the 2-D discrete transform of an $N \times N$ image $x[m,n]$ can be described by

$$X[k,l] = \sum_{m=0}^{N-1} \sum_{n=0}^{N-1} x[m,n] T(k,m;l,n), \quad 0 \le k, l \le N-1. \tag{6-27}$$

If the 2-D transform is orthogonal, the inverse transform is defined by

$$x[m,n] = \sum_{k=0}^{N-1} \sum_{l=0}^{N-1} X[k,l] T^*(k,m;l,n), \quad 0 \le m, n \le N-1. \tag{6-28}$$

Separable Transforms

When the 2-D transform is separable, it can be written as

$$T(k,m;l,n) = T_1(k,m) T_2(l,n). \tag{6-29}$$

Often $\mathbf{T}_1$ and $\mathbf{T}_2$ are identical matrices and are also unitary. In such cases the 2-D discrete transform of $x[m,n]$ can be written as

$$\mathbf{Y} = \mathbf{TXT}. \tag{6-30}$$

The corresponding image can be obtained from the inverse transform as

$$\mathbf{X} = \mathbf{T}^{*\prime} \mathbf{YT}^{*\prime}. \tag{6-31}$$

Basis Image

Just as a 1-D time-domain signal can be expressed as a linear sum of basis functions, an image, which is a discrete-space 2-D signal, can be expressed as a linear sum of basis images. Each basis image is obtained as follows. (1) First obtain the conjugate transpose of the transform matrix. (2) For each column of this matrix, consider the transpose of another column of the same matrix. (3) Multiply the two vectors to get a basis image. Repeat steps 2 and 3 to obtain all the N^2 basis images. Thus, an $N \times N$ block of image pixels can be expressed in terms of the basis images as

$$x[m,n] = \sum_{k=0}^{N-1}\sum_{l=0}^{N-1} X[k,l]A_{k,l}, \quad 0 \le m, n \le N-1. \tag{6-32}$$

where $X[k,l]$ is the transform coefficient and $\mathbf{A}_{k,l}$ is the basis image. For example, the basis images of the 8×8 DCT transform for k = 0, l = 0 and k = 0, l = 1 are given in the following equations.

$$\mathbf{A}_{0,0} = \frac{1}{8}\begin{bmatrix} 1 & 1 & 1 & 1 & 1 & 1 & 1 & 1 \\ 1 & 1 & 1 & 1 & 1 & 1 & 1 & 1 \\ 1 & 1 & 1 & 1 & 1 & 1 & 1 & 1 \\ 1 & 1 & 1 & 1 & 1 & 1 & 1 & 1 \\ 1 & 1 & 1 & 1 & 1 & 1 & 1 & 1 \\ 1 & 1 & 1 & 1 & 1 & 1 & 1 & 1 \\ 1 & 1 & 1 & 1 & 1 & 1 & 1 & 1 \\ 1 & 1 & 1 & 1 & 1 & 1 & 1 & 1 \end{bmatrix} \tag{6-33}$$

$$\mathbf{A}_{0,1} = \begin{bmatrix} 0.1734 & 0.1470 & 0.0982 & 0.0345 & -0.0345 & -0.0982 & -0.1470 & -0.1734 \\ 0.1734 & 0.1470 & 0.0982 & 0.0345 & -0.0345 & -0.0982 & -0.1470 & -0.1734 \\ 0.1734 & 0.1470 & 0.0982 & 0.0345 & -0.0345 & -0.0982 & -0.1470 & -0.1734 \\ 0.1734 & 0.1470 & 0.0982 & 0.0345 & -0.0345 & -0.0982 & -0.1470 & -0.1734 \\ 0.1734 & 0.1470 & 0.0982 & 0.0345 & -0.0345 & -0.0982 & -0.1470 & -0.1734 \\ 0.1734 & 0.1470 & 0.0982 & 0.0345 & -0.0345 & -0.0982 & -0.1470 & -0.1734 \\ 0.1734 & 0.1470 & 0.0982 & 0.0345 & -0.0345 & -0.0982 & -0.1470 & -0.1734 \\ 0.1734 & 0.1470 & 0.0982 & 0.0345 & -0.0345 & -0.0982 & -0.1470 & -0.1734 \end{bmatrix}$$
$$\tag{6-34}$$

Basis images for some of the sinusoidal and nonsinusoidal 2-D unitary transforms are shown in Figure 6-8. For an $N \times N$ transform, there are N^2 basis images.

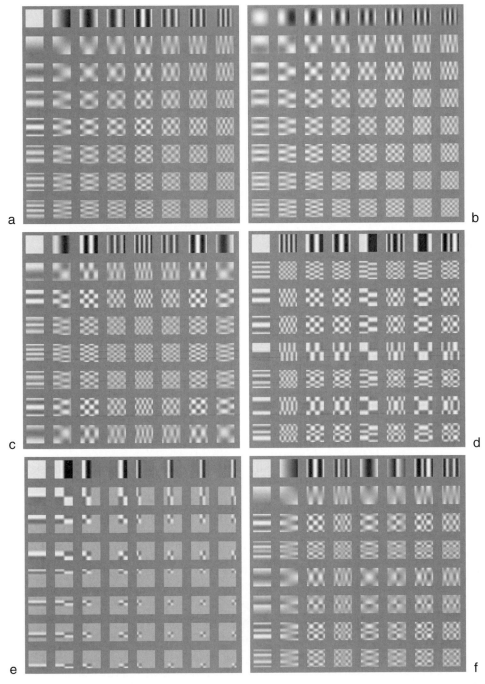

FIGURE

6-8

8×8 basis images of 2-D unitary transforms: (a) DCT, (b) DST, (c) Hartley, (d) Hadamard, (e) Haar, and (f) slant.

FIGURE

6-9

Image reconstruction using 8 × 8 DCT basis images: (a) reconstructed image, using the basis images, $A_{i,j}$, $0 \leq i, j \leq 1$, (b) reconstructed image using the first two rows of the basis images, and (c) reconstructed image using the first four rows of the basis images.

For better viewing purpose, the images in Figure 6-8 are enlarged by a factor of 2 in each dimension and displayed against a darker background. To illustrate the effect of using basis images to reconstruct an image, consider the 2-D DCT of size 8 × 8 pixels. Figure 6-9a is the result of using only 4 out of the 64 basis images. Observe how blocky the image looks. The reconstructed image using the first two rows of the basis images is shown in Figure 6-9b. Figure 6-9c shows the result of reconstructing the image using the first four rows of the basis images. We see that the image in Figure 6-9c is very nearly the same as the original image. Of course, when all the N^2 basis images are used in the reconstruction, the result-

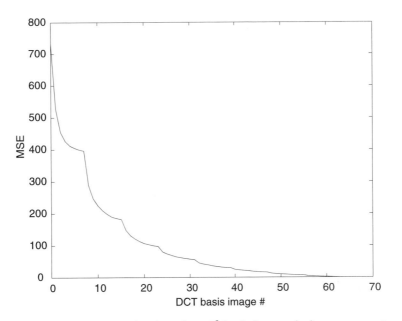

FIGURE   Mean square error using less than N^2 basis images in image reconstruction.
                The transform used is 2-D DCT of size 8×8.

6-10

ing image will be identical to the original image provided infinite precision is used in the arithmetic. The mean square error (MSE) between the original image and the image reconstructed using basis images between 1 and N^2 decreases as the number of basis images used increases. This is illustrated in Figure 6-10 for the cameraman and 2-D DCT of size 8×8. As a comparison, Figure 6-11 shows the MSE for the Hadamard transform. Even though the MSE is zero when all 64 basis images are used, the reduction in the MSE is much faster for the DCT than for the Hadamard transform. Figure 6-12 shows the MSE for the different unitary transforms for the same image of the cameraman. It is seen that the MSE decreases the fastest for the 2-D DCT.

6.2.3   Some Properties of Unitary Transform

Conservation of Energy

The unitary transform has the property that the sum of squares of the pixels in an $N \times N$ block is identical to that of the transform coefficients. Thus,

$$\sum_{m=0}^{N-1}\sum_{n=0}^{N-1}|x[m,n]|^2 = \sum_{k=0}^{N-1}\sum_{l=0}^{N-1}|X[k,l]|^2. \qquad (6\text{-}35)$$

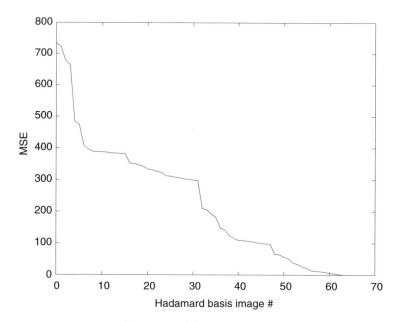

FIGURE

6-11
Mean square error between original and reconstructed images for Hadamard transform of size 8×8.

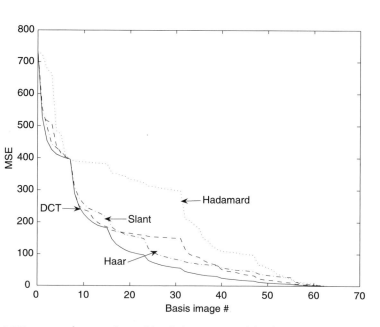

FIGURE

6-12
MSE versus the number of basis images used in the reconstruction.

The only effect of the unitary transformation on the image is to rotate the axes in the transform domain so that they are orthogonal. A further implication is that since the axes are orthogonal, the transform coefficients are independent; each coefficient represents a feature of the image block.

Energy Compaction

Another important property of the unitary transform is that each transform coefficient carries an unequal amount of the energy in the image block. Consider an 8×8 block of pixels whose values follow.

$$\mathbf{x} = \begin{bmatrix} 156 & 159 & 158 & 155 & 158 & 156 & 159 & 158 \\ 160 & 154 & 157 & 158 & 157 & 159 & 158 & 158 \\ 156 & 159 & 158 & 155 & 158 & 156 & 159 & 158 \\ 160 & 154 & 157 & 158 & 157 & 159 & 158 & 158 \\ 156 & 153 & 155 & 159 & 159 & 155 & 156 & 155 \\ 155 & 155 & 155 & 157 & 156 & 159 & 152 & 158 \\ 156 & 153 & 157 & 156 & 153 & 155 & 154 & 155 \\ 159 & 159 & 156 & 158 & 156 & 159 & 157 & 161 \end{bmatrix}$$

(6-36)

The corresponding DCT transform block is given by

$$\mathbf{X} = \begin{bmatrix} 1255 & -2 & 1 & 9 & 2 & 1 & 3 & 0 \\ 4 & -1 & 1 & 1 & -2 & 0 & -2 & 4 \\ 2 & 1 & 3 & -1 & -2 & -2 & 0 & -1 \\ -5 & 0 & -3 & 0 & 1 & -1 & 1 & 0 \\ 3 & 0 & 0 & 1 & 1 & 0 & -2 & 1 \\ -2 & 1 & 1 & -1 & -3 & 0 & 0 & 1 \\ 2 & -1 & 1 & -1 & -2 & -5 & -2 & -1 \\ -3 & 1 & -1 & -2 & -1 & 0 & -4 & 3 \end{bmatrix}$$

(6-37)

It can be verified that the sum of squares of the elements of the matrices in Eqs. (6-36) and (6-37) are equal. However, 99.55% of the total energy is contained in the first (DC) coefficient alone. This shows that almost all the energy in the block is packed into a single DCT coefficient, which is the energy compaction property of a unitary transform. This trend in energy compaction is true for all the unitary transforms, even though not all the energy will be packed in a single coefficient. The distribution of energy decreases rapidly as the coefficient number increases for all the unitary transforms.

Distribution of the Amplitudes of Transform Coefficients

The distribution of the amplitudes of any ac transform coefficient is shown to be a Laplacian density. For the cameraman image, the distribution functions for a few ac coefficients of an 8×8 DCT transform are shown in Figure 6-13.

Unitary Transforms Are Fast Transforms

An N-point unitary transform can be calculated in $O(N\log_2 N)$ operations. Such transforms are called *fast transforms*. As an example, an eight-point 1-D DCT can be calculated using the signal flow diagram, as shown in Figure 6-14a. Note that there are $\log_2(8) = 3$ stages of computation with four multiplications per stage, for a total of 12 multiplications. Due to symmetry of the DCT transform matrix, only 12 multiplications are required instead of 24. A straightforward computation will require 64 multiplications. Thus, DCT is a fast transform. Figure 6-14b shows the signal flow graph of the inverse DCT. Because the 2-D DCT is separable, the same flow graph in Figure 6-14a can be used twice to perform the 2-D DCT of 8×8 block of pixels, once along the rows and then along the columns.

6.3   KARHUNEN–LOEVE TRANSFORM

The unitary transforms described in the foregoing sections have either sinusoidal or sequency basis functions and are independent of the image under consideration. The main purpose of a transform is to express a block of image pixels in the transform domain such that the transform coefficients are completely decorrelated even though the pixels may have correlation. With the transform coefficients completely decorrelated, each one of them then represents an independent feature of the image subblock. All the transforms discussed earlier do not achieve this objective, although the DCT comes very close to achieving this objective. The Karhunen–Loeve (KL) transform, which is also known as the Hotelling transform or the method of principal components, is an optimal transform in the sense that the transform coefficients are completely decorrelated. However, the KL transform is image dependent, meaning that it is calculated from the second-order statistics of an image. More specifically, the KL transform of an image of size $N \times N$ is determined as follows. (1) Determine the covariance matrix $\mathbf{C}_R$ of the image along row dimension. (2) Solve the system of linear equations to obtain the 1-D row transform T_R:

$$\lambda_R(k)T_R(k,m) = \sum_{m'=0}^{N-1} C_R(m,m')T_R(k,m'), \qquad (6\text{-}38)$$

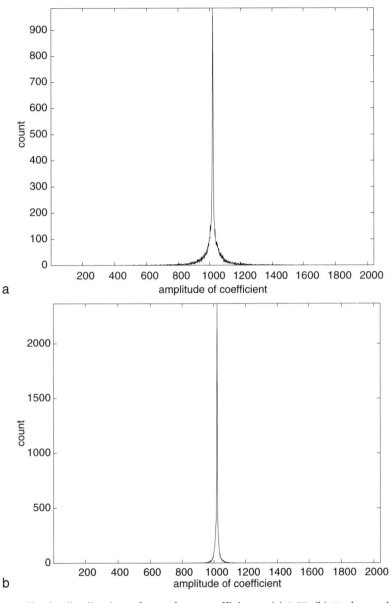

FIGURE

6-13

Amplitude distribution of transform coefficients. (a) DCT, (b) Hadamard, and (c) slant. All the ac coefficients correspond to $k = 0$ and $l = 1$.

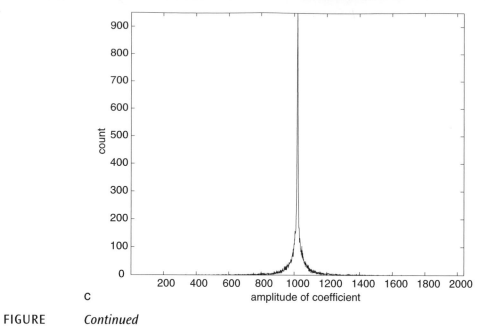

c

FIGURE

6-13

Continued

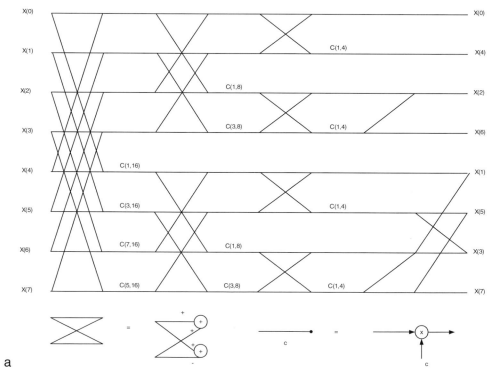

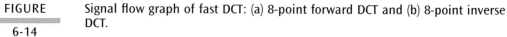

a

FIGURE

6-14

Signal flow graph of fast DCT: (a) 8-point forward DCT and (b) 8-point inverse DCT.

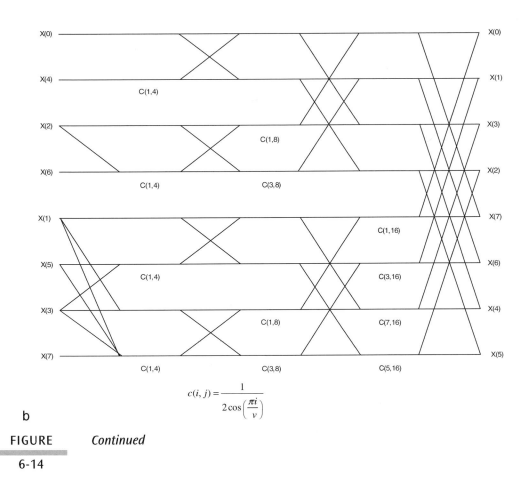

$$c(i, j) = \frac{1}{2\cos\left(\dfrac{\pi i}{v}\right)}$$

b

FIGURE   *Continued*

6-14

where $\lambda_R(k)$ is a constant. (3) Solve a similar system of equations to obtain the column transform T_C:

$$\lambda_C(l)T_C(l,n) = \sum_{n'=0}^{N-1} C_C(n,n')T_C(l,n').$$ (6-39)

In Eq. (6-39) C_C denotes the covariance matrix of the image along column dimension. (4) Transform the image using

$$\mathbf{Y} = \mathbf{T}_R' \mathbf{X} \mathbf{T}_C.$$ (6-40)

6.4   CHOICE OF A TRANSFORM

Given a variety of unitary transforms, how does one choose a particular transform? The choice depends on the application as well as the computational complexity. We will focus on image compression. The intention here is to reduce original image data to the minimum possible with the least amount of distortion. The initial choice will be the KL transform, as it is the optimal one and will yield the highest compression for a given amount of distortion. However, because it is image dependent, we need to calculate the KL transform kernel matrix for each instance of image compression. This may be computationally prohibitive. Also, the KL transform kernel matrix must be stored for each image and the overhead may defeat the optimality property. Therefore, we need to look for other possible suboptimal transforms. As shown from the MSE property of the unitary transforms, the DCT is the best choice for this particular application. It is nearly optimal and is also a fast transform.

6.5   SUMMARY

This chapter defined 1-D and 2-D unitary and orthogonal transforms suitable for image processing applications. Transforms involving both sinusoidal and nonsinusoidal basis functions were described. Examples were provided to show how an image may be expanded in terms of basis images and how the mean square error in the reconstruction process decreases as more and more basis images were used. Finally, the choice of a transform was explained in the context of image compression.

REFERENCES

For detailed discussions on discrete transforms for images, refer to Pratt (1991), Castleman (1996), and Jain (1989). For an understanding of the FFT algorithm, refer to Cooley (1965) and Cochran (1967). For details on algorithm development and analysis of DCT, refer to Ahmed (1974), Narasimha (1978), Chen (1977), and Yip (1980). A comprehensive survey of sinusoidal unitary transforms can be found in Jain (1979). Refer to Hadamard (1893), Walsh (1923), Whelchel (1968), and Pratt (1969) for the development of the Hadamard transform and its application to image coding. Haar transform fundamentals are found in Haar (1955) and Shore (1973). For details on Hartley transform, refer to Hartley (1942) and Bracewell (1983). For a basic understanding of KL transform, refer to Karhunen (1947), Loeve (1948), and Hotelling (1933).

W.K. Pratt, *Digital Image Processing*, 2nd edition, John Wiley & Sons, New York, 1991.

K.R. Castleman, *Digital Image Processing*, Prentice Hall, Englewood Cliffs, NJ, 1996.

A.K. Jain, *Fundamentals of Digital Image Processing*, Prentice Hall, Englewood Cliffs, NJ, 1989.

J.W. Cooley and J.W. Tukey, "An Algorithm for the Machine Calculation of Complex Fourier Series," Math. Comput., Vol. 19, 90, pp. 297–301, 1965.

W.T. Cochran et al., "What is the Fast Fourier Transform?" Proc. IEEE, Vol. 55, 10, 164–1674, 1967.

N. Ahmed, T. Natarajan, and K.R. Rao, "Discrete Cosine Transform," IEEE Trans. Comp., **C-23**, 90–93, 1974.

M.J. Narasimha and A.M. Peterson, "On the Computaion of the Discrete Cosine Transform," IEEE Trans. Comm., **COM-26**, 6:934–936, 1978.

W.H. Chen, C.H. Smith, and S.C. Fralick, "A Fast Computational Algorithm for the Discrete Cosine Transform," IEEE Trans. Comm., **COM-25**, 1004–1009, 1977.

P. Yip and K.R. Rao, "A Fast Computational Algorithm for the Discrete Sine Transform," IEEE Trans. Comm., **COM-28**(2), 304–307, 1980.

A.K. Jain, "A Sinusoidal family of Unitary Transforms," IEEE Trans. Pattern Anal. Macine Intll., **PAMI-1**(4), 356–365, 1979.

J. Hadamard, "Resolution d'une Question Relative aux Determinants," Bull. Sci. Math., Ser. 2, **17**, Part I, 240–246, 1893.

J.W. Walsh, "A Closed Set of Normal Orthogonal Functions," Am. J. Math., **45**(1), 5–24, 1923.

J.E. Whelchel Jr and D.F. Guinn, "The Fast Fourier-Hadamard Transform and Its Use in Signal representation and Classification," EASCON 1968 Convention Record, 561–573, 1968.

W.K. Pratt, H.C. Andrews, and J. Kane, "Hadamard Transform Image Coding," Proc. IEEE, Vol. 57(1), 58–68, 1969.

A. Haar, "Zur Theorie der Orthogonalen Funktionen-System," Inaugural Dissertation, Math. Annalen, **5**, 17–31, 1955.

J.E. Shore, "On the Application of Haar Functions," IEEE Trans. Comm., **COM-21**, 209–216, 1973.

R.V.L. Hartley, "A More Symmetrical Fourier Analysis Applied to Transmission Problems," Proc. IRE, **30**, 144–150, 1942.

R.M. Bracewell, "The Discrete Hartley Transform," J. Opt. Soc. Am., **73**(12), 1832–1835, 1983.

K. Karhunen, "Uber Lineare Methoden in der Wahrscheinlich-Kietsrechnung," Ann. Acd. Sci. Fennicae, Ser. A.1.37, 1947. English Translation by I. Selin, "On Linear Methods in Probability Theory," Doc. T-131, The RAND Corp., Santa Monica, CA, 1960.

M. Loeve, "Fonctions Aleatoires de Second Ordre," in P. Levy, *Processus Stochastiques et Mouvement Brownien*, Hermann, Paris, 1948.

H. Hotelling, "Analysis of a Complex of Statistical variables into Principal Components," J. Educ. Psychol., **24**, 417–441, 498–520, 1933.

7 Wavelet Transform

7.1 INTRODUCTION

Chapter 6 introduced discrete image transforms, which are based on sinusoidal and rectangular basis functions. The basis functions of these block transforms span the width of an image block. In other words, all the basis functions have the same fixed support. When it is required to capture transient behavior of a time-domain signal or spatial activity in an image, conventional transform techniques, such as the Fourier transform, are not adequate. The wavelet transform described in this chapter has its basis functions that have varying width instead of fixed width. This feature of varying width makes the wavelet transform, a powerful tool for signal analysis in general and image processing in particular.

Let us, for a brief moment, consider the familiar one-dimensional Fourier integral transform. It enables us to represent a signal $f(t)$ in terms of sinusoidal waveforms of continuously varying frequencies, all of which exist over the entire interval of observation. Therefore we can only pinpoint the frequencies of the sinusoidal waveforms, which make up the signal, but not the time instants at which these sinusoids are present. Even though the phase of the Fourier transform contains the time information, it is not easy to extract the time information from it. Figure 7-1a shows the time–frequency tile for the Fourier transform. Horizontal tiles with zero width correspond to precise frequencies that persist over the entire time interval.

Now consider a discrete-time signal $x[n]$. This signal can be analyzed by either discrete-time Fourier transform (continuous in frequency) or discrete Fourier transform (DFT), which is discrete in both time and frequency. The result is similar to the Fourier transform, which is that the signal is composed of sinusoids of continuous or discrete frequencies over the entire time interval. Short-time Fourier transform (STFT) was introduced to analyze speech signals, which are nonstationary, i.e., different frequency components evolve over time. The idea here is to block the discrete-time signal into segments (usually overlapping) and then perform DFT on each segment. This gives a spectrum of the signal as a function of time, i.e., frequency content over each time segment. However, the time interval of each segment is fixed and so the precise time of origination of the signal components within the time segment cannot be

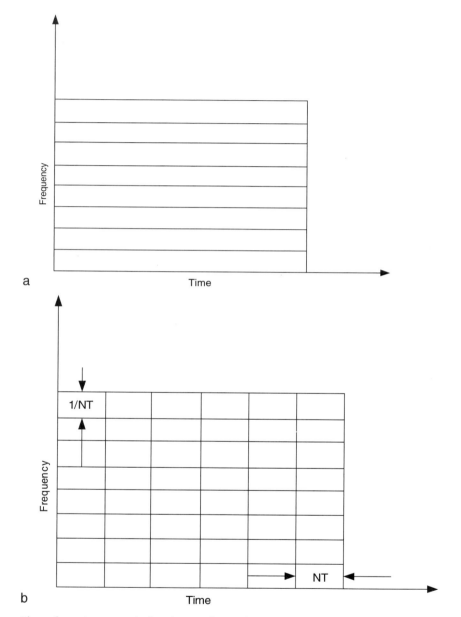

FIGURE

7-1

Time–frequency resolution in Fourier and wavelet transform domains: (a) Fourier transform, (b) STFT, and (c) wavelet transform.

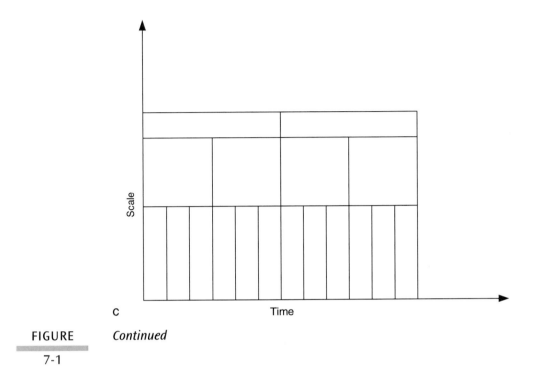

c

Time

FIGURE   *Continued*

7-1

pinpointed, as with the case of the Fourier transform. This is shown in Figure 7-1b. Each rectangular block is a *tile* in the time–frequency plane. If each time segment consists of N samples with uniform spacing of T seconds, then the width of any tile along the time axis equals NT and the width along the frequency axis is $1/NT$. This fixed width of basis functions results in fixed frequency resolution. The area of each tile is a constant. This is shown in Figure 7-1b.

Supposing we analyze the signal $x[n]$ using basis functions of varying width. This results in frequencies of different resolutions. The corresponding time–frequency tiles are shown in Figure 7-1c. Figure 7-1c shows that the tiles have varying widths in both time and frequency axes. This is the basis for the wavelet transform.

7.2   CONTINUOUS WAVELET TRANSFORM

We begin our discussion with 1-D signals. The wavelet transform of a signal resembles the familiar Fourier transform except that the basis functions are wavelets and not complex exponential functions. Qualitatively speaking, a *wavelet*

$\psi(t)$ is a function that wiggles around and dies fast as opposed to a *wave*, which persists indefinitely. All the basis functions $\psi_{s,\tau}(t)$ used in the wavelet transform are generated from a suitable prototype or mother wavelet $\psi(t)$ by dilating (or contracting) and translating it by s and τ, respectively. Thus,

$$\psi_{s,\tau}(t) = \frac{1}{\sqrt{s}}\,\psi\!\left(\frac{t-\tau}{s}\right), \tag{7-1}$$

where s is a scaling factor and τ is a delay or shift factor and the normalizing factor $\frac{1}{\sqrt{s}}$ ensures that all the wavelets have the same energy. Note that in Fourier series analysis, all the basis functions have the same average power, as the basis functions are periodic, whereas wavelets have the same finite energy, as the wavelets are, in general, aperiodic. Figure 7-2 shows a function and its dilates and translates. The signal spreads as the scale factor is increased and shrinks as the scale is decreased. A large scale implies a macroscopic view of the signal being analyzed, whereas a small scale amounts to a microscopic view. Also note that large scale corresponds to slow variation in time, which in turn corresponds to low frequency. Similarly, small scale represents high frequency. Thus, scale is

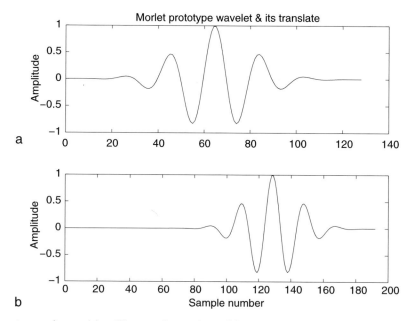

FIGURE
7-2

A wavelet and its dilate and translate: (a) prototype wavelet, (b) its dilate, and translate.

inversely proportional to frequency. Because a wavelet is a damped oscillating function, it does not have a precise frequency but is centered at some frequency with a spread. This center frequency is inversely related to the scale.

Given a signal $f(t)$, its continuous wavelet transform (CWT) is defined as

$$W(s,\tau) = \langle f, \psi_{s,\tau} \rangle = \int_{-\infty}^{\infty} f(t)\psi_{s,\tau}(t)dt. \tag{7-2}$$

In Eq. (7-2), s and τ are the continuous scale and shift factors, and $\langle f, \psi_{s,\tau} \rangle$ denotes the inner product of f and $\psi_{s,\tau}$. The integral is a measure of the area of the product of $f(t)$ and $\psi_{s,\tau}(t)$. Thus, a large value for $W(s,\tau)$ at a specified s and τ means that $f(t)$ has a high degree of similarity to $\psi_{s,\tau}(t)$ and a small $W(s,\tau)$ implies the contrary. The signal $f(t)$ can be recovered from its CWT by the inverse CWT (ICWT), as given by

$$f(t) = \frac{1}{C_\psi} \int_{0}^{\infty} \int_{-\infty}^{\infty} W(s,\tau)\psi_{s,\tau}(t)d\tau \frac{ds}{s^2}. \tag{7-3}$$

The constant in Eq. (7-3) is given by

$$C_\psi = \int_{-\infty}^{\infty} \frac{|\Psi(\omega)|^2}{|\omega|} d\omega < 0, \tag{7-4}$$

where $\Psi(\omega)$ is the Fourier transform of $\psi(t)$. Because the integrant in Eq. (7-4) exists only when $\Psi(0) = 0$, one of the constraints on the wavelets is that they have zero average value. Eq. (7-2) has the familiar form of the Fourier transform. The difference is that the basis functions, which are the wavelets, have different widths (due to different scales) and are not necessarily sinusoidal in shape. The CWT of $f(t)$ is a function of the scale and shift parameters. The scale parameter gives a measure of the frequency of the signal at time instant given by the shift parameter.

7.3   THE WAVELET SERIES

Recall that the Fourier series expansion of a periodic function expresses the signal in terms of an infinite number of sinusoids whose frequencies are integer multiples of the fundamental frequency. In a like manner, it is possible to expand $f(t)$ in a wavelet series if the scale and shift parameters are discrete rather than continuous. In particular, the scale parameter is expressed as a power of 2 (binary scaling) and the shift parameter is allowed to take on integer values (dyadic translations). Then the so-called dyadic wavelets are expressed as

$$\psi_{j,k}(t) = 2^{\frac{j}{2}}\psi(2^j t - k), \quad -\infty < j, k < \infty, \ j, k \in Z. \tag{7-5}$$

Thus, the wavelet series of $f(t)$ can be written as

$$f(t) = \sum_k c(j_0, k)\varphi_{j_0,k}(t) + \sum_{j=j_0}^{\infty} \sum_{k=-\infty}^{\infty} d(j, k)\psi_{j,k}(t). \tag{7-6}$$

The first summation in Eq. (7-6) uses the basis functions $\varphi_{j_0,k}(t)$ for a fixed scale value and the summation is over all possible shift values. In wavelet transform literature the functions $\varphi_{j_0,k}(t)$ are called *scaling* functions and are defined similar to Eq. (7-5), as

$$\varphi_{j,k}(t) = 2^{\frac{j}{2}}\varphi(2^j t - k), \quad -\infty < j, k < \infty, \ j, k \in Z. \tag{7-7}$$

The first summation in Eq. (7-6) is reminiscent of the dc coefficient in the Fourier series expansion. This term corresponds to an approximation of $f(t)$ expressed in terms of the scaling functions $\varphi_{j_0,k}(t)$ at the scale j_0. The difference, however, is that in wavelet series it is a summation and not a single coefficient. The coefficients $c(j_0, k)$ are called the *scaling coefficients*. The second summation in Eq. (7-6) uses the wavelets $\psi_{j,k}(t)$ at all scales starting from j_0, and for all shift values. This is akin to the ac coefficients in the Fourier series expansion, except that in wavelet series the summation is a double summation, over time and scale. The coefficients $d(j,k)$ are called *detail* coefficients, as they add changes about the signal to the approximation.

The coefficients in the wavelet series are obtained from

$$c(j_0, k) = \langle f, \varphi_{j_0,k} \rangle = 2^{\frac{j}{2}} \int_{-\infty}^{\infty} f(t)\varphi_{j_0,k}(t)dt \tag{7-8a}$$

$$d(j, k) = \langle f, \psi_{j,k} \rangle = 2^{\frac{j}{2}} \int_{-\infty}^{\infty} f(t)\psi_{j,k}(t)dt. \tag{7-8b}$$

Because the wavelet expansion is an infinite series, we have an overcomplete expansion for $f(t)$. A complete reconstruction of $f(t)$ will, therefore, require, in general, all the terms in the expansion.

Example 7.1

Compute the wavelet series of the signal $f(t) = 2(1 - t), 0 \le t \le 1$ starting at scale 0 using Haar scaling functions and wavelets.

Solution

Haar scaling functions and wavelets are one of the oldest known such functions and are the simplest ones as well. Hence we choose them here to describe the process of computing the wavelet series.

Haar scaling and wavelet functions at levels 0 and 1 are shown in Figure 7-3. At each level j, there are $N = 2^j$ scaling functions and wavelets. The scaling functions and the wavelets at level j and shift k are denoted $\varphi_{j,k}(t)$ and $\psi_{j,k}(t)$, respectively. If we start at level $j_0 = 0$, then the scaling coefficient is obtained from

$$c(0,0) = \langle f, \varphi_{0,0} \rangle = \int_0^1 f(t)\varphi_{0,0}(t)dt = \int_0^1 2(1-t)dt = 1.$$

Note that there is only one scaling function at level 0 and hence one scaling coefficient. The detail coefficient at level 0 is found from

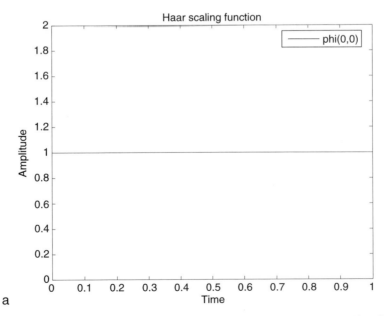

a

FIGURE 7-3   Haar scaling functions and wavelets of Example 7.1: (a) Haar scaling function at level 0, (b) wavelets at levels 0 and 1, and (c) wavelets at level 2. At each level j there are 2^j wavelets of width 2^{-j}.

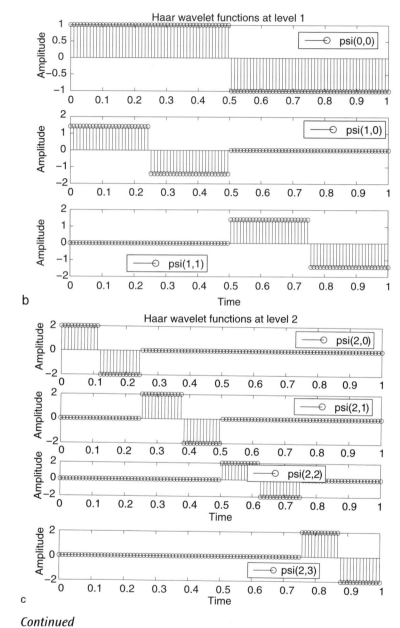

b

c

FIGURE   *Continued*

7-3

$$d(0,0) = \langle f, \psi_{0,0} \rangle = \int\limits_{0}^{1/2} 2(1-t)dt - \int\limits_{1/2}^{1} 2(1-t)dt = 2\left[t - \frac{t^2}{2} \right]_{0}^{1/2} - 2\left[t - \frac{t^2}{2} \right]_{1/2}^{1} = \frac{1}{2}.$$

Again, note that there is only one wavelet at level 0 and so only one detail coefficient. The wavelet series expansion of $f(t)$ at level 0, i.e., the reconstruction of $f(t)$ at level 0 using $c(0,0)$ and $d(0,0)$, is expressed as

$$\hat{f}(t) = \varphi_{0,0}(t) + \frac{1}{2} \psi_{0,0}(t), \quad 0 \le t \le 1.$$

Next, the level 1 detail coefficients are determined as follows

$$d(1,0) = \langle f, \psi_{1,0} \rangle = \int\limits_{0}^{1/4} 2(1-t)dt - \int\limits_{1/4}^{1/2} 2(1-t)dt = \frac{\sqrt{2}}{8}$$

$$d(1,1) = \langle f, \psi_{1,1} \rangle = \int\limits_{1/2}^{3/4} 2(1-t)dt - \int\limits_{3/4}^{1} 2(1-t)dt = \frac{\sqrt{2}}{8}.$$

The reconstruction of $f(t)$ at level 1 is now found to be

$$\hat{f}(t) = \varphi_{0,0}(t) + \frac{1}{2} \psi_{0,0}(t) + \frac{\sqrt{2}}{8} \psi_{1,0}(t) + \frac{\sqrt{2}}{8} \psi_{1,1}(t)\varphi_{1,1}(t), \quad 0 \le t \le 1.$$

Extending to level 2, the detail coefficients are obtained as

$$d(2,0) = \langle f, \psi_{2,0} \rangle = \int\limits_{0}^{1/8} 2(1-t)dt - \int\limits_{1/8}^{1/4} 2(1-t)dt = \frac{1}{16}$$

$$d(2,1) = \langle f, \psi_{2,1} \rangle = \int\limits_{1/4}^{3/8} 2(1-t)dt - \int\limits_{3/8}^{1/2} 2(1-t)dt = \frac{1}{16}$$

$$d(2,2) = \langle f, \psi_{2,2} \rangle = \int\limits_{1/2}^{5/8} 2(1-t)dt - \int\limits_{5/8}^{3/4} 2(1-t)dt = \frac{1}{16}$$

$$d(2,3) = \langle f, \psi_{2,3} \rangle = \int\limits_{3/4}^{7/8} 2(1-t)dt - \int\limits_{7/8}^{1} 2(1-t)dt = \frac{1}{16}.$$

Finally, the signal reconstruction at level 2 is written as

$$\hat{f}(t) = \varphi_{0,0}(t) + \frac{1}{2}\psi_{0,0}(t) + \frac{\sqrt{2}}{8}\psi_{1,0}(t) + \frac{\sqrt{2}}{8}\psi_{1,1}(t) + \frac{1}{16}\psi_{2,0}(t)$$
$$+ \frac{1}{16}\psi_{2,1}(t) + \frac{1}{16}\psi_{2,2}(t) + \frac{1}{16}\psi_{2,3}(t), \quad 0 \le t \le 1$$

The given function and the various reconstructions of it are shown in Figure 7-4. Observe how the reconstruction gets closer and closer to the actual function as more and more details are added to the approximation.

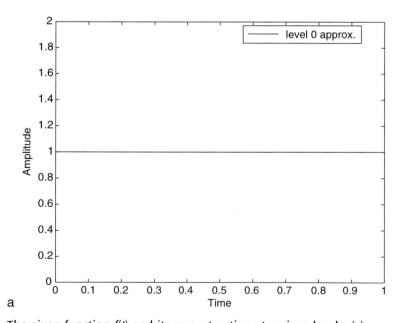

a

FIGURE

7-4

The given function $f(t)$ and its reconstruction at various levels: (a) approximation to $f(t)$ at level 0, (b) details of $f(t)$ at level 0, (c) reconstruction of $f(t)$ at level 0, (d) details at level 1, (e) reconstruction of $f(t)$ at level 1, (f) details at level 2, and (g) reconstruction of $f(t)$ at level 2.

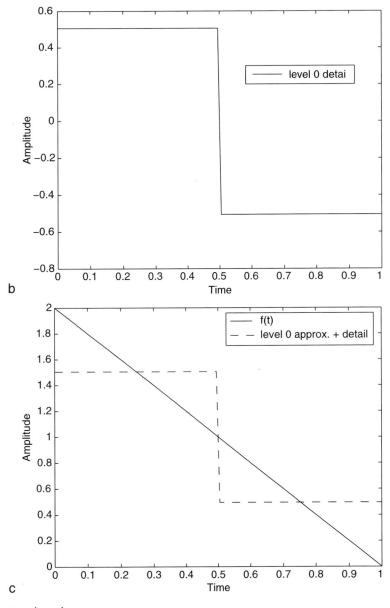

b

c

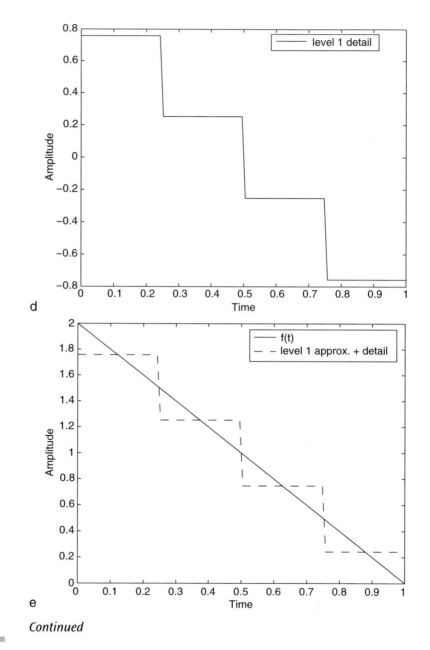

d

e

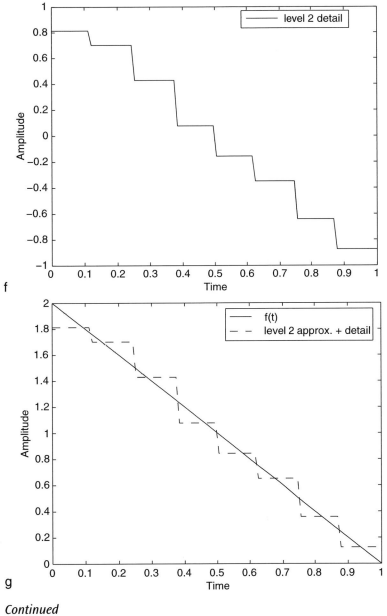

f

g

7.4   DISCRETE WAVELET TRANSFORM

If the signal, scaling functions and the wavelets are discrete in time, then the wavelet transform pair can be expressed as summations, in which case we have what is known as the *discrete wavelet transform* (DWT). Thus, the DWT of a discrete-time signal $x[n]$, $0 \leq n \leq N-1$ can be written as

$$W_\varphi(j_0, k) = \frac{1}{\sqrt{N}} \sum_{n=0}^{N-1} x[n]\varphi_{j_0,k}[n] \tag{7-9a}$$

$$W_\psi(j, k) = \frac{1}{\sqrt{N}} \sum_{n=0}^{N-1} x[n]\psi_{j,k}[n] \tag{7-9b}$$

for $j \geq j_0$. The inverse DWT, which recovers the signal from the transform coefficients, is given by

$$x[n] = \frac{1}{\sqrt{N}} \sum_k W_\varphi(j_0, k)\varphi_{j_0,k}[n] + \frac{1}{\sqrt{N}} \sum_{j=j_0}^{\infty} \sum_k W_\psi(j, k)\psi_{j,k}[n]. \tag{7-10}$$

Note that in Eq. (7-10) the summation over the scale parameter in the second term has an infinite number of terms. However, in practice the upper limit for the scale is fixed at some value, J. Also, the starting scale value is set to 0, i.e., $j_0 = 0$. Thus, the DWT coefficients are determined for $j = 0, 1, \ldots, J-1$ and $k = 0, 1, \ldots, 2^j - 1$.

7.5   IMPLEMENTATION OF THE DISCRETE WAVELET TRANSFORM

This section describes a computationally efficient method of computing the DWT of a signal $x[n]$, $0 \leq n \leq N-1$, which uses a two-channel subband coder. To begin with, we can express the scaling function at scale j as a linear combination of level $j+1$ scaling functions by

$$\varphi[2^j n - k] = \sum_m h_0[m]\sqrt{2}\varphi[2(2^j n - k) - m]. \tag{7-11}$$

Using the substitution $l = m + 2k$ in Eq. (7-11), we obtain

$$\varphi[2^j n - k] = \sum_l h_0[l - 2k]\sqrt{2}\varphi[2^{j+1} n - l]. \tag{7-12}$$

We can similarly express the wavelets as

$$\psi[2^j n - k] = \sum_l h_1[l - 2k]\sqrt{2}\varphi[2^{j+1} n - l].$$ (7-13)

where the coefficients $h_0[n]$ and $h_1[n]$ are related to the wavelets. Using Eq. (7-12) in Eq. (7-9a) with some algebraic manipulation, we arrive at

$$W_\varphi(j,k) = \frac{1}{\sqrt{N}} \sum_n h_0[n - 2k]W_\varphi(j+1,n).$$ (7-14)

Eq. (7-14) says that the scaling function coefficients at scale j are obtained by convolving the scaling coefficients at the next scale $j + 1$ with the time-reversed scaling filter $h_0[-n]$ and retaining every other output sample. Similarly, the wavelet coefficients at scale j are the result of convolving the scaling coefficients at scale $j + 1$ with the wavelet filter $h_1[-n]$ and retaining every other output sample. This is expressed as

$$W_\psi(j,k) = \sum_n h_1[n - 2k]W_\varphi(j+1,n).$$ (7-15)

Figure 7-5 shows an implementation of Eqs. (7-14) and (7-15) as a bank of filters and downsamplers. This is also the well-known two-channel subband coder.

One can iterate the two-channel filtering and down sampling at the output of the scaling coefficients to obtain a multistage DWT, as shown in Figure 7-6,

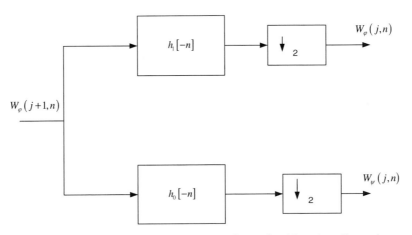

FIGURE   A fast computation of DWT using a two-channel subband coding scheme.

7-5

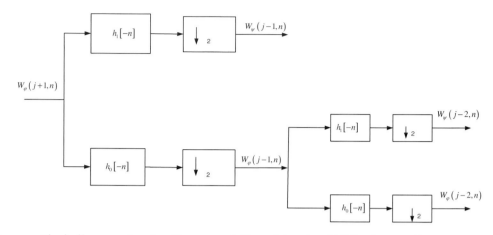

FIGURE

7-6

Block diagram showing the computation of two-level DWT of a 1-D discrete-time signal using the iterative two-channel subband coding scheme.

which is a two-stage DWT. Typically, the initial scale is the highest scale (or lowest level) and the scaling coefficients correspond to the original signal $x[n]$ itself and the DWT scaling and detail coefficients are computed at different lower scales by iterating the two-channel filtering scheme. The filters $h_0[-n]$ and $h_1[-n]$ are generally of the low-pass and high-pass types, respectively. This scheme of computing the DWT of a signal is usually known as the *fast wavelet transform* (FWT).

The inverse DWT reconstructs the signal and can also be implemented in a subband decoding fashion. One starts from the lowest scaling (low-pass) and detail (high-pass) DWT coefficients, inserts zeros at every other sample, filters them through filters $g_0[n]$ and $g_1[n]$, respectively, and adds the two outputs to synthesize the scaling coefficients at the next higher scale. This is shown in Figure 7-7. It can be shown that the reconstruction filters are the time-reversed version of the analysis filters. Figure 7-8 shows the computational scheme for the IDWT corresponding to the two-stage DWT of Figure 7-6.

Example 7.2

Consider the signal $x[n]$ used in Example 7.1 and let the length of $x[n]$ be 8. Obtain a three-level DWT of $x[n]$ using the Haar filter banks and fast algorithm described earlier.

Solution

The fast algorithm to compute the DWT using the two-channel subband coding scheme is shown in Figure 7-9. Because $N = 8$, there are $\log_2(N) = \log_2(8) = 3$ stages of computation. At each stage the number of samples at the output of

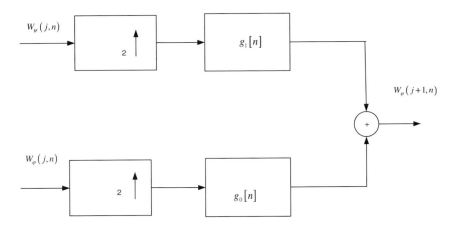

FIGURE

7-7

A fast computation of IDWT using a two-channel subband decoding scheme.

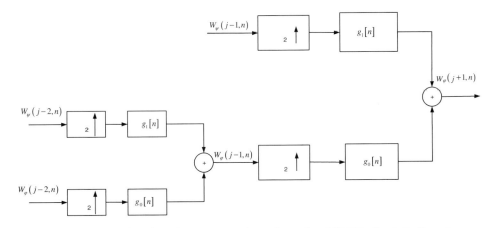

FIGURE

7-8

Block diagram showing the computation of two-level IDWT of a 1-D discrete-time signal using the iterative two-channel subband decoding scheme.

each filter is half that of the number of samples at the input. In this implementation of the fast DWT algorithm, we have one approximation coefficient at the lowest level, which is 3 in this case, and a sequence of three detail coefficients. The inverse DWT is implemented as shown in Figure 7-9b. Figure 7-10a shows a plot of the DWT coefficients. Comparing these coefficient values to the ones obtained in Example 7.1, we note that the coefficient values differ from those of Example 7.1 by the factor $2^{j/2}$. This is because the scaling and wavelet functions in Example 7.1 have the value $2^{j/2}$ incorporated in them. The recon-

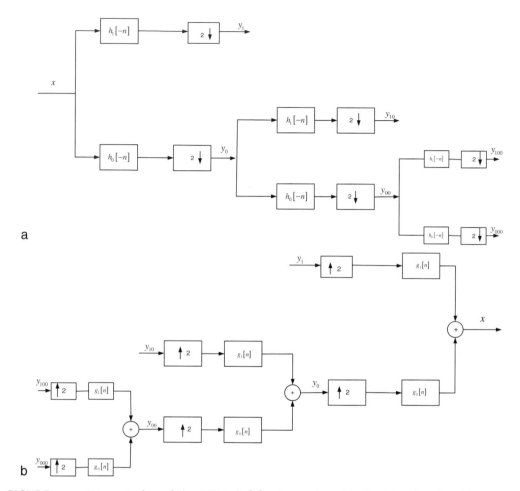

FIGURE

7-9
Computation of the DWT of $x[n]$ using a three-level subband coder: (a) forward DWT and (b) inverse DWT.

structed signal obtained from Figure 7-9b is shown in Figure 7-10b, which is exactly the signal we started with.

7.6 RELATIONSHIP OF SCALING AND WAVELET FILTERS TO WAVELETS

So far we have not mentioned how to design the analysis and synthesis filters used to implement the DWT. There has been a considerable amount of work done in the area of subband coding with perfect reconstruction (PR)

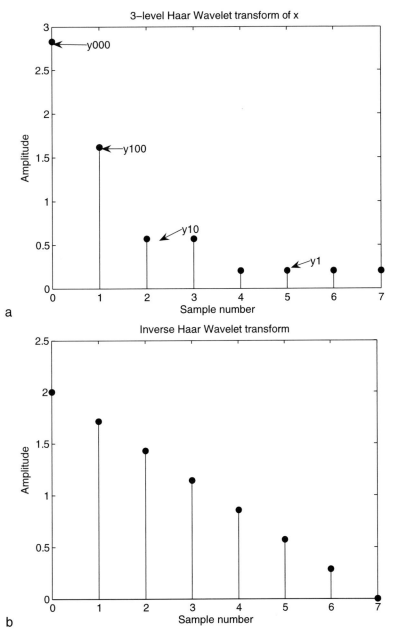

FIGURE

7-10

DWT coefficients of $x[n]$ in Example 7.1: (a) DWT coefficients and (b) reconstructed signal.

properties. It has been shown that in a two-channel subband coder the synthesis filters $g_0[n]$ and $g_1[n]$ must satisfy what is known as the *power complementary condition* property, which is

$$\left|G_0(e^{j\omega})\right|^2 + \left|G_1(e^{j\omega})\right|^2 = 2. \tag{7-16}$$

There are two possible wavelet expansions one could use: *orthogonal* and *biorthogonal*. Depending on the type of wavelet transform that is being implemented, the filter bank must satisfy a set of conditions. These conditions are described in the following.

7.6.1   Orthogonal Discrete Wavelet Transform

In a two-channel subband coding scheme that implements an orthogonal wavelet transform with perfect reconstruction, the filter bank must satisfy the following.

1. The filter length L is even.
2. $g_0[n]$ and $h_0[n]$ satisfy the power complementary condition, namely Eq. (7-16).
3. $g_0[n]$ and $h_0[n]$ are time reversed and modulated versions of each other, which is equivalent to $h_0[n] = (-1)^n g_0(-n)$.
4. $g_1[n]$ and $h_1[n]$ are time reversed and modulated versions of each other.
5. $h_1[n] = (-1)^{n+1} h_0[L-1-n]$.
6. $g_1[n] = (-1)^{n+1} g_0[L-1-n]$.
7. $\sum_n h_0[n] = \sum_n g_0[n] = \sqrt{2}$.

The only problem with the orthogonal filter bank is that the FIR filters do not have a linear phase characteristic.

   A number of techniques have been advanced for the design of filters satisfying the aforementioned conditions. A four-tap orthogonal FIR filter bank due to Daubechie has the impulse responses as shown in Table 7.1. Observe that $g_0[n]$ and $h_0[n]$ sum up to $\sqrt{2}$. The filter impulse responses are shown in Figure 7-11a. The magnitude of the frequency response of the synthesis filters is shown in Figure 7-11b. Note the dc response of the low-pass filter, which is $\sqrt{2}$, as per property 7. A condition equivalent to the power complementary condition in the time domain is that the sum of the convolutions of the low-pass filters $g_0[n]$ and $h_0[n]$ and its modulated version add up to an impulse of strength 2, and a similar condition holds good with respect to the high-pass filters, as given by

Table 7-1. Daubechie's Four-Tap Orthogonal FIR Filter Bank

$g_0[n]$	$g_1[n]$	$h_0[n]$	$h_1[n]$
0.4830	−0.1294	−0.1294	−0.4830
0.8365	−0.2241	0.2241	0.8365
0.2241	0.8365	0.8365	−0.2241
−0.1294	−0.4830	−0.4830	−0.1294

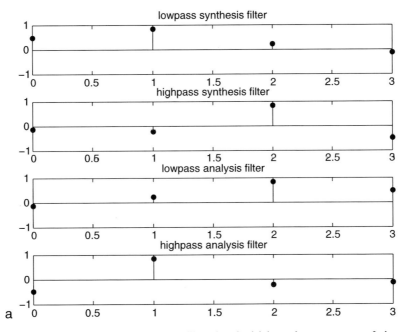

FIGURE
7-11

Daubechie's four-tap orthogonal filter bank: (a) impulse response of the analysis and synthesis filters and (b) magnitude of the frequency response of the synthesis filters.

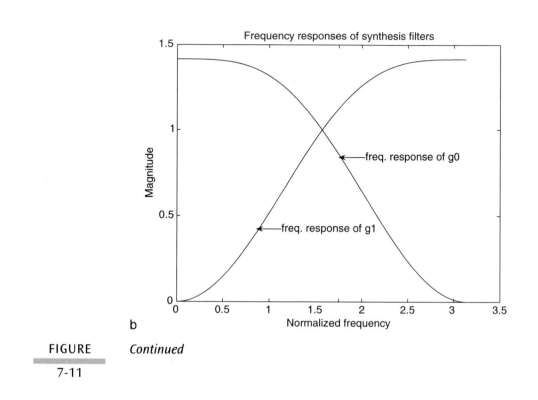

b

FIGURE   *Continued*

7-11

$$\sum_k g_i[k]h_i[n-k] + (-1)^n \sum_k g_i[k]h_i[n-k] = 2\delta[n], \quad i = 0,1. \tag{7-17}$$

The convolutions of the cross filters will be equal to zero. These conditions are depicted in Figure 7-12.

7.6.2   Biorthogonal Discrete Wavelet Transform

In the case of the two-channel filter bank realizing a biorthogonal DWT, the following conditions hold good for the analysis and synthesis filters.

1. The filter length is even.
2. The filters can have linear phase.
3. $g_0[n]$ and $h_0[n]$ are not time reversed.
4. Similarly, $g_1[n]$ and $h_1[n]$ are not time reversed.
5. $h_0[n]$ and $g_1[n]$ are modulated versions of each other, i.e., $g_1[n] = (-1)^n h_0[n]$.

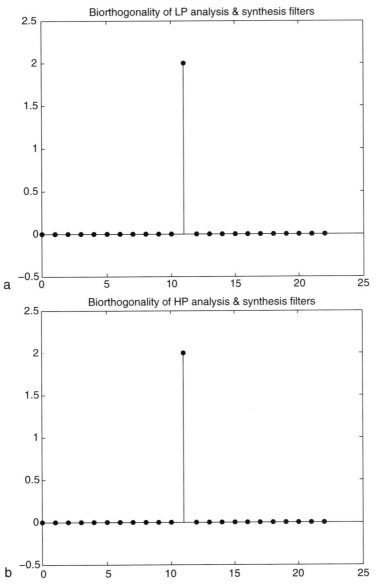

FIGURE

7-12

Orthogonality condition in the time domain: convolution sums of (a) $g_0[n]$ and $h_0[n]$ and its modulated version, (b) $g_1[n]$ and $h_1[n]$ and its modulated version, (c) $g_0[n]$ and $h_1[n]$ and its modulated version, and (d) $g_1[n]$ and $h_0[n]$ and its modulated version.

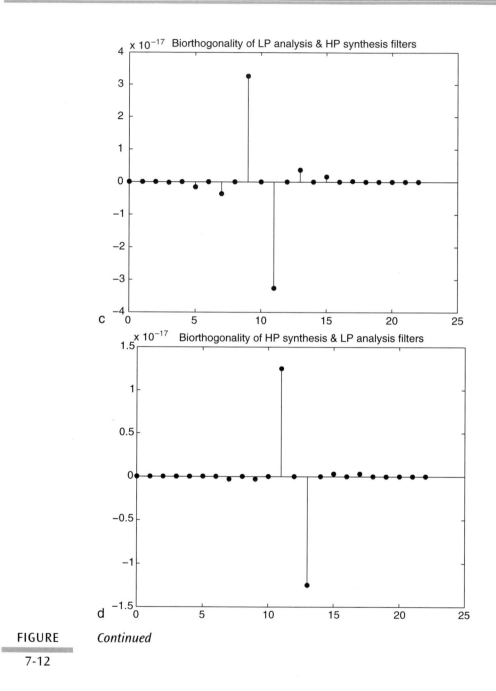

FIGURE

7-12

Continued

6. Similarly, $g_0[n]$ and $h_1[n]$ are modulated versions of each other with one sign change, i.e., $h_1[n] = (-1)^{n+1} g_0[n]$.

7. $\sum_n h_0[n] = \sum_n g_0[n] = \sqrt{2}$.

An example of a biorthogonal filter bank is illustrated in Figure 7-13. The filter impulse responses are listed in Table 7-2. Note that the power complementary condition does not hold good in this case, as evidenced from Figure 7-13.

7.6.3   Construction of Wavelets

Section 7.5 showed how to compute the DWT of a discrete-time signal through repeated use of a two-band subband coder, each time applying subband coding to the low-pass signal. The only thing that mattered in the computation of the DWT was the filter bank, which had the properties listed in the previous two sections. However, the shape of the wavelet as a result of repeating the two-band subband coding scheme is intimately related to the reconstruction filters. In fact, the underlying wavelet can be obtained as follows.

1. Start with the low-pass filter $g_0[n]$.
2. Modulate $g_0[n]$, which amounts to $(-1)^n g_0[-n]$. This becomes the high-pass filter $g_1[n]$.
3. Insert zeros between the samples of $g_1[n]$. This is called *upsampling*.
4. Convolve the upsampled signal with $g_0[n]$.

If this procedure is repeated many times, the resultant curve approaches the shape of a wavelet. The wavelet shape will be dependent on the filter $g_0[n]$ chosen.

One can obtain the scaling function in a manner similar to that of the wavelet function except that one should use the low-pass filter instead of the high-pass filter. As an example, the Daubechie wavelet "db6" is shown in Figure 7-14 for one through four iterations. Figure 7-14 also shows the corresponding scaling functions. As seen from Figure 7-14, the wavelet shape quickly reaches a steady shape. It is to be pointed out that the number of samples will increase with the iteration due to the convolution. Using the same procedure, a biorthogonal wavelet "bior5.5" is generated and is shown in Figure 7-15.

7.7   TWO-DIMENSIONAL DISCRETE WAVELET TRANSFORM

Because images are two dimensional, it is necessary to apply the wavelet transform in the horizontal and vertical dimensions. There are two possible ways to

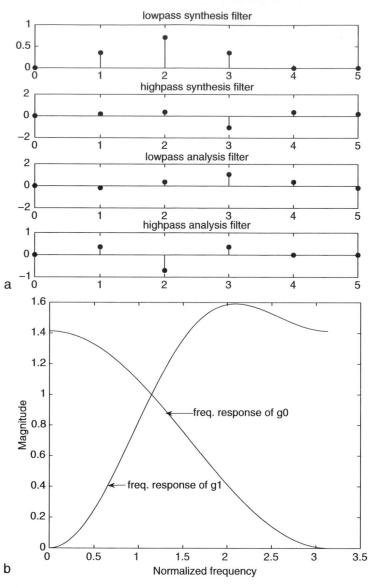

FIGURE 7-13 A four-tap biorthogonal filter bank: (a) impulse response of the analysis and synthesis filters and (b) magnitude of the frequency response of the synthesis filters.

Table 7-2. Six-Tap Biorthogonal Filter Bank

$g_0[n]$	$g_1[n]$	$h_0[n]$	$h_1[n]$
0	0	0	0
0.3536	0.1768	−0.1768	0.3536
0.7071	0.3536	0.3536	−0.7071
0.3536	−1.0607	1.0607	0.3536
0	0.3536	0.3536	0
0	0.1768	−0.1768	0

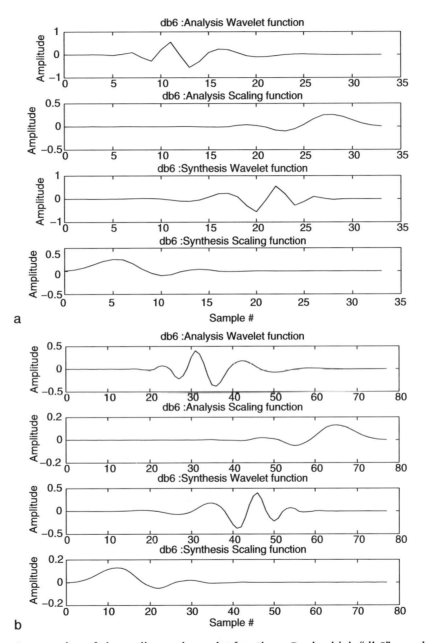

FIGURE 7-14

Construction of the scaling and wavelet functions. Daubechie's "db6" wavelets and scaling functions are shown: (a) iteration #1, (b) iteration #2, (c) iteration #3, and (d) iteration #4.

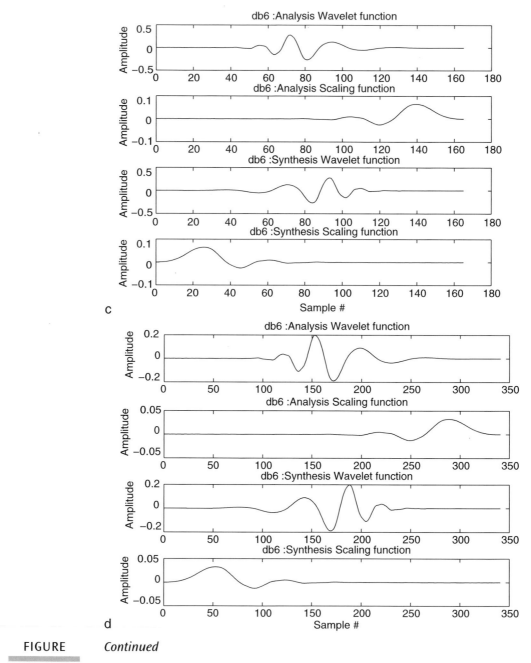

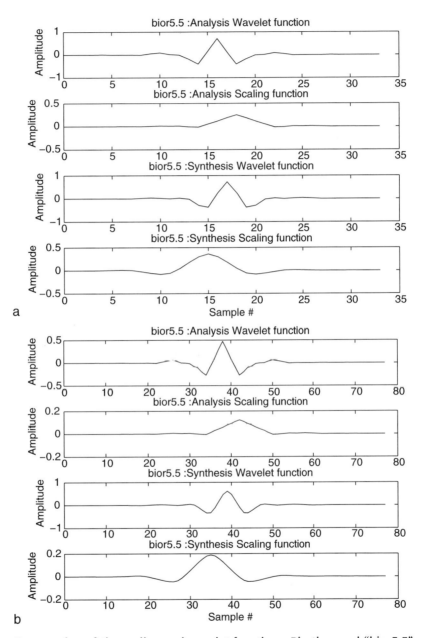

a

b

FIGURE

7-15

Construction of the scaling and wavelet functions. Biorthogonal "bior5.5" wavelets and scaling functions are shown: (a) iteration #1, (b) iteration #2, (c) iteration #3, and (d) iteration #4.

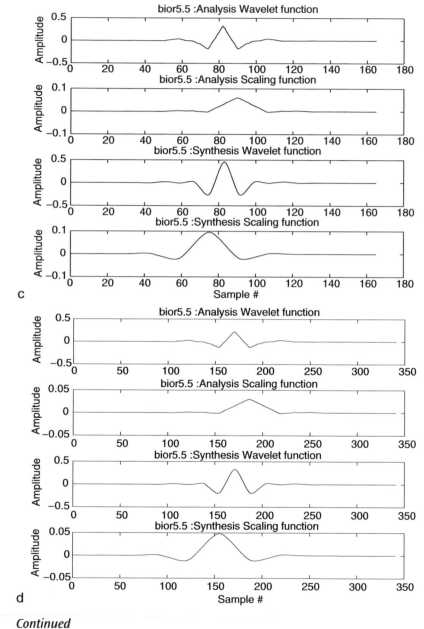

do this. One is to apply the ideas developed for the one-dimensional signals to the 2-D case, one dimension at a time. This is the simplest and most straightforward method and is the often-used method in practice. The advantages are that all the required tools are readily available and that implementation is easy. The second or alternative way to compute the 2-D wavelet transform is to develop all the ideas in two dimensions as a whole. That is, the procedure is no longer applied one dimension at a time. Instead, it is applied to the two dimensions. Although this may be better from the point of view of exploiting the image characteristics, the main difficulty lies in the design of filters that are truly two dimensional. It also increases the computational complexity. For this reason, we will restrict our discussion to separable 2-D wavelet transform. Further, our interest is in digital image processing. Therefore, our discussion narrows down to 2-D DWT rather than wavelet series or continuous wavelet transform.

As pointed out in Chapters 2 and 4, if the basis functions used in a transform are separable, then that transform can be carried out in a row–column fashion, i.e., it can be computed along the rows first and then along the column of the row-transformed image. In terms of the two-channel filter bank scheme, we pass each row of the image through low-pass and high-pass filters and downsample the filtered signals by two. This creates the DWT of the image in the horizontal dimension. Next we pass this row-transformed image through the same low-pass and high-pass filters, but now the columns, followed by downsampling by two, which yields the true 2-D DWT of the image.

Let us illustrate this idea by an example. Consider an image $x[m,n]$, $0 \leq m,n \leq N - 1$. Filtering it by the 1-D filters H_0 and H_1 along the rows followed by downsampling by 2 results in the approximation and detail DWT coefficients each of size $N \times \dfrac{N}{2}$, as shown in Figure 7-16a. Next the procedure is repeated along the columns for each of the $N \times \dfrac{N}{2}$ coefficients. This produces four components, each of size $\dfrac{N}{2} \times \dfrac{N}{2}$, labeled LL, LH, HL, and HH. We can place these four components as shown in Figure 7-16b for compact representation of the DWT coefficients. This realizes one level of the 2-D DWT of the input image. Figure 7-16c shows the four components of the DWT coefficients in the 2-D frequency plane. Note that π corresponds to half the normalized sampling frequency.

The inverse 2-D DWT can be computed according to the block diagram shown in Figure 7-17. The four components are first upsampled by 2 along the column dimension, filtered along the columns by the respective synthesis or reconstruction filters, and the outputs are added. This results in two partially reconstructed image of size $N \times \dfrac{N}{2}$. Next these two components are

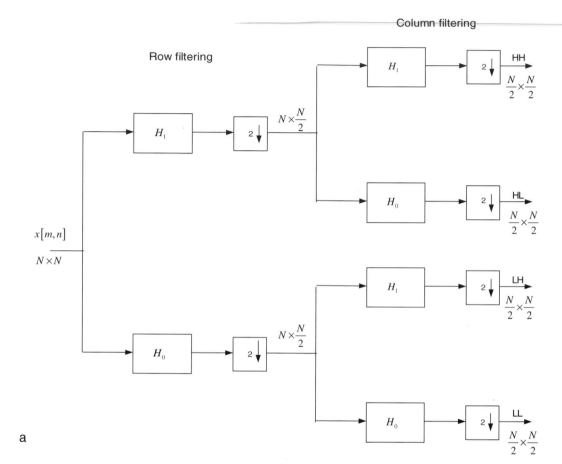

Row filtering

Column filtering

FIGURE

7-16

Computation of 2-D DWT via subband coding scheme: (a) analysis filter bank, (b) placement of the four 2-D DWT coefficients, and (c) resulting 2-D frequency spectral division.

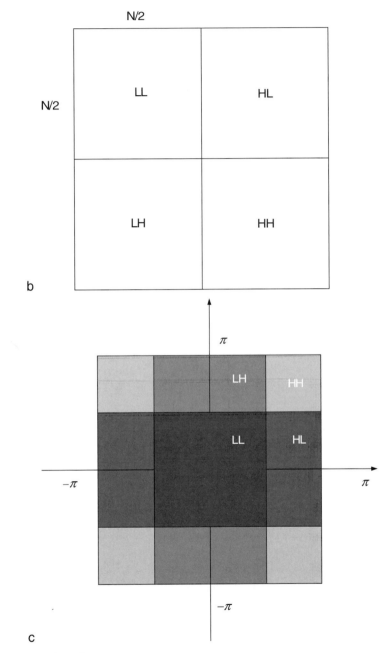

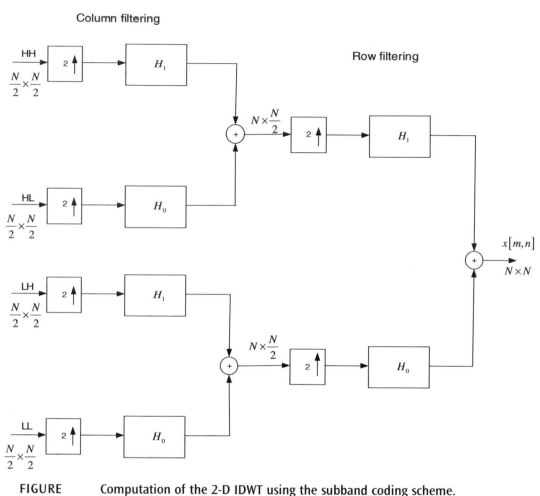

Column filtering

Row filtering

FIGURE Computation of the 2-D IDWT using the subband coding scheme.

7-17

upsampled by 2 along the rows, filtered by the low-pass and high-pass filters, and then the outputs are added to produce the original image of size $N \times N$.

It should be pointed out that the row–column order in which the image is reconstructed is not important. We can iterate this procedure one more time on the LL coefficients to achieve second-level 2-D DWT and so on. Similarly, in reconstructing the image from the 2-D DWT coefficients, the highest level coefficients are synthesized first, then the next lower level, and so on.

An example of a four-level, 2-D DWT of a real image is shown in Figure 7-18 using both orthogonal and biorthogonal wavelets. Figure 7-18a corresponds to the orthogonal wavelet called db2. The biorthogonal case is shown in Figure

a   b

FIGURE

7-18

A four-level 2-D DWT of a real image using (a) orthogonal wavelet "db2," with a FIR filter length of 4, and (b) biorthogonal wavelet "bior5.5," with a filter length of 6. The amplitudes of the DWT coefficients are scaled to be in the range 0 to 255 for better visibility.

7-18b, which uses the bior5.5 wavelet. In both cases the DWT approximation and detail coefficients are scaled to fit into the intensity range of 0 to 255. Otherwise the detail coefficients will not be visible. It is seen from Figure 7-18 that the HL coefficients capture the horizontal edges more effectively while the LH coefficients capture the vertical edges. The HH coefficients retain edges with diagonal orientation. These three components, in essence, represent finer details in the image in the form of intensity transitions. On the other hand, the LL coefficients represent an approximation of the image at a lower resolution.

It is also interesting to look at some statistics of the various DWT coefficients. Histograms of the detail coefficients at the four levels for the orthogonal case are shown in Figures 7-19a through 7-19d. The corresponding quantities for the biorthogonal case are shown in Figures 7-20a through 7-20d, respectively. Each such figure shows the histograms of the amplitudes of the detail coefficients at a particular level. These figures show that the range of the coefficient amplitude increases as the level increases. The reason for this is that at level 1, for instance, the wavelets capture the macroscopic properties of the image. At the highest level, which is 4 in this case, the wavelets capture microscopic properties of the image. The mean and standard deviations of the approximation and detail coefficients for the orthogonal and biorthogonal cases are listed in Tables 7-3 and 7-4, respectively. For a better perspective, standard deviations of the 2-D DWT coefficients for the four different wavelets at the four levels are shown as bar charts in Figures 7-21a through 7-21d. Since at level 4 we have both

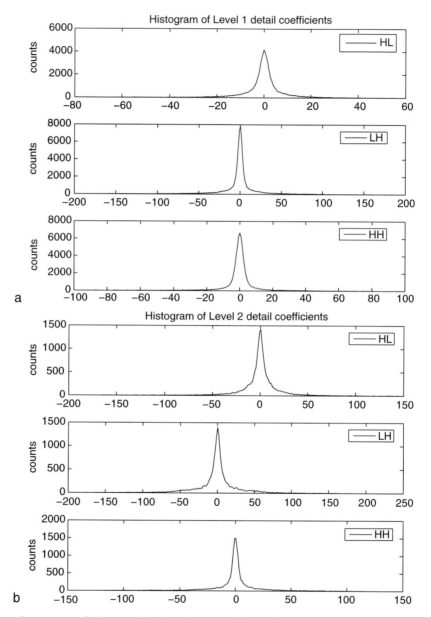

FIGURE

7-19

Histograms of the amplitudes of the detail coefficients for the four-level, orthogonal 2-D DWT in Figures 7-18a: (a) level 1 details, (b) level 2 details, (c) level 3 details, and (d) level 4 details.

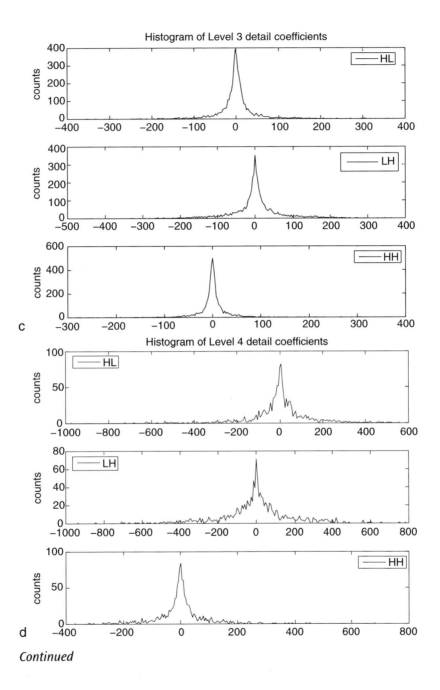

FIGURE

7-19

Continued

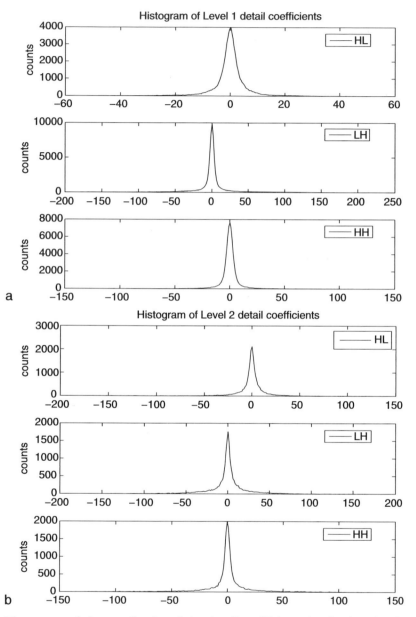

FIGURE
7-20

Histograms of the amplitudes of the detail coefficients for the four-level, biorthogonal 2-D DWT in Figures 7-18b: (a) level 1 details, (b) level 2 details, (c) level 3 details, and (d) level 4 details.

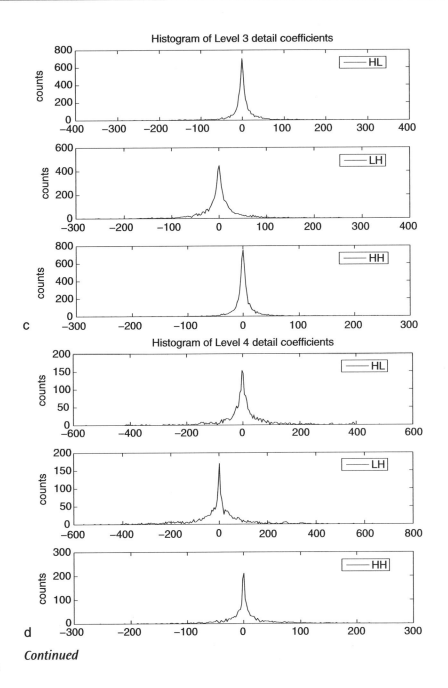

c

d

FIGURE   *Continued*

7-20

Table 7-3. Mean and Standard Deviations of Detail DWT Coefficients for the Orthogonal Wavelet "db2"

Coefficient type	Level #	μ	σ
LL	4	1897	776
HL	4	−3	137
LH	4	−3	181
HH	4	0	83
HL	3	0	52
LH	3	1	65
HH	3	0	34
HL	2	0	20
LH	2	0	30
HH	2	0	23
HL	1	0	8
LH	1	0	23
HH	1	0	9

Table 7-4. Mean and Standard Deviations of Detail DWT Coefficients for the Biorthogonal Wavelet "bior5.5"

Coefficient type	Level #	μ	σ
LL	4	1870	678
HL	4	1	87
LH	4	−3	111
HH	4	0	40
HL	3	0	40
LH	3	0	42
HH	3	0	26
HL	2	0	14
LH	2	0	22
HH	2	0	21
HL	1	0	6
LH	1	0	24
HH	1	0	10

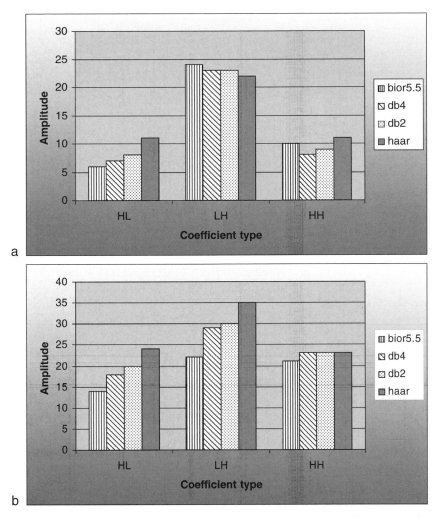

FIGURE

7-21

Bar chart showing standard deviations of the orthogonal and biorthogonal, 2-D DWT coefficients against the coefficient types: (a) level 1, (b) level 2, (c) level 3, and (d) level 4.

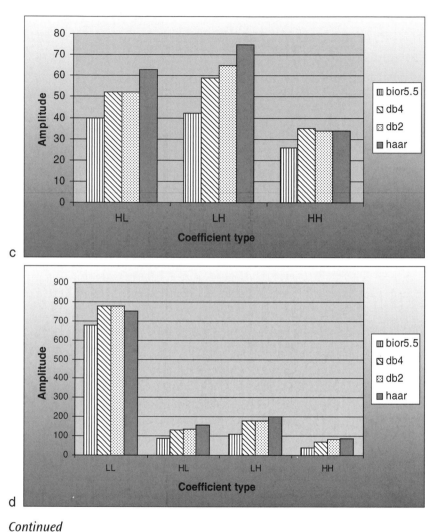

approximation and detail coefficients, the chart in Figure 7-21d has four entries instead of three, as in the rest of the charts. From the tables and charts we see that the standard deviations (or variances) of the 2-D DWT coefficients have the smallest values for the biorthogonal wavelet "bior5.5" and the largest values for Haar wavelets. We will later see that the amount by which data can be compressed, using wavelets, depends on the variance of the DWT coefficients: the smaller the variance, the larger the compression. From this angle it is interesting to note that the biorthogonal wavelet will have a better compression capability than the Haar wavelet. Thus, the choice of a particular wavelet influences the compression characteristics.

7.8 SUMMARY

This chapter described the ideas behind time-scale analysis of signals. More specifically, we introduced the definition of the continuous wavelet transform and then discussed wavelet series expansion of signals. For discrete-time signals, discrete wavelet transform is used. We have shown how the DWT can be computed via subband coding procedure for fast implementation of the transform. It was shown that by repeatedly filtering and subsampling the approximation component, one obtains the DWT of a signal. Some examples were given to illustrate the computational procedure. We next extended the wavelet transform to images and demonstrated how the 2-D DWT can be computed using separable transform. With these tools we have, especially the unitary block transforms and wavelet transforms, we will introduce the main idea behind image compression in the next chapter.

REFERENCES

Interested readers can find a wealth of information on the original works in wavelets in Myer (1987, 1990, 1992) and, Daubechies (1988, 1990, 1992, 1993, 1996). Classical work in multiresolution analysis can be found in Mallat (1987, 1989, 1998). Excellent textbooks abound in this field, notably Vetterli and Kovacevic (1995) and Burrus et al. (1998). References on STFT can be found in Allen (1977) and Portnoff (1980).

Textbooks on image processing, such as Gonzalez and Woods (2002) and Castleman (1996) contain well-written chapters on wavelet transform.

Critical to DWT implementation, subband coding theory, which was originally applied to speech coding, may be found in Crochiere (1976) and Croisier et al. (1976). Theory of perfect reconstruction filter banks is developed in Smith and Barnwell (1984), Smith and Barnwell (1986), Mintzer (1985), Vaidyanathan (1987, 1993), and Nguyen and Vaidyanathan (1989).

Y. Meyer, "L'analyses par Ondelettes." Pour la Science, 1987.

Y. Meyer, *Ondelettes et ope'rateurs*, Hermann, Paris, 1990.

Y. Meyer, Wavelets and Applications: Proceedings of the Intl. Conf., Marseille, France, Mason, Paris, and Springer-Verlag, Berlin, 1992.

I. Daubechies, "Orthoginal Bases of Compactly Supported Wavelets," Commun. On Pure and Applied Math., Vol. 41, pp. 909–996, 1988.

I. Daubechies, "The Wavelet Transform, Time-Frequency Localization and Signal Analysis," IEEE Trans. On Inf. Theory, Vol. 36, No. 5, pp. 961–1005, 1990.

I. Daubechies, *Ten Lectures on Wavelets*, Society for Industrial and Applied Mathematics, Philadelphia, PA, 1992.

I. Daubechies, "Orthonormal bases of compactly supported wavelets II, variations on a theme," SIAM J. Mathematical Analysis, Vol. 24, No. 2, pp. 499–519, 1993.

I. Daubechies, "Where do we go from here"—a personal point of view," Proc. IEEE, Vol. 84, No. 4, pp. 510–513, 1996.

S. Mallat, "A compact multiresolution representation: The wavelet model," Proc. IEEE Computer Society Workshop on Computer Vision, IEEE Computer Society Press, Washington, DC, pp. 2–7, 1987.

S. Mallat, "A theory of multiresolution signal decomposition: The wavelet representation," IEEE Trans. Pattern Anal. Mach. Intll., Vol. PAMI-11, pp. 674–693, 1989.

S. Mallat, "Multiresolution approximation and wavelet orthonormal bases of L^2." Trans. American Mathematical Society, Vol. 315, pp. 69–87, 1989.

S. Mallat, "Multifrequency channel decomposition of images and wavlet models." IEEE Trans. Acoustic, Speech, and Signal Processing, Vol. 37, pp. 2091–2110, 1989.

S. Mallat, *A Wavelet Tour of Signal Processing*, Academic Press, Boston, MA, 1998.

M. Vetterli and J. Kovacevic, *Wavelets and subband coding*, Prentice Hall PTR, Englewood Cliffs, NJ, 1995.

C.S. Burrus, R.A. Gopinath, and H. Guo, *Introduction to Wavelets and Wavelet Transforms*, Prentice Hall, Upper Saddle River, NJ, 1998.

J.B. Allen, "Short term spectral analysis, synthesis, and modification by discrete Fourier transform," IEEE Trans. Acoust., Signal, and Speech Proc., Vol. 25, pp. 235–238, June 1977.

M.R. Portnoff, "Representation of digital signals and systems based on short-time Fourier analysis," IEEE Trans. Acoust., Signal, and Speech Proc., Vol. 28, pp. 55–69, February 1980.

R.C. Gonzalez and R. E. Woods, *Digital Image Processing*, 2nd edition, Prentice Hall, Upper Saddle River, NJ, 2002.

K.R. Castleman, *Digital Image Processing*, Prentice Hall, Englewood Cliffs, NJ, 1996.

R.E. Crochiere, S.A. Weber, and J.L. Flanagan, "Digital coding of speech in sub-bands," Bell System Technical Journal, 55(8), pp. 1069–1085, October 1976.

A. Croisier, D. Esteban, and C. Galand, *Perfect channel splitting by use of interpolation/ decimation/tree decomposition techniques*, Intl. Conf. On Inform. Sciences and Systems, pp. 443–446, Patras, Greece, August 1976.

M.J.T. Smith and T.P. Barnwell III, "A procedure for designing exact reconstruction filter banks for tree structured sub-band coders," Proc. IEEE Intl. Conf. Acoust., Speech, and Signal Proc., San Diego, CA, March 1984.

M.J.T. Smith and T.P. Barnwell III, "Exact reconstruction for tree-structured subband coders," IEEE Trans. Acoust., Signal, and Speech Proc., 34(3), pp. 431–441, June 1986.

F. Mintzer, "Filters for distortion-free two-band multirate filter banks," IEEE Trans. Acoust., Signal, and Speech Proc., 33(3), pp. 626–630, June 1985.

P.P. Vaidyanathan, "Quadrature mirror filter banks, M-band extensions and perfect reconstruction techniques," IEEE ASSP Mag., 4(3), pp. 4–20, July 1987.

T.Q. Nguyen and P.P. Vaidyanathan, "Two-channel perfect reconstruction FIR QMF structures which yield linear phase analysis and synthesis filters," IEEE Trans. Acoust., Signal, and Specch Proc., 37(5), pp. 676–690, May 1989.

P.P. Vaidyanathan, *Multirate Systems and Filter Banks*, Prentice Hall, Englewood Cliffs, NJ, 1993.

8 | Image Compression

8.1　INTRODUCTION

So far we have described several image processing methods that enable us to modify a given image so that a specific image characteristic is altered. This chapter describes another image processing method used in compressing images. Thus, image compression is a digital process by which the amount of data (in bits) in a given image is reduced to as low as desired. The need for image compression stems from the fact that more and more image and video data are used for transmission and storage in this Internet age. As more and more TV channels are introduced, transmission bandwidth becomes very precious. For example, the data rates for SDTV and HDTV are shown in Table 8-1. As shown in Table 8-1, raw video data rates range from about 20 to 120 MB/s. However, the transmission channel bandwidths are around 4 and 8 MHz, respectively, for SDTV and IIDTV, hence the need for data compression. In fact the required compression ratios for the two TV systems are about 20:1 and 60:1. The term *compression ratio* used earlier refers to the ratio of the number of bits in the original digital source data to that in compressed digital data.

At this point it is worth mentioning the difference between the terms bandwidth and data compression. Bandwidth compression refers to an analog signal, whose bandwidth is reduced from that of the original signal. Obviously, this can be achieved by filtering the analog signal through an appropriate filter. Data compression, however, refers to a process of reducing the data rate of a digital signal. Data compression does not necessarily reduce the signal bandwidth. Consider, for instance, a speech signal in telephony. The speech signal in native form has a bandwidth of about 4kHz. Therefore, a transmission medium supporting a maximum of 4kHz is enough to carry the analog speech signal. If the same speech signal is to be conveyed through digital means, then it has to be sampled at least at a rate of 8kHz (Nyquist frequency) with each sample quantized to 8 bits or more. So, the same analog signal in digital form generates data at a rate of 64K bits/s. In order to transmit this digital signal using digital modulation schemes, a bandwidth of about 32kHz is required. In fact, the speech signal in digital form has expanded its bandwidth over that of the same signal in analog form. Even if we compress the digital speech signal by a factor of two, which gives

Table 8-1. Data Rates for SDTV and HDTV

TV format	Raw data rate bytes/s	Required compression ratio
480i30, SDTV	20,275,200	18:1
576i25, SDTV	20,736,000	22:1
720p60, HDTV	110,592,000	55:1
1080i30, HDTV	124,416,000	62:1

a data rate of 32 K bits/s, it still requires the transmission channel to support a bandwidth of about 16 kHz. Thus, we see that data compression does not reduce the bandwidth of the original signal source, which is analog. However, the converse is true. Despite this fact, converting analog signal into digital signal has many service features that the analog signal cannot offer, which is one of the important reasons for the exploding deployment of digital techniques in almost all communications applications.

Having convinced ourselves the need for image data compression, the question is whether we want any loss of data in the process of compression. That is, there are two broad categories of compression, namely lossless and lossy. In a lossless compression the decompressed and original images are identical. Although this may be a boon for the media industries, the amount of achievable compression ratio is small, typically 2:1. As shown in Table 8-1, this amount of compression is far below the required value. On the other hand, one can achieve any amount of compression if a corresponding loss of information is tolerable. Thus, in a lossy compression scheme, some amount of information is irrecoverably lost at the gain of a large compression ratio. Thus there is a trade-off between compression ratio and resulting information loss. This loss of information manifests in the form of visible distortions in the decompressed image. A lot of effort is therefore required in finding ways to hide such distortions so as to minimize the visible artifacts due to the compression process.

The basic idea behind a digital image compression method is to remove redundant data from the source image. Data redundancy exists either in the spatial domain or, equivalently, in the transform domain. Accordingly, the method of removing data redundancy will differ. Spatial redundancy in an image manifests in the form of closeness in the amplitude of neighboring pixels. Figure 8-1 shows the pixel values along row 128 for the Barbara image. It can be seen from Figure 8-1 that the luminance value of a pixel is very close to its neighbors than to pixels far removed from it. That is, there is predictability in the pixel

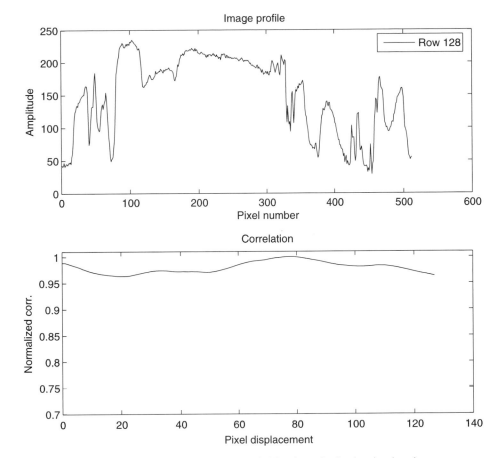

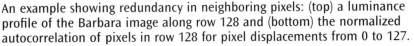

 FIGURE

8-1

An example showing redundancy in neighboring pixels: (top) a luminance profile of the Barbara image along row 128 and (bottom) the normalized autocorrelation of pixels in row 128 for pixel displacements from 0 to 127.

values—the higher the predictability, the larger the redundancy and vice versa. Another way of quantifying spatial redundancy is pixel correlation. This is shown at the bottom of Figure 8-1 where normalized autocorrelation is plotted against pixel displacement. Again, the correlation stays high over large pixel displacements. This is typical of grayscale images. Methods exploiting the spatial redundancy just described are known as *predictive coding*. Predictive coding procedures are described later in the chapter.

An equivalent form of data redundancy exists in the transform domain. This is illustrated in Figure 8-2, which shows the pixel values and the corresponding 1-D DCT values of eight consecutive pixels in row 128 of the Barbara image. In the pixel domain, the eight pixels have very nearly the same value: high

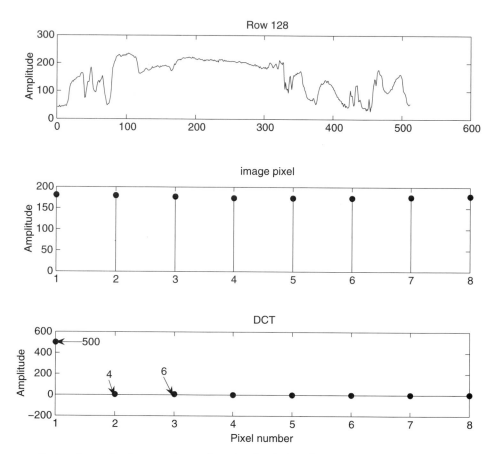

FIGURE

8-2

Redundancy in the transform domain: (top) the pixel profile of the Barbara image along row 128, (middle) values of pixels 128 to 135 of row 128, and (bottom) the 1-D DCT of the eight pixels in the middle graph. The first three coefficients are significant and the rest are discarded.

predictability. In the DCT domain, almost all coefficient values are nearly equal to zero except the dc coefficient. As a result, the first few coefficients are the most important ones. That is to say that most of the information contained in the eight pixels is now packed into the first few DCT coefficients. Thus, the predictability of pixel values has emerged in the form of significant coefficient values—the fewer the number of coefficients with *significant* values, the higher the achievable compression.

What we have described so far pertains to still images wherein the redundancy is in the spatial domain. Alternatively, these still images may be the individual images or frames in a video sequence, in which case the individual images are known as *intraframe* images. Intraframe images in a sequence image occur in time sequence; we can anticipate little or very little changes from frame to frame. This implies that there is high temporal redundancy in the sequence in addition to spatial redundancy. Thus, we can exploit both spatial and temporal redundancies to obtain a higher compression ratio when compressing video images. This forms the basis for the compression of video sequences.

These ideas can be extended to encompass color images as well. However, as shown later, in addition to exploiting pixel redundancies, one can also exploit the human psychovisual effects in reducing the data rate. It is worth pointing out that this visual phenomenon is also applicable to monochromatic images. In either case, the idea is to discard as much irrelevant data as possible without incurring any visible distortion. This is especially important in applications such as digital cinema, where visual effect is the most important factor.

8.1.1 Image Fidelity Criterion

In order to be able to design useful compression systems as well as assess their performances, we need to define a measure of quality of the compression systems. As pointed out, a lossy compression introduces distortions in the decompressed image—the higher the compression ratio, the larger the distortion. From a system design point of view, a quantitative measure will be useful. From a visual point of view, subjective rating will be required. These two measures, in general, may not be correlated and so one or the other measure of performance should be used as the criterion for quality.

8.1.1.1 Quantitative Measures

A simple but often used quantitative measure of assessing image distortions due to lossy compression is the signal-to-noise ratio (SNR) expressed in dB:

$$SNR = 10 \log_{10}\left(\frac{\sigma_s^2}{MSE}\right), dB. \qquad (8\text{-}1)$$

In Eq. (8-1), the signal variance is defined by

$$\sigma_s^2 = \frac{1}{MN}\sum_{m=1}^{M}\sum_{n=1}^{N}(x[m,n]-\mu)^2, \quad \mu = \frac{1}{MN}\sum_{m=1}^{M}\sum_{n=1}^{N}x[m,n] \qquad (8\text{-}2)$$

and the MSE, which is the mean square error between the original image $x[m,n]$ and the compressed/decompressed image $\hat{x}[m,n]$, given by

$$MSE = \frac{1}{MN} \sum_{m=1}^{M} \sum_{n=1}^{N} (x[m,n] - \hat{x}[m,n])^2. \tag{8-3}$$

The disadvantage with this SNR measure is that it is a function of the image variance. Even if the MSE for two images is the same, SNR values can differ if the corresponding variances differ. Another quantitative measure often used in practice is peak SNR (PSNR), which is defined as the ratio of the square of the peak signal to the MSE, expressed in dB:

$$PSNR = 10 \log_{10}\left(\frac{peak^2}{MSE} \right), dB. \tag{8-4}$$

For example, for an 8-bits/pixel grayscale image, the peak value is 255. An advantage of the PSNR is that it is a measure of the MSE with an offset. Therefore, two images having the same grayscale resolution but differing MSE values will have different PSNR values. In either case, the mean square error has been shown not to correlate well with the visual quality. In other words, two images having the same PSNR may not have visually the same quality. Therefore, it is necessary to incorporate the HVS model into the quantitative measure in order to assess the degradations due to compression. However, we will stick with the PSNR in comparing the performance of different compression algorithms because it is much easier to compute.

8.1.1.2   Subjective Measures

As the name implies, subjective evaluation of picture quality depends on the consensus of individuals regarding the appearance of the compressed/decompressed images. There are two broad categories, namely primary and secondary measurements. In primary measurements, a group of individuals takes the test of judging the image quality. In secondary measurements, characteristics of the waveforms of the original and compressed/decompressed images are measured and then the qualitative ratings are determined based on previous calibration.

Category Judgment

This is one of the primary evaluation methods of subjective rating. A group of individuals is presented with a sequence of pictures, which includes original and compressed images in a predetermined order under normal viewing conditions. They then rate these pictures according to one of different multiple choices. These categories may refer to the overall visual quality or degrees of visibility of

Table 8-2. Commonly Used Quality Rating Scales

Overall quality	Visibility of impairments
5 Excellent	5 Imperceptible
4 Good	4 Perceptible but not annoying
3 Fair	3 Slightly annoying
2 Poor	2 Annoying
1 Bad	1 Very annoying

impairments as shown in Table 8-2. These ratings are then converted to a numerical value called a *mean opinion score* (MOS), which is defined as

$$MOS = \frac{\sum_{i=1}^{C} n_i R_i}{\sum_{i=1}^{C} n_i},$$
(8-5)

where R_i is the numerical value corresponding to category i, n_i is the number of judgments in that category, and C is the number of categories in the rating scale.

This chapter describes the basics of both lossless and lossy compression techniques applicable to both still and sequence images. We will cover spatial, transform, and wavelet domain methods of compression. We will start with still image compression and then extend the techniques to the temporal domain.

8.2   LOSSLESS COMPRESSION

As pointed out earlier, lossless compression yields only a modest amount of compression, which may not be sufficient for many applications. However, its use is prolific in all lossy compression schemes, as it provides a means for coding the signals after the removal of the redundancy. We use the term *coding* and *compression* interchangeably. In the field of information theory, compression is also referred to as *source coding*. It is appropriate to introduce some basic elements of information theory at this point.

8.2.1   Elements of Information Theory

The information we are talking about is not semantic information, but one of quantitative in nature. A source of information consists of an alphabet of symbols and messages occur as a sequence of symbols belonging to this alphabet. For example, consider a grayscale image with 8 bits/pixel. When the image pixels are transmitted in a sequence, each pixel is represented by a code corresponding to its luminance value. Because only 8 bits are used to represent the pixel values, the source alphabet has 256 symbols. If we consider each pixel as a message, then each message carries a certain amount of information. In accordance with our daily experience, a measure of information carried by a message symbol has been defined as the negative logarithm of its probability of occurrence. The unit of information depends on the base of the logarithm used. Thus, if a message m_i of a source occurs with a probability p_i, then the information content associated with it is expressed as

$$I_i = -\log_2(p_i), \text{ bits.} \tag{8-6}$$

Thus, a message that never occurs has an infinite amount of information, whereas a message that always occurs has zero amount of information. In terms of assigning a code for a message symbol, the implication of Eq. (8-6) is that a rarely occurring message symbol will have a long code length (if I_i is not an integer, then we assign a code whose length equals the integer value of I_i) whereas a frequently occurring one will have a shorter code length.

Because a source is expected to produce a long sequence of message symbols, we need to know the average amount of information that a source symbol carries. This is the source *entropy*, which is the average amount of information content per source symbol. It is expressed as

$$H = -\sum_i p_i \log_2(p_i), \text{ bits/symbol.} \tag{8-7}$$

Entropy is a useful measure, which refers to the minimum number of bits needed to code the source symbols. It also points to the average amount of uncertainty per source symbol. If all the source symbols are equally uncertain, then the source entropy will be a maximum. Table 8-3 lists a few grayscale images and corresponding entropies. All the images listed in Table 8-3 are 8-bit images. Figure 8-3 shows the original image and its normalized histogram. Its entropy is found to be 6.56 bits/pixel. Another image and its normalized histogram are shown in Figure 8-4. This image has an entropy of 7.63 bits/pixel. As expected, the histogram of the image in Figure 8-4 is much wider than that in Figure 8-3, with the result that the entropy of the farmer is higher.

With this brief introduction we now describe lossless coding methods used in image and video compression.

Table 8-3. Entropy of a Few Source Images

Image	Entropy, bits/pixel
Table tennis	6.56
Masuda	7.02
Barbara	7.63
Baboon	7.14
Cornfield	7.13

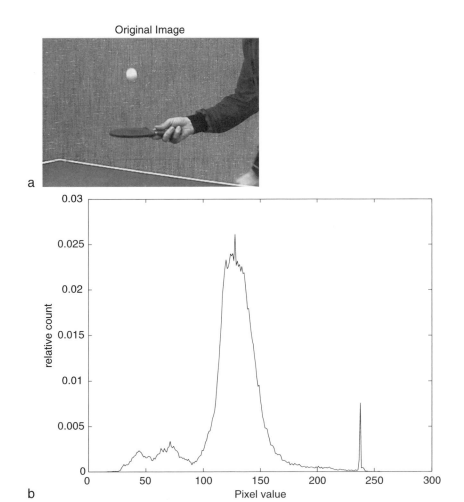

a

b

FIGURE

8-3

Source image and its histogram: (a) table tennis scene #1 and (b) its
normalized histogram. The grayscale resolution of the image is 8 bits/pixel.
The entropy is 6.56 bits/pixel.

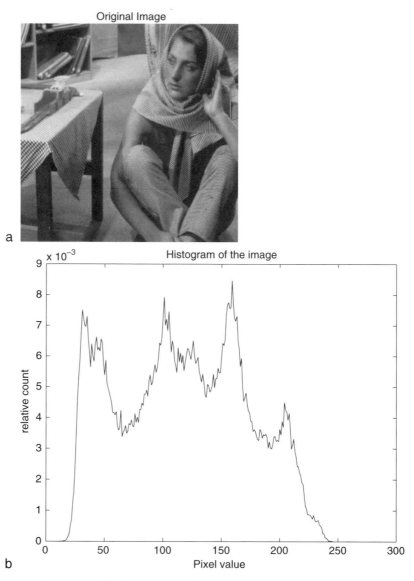

b

FIGURE

8-4

Source image and its histogram: (a) Barbara image and (b) its normalized histogram. The grayscale resolution of the image is 8 bits/pixel. The entropy is 7.63 bits/pixel.

8.2.2   Huffman Coding

Huffman codes are variable-length codes that are optimum for given source symbol probabilities. Huffman codes are also called *prefix* codes because no code can be a prefix to any other code in the code set. The Huffman coding procedure can be described as follows. Assume a data source with a finite alphabet and corresponding symbol probabilities.

1. Sort the symbol probabilities in descending order. Treat each symbol in the ordered list as a terminal node.

2. Merge the two least probable nodes to form a new node whose probability is the sum of the two probabilities of the merged nodes. Assign 1 and 0 to the two branches that lead to a single node. This assignment of 1 and 0 is arbitrary.

3. Repeat step 2 until left with a single node.

4. The Huffman codes for the symbols are then obtained by reading the branch digits sequentially from the root node to the terminal node pointing to the symbols.

Example 8.1

Find the Huffman codes for the source with an alphabet of five symbols with probabilities of 0.5, 0.25, 0.15, 0.07, and 0.03. Determine the source entropy and the average code length.

Solution

Let the source symbols be denoted by s_i, $1 \leq i \leq 5$ and the corresponding probabilities by p_i. First, sort the symbols and probabilities according to a descending order of the probabilities, as shown in Figure 8-5. Consider the sorted symbols as the terminal nodes of the code tree. Next, combine the two nodes with symbols s_5 and s_3 with corresponding probabilities of 0.03 and 0.07 to form a single node s_3' whose sum equals 0.1. Assign 1 to the top branch and 0 to the bottom branch, as shown in Figure 8-5. This leaves us with the three symbols s_1, s_4, and s_2 and the newly formed node for a total of four nodes. Now combine the symbol nodes s_2 and s_3' to form a single node s_2' whose probability is the sum of 0.1 and 0.15. Assign a 1 to the top branch and a 0 to the bottom branch. At this stage we have three symbols, namely s_1, s_4, and s_2'. Note that the number of nodes decreases by 1 at each stage of the procedure. Once again we form a single node s_4' by combining the symbol nodes s_4 and s_2'. The probability of the new node s_4' equals 0.5. Again, we assign 1 and 0 to the top and bottom branches of this node, respectively. Finally the symbol nodes s_1 and s_4' are combined to form a single node s_1' whose probability equals 1. This node is called the *root* node, as we are left with only one node s_1'. At this point the procedure is terminated.

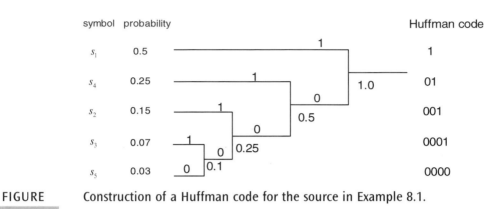

FIGURE

8-5

Construction of a Huffman code for the source in Example 8.1.

The entropy of this source is found from

$$H = -\sum_{i=1}^{5} p_i \log_2 p_i = 1.8309 \text{ bits/symbol}. \tag{8-8}$$

The average length $\overline{L}$ of the Huffman codes for this source is found from

$$\overline{L} = \sum_{i=1}^{5} l_i p_i = 1 \times 0.5 + 2 \times 0.25 + 3 \times 0.15 + 4 \times (0.07 + 0.03) = 1.85 \text{ bits/symbol} \tag{8-9}$$

Huffman codes are optimal for this source, although the average code length is slightly greater than the entropy. The reason for this discrepancy is the fact that the negative of the logarithm to the base 2 of the individual probability is not an integer. If the probabilities of the source symbols are of the form 2^{-m}, with m being positive integers, then the average code length will be exactly equal to the source entropy.

A measure of how close the Huffman coding is to the source entropy is the coding efficiency η, which is defined as

$$\eta = \frac{H}{\overline{L}}. \tag{8-10}$$

For the source in this example, the coding efficiency is 98.97%.

In addition to being optimal, the Huffman code is uniquely decodable. When a sequence of messages is transmitted, the receiver decodes the received bits one at a time. Consider, for example, the received message sequence $s_4 s_1 s_3 s_2$ and the corresponding code sequence 0110001001. After receiving the first bit in the sequence, which is 0, the receiver compares it to the codes in the codebook. Because it is not a valid code, it takes in the next received bit and the first two bits 01 correspond to the code for the message s_4. Next the third received bit 1 is compared against the codes in the library. It is a valid code and the receiver decodes it as message s_1. Continuing further, the receiver decodes the next four consecutive bits as message s_3. Finally, the message s_2 is decoded using the bits 001. We see from this example that the receiver needs a buffer to store the received bits in order to be able to decode the message. Designing a buffer of proper size by itself is another topic of interest in video coding systems.

The foregoing discussion implicitly assumed the existence of a Huffman codebook or that we generated a hypothetical source whose probability model is known. In practice, one estimates the source model by collecting a large number of source data and then determining the probabilities from the data. From these data, which are representative of the sources to be encountered, Huffman codes are designed. Once the library of Huffman codes is built, both the transmitter and the receiver have the same copy of the library.

If the statistics of the source are expected to change frequently, then fixed design of the Huffman codes is not efficient. We need to adapt the Huffman coder to be able to build the codes on the fly from the incoming messages. This is done using *adaptive* Huffman coding. Readers interested in adaptive Huffman coding should refer to the references at the end of the chapter.

8.2.3   Run-Length Coding

In a binary source we may encounter situations where a particular symbol repeats itself many times before being interrupted by the other symbol. Consider, for example, a message sequence that has four consecutive zeros followed by 1. Then it is more efficient to code the length of the run of zeros, which is 4, as a single code than to code every zero four times. This is known as *run-length coding* (RLC). RLC is used routinely in image and video compression schemes. More specifically, in transform coding, where the transform coefficients are quantized, a large number of consecutive zeros are encountered before a nonzero amplitude is encountered. Then the encoder codes the run of consecutive zeros using Huffman codes. For example, consider the quantized coefficient matrix shown here:

$$
\begin{matrix}
88 & 1 & 0 & 0 \\
5 & 0 & 0 & 0 \\
-2 & 1 & 0 & 0 \\
0 & 0 & 0 & -1
\end{matrix}
$$

If the coefficient values are transmitted serially from left to right, top to bottom, then we hit run lengths of 2, 3, and 5. In video coding standards, zigzag scanning of the coefficients is implemented as it increases the run lengths. If we use such a zigzag, scanning pattern, then we encounter run lengths of 4 and 6. This is more efficient than raster scanning the coefficients. Of course, one has to generate the codes for the various run lengths to be encountered when coding a class of source data.

8.2.4   Arithmetic Coding

It is shown that the average length $\overline{L}$ of Huffman codes is bounded between the source entropy and entropy plus one bit per symbol, i.e.,

$$H \le \overline{L} < H + 1. \qquad (8\text{-}11)$$

However, instead of Huffman coding a symbol at a time, if we code a sequence of symbols of length m as a single symbol, then the average length of the Huffman code is bounded by

$$H \le \overline{L} < H + \frac{1}{m}. \qquad (8\text{-}12)$$

This suggests that the average code length approaches the source entropy, as the symbol sequence length m is made large. The problem with this is that the Huffman table needs to store the codes of all length m sequences, which is 2^m in size. For example, if m equals 16, then we have to store 65536 codes, which is prohibitively large from both a storage and an implementation point of view for any practical application.

In arithmetic coding, large-length symbol sequences can be used without having to store all the 2^m code words. In arithmetic coding, a tag is sent for the entire message sequence instead of sending a symbol or group of symbols. The code corresponding to the tag is the truncated binary representation of the tag value, which falls in the half-open interval $[0,1)$. This is best understood by the following example.

Example 8.2

Consider a discrete source with an alphabet $\{s_1,s_2,s_3,s_4\}$ and corresponding probabilities of 0.4, 0.3, 0.2, and 0.1, respectively. Let us assume the encoding sequence to be $s_2 s_3 s_1 s_4 s_2$. Initially the interval $[0,1)$ is divided in proportion to the

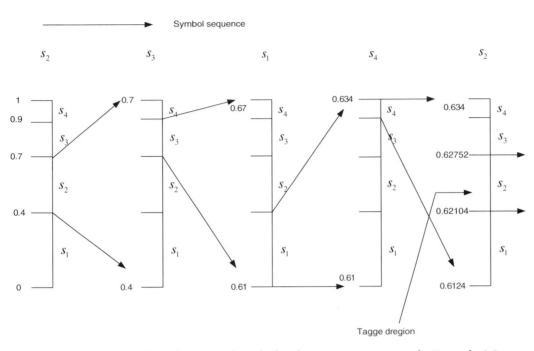

Symbol sequence

S_2 S_3 S_1 S_4 S_2

Tagge dregion

FIGURE   Construction of arithmetic code for the message sequence in Example 8.2.

8-6

symbol probabilities as shown in Figure 8-6. With the arrival of the first symbol s_2, the interval $[0.4,0.7)$ is then divided in the same proportion as in the initial step. Note that the interval after encoding the first symbol is uniquely different from that of the prior interval. When the second symbol s_3 is received, the interval is narrowed to $[0.61,0.67)$. This interval is again divided in proportion to the symbol probabilities to prepare for the arrival of the next symbol in the sequence to be coded. Since the third symbol is s_1, in the next interval the tag resides in $[0.61,0.634)$. When the fourth symbol s_4 is received, the tag interval becomes $[0.6124,0.634)$. After the arrival of the last symbol s_2 in the sequence, the final tag lies in the interval $[0.62104,0.62752)$. Any value in this interval may be used for the tag value because this interval is unique. We will choose the midpoint of the interval, which is 0.62428. The arithmetic code for this sequence of length 5 is then the binary representation of the tag value.

Even though arithmetic coding does not require the storage of codes of all the 2^m sequences, its drawback is the need for higher precision to represent the tag value. Also, an end of sequence symbol has to be transmitted so that the decoding can be terminated when the sequence is decoded. These two factors prevent the performance of arithmetic coders from reaching the source entropy value.

8.2.5   Golomb–Rice (GR) Coding

As pointed out earlier, Huffman coding is well suited to coding sources with a large alphabet, as in RLC. As shown later, there are situations where one has to code differential signals, as in predictive coding. These residual signals tend to have a double-sided exponential distribution, which is termed Laplacian. We have seen examples of such distributions in the chapter on wavelets where the detail coefficients at the first level of the 2-D DWT tend to exhibit this characteristic. Further, when simple differencing is used in image pixel prediction, the residuals will be integers. An example of simple differencing of two consecutive frames and the histogram of the difference image are shown in Figure 8-7. As can be seen from Figure 8-7d, the histogram of the difference image has a double-sided exponential shape. It has been shown that under these circumstances, Golomb–Rice coding of the residual signals is simpler and more efficient than either Huffman or arithmetic coding.

GR coding is a method of representing positive integers using a base value that is a power of 2. Let n be a positive integer and let $m = 2^k$; k is a positive integer. Let Q and R be the quotient and remainder after dividing n by m: $Q = \left\lfloor \dfrac{n}{m} \right\rfloor$, $R = n - m \times Q$. Then the GR code for n is obtained by concatenating the unary code of Q with the k least significant bits in the binary representation of n. Note that the unary code of Q has $Q + 1$ number of bits. Thus, the length of the GR code is $Q + 1 + k$. Table 8-4 shows integers 0 through 10 and the corresponding GR codes. The digits in bold face correspond to the k least significant bits in the binary representation of n. The 1 bit in the remainder of the code is a terminating bit. That is, we count the number of zeros up to the 1 bit.

Because the residual signals in a predictive coding system have both positive and negative integer values, we need to map the negative values to positive ones uniquely. This may be done by the following mapping rule:

$$M(e) = \begin{cases} 2e, & e \geq 0 \\ 2|e| - 1, & e < 0 \end{cases},\qquad (8\text{-}13)$$

where e is the actual residual signal. From Eq. (8-13), it is easy to see that all positive integer values of e map to even positive integers and negative integer values of e map to odd positive integers.

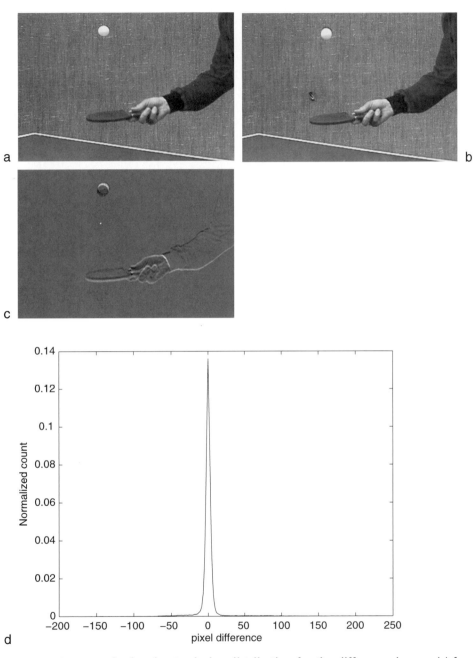

FIGURE

8-7

An example showing Laplacian distribution for the difference image: (a) frame 5, (b) frame 6 of a table tennis sequence image, (c) difference image, and (d) normalized histogram of the difference image. The original images of frames 5 and 6 are courtesy of the Center for Image Processing Research, Rensselaer Polytechnic Institute.

Table 8-4. GR Codes of Integers for $m = 2^2$

n	Q	R	GR code
0	0	0	100
1	0	1	101
2	0	2	110
3	0	3	111
4	1	0	0100
5	1	1	0101
6	1	2	0110
7	1	3	0111
8	2	0	00100
9	2	1	00101
10	2	2	00110

The GR encoding procedure can be described as follows. Given $m = 2^k$,

1. Map the residuals to positive values as per Eq. (8-13).
2. Find the quotient Q and remainder R after dividing the mapped residual signal by m.
3. Concatenate the unary code of Q and the k least significant bits of the binary representation of the mapped residual signal.

Using the aforementioned coding procedure, a few differential frames from the *Trevor* sequence have been encoded. Figures 8-8a and 8-8b show the originals of frames 5 and 6, respectively, of the *Trevor* sequence. The difference between frames 6 and 5 is shown in Figure 8-8c along with its histogram in Figure 8-8d. The encoded bit rate is 4.35 bits/pixel. The original images all have 8 bits/pixel. The bit rates for a few difference frames of the *Trevor* sequence are tabulated in Table 8.5. For the 10 differential images the average GR encoding rate is 4.357 bits/pixel with a mean compression ratio of 1.836. As shown later, using motion detection and estimation, we can get a higher compression ratio on these same differential images. Thus, Golomb–Rice coding is optimal for exponentially distributed, integer, differential images and is very simple to implement at both the encoder and the decoder. Further, there is no need to store a large set of codes, as is the case with Huffman codes.

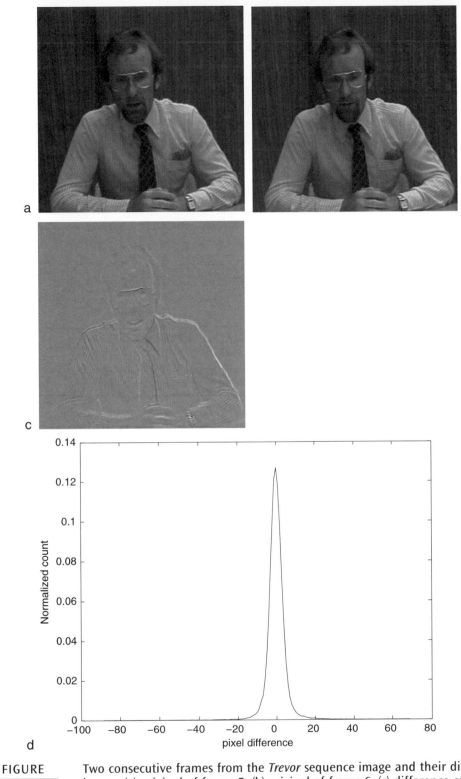

FIGURE

8-8

Two consecutive frames from the *Trevor* sequence image and their difference image: (a) original of frame 5, (b) original of frame 6, (c) difference of frames 6 and 5, and (d) normalized histogram of the differential image. The original images in a and b are courtesy of the Center for Image Processing Research, Rensselaer Polytechnic Institute.

Table 8-5. Lossless Encoding Rates for the *Trevor* Sequence Image Using Golomb–Rice Coding

Frame #i + 1 – frame #i	Bits/pixel
6–5	4.35
7–6	4.37
8–7	4.36
9–8	4.40
10–9	4.38
11–10	4.38
12–11	4.35
13–12	4.33
14–13	4.33
15–14	4.32
Average bit rate	4.357
Mean comp. ratio	1.836

8.3   PREDICTIVE CODING

In the lossless coding methods just described, symbols are encoded independent of other symbols occurring in the message sequence. This is commonly referred to as memoryless encoding. However, image pixels in a spatial neighborhood have high correlation. As mentioned earlier in this chapter, pixel correlations can be removed by being able to predict pixel values based on the neighboring pixel values. This is the basis for all predictive coding procedures.

8.3.1   One-Dimensional DPCM

Consider a 1-D signal $x[n]$, which may correspond to a row or column of an image. Its predicted value is $\hat{x}[n]$, as shown in Figure 8-9a. The differential pixel value $e[n]$ is given by

$$e[n] = x[n] - \hat{x}[n]. \tag{8-14}$$

As shown in the previous section, this differential signal has a variance that is, in general, a fraction of the actual signal variance and so requires fewer bits of representation and hence the compression. If we encode the differential signal in a lossless fashion, we realize a lossless predictive coding procedure. However,

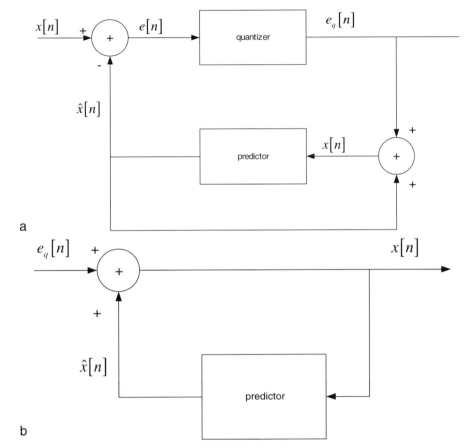

First-order DPCM: (a) encoder and (b) decoder.

the intent of this section is to describe lossy predictive coding methods. Incidentally, this scheme of encoding differentials is called differential pulse code modulation (DPCM). There are two subsystems in the DPCM that have to be designed. First the predictor, which is assumed to be linear and may be characterized by

$$\hat{x}[n] = f(\hat{x}[n-1], \hat{x}[n-2], \ldots), \tag{8-15}$$

i.e., the current pixel value is estimated from the previously estimated pixel values based on the estimation rule $f(.)$. Because we are interested in a linear estimator, we can express the estimate of the current pixel value as a weighted sum of the previously estimated pixel values. In general, one can use p previously predicted pixel values to estimate the current pixel value. Thus, Eq. (8-15) can be written more explicitly as

$$\hat{x}[n] = \sum_{i=1}^{p} \alpha_i \hat{x}[n-i].\tag{8-16}$$

The weights in Eq. (8-16) are real. Because we are using p previously predicted pixel values in the prediction of the current pixel value, the linear predictor is called the pth-order predictor. From Eq. (8-14) we note that the current prediction error signal will have the least value when the predictor is perfect or the best. Therefore, for the overall prediction to be optimal, we need to choose the weighting coefficients such that a certain optimality criterion is met. For linear predictors the optimality criterion often used is minimization of the MSE between the original signal and the predicted signal. Even though this criterion may not be the best choice from a human visual perception point of view, this is the preferred criterion for mathematical tractability.

Observe from Figure 8-9a that the predictor uses *quantized* pixel values to estimate the current pixel value. Because quantization incurs loss of information contained in the actual pixel values and because it is a nonlinear process, the task of computing the optimal weighting coefficients based on the previously predicted pixels is daunting. Therefore one uses actual pixel values instead of the previously predicted values in order to compute the optimal weights. The drawback of using previously predicted pixels in the predictor is that the errors tend to accumulate and render reconstructed images useless after decoding several frames. This calls for a frequent use of *key* frames to reset the accumulated errors.

It can be shown that for a first-order linear predictor the optimal coefficient α is found to be

$$\alpha^* = \rho,\tag{8-17}$$

where ρ is the correlation coefficient of the signal. For images, it is the correlation coefficient along the row or column dimension, depending on how the 1-D DPCM is used. With the optimal predictor in place, the resulting minimum MSE or the prediction variance can be obtained as

$$\sigma_e^2 = (1 - \rho^2)\sigma_x^2,\tag{8-18}$$

where σ_x^2 is the variance of the signal. For typical images, the correlation coefficient is around 0.95. The prediction error variance is, therefore, only about 10% of the signal variance. The effectiveness of the linear predictor is usually expressed in terms of a prediction gain, G_p, and is defined as the ratio of the variances of the signal and prediction error, which is expressed as

$$G_p = \frac{\sigma_x^2}{\sigma_e^2} = \frac{1}{1-\rho^2}. \tag{8-19}$$

The prediction gain tells us how much reduction in the signal variance we have achieved relative to the variance of the original signal.

One can use a higher order prediction to improve the performance of the DPCM. However, the improvement depends on whether the signal statistics really correspond to higher orders. Images are typically what are termed as first-order Markov fields, which essentially means that a current pixel is dependent only on the previous pixel, i.e., a first-order prediction. Hence, the improvement achieved in using predictors higher than first order is not significant. The typical reduction in bit rate, achieved by a first-order 1-D DPCM over that of a PCM signal, is about 2 bits.

Figure 8-9 shows that both the encoder and the decoder are operating in synchronism, i.e., the encoder loop has the decoder built into it. By following the signal flow, we can show that the error in reconstructing the signal equals the quantization error:

$$x[n] - \tilde{x}[n] = q[n] \tag{8-20}$$

$$q[n] = e[n] - e_q[n] \tag{8-21}$$

where $e_q[n]$ is the quantized error signal. Because the error between actual and reconstructed pixels equals the quantization error, the quantizer must be designed in an optimal fashion. Chapter 4 showed that the optimal quantizer is the nonuniform, PDF- optimized Lloyd–Max quantizer. In many practical schemes, one can simply use uniform quantizers, which get the job done fairly well and are also very simple to implement.

The prediction gain for optimal first- and second-order 1-D DPCM coders is shown in Table 8-6 for a few grayscale images. All the original images have 8 bits/pixel, grayscale resolution. Depending on the image detail, the prediction gain varies from around 5 to 17 dB. The baboon image has a lot of edges so the prediction gain is far below the expected value of about 10 dB.

8.3.2   Adaptive DPCM

The predictor used in the 1-D DPCM is a fixed predictor, which implies that the predictor coefficients are predetermined and stay fixed for at least a single

Table 8-6. Prediction Gain in dB for First- and Second-Order DPCM

Image	First order	Second order
Barbara	6.57	6.8
Baboon	5.35	5.35
Cameraman	8.16	8.16
Masuda	17.54	17.66
Cornfield	8.32	9.32
Yacht	12.07	13.09
Average	9.67	10.06

image. The disadvantage of a fixed predictor is that when the statistics change from image to image or even within an image, the prediction is not efficient. What we mean by this statement is that when a pixel falls on a boundary between two homogeneous regions, the predictor is unable to follow the boundary condition. This is because we chose the minimum MSE as the criterion of optimality. Because the predictor fails to follow the boundary, the resulting prediction error tends to be large. When such pixel errors are quantized by a quantizer with a small number of bits of quantization, the edges are not reconstructed well. This manifests as jagged edges in the reconstructed images.

A way around this difficulty is to adapt either the predictor or the quantizer to the changing statistics of the images to be encoded. Adapting the predictor means that the weighting coefficients have to be updated either for each input image or for regions within an image. This is avoided for two reasons: extra storage memory is required and the updated weighting coefficients have to be carried out on the fly and conveyed to the receiver. However, adapting the quantizer is much easier to implement. Two such adaptive predictive coders, called adaptive differential PCM (ADPCM), are shown in Figures 8-10 and 8-11. The predictive coder in Figure 8-10 is known as *adaptive gain control* ADPCM. In this scheme the quantizer is designed for a fixed unit variance signal. However, its input is normalized before quantization and denormalized after quantization. This normalization factor, which is the instantaneous standard deviation of the quantized signal, can be computed recursively by

$$\sigma_{\hat{e}}^2[n+1] = (1-\gamma)\hat{e}^2[n] + \gamma\sigma_{\hat{e}}^2[n] \qquad (8\text{-}22)$$

with $\sigma_{\hat{e}}^2[0] = \hat{e}^2[0]$ and $0 \leq \gamma \leq 1$.

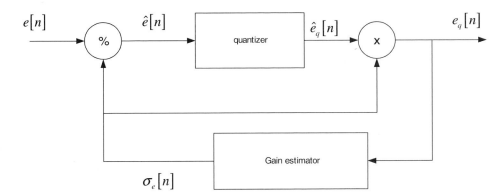

FIGURE

8-10

Block diagram of an adaptive gain control DPCM.

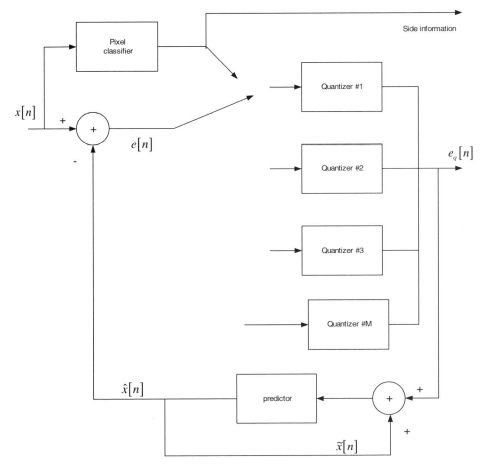

FIGURE

8-11

Block diagram of a switched quantizer ADPCM.

As an alternative to adaptive gain control DPCM, one can use a number of quantizers, one for each class of the image pixel. The actual quantizer used for the current pixel depends on the class to which the current pixel belongs. This is called a *switched quantizer* ADPCM because the quantizer in actual use for the current pixel is switched between a number of quantizers based on the pixel class information. This calls for a pixel classifier, which assigns the current pixel one of a predetermined number of classes. Thus, there are as many quantizers as there are pixel classes. Of course, this class information has to be conveyed to the decoder in order for it to use the appropriate dequantizer for the reconstruction.

8.3.3   Two-Dimensional DPCM

The 1-D or line-by-line DPCM discussed in the previous section takes advantage of the pixel correlation in one dimension only. Because image pixels have correlation in both spatial dimensions, it is to our advantage to exploit the 2-D correlation. One can, therefore, perform the prediction of a pixel value based on a neighborhood of pixels centered on the pixel being predicted. The resulting coder is then called a 2-D DPCM. For a 2-D DPCM, the predictor can be expressed by

$$\hat{x}[m,n] = \sum_{(k,l)\in W} \sum \alpha(k,l)x[m,n], \tag{8-23}$$

where w is a causal 2-D window centered on $[m,n]$. Causality implies that the pixels used in the prediction should be to the left and top of the current pixel. Using the same optimality criterion as in the case of the 1-D DPCM, we can compute the optimal predictor coefficients so that the MSE between actual and predicted pixels is a minimum.

The choice between 1-D and 2-D DPCM depends on issues relating to implementation. Two-dimensional DPCM requires a larger storage memory as well as computational complexity. Typically, the bit rate reduction in using 2-D DPCM is not very significant and, therefore, we are better off using the 1-D DPCM.

8.4   TRANSFORM CODING

Figure 8-12 shows a block diagram depicting the transform coder. In this type of image compression, the encoder operations can be described as follows. The image to be compressed is divided into $N \times N$ nonoverlapping blocks. Next the

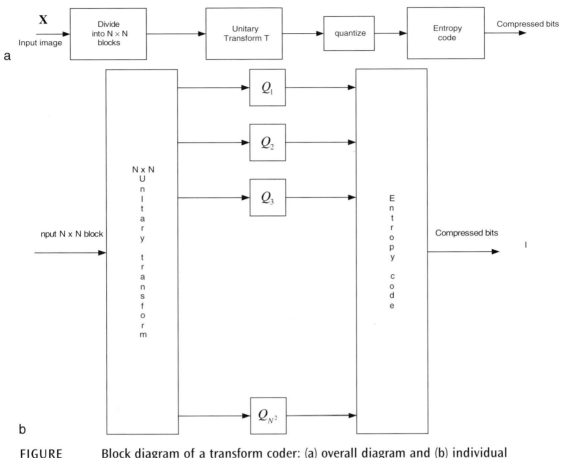

FIGURE
8-12

Block diagram of a transform coder: (a) overall diagram and (b) individual quantizers.

unitary transform of each subblock is computed and then the transform coefficients are quantized using a quantizer for each coefficient. Thus, there are N^2 number of quantizers. The quantized coefficients are run length encoded and the various RLC symbols are then entropy coded for transmission or storage. It should be pointed out that the N^2 number of quantizers used is from the viewpoint of explanation and not necessarily the number of distinct hardware entities. At the decoder, the symbols are decoded first and then each transform block is dequantized and inverse transformed and rearranged to form the image.

The parameters of a transform coder are the unitary transform, quantizer, and entropy coder. Each one of the parameters is discussed further in the following.

8.4.1   Choice of a Transform

Several unitary and orthogonal transforms were defined in the last chapter. It has been shown that for a given image, the KL transform performs the best in the sense that it achieves complete decorrelation of the transform coefficients. To rephrase, the KL transform has the best energy compaction property. However, it is image dependent. On the other hand, the DCT is very nearly equivalent to the KL transform, is image independent, and a real transform as well. It is also a fast transform. Therefore, the DCT is used as the image transform of choice in JPEG and MPEG image compression standards.

8.4.2   Optimal Bit Allocation

In a transform coder, the 2-D unitary transform, such as the DCT, Hadamard, and so on, is fixed for the system. Depending on image details, there can be significant variations in the amplitudes of the transform coefficients from block to block. Because the bit rate is fixed in an encoding system, we need to assign bits to the quantizers in an optimal fashion so that we obtain the least overall distortion for the given bit budget. Such a task of assigning bits to quantizers with a constraint on the available bits per pixel is known as the *optimal bit allocation* procedure or algorithm. It can be stated as follows.

Problem Statement

Given a unitary transform matrix, **A**, and an overall average bit rate R bits/pixel, where $R = \dfrac{1}{M}\sum_{k=0}^{M-1} R_k$, $M = N^2$, find the quantizer bits R_k, $0 \le k \le M - 1$ such that the overall MSE between the input and the reconstructed image is minimized. Because the transform is unitary, by its energy conservation property the overall MSE equals the sum of the variances of the quantizers.

Denoting the MSE of the kth quantizer by σ_{qk}^2, the total mean square error σ_q^2 due to all the quantizers is the sum of the individual quantizers, given by

$$\sigma_q^2 = \sum_{k=0}^{M-1} \sigma_{qk}^2. \tag{8-24}$$

The individual quantizer error variance for large bit rate is proportional to the quanitzer input signal variance, and the number of bits and can be expressed as

$$\sigma_{q_i}^2 = C2^{-2R_i}\sigma_i^2. \tag{8-25}$$

In Eq. (8-25) we assumed without loss of generality that the constant of proportionality is the same for all the quantizers. The solution to this constrained minimization problem is obtained using the Lagrange multiplier method. More specifically, we set the cost function J as

$$J = \sum_{i=1}^{M} C 2^{-2R_i} \sigma_i^2 - \lambda \left(R - \frac{1}{M} \sum_{i=1}^{M} R_i \right),$$
(8-26)

where λ is the Lagrange multiplier. By setting the partial derivatives of J with respect to the individual quantizer bits R_i to zero and solving for R_i, it can be shown that the optimal bit allocation is given by

$$R_k = R + \frac{1}{2} \log_2 \frac{\sigma_k^2}{\left(\prod_{i=0}^{M-1} \sigma_i^2 \right)^{1/M}}.$$
(8-27)

According to Eq. (8-27), the ith coefficient gets bits less than or greater than the overall average bit depending on whether its variance is less than or greater than the geometric mean of the coefficient variances. A problem with this bit allocation rule is that the quantizer bits are not guaranteed to be integers and some quanitizer bits may even be negative.

As an example, for an 8×8 DCT and an average bit rate of 1 bit/pixel, the optimal bit assignment for the Barbara image is found to be

6	3	2	2	2	2	1	0
3	2	2	2	2	2	1	0
2	1	1	1	2	2	2	1
1	1	1	1	2	2	1	0
0	0	1	1	1	1	1	0
0	0	0	0	0	0	0	0
0	0	0	0	0	0	0	0
0	0	0	0	0	0	0	0

In this assignment, all quantizers with negative bits are assigned zero bits and all noninteger bits are truncated to integer values. The resulting bit rate comes out to be 0.91 bit/pixel. Because we have some room for additional bits and because the dc coefficient is more important, we can assign 12 bits instead of 6 for the dc coefficient. This brings the average bit rate to 1 bit/pixel.

An alternative approach to the bit allocation rule in Eq. (8-27) is the integer bit allocation procedure, which assigns positive, integer bits to the quantizers and is described as follows. Let us assume that we have found the variances of the $N \times N$ transform coefficients of a given image. Then,

1. Set all quantizer bits to zero at the initial step, $R_k^{(0)} = 0$, $1 \le k \le M$; $M = N^2$. Set step $j = 1$. Let $R_T = M.R$ be the total bits available for the M quantizers.
2. Sort the coefficient variances and denote the maximum variance by σ_i^2.
3. Set $R_i^{(j)} = R_i^{(j-1)} + 1$ and $\sigma_i^2 \leftarrow \dfrac{\sigma_i^2}{2}$.
4. $R_T \leftarrow R_T - 1$. If $R_T = 0$, quit, otherwise $j \leftarrow j + 1$ and go to step 2.

For the same image as in the noninteger case just given, the integer bit allocation procedure results in the bit assignment as shown here.

10	5	3	2	2	2	1	0
5	3	2	2	2	2	1	0
2	2	1	2	2	3	2	0
0	0	1	1	2	2	1	0
0	0	0	0	1	0	0	0
0	0	0	0	0	0	0	0
0	0	0	0	0	0	0	0
0	0	0	0	0	0	0	0

8.4.3   Quantizer Design

After determining the bit assignment for the quantizers, we need to design optimal quantizers with respective bits. Recall from Chapter 4 that the design of an optimal quantizer amounts to the computation of the decision intervals and corresponding reconstruction levels using the Lloyd–Max algorithm. Thus, the quantizers have nonuniform decision intervals and reconstruction levels. As shown earlier, all the DCT coefficients, except the dc coefficient, tend to have a Laplacian distribution for their amplitudes. Fortunately, the decision intervals and corresponding reconstruction levels for a given number of quantizer bits and input PDF have been tabulated. These values are calculated for an input with zero mean value and unit variance. In order for us to design optimal quantizers, all we need to do is to scale the tabulated values by the standard deviation of the respective DCT coefficients to be quantized. However, in practice one simply uses a uniform quantizer for ease of implementation either in hardware or software. The resulting loss in PSNR may not be significant if the compressed bit rate is high enough. When a uniform quantizer is employed, a DCT coefficient is quantized by simply dividing it by a corresponding quantization *step size* in the following manner:

$$\hat{X}(k,l) = \left\lfloor \frac{X(k,l)}{Q(k,l)} + 0.5 \right\rfloor \cdot Q(k,l), \quad 0 \le k, l \le N-1, \qquad (8\text{-}28)$$

where $X(k,l)$ and $\hat{X}(k,l)$ are the actual and quantized/dequantized DCT coefficients, $Q(k,l)$ is the corresponding step size of a uniform quantizer, and $\lfloor x \rfloor$ is the largest integer less than x. One can scale the step size of the coefficients by the same scale factor to increase or decrease the amount of compression to be obtained. It should be pointed out that the quantization steps just described are based purely on a quantitative measure, which is the MSE, but we know from earlier discussions that the MSE does not correlate well with human visual judgment. As discussed later in the chapter, the JPEG compression standard uses a quantization matrix that is determined experimentally, based on the threshold of visibility of distortion. A quantization step size used in the JPEG standard for quantizing the DCT coefficients of the luminance component is shown in Table 8-7. Again, scaling this quantization matrix by a scale factor we can vary the resulting compression of the image.

An example of compressing and decompressing an image using DCT-based transform coder is shown in Figure 8-13a for the case of noninteger bit assignment. The average bit rate is set at 0.5 bit/pixel. The PSNR is about 32 dB. The same image is compressed and decompressed using the integer bit assignment procedure at the same 0.5 bit/pixel and is shown in Figure 8-13b. As a comparison, the same image is quantized using the JPEG quantization matrix given in Table 8-6 and is shown in Figure 8-13c.

Table 8-7. JPEG Quantization Matrix for *Y* Component

16	11	10	16	24	40	51	61
12	12	14	19	26	58	60	55
14	13	16	24	40	57	69	56
14	17	22	29	51	87	80	62
18	22	37	56	68	109	103	77
24	35	55	64	81	104	113	92
49	64	78	87	103	121	120	101
72	92	95	98	112	100	103	99

FIGURE
8-13

Compressing/decompressing an image using DCT-based TC. (a) Optimal bit allocation and uniform quantization. The average bit rate is set to 0.5 bit/pixel. No RLC/entropy coding is used. PSNR = 35 dB. (b) Compression using integer bit assignment. (c) Compression using the quantization matrix of JPEG standard. PSNR = 32.5 dB.

Coding Gain

When comparing coding rates between two schemes, a quantity called the coding gain is a useful measure and is defined as the ratio of distortions due to the two coders. A scalar quantizer with R bits/pixel (number of quantization levels is assumed large) introduces signal distortion due to quantization, which can be expressed as

$$D(R) = K \cdot 2^{-2R} \cdot \sigma_x^2, \tag{8-29}$$

where K is a constant of the quantizer and σ_x^2 is the input signal variance. This distortion versus rate actually pertains to a PCM coder. For a transform coder with a given 2-D unitary transform T of size $M = N^2$ and M scalar quantizers with optimal bit allocation, it can be shown that the total distortion due to quantization is given by

$$D_T = K \cdot 2^{-2\bar{R}} \left(\prod_{i=1}^{M} \sigma_i^2 \right)^{1/M},$$ (8-30)

where $\bar{R}$ is the average bit rate in bits/pixel and σ_i^2 is the variance of the ith transform coefficient. Using Eqs. (8-29) and (8-30) with the bit rate for the PCM to be $\bar{R}$, we get the coding gain for the transform coder to be

$$G_C = \frac{D_{PCM}}{D_T} = \frac{\sigma_x^2}{\left(\prod_{i=1}^{M} \sigma_i^2 \right)^{1/M}} = \frac{\frac{1}{M} \sum_{i=1}^{M} \sigma_i^2}{\left(\prod_{i=1}^{M} \sigma_i^2 \right)^{1/M}}.$$ (8-31)

Equation (8-31) shows that the coding gain for the transform coder over that of the PCM coder is the ratio of the arithmetic mean of the coefficient variances to the geometric mean of the variances. The coding gain for the 2-D DCT transform coder, for the same set of images used in predictive coding scheme, is listed in Table 8-8. The variations seen in the coding gain among the images are due to the image content. It is well known that the DCT is more efficient in its energy compaction property when the pixels are highly correlated. Hence we see a high

Table 8-8. Coding Gain for DCT-Based Transform Coder

Image	Coding gain in dB			
	4 × 4	*8 × 8*	*16 × 16*	*32 × 32*
Barbara	10.94	12.85	14.31	15.47
Baboon	5.75	6.51	6.89	7.13
Cameraman	10.97	12.18	12.82	13.35
Masuda	24.27	27.25	28.62	29.35
Cornfield	11.98	14.64	16.13	16.92
Yacht	16.45	19.40	20.94	21.74
Average	13.39	15.47	16.62	17.33

coding gain for the Masuda image, which has very little active regions, whereas the baboon image has a lot of cluttered areas with a consequent low correlation. Comparing the values in Tables 8-6 and 8-8, we find that the 8×8, DCT coder yields an improvement of about 6 dB in coding gain over the 1-D predictive coder. This implies that at the same average bit rate, the DCT coder improves the SNR by 6 dB, which is significant. Of course, the DCT coder has a higher complexity of implementation than the predictive coder. A further examination of Table 8-8 shows that the 2-D DCT coder improves coding gain with increasing block sizes. For example, there is a 4-dB improvement in the average coding gain using a 32×32 block instead of a 4×4 block for the 2-D DCT. However, the improvement in the coding gain is not significant in using a 32×32 size DCT instead of an 8×8 size DCT. The increase in complexity, however, is significant. Therefore, in practice, only 8×8 DCT is used.

8.4.4   Entropy Coder

Once the transform coefficients are quantized, we need to assign a code to each one of the coefficients before transmission or storage. By the very energy compaction property of the unitary transform, most of the coefficients in a block will be zero after quantization. Instead of coding each quantized coefficient individually, there is more to be gained if we use RLC of the zero runs. Because the coefficients form a 2-D array, we need to scan the coefficient array in a manner as to convert it to a 1-D array. One can use a raster scanning order from left to right and top to bottom. However, statistics show that larger lengths of zero runs are encountered if the scanning pattern is zigzag, as shown in Figure 8-14. These run lengths and nonzero coefficients are Huffman coded, which results in variable length binary codes. With a constant bandwidth channel, the Huffman-coded bit stream must be buffered and then transmitted serially.

Let us explain the entropy coding procedure with the help of an example. Consider an 8×8 block of pixels as shown in Table 8-9. Its DCT coefficients are shown in Table 8-10. Using the JPEG quantization matrix in Table 8-7, the quantized DCT coefficients are shown in Table 8-11. As expected, most of the coefficients become zero after quantization. If we scan the quantized coefficients in a raster order, we get the sequence of nonzero coefficient values and zero runs as 64, −9, 8, 1, −1, [3], −1, [7], 1, [1], −1, 1, [44]. Here the length of zero run is denoted [.]. If we use the zigzag scanning pattern shown in Figure 8-14, we obtain the sequence as 64, −9, −1, 1, [1], 8, 1, [5], −1, [1], −1, [2], 1, [46]. Although it is not obvious from this example that the zigzag scan results in larger zero runs, in general, the zigzag scan is found to be more efficient in yielding larger zero runs and, as a consequence, higher compression.

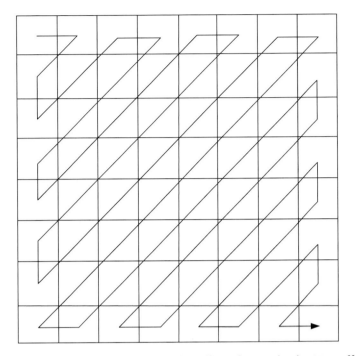

FIGURE

8-14

A zigzag pattern for run length coding of quantized DCT coefficients.

Table 8-9. An 8 × 8 Pixel Block

126	119	112	115	122	137	149	153
123	115	113	114	119	135	151	152
125	116	114	113	114	134	150	154
122	120	119	111	110	130	152	155
126	121	117	110	112	134	150	157
124	122	112	112	110	134	158	152
127	121	113	110	116	140	160	156
127	116	113	114	122	151	155	151

In this example, we encounter runs of length 44 and 46 in the raster and zigzag scans, respectively. It is much less efficient to generate Huffman codes for such large zero runs. Remember that if we allow such large run lengths, then the Huffman table must contain codes for all run lengths. Hence, in practice, an *end of block* (EOB) code of shorter length is used to signal that the rest of the quantized coefficients are zero in that block.

Table 8-10. Rounded 2-D DCT of Pixels in Table 8-9

1030	−99	78	10	−16	15	0	−3
−7	4	−4	−6	8	−2	0	2
7	−5	−9	14	3	−1	1	−1
0	2	4	−2	−1	−1	−5	0
2	2	−3	0	1	−3	4	0
1	0	4	−3	−2	0	−3	1
−1	1	−2	2	0	1	0	−3
2	0	2	2	3	−2	3	0

Table 8-11. Coefficients Quantized using the JPEG Quantization Matrix in Table 8-7

64	−9	8	1	−1	0	0	0
−1	0	0	0	0	0	0	0
1	0	−1	1	0	0	0	0
0	0	0	0	0	0	0	0
0	0	0	0	0	0	0	0
0	0	0	0	0	0	0	0
0	0	0	0	0	0	0	0
0	0	0	0	0	0	0	0

In the JPEG compression standard the quantized dc and ac coefficients are encoded in slightly different ways, as described in the following manner: The dc DCT coefficients are proportional to the average values of the respective pixel blocks. Because neighboring block averages have high correlation and the quantized dc coefficients have even more, one can hope to achieve higher compression if the differences of consecutive dc coefficients, instead of the actual quantized values, are encoded. This is actually a lossless predictive coding of the quantized dc coefficients, except that the prediction is simply the difference of the current and previous block dc DCT values. The difference values are mapped according to category and size, as shown in Table 8-12. Each category has twice the number of entries in the preceding category. Thus, if the differential dc value is 9, then its category is 4. Then the code for the dc differential value 9 will be the Huffman code for the category 4 followed by 4 bits to indicate its position in the category, which contains 16 elements.

The quantized ac coefficients are coded by grouping the run length and the size of the nonzero coefficient that broke the run as a pair and replacing the

Table 8-12. Category/Range Representation of the dc Differential

Category	Difference values
0	0
1	−1, 1
2	−3, −2, 2, 3
3	−7, −6, −5, −4, 4, 5, 6, 7
4	−15 .... −8, 8, ... 15
5	−31 .... −16, 16 31
6	−63 ..... −32, 32, ... 63
7	−127 ..... −64, 64 127
8	−255 .... −128, 128 255
9	−511 .... −256, 256 511
10	−1023 .... −512, 512 1023
11	−2047 .... −1024, 1024 2047
12	−4095 ...... −2048, 2048 4097
13	−8191 .... −4096, 4096 8191
14	−16383 .... −8192, 8192 16383
15	−32767 .... −16384, 16384 32767

pair by the corresponding Huffman code. The amplitude part of the ac coefficients is divided into 15 categories, similar to the dc coefficients, except that we now have categories 1 through 15. For example, (0,2) denotes a run of length zero and the nonzero ac coefficient of size 2. Similarly, the pair (1,4) corresponds to a run of length 1 followed by the coefficient size 4. The run length/size and corresponding Huffman codes for a few values are listed in Table 8-13. The EOB corresponds to the run length/size pair (0,0). Further, to reduce the Huffman table size for the run length/size pair, JPEG uses a fixed-length code for run lengths beyond 14. Any pair with a run length of 15 or greater is given a fixed-length code ZRL followed by the binary number representing the value in excess of 15.

Now look at the coefficients after the zigzag scan. If the difference dc coefficient value is 2, then its category is 2. The corresponding Huffman code is found to be 100. Because the amplitude of the difference dc coefficient is 2, its binary code is 10. Thus, the differential dc coefficient is Huffman coded with 10010. Next we encode the ac coefficient values. The first ac coefficient value is

Table 8-13. Run Length (RL)/Amplitude (amp.) and Huffman Codes

RL/amp.	Code word	RL/amp.	Code word		RL/amp.	Code word
0/0 (EOB)	1010	1/1	1100	...	15/0 (ZRL)	11111111001
0/1	00	1/2	11011	...	15/1	111111111110101
0/2	−1	1/3	1111001	...	...	...
0/3	100	1/4	111110110	...	...	...
0/4	1011	1/5	11111110110	...	...	...
0/5	11010	...	....	...	...	...

−9. Because −9 is followed by a run length of zero, we use the code word corresponding to 0/1 from Table 8-13, which is 00. Because −9 is the seventh entry in category 4 of Table 8-12, we pick the code 011 and append it to the code 00. Thus, the ac coefficient −9 will be coded as 00011. Similarly, we can obtain the codes for the other values of the coefficients.

8.4.5   Variable Block Size DCT Coder

A disadvantage of using fixed size DCT for image compression is that areas with details suffer severe degradation for a specified bit budget, especially at low to moderate bit rates. The HVS is more sensitive to busy areas than to regions with little or no details. This causes one to more easily notice degradations in flat areas than in busy areas. Thus, if we use smaller block size in areas of high activity and quantize more aggressively, we can hide the quantization noise amidst cluttered details and we will not be able to notice any distortions. Similarly, we can choose larger block size for areas with little activity and use light to moderate quantization. The overall effect is to achieve good quality at high compression.

One possible way to use variable block size is to decompose a larger block, say 16×16, into four 8×8 subblocks. Then each 8×8 subblock can be divided into four 4×4 subblocks and 4×4 blocks into 2×2 blocks. This type of block decomposition is known as a *quadtree* decomposition. Once the quadtree decomposition of each major block is done, then the 2-D DCT of the individual subblocks are computed, quantized, and entropy coded. If all the blocks are fully decomposed, i.e., down to 2×2 pixels, then there is no need to inform the decoder about the decomposition. However, if the block decomposition is adaptive, then not all major blocks are decomposed fully and different combinations of block division are possible. In such cases, side information must be communicated to the decoder as to how a given major block is decomposed so that the decoder can perform decoding of the compressed data properly.

An adaptive quadtree decomposition of a major block can be achieved based on a suitable criterion. A simple and mathematically tractable criterion is the block variance. Although it is a known fact that the variance does not correlate well with the HVS, it, nevertheless, is useful in determining the activity in a block—the larger the variance, the more active a block. So we compute the variance of a major block of size $N \times N$ pixels in question and compare it with a threshold. If the block variance exceeds the threshold, then divide the major block into 4 $N/2 \times N/2$ blocks. If not, do not divide it and send side information to the decoder. If the decision was to subdivide, then consider each $N/2 \times N/2$ subblock sequentially for further division. Continue the process until we are left with 2×2 blocks and send the quadtree decomposition information to the decoder.

An alternative criterion for quadtree decomposition is to use perceptually significant measures. We know that our visual perception is not isolated but depends on the surround. Therefore, we can subdivide a block if its local contrast ratio exceeds a threshold. A local contrast ratio is defined as the ratio of the mean of the neighborhood to the mean of the block under consideration. Thus, blocks with higher local contrast are perceptually more significant than those with lesser local contrast. The author of this book has developed such an adaptive, block decomposition scheme suitable for use in HDTV compression. It was found that the use of local contrast in block decomposition achieved a superior visually lossless image compression at around 40-Mb/s rates. Yet another approach to variable block size DCT coding that uses a visual masking model is described later in this chapter.

8.5   COMPRESSION IN THE WAVELET DOMAIN

Compression in the wavelet domain is similar to compression in the transform domain. First the 2-D DWT of the image to be compressed is computed. Then the coefficients in each scale or level are quantized and the quantized coefficients are entropy coded for transmission or storage. The performance of the wavelet coder depends on a number of factors. The wavelet transform compacts the input image's energy into the coefficients. Different wavelets have different energy-compacting characteristic. Thus, we need to choose the appropriate wavelet. Having fixed a wavelet, the next parameter that governs the coder performance is the quantizer. Because there are $3*L$ number of detail coefficients and one approximation for an L-level 2-D DWT, we encounter a situation similar to the TC regarding the design of the quantizers. The same optimal bit allocation rule used for the TC can also be employed here. Coefficients belonging to a given scale and orientation are quantized by the quantizer with the same number of bits. The approximation coefficients must be treated differently than the detail coefficients as they are more important. In other words, the approximation coefficients are quantized very lightly. These two issues are addressed in this section.

8.5.1   Choice of Wavelets

As we have seen before, the two-dimensional DWT is implemented as a tree-structured or octave-band subband coder. The image is first filtered by low-pass and high-pass filters and decimated by a factor of 2 in both horizontal and vertical directions. The low-pass wavelet coefficients are again filtered by the two filters and decimated. This process of filtering and subsampling the low-pass coefficients is iterated a number of times to obtain a multilevel 2-D DWT. We have also seen the relationship between the wavelet and the filters in the subband coder. Thus, the choice of a wavelet boils down to the choice of the low-pass and high-pass filters.

Linear or Nonlinear Phase

First, we assume that we are going to use FIR filters to compute the DWT. Having said that, the linear phase is preferred in imaging applications. Filters with a nonlinear phase response tend to distort the edges. Unfortunately, orthogonal wavelet transform is not possible with linear phase FIR filters. However, in subband coding the two FIR filters are designed to have perfect reconstruction of the image and therefore the filter phase is of no concern. This perfect reconstruction property still holds when the coefficients are quantized finely—a high bit rate.

Filter Length

From an implementation point of view, shorter length filters are preferred—a shorter length means fewer multiplications per pixel. Long filters introduce the annoying artifact known as *ringing*. Because ringing is a high-frequency phenomenon, quantization of high-frequency coefficients will make the ringing artifact worse. Hence, short filters are preferred.

Smoothness of Filter

A FIR filter is called regular or smooth if its repeated iteration results in a continuous function. Also, a smooth filter bank introduces much less compression artifacts. Because the 2-D DWT is implemented by iterating the low band, quantization noise in the highest level will propagate to the lower level coefficients—quantization noise in a pixel at level j will spread to four times the area in the next lower level. Therefore, smooth filters should be used to minimize compression artifacts. In an orthogonal wavelet system, the analysis and synthesis filter banks have the same length. In a biorthogonal wavelet system, the two filters have unequal lengths. In such a case, it is preferable to use shorter analysis filters and longer synthesis filters, which tend to introduce less objectionable distortion in the reconstructed images.

Orthogonality

In orthogonal wavelets, image energy is conserved. This implies that the total distortion due to quantization is equal to the sum of the distortions of the different scales. It also implies that the coefficients in different scales are independent, thus allowing us to quantize the individual scales differently. This in turn implies that we can use the optimal bit allocation rule developed for the transform coder. However, this shortcoming is not crucial in image compression.

The variances of the coefficients at different scales of a four-level 2-D DWT using a number of wavelets for the Barbara image are shown in Table 8-14. Using Table 8-14, we find that the Daubechies' "db4" wavelet has the maximum coefficient variance for the highest level, approximation coefficients, whereas the biorthogonal wavelet "bior5.5" has the least variance. These values are shown in Figures 8-15a. Figure 8-15b shows the variances of the detail coefficients.

Coding Gain

As pointed out, for an orthogonal DWT the coefficients in different scales and orientation are uncorrelated. We can therefore express the coding gain for the DWT over PCM as the ratio of the mean and geometric variances of the coefficients as given by Eq. (8-31). Table 8-15 lists the coding gain for a few images and wavelets. As expected, the Haar wavelet performs the poorest because it lacks smoothness. Remember that the coding gain is also image dependent. Because the baboon image is cluttered, it has the least coding gain over all the wavelets.

Table 8-14. Variances of Four-Level 2-D DWT Coefficients for the Barbara Image

Scale #/ orientation	db2	db4	Haar	bior5.5	coif2
1	602260	604350	563160	460000	585260
2	18670	17560	24330	7560	17620
3	32740	31520	41060	12430	28690
4	6860	4990	7560	1580	4370
5	2736	2737	3908	1609	3134
6	4161	3518	5589	1764	3378
7	1156	1216	1187	688	1304
8	393	317	564	197	331
9	888	831	1253	502	835
10	525	522	509	451	502
11	71	48	125	36	47
12	518	546	502	566	537
13	88	63	121	92	62

8.5.2   Quantization

As in transform coding, the DWT coefficients are quantized before entropy coding them. Because the variances differ significantly between detail and approximation coefficients, we allocate quantization bits to the coefficients in accordance with the optimal bit assignment rule, as discussed earlier. Once the quantizer bits are known, there are two approaches to the design of the quantizers. We can use uniform quantizers at the expense of PSNR, but the implementation is simpler. The second approach is to use the Lloyd–Max algorithm to design the quantizers optimized to the PDF of the coefficients in different scales and orientations. However, the implementation is more complex.

Another approach to the design of quantizers is to simply use the quantization matrix, which is designed on the basis of the importance of the different scales and coefficients. This method is used in the JPEG2000 standard.

8.5.3   Zero-Tree Wavelet Coding

A majority of the coefficients in a 2-D DWT of an image has zero or very nearly zero values. However, coding the positional locations of the coefficients with

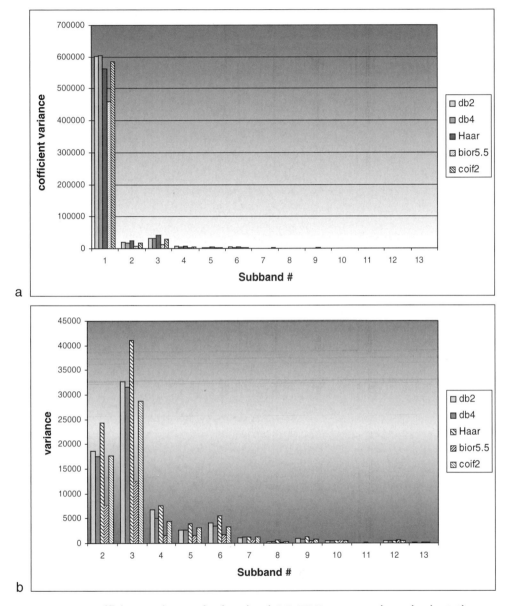

FIGURE

8-15

Coefficient variance of a four-level 2-D DWT versus scale and orientation: (a) all scales and (b) only detail coefficients. The image is Barbara. Scales are numbered sequentially starting with the highest level. Coefficient orientations are counted clockwise in each level.

Table 8-15. Coding Gain for 2-D DWT

Image	db2	db4	Haar	bior5.5	coif2
Barbara	13.82	14.31	12.78	14.93	14.21
Baboon	9.37	9.71	9.11	10.03	9.34
Cameraman	13.29	13.18	12.50	13.32	12.59
Masuda	22.80	23.72	20.86	25.16	23.72
Cornfield	10.34	10.66	9.60	11.38	10.75
Yacht	14.64	15.03	13.39	15.76	15.13
Mean	14.04	14.44	13.04	15.10	14.29

significant values can consume a large portion of the allocated bits. Zero-tree coding is an efficient way of representing the locations of the significant DWT coefficients. Embedded coding refers to a coded bit stream containing all lower rate codes whereby an encoder (or decoder) can stop coding (or decoding) at any time to achieve a target rate exactly. Embedded zero-tree wavelet (EZW) coding is, therefore, a coding scheme that represents the positions of the significant coefficients very efficiently and contains all lower rate codes implicitly so that the encoder (or decoder) can stop encoding (or decoding) until a certain target rate is reached. A coefficient x is said to be significant with respect to a specified threshold T if $|x| \geq T$.

Before we describe the EZW coding procedure, let us define a few terms. The various scales and orientations of the coefficients in a level-N 2-D DWT are denoted LL_N, HL_N, LH_N, HH_N, LL_{N-1}, HL_{N-1}, LH_{N-1}, HH_{N-1}, and so on, as shown in Figure 8-16. This wavelet decomposition is known as tree-structured or hierarchical wavelet decomposition. With the exception of the detail coefficients at the lowest level (finer resolution), every coefficient at a given scale and orientation can be related to a set of coefficients at the next higher scale (lower level) and similar orientation. The coefficient at the larger scale is called the *parent* whose *children* are the coefficients in the next finer scale, spatial location, and same orientation. *Descendants* are those coefficients at all finer scales and same orientation as the corresponding parent, which is in the coarsest scale. Similarly, for a given child, the set of all coefficients at all higher levels of similar orientation corresponding to the same location are called the *ancestors*. All parents, with the exception of the low-low band, have four children. For the low-low band, each parent has only three children.

3LL	3HL		
3LH	3HH	2HL	1HL
2LH		2HH	
1LH		1HH	

FIGURE 8-16   Depiction of a three-level 2-D wavelet decomposition.

Coding Significance Map

In EZW the scanning order of the coefficients is important and is such that no child node will be scanned before its parent. This scanning order is shown Figure 8-17. As pointed out earlier, the EZW algorithm encodes the positions and magnitudes of the significant coefficients. It can be described as follows. Four symbols are used to convey the position and sign of a significant coefficient, namely ZTR for zero-tree root, IZ for isolated zero, POS for positive significant, and NEG for negative significant. Given a threshold value T, a coefficient is a member of a zero-tree if it and all its descendants are insignificant with respect to T. An element of a zero tree for the given T is a zero-tree root if it is not the descendant of a previously found zero-tree root for that T. A flowchart of the algorithm to code the position of the significant coefficients is shown in Figure 8-18.

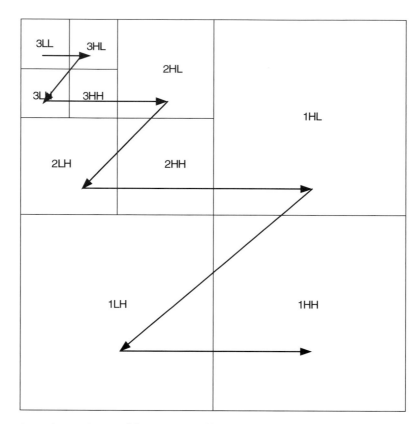

FIGURE   Scanning order used in EZW encoding of the significance map.

8-17

Successive Approximation

The second step in EZW coding is successive approximation of the significant coefficients. This successive approximation enables one to reconstruct the image with better and better quality (lower distortion) with increasing bit rate. Thus, EZW is a progressive coding scheme, which progressively improves the image quality by using more and more bits. In order to perform embedded coding, the significant coefficients are quantized using successive approximation. A sequence of thresholds $T_0, \ldots, T_{N-1}$ is used in locating significant coefficients. The thresholds are halved successively, i.e., $T_k = \dfrac{T_{k-1}}{2}$, with the initial threshold chosen such that $T_0 \geq \dfrac{|x|_{\max}}{2}$.

At the encoder (or decoder), two separate lists are maintained, one for the significance map called the *dominant* list and the other for the magnitudes of

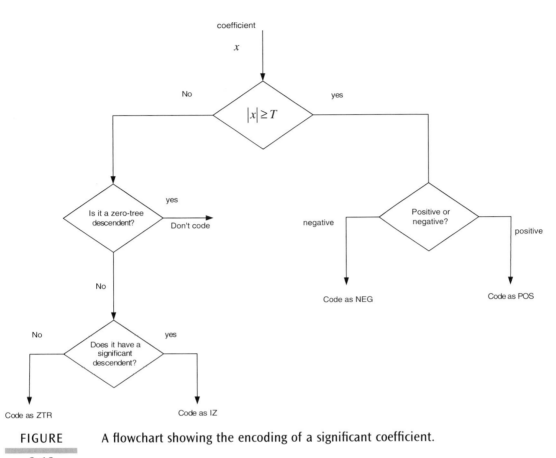

FIGURE

8-18

A flowchart showing the encoding of a significant coefficient.

the significant coefficients called the *subordinate* list. At any stage in the encoding process, the dominant list contains the positions of the coefficients that are yet to be found significant in the same relative order as the initial scan. That is, all the coefficients in a given level will appear in the initial dominant list prior to the coefficients in the next level. The subordinate list will contain the magnitudes of those coefficients that have been found to be significant. For each given threshold, the two lists are scanned only once.

In a dominant pass, coefficients in the list are compared to the threshold T_k to determine if they are significant and their sign if they are found significant. This significance map is zero-tree encoded using one of the four symbols mentioned before. Whenever a coefficient is encoded as significant, its magnitude will be appended to the subordinate list and that coefficient in the DWT space is set to zero so that it is not coded again.

Following a dominant pass, a subordinate pass takes place. In a subordinate pass, all the coefficient magnitudes are scanned and the quantization intervals

63	-34	49	10	7	13	-12	7
-31	23	14	-13	3	4	6	-1
15	14	3	-12	5	-7	3	9
-9	-7	-14	8	4	-2	3	2
-5	9	-1	47	4	6	-2	2
3	0	-3	2	3	-2	0	4
2	-3	6	-4	3	6	3	6
5	11	5	6	0	3	-4	4

FIGURE 8×8 2-D DWT coefficients used to explain the EZW encoding procedure.

8-19

(step sizes) are halved to refine the quantization to an additional bit of precision. The magnitudes fall at any point within the quantization intervals. For practical reasons, we take the magnitude to be represented by the midpoint of the respective interval. This refinement information is encoded as a single bit, a "1" bit if the magnitude is in the upper half of the quantization interval and a "0" if it falls in the lower half of the interval. This string of binary symbols produced during the subordinate pass is entropy encoded. This alternating process of scanning the two lists continues until a target bit rate is met.

Example

The EZW coding procedure is best explained by a simple example. Let us consider a three-level 2-D DWT of 8×8 pixels as shown in Figure 8-19. This example is given in Shapiro's paper. The initial threshold is chosen to be $T_0 = 32$, as it is

Table 8-16. Significance Map in the First Dominant Pass

Scale and orientation	Coefficient value	Encoded symbol	Reconstructed value
LL3	63	POS	48
HL3	−34	NEG	−48
LH3	−31	IZ	0
HH3	23	ZTR	0
HL2	49	POS	48
HL2	10	ZTR	0
HL2	14	ZTR	0
HL2	−13	ZTR	0
LH2	15	ZTR	0
LH2	14	IZ	0
LH2	−9	ZTR	0
LH2	−7	ZTR	0
HL1	7	Z	0
HL1	13	Z	0
HL1	3	Z	0
HL1	4	Z	0
LH1	−1	Z	0
LH1	47	POS	48
LH1	−3	Z	0
LH1	−2	Z	0

greater than half the largest coefficient magnitude. Because 63 is larger than 32, it is assigned a symbol POS. Table 8-16 shows the first pass of the dominant list. The last column shows what the reconstructed value of this coefficient would be at this pass. The next coefficient in the scanning has a value of −34, which is found to be significant and negative. Therefore, it is assigned a symbol NEG, as shown in the list. Its approximate value is −48. The third element encountered is −31. Even though it is insignificant for this pass, there is a descendant with a value of 47 in the LH_1 scale that is significant with respect to the threshold value of 32. Hence the coefficient with a value of −31 is an isolated zero tree and is assigned the symbol IZ. Because it is insignificant, its reconstructed value would be zero. The fourth element in the scan is found to be insignificant (23 is less than 32) along with its descendants in HH_2 and HH_1 scales so it is assigned the zero-tree root symbol ZTR. Because the coefficient with the value 23 is zero-tree root, all its descendants will not appear in the dominant list at this pass. Next we encounter the value 49 in the HL_2 scale and it gets the symbol POS because it is significant and positive. Its reconstructed value would be 48. The element with value 48 in the same scale is a zero-tree root as its children (−12, 7, 6, −1) are insignificant as well so we assign it the symbol ZTR. Similarly, the coefficients 14 and −13 are assigned the symbol ZTR. Next, the coefficients 15, −9, and −7 in the LH_2 scale are assigned the symbol ZTR because they and their children are insignificant. However, the coefficient with value 14 is assigned the symbol IZ because one of its children 47 is significant. Following the scanning pattern, the next set of values in the dominant list are 7, 13, 3, and 4, whose parent is the coefficient in the HL_2 scale with value 49 and because they are all insignificant, we assign them the symbol Z. Note that these have no children and so get the zero symbol. Finally, the four coefficients −1, 47, −3, and 2 in the LH_1 scale get, respectively, the symbols Z, POS, Z, and Z. This completes the first dominant pass with a threshold value of 32.

We found four significant coefficients during the first dominant pass with a corresponding threshold value of 32 and a quantization interval of [32, 64). Now we enter the subordinate pass to refine the quantization intervals and encode the magnitudes with one bit. The interval [32, 64) is divided into two subintervals: [32, 48) and [48, 64). The value 63 falls in the upper half of the interval [32, 64) and will be encoded with a symbol "1". The magnitude value 34 is coded with symbol "0" as it is in the lower half of the interval. Continuing further, the magnitudes 49 and 47 will be coded with symbols "1" and "0", respectively. The first pass of the subordinate list is shown in Table 8-17. The list also shows the reconstructed values at the end of the subordinate pass. One can see that the reconstructed values are getting closer to the actual values. The magnitudes are reordered at this time so that the decoder can decode unambiguously. We set the coefficients of significance to zero before moving on to the next pass.

In the second dominant pass the threshold is set at 16 because the largest magnitude is found to be 31. Following the same procedure, the dominant list at the end of the second pass is obtained as shown in Table 8-18. In this list we find two significant values, namely −31 and 23. Moving to the second subordi-

Table 8-17. First Subordinate List

Coefficient magnitude	Code symbol	Reconstructed value
63	1	56
34	0	40
49	1	56
47	0	40

Table 8-18. Second Dominant Pass: $T = 16$

Scale and orientation	Coefficient value	Encoded symbol	Reconstructed value
LH3	−31	NEG	−24
HH3	23	POS	24
HL2	10	ZTR	0
HL2	14	ZTR	0
HL2	−13	ZTR	0
LH2	15	ZTR	0
LH2	14	ZTR	0
LH2	−9	ZTR	0
LH2	−7	ZTR	0
HH2	3	ZTR	0
HH2	−12	ZTR	0
HH2	−14	ZTR	0
HH2	8	ZTR	0

Table 8-19. Second Subordinate List

Coefficient magnitude	Code symbol	Reconstructed value
63	1	60
49	0	52
47	1	44
34	0	36
31	1	28
23	0	20

nate pass (Table 8-19), we add these two newly found magnitudes to the subordinate list. Next, each quantization interval is halved and the magnitudes are assigned the symbols "0" or "1" depending on where the magnitude values fall. Thus, the magnitudes appear as 63, 49, 47, 34, 31, and 23, in that order. Correspondingly, the code sequence for the magnitudes will be 101010. One can stop at this stage or continue further depending on the allowed target bits or distortion, as the case may be. Finally, the symbols in the dominant lists are encoded using adaptive arithmetic coding.

8.5.4   JPEG2000 Standard

The JPEG2000 standard is a wavelet-based, compression standard for still images. The standard allows both lossless and lossy compression of images. The lossless case is called *reversible* and the lossy one *irreversible*. In this standard, an image can have many components, typically three components (R, G, and B) corresponding to a color image. The essential, overall encoding procedure in the JPEG2000 standard is as follows.

1. The image to be compressed is split into its components.
2. The component images are divided into rectangular blocks called *tiles*. A component may have just one tile, in which case it is encoded as a whole. A component tile is the basic unit of the encoder or decoder, just as a macro block in MPEG.
3. Each tile is transformed into the wavelet domain using a 2-D DWT. The number of levels in the transformed image is variable.
4. The approximation and detail coefficients of the DWT image are quantized and grouped into *code blocks*. The quantization is embedded, which means that one can decode the compressed bits partially to achieve any desired level of accuracy or quality.
5. The quantized coefficients are entropy coded using adaptive arithmetic coding.
6. Markers are added to the bit stream as an error resilience measure. Error resilience enables the decoder to reconstruct those portions that are in error during wireless transmission of the bit stream.

Simplified block diagrams of the JPEG2000 encoder and decoder are shown in Figures 8-20a and 8-20b, respectively. The preprocessing functions perform component splitting, tiling, dc level shifting, and component transformation. The rest of the encoding operations are the 2-D DWT, quantization of the DWT coefficients, and entropy coding of the quantized coefficients. The decoder performs these operations in the reverse order. We now describe briefly the individual functions.

Tiling

Each component of an input image to be compressed is divided into *tiles* or blocks. All tiles in all the components must be of the same size. Also, all components are of the same size. There may be only one tile in the whole component, which means that the whole component is compressed as a single block.

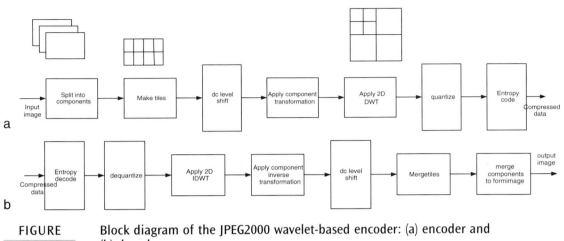

a

b

FIGURE   Block diagram of the JPEG2000 wavelet-based encoder: (a) encoder and
8-20   (b) decoder.

Tiling an image introduces blocking artifacts as in the transform coder, at low bit rates. It is, therefore, a good practice not to tile an image component into too small a size. A tile is a basic unit, just as a macro block is a basic unit in MPEG standard. Each tile is compressed independently.

DC Level Shifting

The samples in each tile are dc level shifted. DC level shifting means simply subtracting $2^P - 1$ from each sample in every tile, where P is the precision of a component. The effect of dc level shifting is to represent unsigned integers in two's complement integer format.

Component Transformation

Next, the components are transformed to a new color coordinate space. This is optional in the standard. As observed in Chapter 3, compressing a color image in the RGB space is not very efficient in terms of achievable compression ratio due to higher correlation among the RGB components. A suitable color space for more efficient compression is the luminance and chrominance space. Two component transformations are available in the standard: one for reversible transformation and the other for irreversible transformation. The irreversible component transformation (ICT) uses the following 3×3 linear transformation:

$$\begin{bmatrix} Y \\ Cr \\ Cb \end{bmatrix} = \begin{bmatrix} 0.299 & 0.587 & 0.114 \\ 0.5 & -0.41869 & -0.08131 \\ -0.16875 & -0.33126 & 0.5 \end{bmatrix} \begin{bmatrix} R \\ G \\ B \end{bmatrix}. \tag{8-32}$$

The corresponding inverse relationship is given by

$$\begin{bmatrix} R \\ G \\ B \end{bmatrix} = \begin{bmatrix} 1.0 & 1.402 & 0 \\ 1.0 & -0.71414 & -0.34413 \\ 1.0 & 0 & 1.772 \end{bmatrix} \begin{bmatrix} Y \\ Cr \\ Cb \end{bmatrix}. \tag{8-33}$$

As can be seen from Eqs. (8-32) and (8-33), rounding the components to integers in the forward and inverse transformations cause errors, which result in the loss of information even in the absence of quantization.

Reversible component transformation (RCT) is used for both lossless and lossy compression of images. Therefore the component transformation should be such that it introduces no rounding errors in the forward and inverse conversion processes. As a result, it has the form of the YUV color space transformation, where U and V are the color differences. The forward and inverse component transformations for the RCT are given by

$$\begin{bmatrix} Y \\ V \\ U \end{bmatrix} = \begin{bmatrix} \left\lfloor \dfrac{R + 2G + B}{4} \right\rfloor \\ R - G \\ B - G \end{bmatrix} \tag{8-34}$$

$$\begin{bmatrix} G \\ R \\ B \end{bmatrix} = \begin{bmatrix} Y - \left\lfloor \dfrac{U + V}{4} \right\rfloor \\ V + G \\ U + G \end{bmatrix}, \tag{8-35}$$

where $\lfloor x \rfloor$ is the floor operation. Note the ordering in Eq. (8-35). Once the green component is found, the red and blue components can be recovered using green and U and V components.

Wavelet Transform

A 2-D discrete wavelet transform is applied to each tile. The number of levels of the DWT is variable and is left to the encoder, which determines the number of levels to use based on the image characteristics and compression ratio to be achieved. Only dyadic decompositions are allowed in part I of the standard. Dyadic decomposition means that each subband has half the number of rows and columns of the previous lower level band.

The 2-D DWT is separable and is implemented in a row–column fashion of a two-channel subband coder. The first level results in four subbands denoted

Table 8-20. Daubechies 9/7 Analysis/Synthesis Filter Impulse Responses

Sample index	Analysis filter bank		Synthesis filter bank	
	Low pass	High pass	Low pass	High pass
0	0.6029490182	1.1150870525	1.1150870525	0.6029490182
±1	0.2668641184	−0.5912717631	0.5912717631	−0.2668641184
±2	−0.0782232665	−0.0575435263	−0.0575435263	−0.0782232665
±3	−0.0168641184	0.0912717631	−0.0912717631	0.0168641184
±4	0.0267487574			0.0267487574

Table 8-21. Le Gall's 5/3 Analysis/Synthesis Filter Impulse Responses

Sample index	Analysis filter bank		Synthesis filter bank	
	Low pass	High pass	Low pass	High pass
0	6/8	1	1	6/8
±1	2/8	−1/2	1/2	−2/8
±2	−1/8			−1/8

1LL, 1HL, 1LH, and 1HH. The numeral 1 denotes the level number of the subband, the first letter L or H denotes low pass or high pass in the row dimension, and the second letter denotes the column dimension. Because a tree-structured decomposition is used, the 1LL band is again decomposed into the next level subbands 2LL, 2HL, 2LH, and 2HH. This process of decomposition of the LL band is repeated N times to obtain an N-level 2-D DWT of the component tiles. For the irreversible transform the default 1-D filter bank used in the standard is the Daubechies 9/7 filter. The analysis low-pass filter has nine taps and the high-pass filter has seven taps. The synthesis low-pass filter has seven taps whereas the synthesis high-pass filter has nine taps. The default filter for the reversible transform is the Le Gall's 5/3-tap filter. The filter impulse responses are listed in Tables 8-20 and 8-21 for the two cases.

Figure 8-21 shows the frequency responses and phase responses of the analysis and synthesis filters for the irreversible transform. Similar responses are shown in Figure 8-22 for the reversible transform.

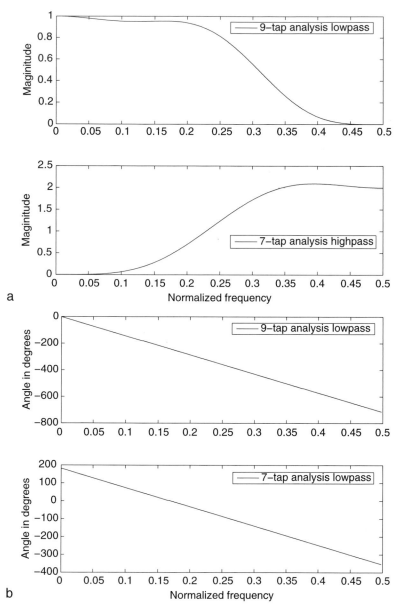

FIGURE

8-21

Frequency responses of default Daubechies's filters for the irreversible transform: (a) magnitude response of 9/7 analysis filters, (b) corresponding phase responses, (c) magnitude response of 9/7 synthesis filters, and (d) corresponding phase response.

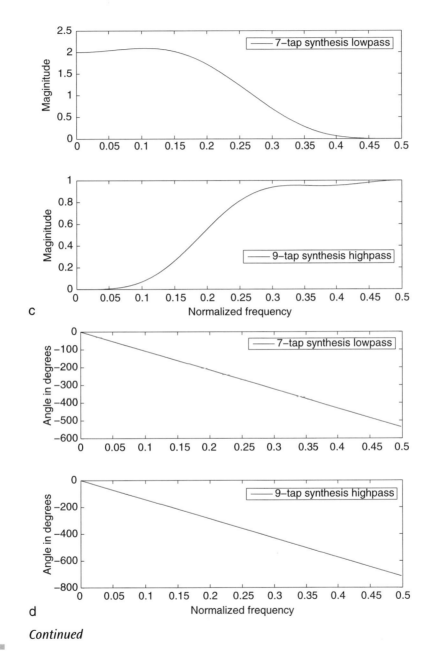

FIGURE

8-21

Continued

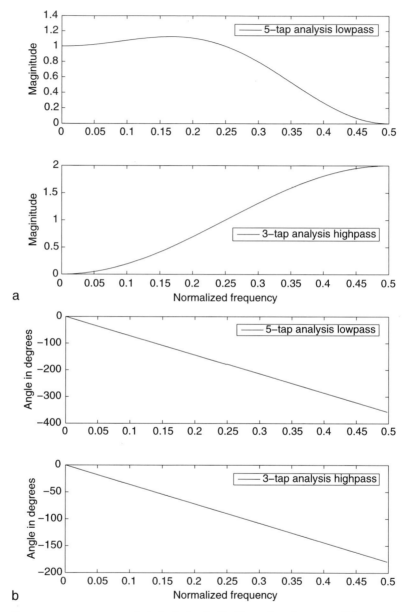

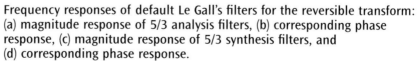

FIGURE

8-22

Frequency responses of default Le Gall's filters for the reversible transform:
(a) magnitude response of 5/3 analysis filters, (b) corresponding phase
response, (c) magnitude response of 5/3 synthesis filters, and
(d) corresponding phase response.

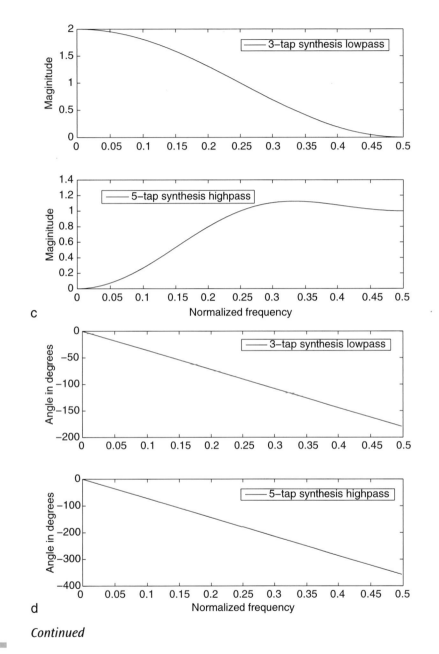

FIGURE

8-22

Continued

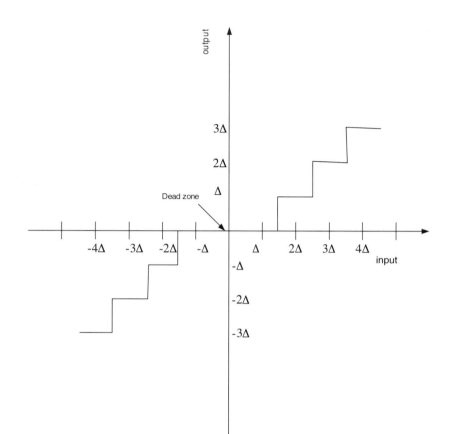

FIGURE

8-23
A uniform quantizer with a dead zone of width 2Δ and a step size Δ.

Quantization

The 2-D DWT coefficients are quantized to reduce their dynamic range in order to compress the amount of data. JPEG2000 uses uniform scalar quantization with a dead zone of fixed size in part I. In part II trellis-coded quantization is also allowed. A uniform scalar quantizer with a dead zone has decision intervals of constant width Δ except in the dead zone, whose width is 2Δ, as shown in Figure 8-23. The reconstruction levels are the midpoints of the decision intervals, except in the dead zone. We can formally express the uniform quantization process as

$$q_b = sign(x_b) \left\lfloor \frac{|x_b|}{\Delta_b} \right\rfloor, \tag{8-36}$$

where x_b is the actual coefficient value in a subband, Δ_b is the step size for the subband, q_b is its quantized value, and $\lfloor x \rfloor$ is the floor operation. The uniform quantizer assigns the index of the decision interval in which x_b falls. The inverse quantization or *dequantization* of q is given by

$$\hat{x}_b = \begin{cases} 0, & q_b = 0 \\ sign(q_b)\left(|q_b| + \dfrac{1}{2}\right)\Delta_b, & q_b \neq 0 \end{cases}. \tag{8-37}$$

The standard allows for one quantization step size per subband. The step size of each subband depends on its dynamic range, which in turn depends on the bit width of the original image and on the filter used in implementing the 2-D DWT.

The JPEG2000 standard uses the uniform quantization with a dead zone in an *embedded* fashion. As pointed out earlier, embedded quantization means that each bit plane, starting with the most significant bit, of the quantized coefficients is encoded separately. This allows one the ability to reconstruct the image with progressively improving quality or precision. The uniform quantizer in Eq. (8-36) lends itself to bit plane coding. Assume that a uniform quantizer with a dead zone has M reconstruction levels, where $M = 2^m$. Then the quantizer dynamic range is $2^m\Delta$. Because $2^m\Delta = 2^{m-n}2^n\Delta = 2^{m-n}\Delta'$, and where $\Delta' = 2^n\Delta$, a uniform quantizer with $M' = 2^{m-n}$ levels has a step size $\Delta' = 2^n\Delta$. Thus, if only $m - n$ bits instead of m bits of quantization are used in the reconstruction, then the quantizer step size is scaled by 2^n.

Entropy Coding

The quantized wavelet coefficients are entropy coded using an adaptive arithmetic coding scheme. The JPEG2000 standard has many provisions built into it in forming the coded bit stream to achieve spatial and SNR scalability, random access, error resilience, most importantly *region of interest* (ROI) coding, and possible inclusion of intellectual property rights. In order to realize these features, it divides the quantized coefficient tiles into *precincts* and *code blocks*. A code block is the basic unit that carries the coded bit stream. A precinct is a group of rectangular blocks spatially colocated at the different orientations within a subband. A typical size of a precinct is 64×64 and the minimum size allowed is 32×32. A code block is a rectangular sub-region of a precinct (see Figure 8-24).

For the purpose of entropy coding, code blocks are scanned in a raster order. Within each code block, each bit plane is scanned in a particular order as shown in Figure 8-25. As seen from Figure 8-25, scanning starts with the first four bits of the first column. Next the first four bits of the second column are scanned and the process is continued until the width of the code block is scanned. After scanning the first four bits of the code block, the second scan starts with the second four bits of the first column, etc.

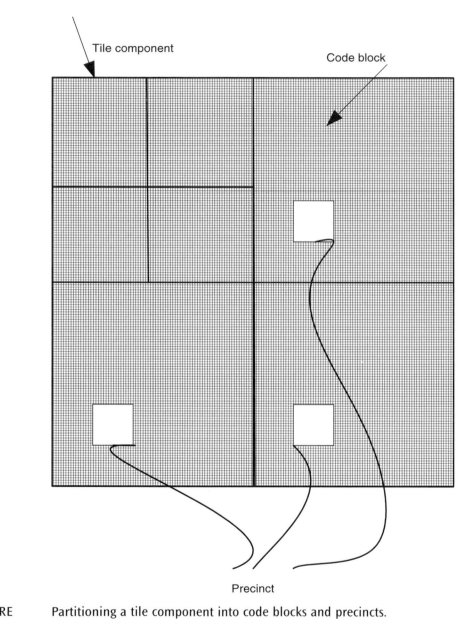

FIGURE   Partitioning a tile component into code blocks and precincts.

8-24

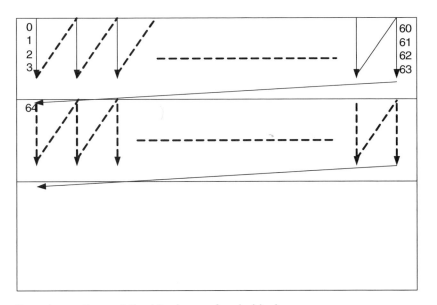

FIGURE

8-25

Scanning pattern of the bit planes of code blocks.

8.6   VIDEO CODING PRINCIPLES

All the compression techniques discussed so far pertain to still images. Video and movie pictures are motion images, which consist of a sequence of still images creating the illusion of motion. Because these sequences are captured at say 24 FPS rate for the movie, there is considerable redundancy between successive frames in the sequence. Of course, this correlation vanishes when scene changes occur. Therefore, one can reduce data in sequence images by exploiting the *interframe* or temporal correlation. This is often done by coding the difference of images rather than coding each individual frames. However, simple differencing may still contain sufficient amount of data if there is motion of objects between consecutive frames. As a result, we need to estimate the amount of motion that the objects have undergone and compensate for the estimated motion before subtracting the frames. This is known as *motion compensated prediction*. When consecutive image frames are subtracted after motion compensation, the resulting difference images have a much reduced dynamic range and result in a large compression ratio.

Interframe correlation can also be reduced in the frequency domain. Specifically, the phase function of the Fourier transform contains information regarding the temporal shifts of objects in a scene. However, extracting the temporal displacements from the incremental phase function of the Fourier spectrum is not as simple and accurate as the spatial domain approach. The Fourier domain idea is also applicable to other transforms, such as the DCT.

One can also implement the idea of temporal correlation reduction using wavelet transform. In this case, the wavelet transform is carried out in the temporal dimension. Another approach is to apply three-dimensional DCT to exploit both spatial and temporal correlation in a sequence image to achieve high compression ratios that cannot be obtained by either spatial or temporal techniques alone.

This section describes the basic principles behind some of these interframe, coding techniques and paves the way for introduction of the MPEG standard.

8.6.1   Temporal Prediction in the Pixel Domain

A block diagram illustrating the idea of a predictive coder suitable for compressing a sequence image is shown in Figure 8-26. As seen from Figure 8-26, the system estimates the amount of motion that a current pixel in the current frame to be encoded undergoes relative to the reference frame. The reference frame is the previously encoded frame. The amount of motion is conveyed as a vector whose elements are the x and y displacements relative to the current pixel location. This is shown in Figure 8-27. The pixel in the reference frame with this offset is then subtracted from the current pixel and the differential is quantized and entropy coded. The *motion vector* is also entropy coded as side information, which is used by the decoder in reconstructing the image. We have already discussed quanization and entropy coding in the context of still image compression so let us focus our attention on motion estimation.

8.6.1.1   *Motion Estimation*

Objects in a scene are imaged onto a plane. Therefore the motion in the image plane is the apparent motion. Estimating motion between two consecutive frames in the spatial domain can be achieved by detecting changes in the pixel values. However, these changes may be due to variations in lighting conditions, electronic noise, or apparent motion of objects. Moreover, object motion in the 3-D space could be translational or rotational due to rigid body motion. Thus, motion estimation in a 2-D image plane is not a simple task. It is even more complicated if the motion is due to deformable bodies, where pixels within an object could undergo translational motion.

We make the assumptions that the object motion is a simple translational (up, down and left, right) one and that it is small. With these simplifying

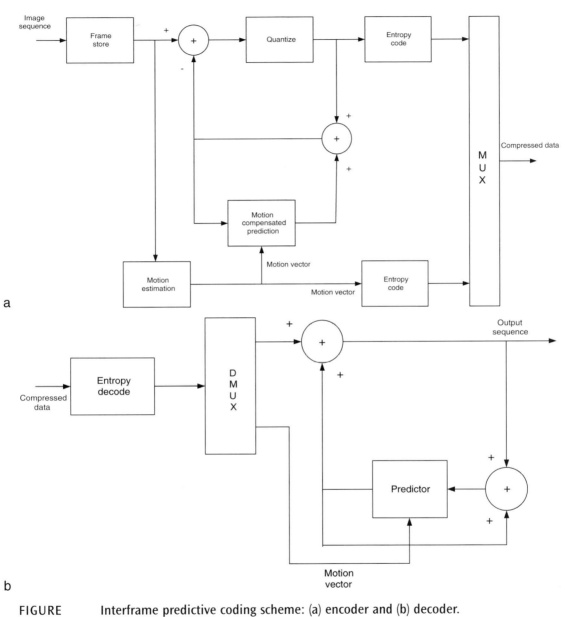

FIGURE   Interframe predictive coding scheme: (a) encoder and (b) decoder.

8-26

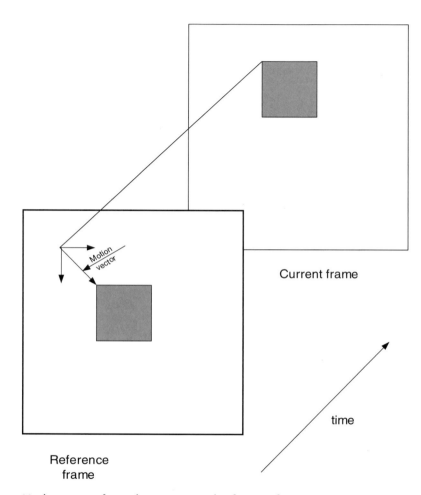

Current frame

Motion vector

Reference frame

time

FIGURE

8-27

Motion vector from the current and reference frames.

assumptions, we can detect the displacement of a pixel in the current frame from that in a reference frame by matching a rectangular region containing the current pixel in the current frame with a larger region in the reference frame. This larger region is called the *search* window. Given the sizes of the two rectangular regions, motion estimation depends on the criterion used to match the two blocks. The minimum mean square error is the traditional matching criterion used, as it is mathematically tractable. However, the matching process involves multiplications and, depending on the matching block and search window sizes, the computational burden can be overwhelming. In practice, therefore, *mean absolute difference* (MAD) is used as the matching criterion. MAD, which is found to be adequate, is expressed as

$$MAD(m,n) = \frac{1}{N^2} \sum_{i=0}^{N-1} \sum_{j=1}^{N-1} |x_t[m+i,n+j] - x_{t-1}[m+r+i,n+s+j]|, \, -P \le r, s \le P,$$

(8-38)

where x_t and x_{t-1} are the current and previous frames, respectively, $[m,n]$ is the current pixel location, $[r,s]$ is the displacement within the search window, and $N \times N$ is the block size. Here we assume the search area to be a rectangular region of size $P \times P$ pixels. The displacement vector $\Delta = (\delta x, \delta y)$ relative to $[m,n]$ is that value for which MAD in Eq. (8-38) is a minimum over the search area. Typical values for N and P are 16 and 8, respectively.

Block matching as just defined is optimal for the given criterion, as it exhaustively searches all the pixels within the search area. However, it is computationally intensive. Several suboptimal procedures for block matching have been advanced, all of which are aimed at reducing the number of searches required to arrive at the result.

The motion estimation just described has an accuracy of one pixel. This is usually not sufficient to achieve higher compression. Therefore, motion displacements to fractional pixel accuracy can be achieved by first interpolating pixel values between appropriate fractional pixels and then applying the block matching technique. Such techniques are used in the MPEG standard.

8.6.2   Wavelet-Based Interframe Coding

The wavelet-based spatiotemporal scheme uses subbands at different scales to estimate the motion vectors. Each frame of image in the sequence is subband coded to a specified number of levels. The assumption is that moving areas in the subbands remain highly correlated. Thus, motion displacements are calculated from the detail coefficients at the highest levels first using the block matching technique. The displacement estimates are then refined at the next higher resolution using the values obtained in the previous lower resolution subbands and so on. One such refinement procedure is given by

$$\mathbf{mv}_{l-1} = 2\mathbf{mv}_l + \Delta\mathbf{mv}_l,$$

(8-39)

where $\mathbf{mv}_l$ is the motion vector at level l and $\Delta\mathbf{mv}_l$ is the incremental displacement at level l. Because the subbands are obtained using dyadic sampling, we use block sizes of increasing size from higher level to lower level. A block diagram of interframe coding in the wavelet domain is shown in Figure 8-28.

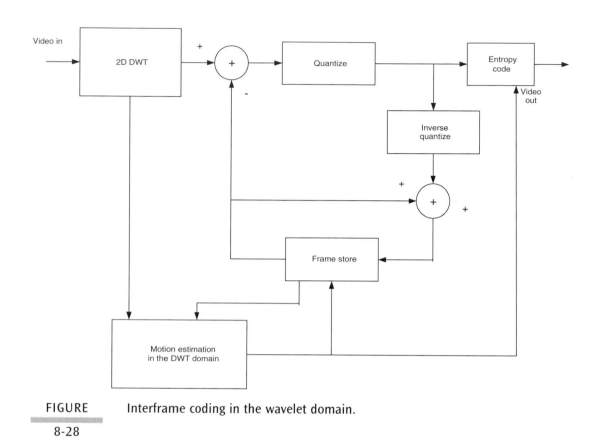

FIGURE

8-28

Interframe coding in the wavelet domain.

8.6.3   Interframe Coding Using Three-Dimensional DCT

An alternative method of exploiting spatiotemporal correlation in video images is to apply three-dimensional DCT. As shown earlier, with DCT being very close to the optimal KL transform in its decorrelation property, it is a good candidate for video compression. The intent is to apply the DCT to a group of temporally adjacent frames in the spatial and temporal dimensions. This generates a sequence of 2-D DCT coefficients, most of which tend to zero after quantization. This, therefore, yields much higher compression than just spatial domain coding alone.

An interframe video coding based on 3-D DCT is shown in Figure 8-29. It consists of a subsystem that detects scene changes and accordingly adjusts the number of frames to be used in computing the 3-D DCT. The rest of the system contains the quantizer and entropy coder. A brief description of the system follows.

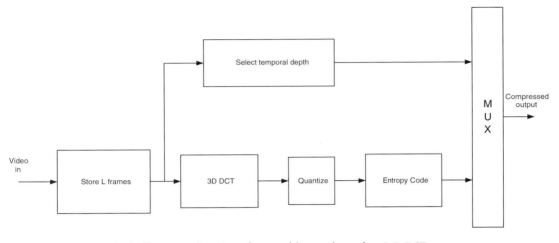

FIGURE   Block diagram of an interframe video coder using 3-D DCT.

8-29

8.6.3.1   *Temporal Depth*

As we know from the properties of the DCT, high energy compaction is achieved by the DCT when pixels are highly correlated. In a video or movie, a scene change creates a frame that is not well correlated with the other frames in the previous scene. A scene change may be detected in a number of ways. One of them is to compute the correlation coefficient between successive frames and, if the correlation coefficient falls below a threshold, a scene change is signaled. We need to use a number of frames in the temporal dimension that are well correlated between scene changes. If we use a large number of frames in computing the 3-D DCT, a large frame store is needed. This creates latency in the system, which may not be acceptable. However, too few frames will not yield good compression ratios. Thus, there is a trade-off between *temporal depth*, i.e., number of consecutive frames in the 3-D stack, and system resource and latency.

8.6.3.2   *Three-Dimensional DCT*

For a group of frames $x[m,n,t]$, $0 \leq t \leq L-1$, the 3-D DCT is defined as

$$X(u,v,w) = \frac{\alpha(u)\beta(v)\gamma(w)}{N\sqrt{L}} \sum_{t=0}^{L-1} \sum_{m=0}^{N-1} \sum_{n=0}^{N-1} x[m,n,t]\cos(\theta_1)\cos(\theta_2)\cos(\theta_3), \quad (8\text{-}40)$$

where $0 \leq u,v \leq N-1$, $0 \leq w \leq L-1$, $\theta_1 = (2m+1)\dfrac{\pi u}{2N}$, $\theta_2 = (2n+1)\dfrac{\pi v}{2N}$, $\theta_3 = (2t+1)\dfrac{\pi w}{2L}$ and

$$\alpha(k) = \begin{cases} 1, & k = 0 \\ \sqrt{2}, & k \neq 0 \end{cases}.$$

An alternative method of computing the 3-D DCT of the group of frames is to express it in terms of the first frame in the group and a sequence of differential frames. To see how this is done, define the consecutive differential frames as

$$d[m,n,t] = x[m,n,t] - x[m,n,t-1]. \tag{8-41}$$

We can then express a frame at time t in terms of the first frame in the group and the differentials as

$$x[m,n,t] = x[m,n,0] + \sum_{s=0}^{t} d[m,n,s], \quad 0 \leq t \leq L-1, d[m,n,0] \equiv 0. \tag{8-42}$$

Using Eq. (8-42) in Eq. (8-40), we can show that the 3-D DCT of the group is given by

$$X(u,v,w) = \sqrt{L} X_{2D}(u,v)\delta(w) + D(u,v,w), \tag{8-43}$$

where $X_{2D}(u,v)$ is the usual 2-D DCT of the first frame in the group, $\delta(w)$ is the unit impulse, and $D(u,v,w)$ is the 3-D DCT of the differential frames and is given by

$$D(u,v,w) = \frac{\alpha(w)}{\sqrt{L}} \sum_{t=0}^{L-1} \left\{ \sum_{s=0}^{t} D_{2D}(u,v,s) \right\} \cos\left(\frac{(2t+1)\pi w}{2L} \right) \tag{8-44}$$

where $D_{2D}(u,v,s)$ is the 2-D DCT of the sth differential frame in the group. We interpret Eq. (8-43) as consisting of two components: the 2-D DCT of the first frame (akin to the intraframe in the parlance of pixel domain prediction) and the 2-D DCT of successive frame differentials (analogous to P frames in MPEG). If there is no motion, then all the differentials will be nearly zero and most of the energy in the sequence will be contained in the DCT of the first frame. If there is motion, then the differentials will carry the motion information, which will manifest as significant coefficient values. Thus, the 3-D DCT as expressed in Eq. (8-43) will be able to track the motion.

8.6.3.3   Quantization

Because the 3-D DCT consists of the 2-D DCT of the first frame and the differentials, we can use perceptually weighted uniform quantizers as used in the MPEG standard.

8.6.3.4   Zigzag Scanning

Because we have added an extra dimension to the DCT, there are many possible scanning patterns to consider that will result in larger zero runs. One straightforward extension of the 2-D scanning procedure is to scan across the temporal dimension first and then across the spatial dimensions.

8.6.3.5   Entropy Coding

Huffman coding similar to the one used in JPEG and MPEG may be used or adaptive Huffman coding may be more efficient in this case.

8.6.4   Role of Human Visual Perception in Image and Video Coding

So far our discussion has been on techniques of redundancy removal in images without any reference to an observer. After all, in almost all imaging applications, a human is the end user. Therefore, it is imperative that a coding system takes into consideration the peculiarities of the HVS so that *irrelevant* data need not be coded. What is irrelevant is based on the characteristics of the HVS so that discarding such data will not incur any visual impairment in the reconstructed images.

We have already described some of the HVS phenomena, such as contrast sensitivity, trichromatic model, and opponent color perception in Chapter 3. This section focuses on two aspects of visual perception in the context of video coding, namely the threshold of visibility and masking phenomenon. Visibility threshold is used to determine the quantization step sizes of the uniform quantizers used in both DCT and wavelet-based coding systems. The masking phenomenon is useful in determining how different areas of an image should be treated in terms of visual importance.

8.6.4.1   Quantization Matrix for DCT Domain Coding

The default quantization matrix for the luminance image used in the JPEG standard was arrived at by experimentation. However, we can use an appropriate analytical model to determine the quantization matrix. In one such instance, a luminance-only detection model is used that approximates the log of the contrast sensitivity function by a parabola in the log spatial frequency. This luminance-only threshold as a function of the spatial frequency is given by

$$\log T_Y(m,n) = \log \frac{s \cdot B_Y}{r_Y + (1-r_Y)\cos^2 \theta_{m,n}} + k_Y (\log f(m,n) - \log f_Y)^2, \quad 0 \le m,n \le N-1$$

$$(8\text{-}45)$$

where $T_Y(m,n)$ is the threshold of visibility (inverse of sensitivity) for the luminance component at the spatial frequency $f(m,n)$ associated with the m, nth DCT coefficient, $s.B_Y$ is the minimum luminance threshold that occurs at the spatial frequency f_Y, and k_Y determines the steepness of the parabola, and $0 < r_Y < 1$. The spatial frequency is related to the pixel size and is expressed as

$$f(m,n) = \frac{1}{2N} \sqrt{\left(\frac{m}{W_x}\right)^2 + \left(\frac{n}{W_y}\right)^2}, \tag{8-46}$$

where W_x and W_y are the horizontal and vertical sizes of a pixel in degrees of visual angle, respectively. The function $\theta_{m,n}$ is defined by

$$\theta_{m,n} = \arcsin\left\{\frac{2f(m,0)f(0,n)}{f^2(m,n)}\right\}. \tag{8-47}$$

For a given viewing condition, the quantization step size for the m, nth DCT coefficient is determined as follows. For a linear display the change in luminance ΔY per unit quantization with L quantization levels is

$$\Delta Y = \frac{Y_{max} - Y_{min}}{L}, \tag{8-48}$$

where Y_{max} and Y_{min} are the maximum and minimum display luminance values. This ΔY divides into the threshold to yield the quantization matrix and is expressed by

$$Q_{m,n} = \frac{T(m,n)}{\alpha_m \alpha_n \left(\dfrac{\Delta Y}{2}\right)}. \tag{8-49}$$

In Eq. (8-49),

$$\alpha_m = \begin{cases} \sqrt{\dfrac{1}{N}}, & m = 0 \\ \sqrt{\dfrac{2}{N}}, & m \ne 0 \end{cases}.$$

Equation (8-49) gives us the flexibility to design the quantization matrix for the luminance component of an image for varying viewing conditions.

By extending the threshold of the detection model to the chrominance components, it is possible to design quantization matrices for all three components of an image in any color space for any viewing condition. That is, given the quantization matrices in the RGB space, one can obtain the corresponding matrices in any other color space, such as the Y, Cr, Cb space through appropriate color space conversion. References are provided for further details on this topic in the reference section.

8.6.4.2   *Quantization Matrix for Wavelet Domain Coding*

Similar results have been advanced for the design of quantization matrices to be used in wavelet domain compression. In particular, quantization step sizes for the 2-D DWT coefficients at different levels and orientations have been reported for the case of Daubechies 9/7 wavelets. More specifically, this work uses a luminance threshold model, which is defined by

$$\log Y = \log a + k(\log f - \log g_\theta f_0)^2. \tag{8-50}$$

Clearly this is a parabola in $\log Y$ versus $\log f$ space and the orientation θ can take on the values 1, 2, 3, or 4 corresponding to the LL, HL, LH, and HH bands. The constant parameters were determined to be $a = 0.495$, $k = 0.466$, $f_0 = 0.401$, $g_1 = 1.501$, $g_3 = 0.534$, and $g_2 = g_4 = 1$. The threshold functions for the chrominance components Cb and Cr have similar model equations to the luminance component. It was found that the threshold of visibility of the noise pattern for the Cr channel was two times larger than the luminance channel and that the Cb channel was two times larger than the Cr channel. Using these models, the quantization step size for the DWT coefficients at level l and orientation θ is found to be

$$Q_{l,\theta} = 2\frac{Y_{l,\theta}}{A_{l,\theta}} = \frac{2}{A_{l,\theta}} a \cdot 10^{k\left(\log\left(\frac{2^l f_0 g\theta}{r^2}\right)\right)}, \tag{8-51}$$

where $A_{l,\theta}$ are the basis function amplitudes and r is the display resolution in pixels/degree of visual angle and is related to the frequency and DWT level through

$$f = r2^{-l} \text{ cycles/degree}. \tag{8-52}$$

Using this method, the authors have determined the quantization step sizes of uniform quantizers, which are shown in the Table 8-22. The orientations are LL, HL, HH, and LH corresponding to the numbers 1, 2, 3, and 4, respectively.

Table 8-22. Step Sizes of Uniform Quantizers for Four-Level 9/7 2-D DWT for a Display Resolution of 32 Pixels/Degree

Component	Orientation	Level			
		1	2	3	4
Y	1	14.05	11.11	11.36	14.5
	2	23.03	14.68	12.71	14.16
	3	58.76	28.41	19.54	17.86
	4	23.03	14.69	12.71	14.16
Cb	1	55.25	46.56	48.45	59.99
	2	86.79	60.48	54.57	60.48
	3	215.84	117.45	86.74	81.23
	4	86.79	60.48	54.57	60.48
Cr	1	25.04	19.28	19.67	25.6
	2	60.02	34.34	27.28	28.5
	3	184.64	77.57	47.44	39.47
	4	60.02	34.34	27.28	28.5

An example of compressing a color image in the wavelet domain using the quantization step sizes listed in Table 8-22 is shown in Figure 8-30. The wavelet used in this example is Daubechies' "db4" filter bank, and the number of levels of wavelet decomposition used is 2. Although the quantization matrix listed in Table 8-22 is for the Daubechies' 9/7 filter bank, it performs reasonably well for the case of the "db4" wavelet. Another example of compressing a luminance image is shown in Figure 8-31. The same parameters are used in this example as in the previous one.

8.6.4.3   Use of Spatial and Temporal Masking Models

Chapter 3 described an HVS model that predicts masking phenomena in image and video signals. Spatial masking refers to an elevated threshold of visibility of noise in the vicinity of sharp edges. Typically, the eye tolerates more noise variance on the darker side of an edge and somewhat less on the brighter side. This is valid when the contrast is high. This is shown in Figure 8-32. In the low contrast case, the visibility of impairments is higher on the bright side of an edge. A similar masking effect occurs in the temporal domain. When a flash of noise for a brief duration is superimposed on a uniform background field that suddenly changes from dark to bright or from bright to dark, the visibility

FIGURE

8-30

Image compression in the wavelet domain using the quantization matrix of Table 8-22. Input Lena image is RGB 4:4:4 with 24 bits/pixel. The wavelet used is "db4" and the number of levels of 2-D DWT is 2. The PSNR for the Y, Cb, and Cr components are 37.50, 35.63, and 38.98 dB, respectively.

a   b

FIGURE

8-31

A black and white image compressed in the wavelet domain using uniform quantization with step sizes listed in Table 8-22. The wavelets and the number of levels used are the same as in Figure 8-30. The pixel depth is 8 bits/pixel. The PSNR is 30.87 dB. (a) Original image and (b) quantized/ dequantized image.

threshold is elevated for a brief period of time. The point is that such masking thresholds can be estimated using the model described in Chapter 3. In what way is this model useful in image and video compression? The answer lies in the fact that use of such a model will enable us to determine the regions in an image

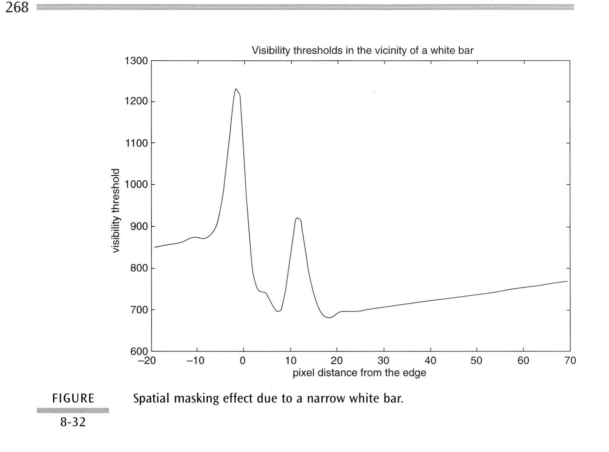

FIGURE   Spatial masking effect due to a narrow white bar.

8-32

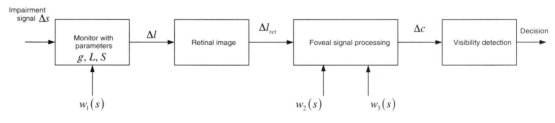

FIGURE   A linearized HVS masking model to detect noise visibility in images.

8-33

that are perceptually important that should be compressed at higher quality to achieve a visually lossless compression. Applications such as digital cinema and medical imaging call for visually lossless compression of image and video signals.

A visual model that can be used to determine the areas of importance in an image is shown in Figure 8-33. This is a linear model, although it is well known that the HVS is nonlinear. However, the justification to use a linearized model is that the impairments are small compared to the signal and that the visual system responds incrementally to such impairments around a strong signal. The model starts with a display monitor, as the images are viewed from a monitor. Because visual experience depends on viewing conditions, we assume standard viewing conditions. As shown from Figure 8-33, the model consists of three multipliers, of which the first one depends on the monitor and its input video signal and the rest depends on the visual system parameters. More specifically, the weights are given by

$$w_1 = \gamma L(s + S)^{\gamma - 1} \tag{8-53a}$$

$$w_2 = \frac{1}{l_{inh} + K_{sat} \times Max\{(l_{rec} - l_{inh}), 0\}} \tag{8-53b}$$

$$w_3 = c_{AGC} \tag{8-53c}$$

In Eq. (8-53a), γ, L, and S are constants specific to a display monitor. Typical values for an 8-bit monitor are 2.2, 0.00035 cd/m^2, and 15, respectively, for the three parameters. The signal l_{rec} is the photoreceptor response and l_{inh} is the inhibitor response. As seen from Figure 8-33, the automatic gain control (AGC) mechanism produces a response c_{AGC} to the retinal signal, which accounts for the masking phenomena due to its limiting characteristics. All signal quantities in Eq. (8-53) are spatiotemporal. Once the weights are calculated as a function of the input video signal, we add noise to the system that undergoes through the same system blocks as the signal. The noise level is increased until the impairment is detected by the system. The impairment detection consists of summing the square errors over a small spatial extent and integrating over time. If this value exceeds a threshold, then the noise is visible. We can, therefore, determine the masking signal required in different areas of an image at the threshold of visibility. We can also, in a similar manner, determine the masking signal in the temporal domain.

We discussed briefly the idea of adaptive, variable block size DCT in the section on transform coding of images, where we used block variance as a criterion for subdivision. Here, we describe a procedure for quadtree decomposition based on the linear visual masking model as described earlier.

The decomposition procedure is described as follows.

1. For a specific monitor and normal viewing conditions, compute the monitor light output as a function of its input pixel values.

2. Compute the weight w_1 using Eq. (8-53a).

3. Scan the image from left to right, top to bottom. For each $N \times N$ block of pixels, compute the mean and contrast ratio over a suitably chosen spatial neighborhood.

4. Find the inhibitor response l_{inh} at each pixel location by convolving the monitor light output with g_{inh} and then adding a bias L_a.

5. Compute the weights w_2 and w_3 from Eqs. (8-53b) and (8-53c), respectively.

6. Next, compute the impairment metric D by summing the squares of Δc_{sat} over the $N \times N$ block.

7. Split the $N \times N$ block into 4 $N/2 \times N/2$ blocks if the metric Δc_{sat} exceeds a threshold. Repeat steps 6 and 7 until 2×2 pixel blocks are left. If not, do not split the block and go to the next $N \times N$ block in the scan order.

The author of this book has tried out this adaptive block decomposition using this procedure for DCT coding of motion pictures for digital cinema. This scheme has resulted in better and visually meaningful block decomposition with visually lossless quality of reconstruction in the 40-Mb/s range.

8.6.5   MPEG Standard

Overview

MPEG is an acronym for Moving Picture Experts Group. It is a group formed under the auspices of the International Organization for Standardization (ISO) and the International Electrotechnical Commission (IEC). MPEG was given formal status within ISO/IEC. Original work started by the MPEG group culminated in a standard called MPEG-1. The MPEG-1 standard itself comprises five parts: 1, systems; 2, video; 3, audio; 4, compliance testing; and 5, software simulation. MPEG-1 has been targeted for multimedia applications. It was optimized for compressing progressive images of size 352×240 at 30 FPS at data rates of about 1.5 Mb/s. The standard does not support interlaced video. MPEG-1 delivers an image quality comparable to VHS.

With increasing demand for digital TV, the MPEG group came up with a second standard called MPEG-2 aimed at broadcast TV. It supports interlaced scanning, larger picture sizes, and data rates at 10 Mb/s or higher. MPEG-2 is deployed for the distribution of digital television, including SDTV, DVD, and HDTV. The MPEG-2 video part of the standard defines five *profiles* to support a wide range of capabilities from MPEG-1 to very advanced HDTV compression. A straightforward extension of MPEG-1 is the main profile (MP) in MPEG-2.

The MPEG-4 standard is aimed at very low data rates as well as content-based interactivity and universal access, which includes error-prone wireless networks. MPEG-7 and MPEG-21 are in the developmental stage. MPEG-7, titled *multimedia content description interface*, will standardize the description of the various types of multimedia metadata information. However, the role of MPEG-21 is to establish an open framework for multimedia delivery and use, thereby enabling the use of multimedia resources covering a broad spectrum of networks and devices.

In what follows, we will attempt to describe the basic ideas behind the video compression part of MPEG-1 and MPEG-2 standards. The MPEG standards documents are grouped into two classes. The *normative* sections define the actual standard. Actually, the standard only defines the compressed bit stream and the decoder simply follows the standards rule in reconstructing the video. The *informative* section of the standards contains the necessary background information on the encoding/decoding principles.

MPEG VideoTerminology

In MPEG terminology, a picture is a frame of image with its components, namely Y, Cb, and Cr. The video sequence comprises group of pictures (GOP). Each GOP consists of three types of pictures, which are termed I, P, and B. I pictures (intracoded pictures) are coded by themselves without any reference pictures. These are also called *key frames*. Key frames are typically the frames that occur at scene changes. Therefore, a key frame has very little correlation with the frames in the previous scene. P pictures (predictive-coded pictures) are coded with reference to preceding I or P pictures in the sequence. However, B pictures (bidirectionally predictive-coded pictures) are coded with reference to both preceding and future I or P pictures in the GOP. A typical GOP in a video sequence at the encoder side is shown in Figure 8-34.

When the pictures in a GOP are decoded, the ordering of the decoded pictures within the GOP has to be changed before displaying, as shown in Figure 8-35. This is because the B pictures depend on both previous and future pictures.

The basic encoding/decoding unit of an MPEG picture is the *macroblock*. It consists of a 16 × 16 block of pixels from the luminance component and an 8 × 8 block from each of the chrominance components. This arrangement of a macroblock is shown in Figure 8-36.

In order to accommodate rate control strategy for constant output bit rate and signaling changes to coding parameters, each picture in the sequence is divided into slices. A slice is made up of several contiguous macroblocks in raster scan order, as shown in Figure 8-37.

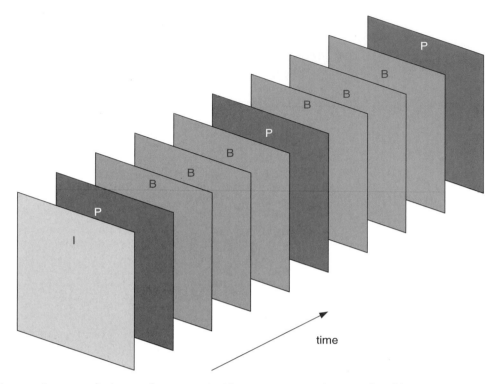

FIGURE   A group of pictures in an MPEG video sequence at the encoder side.

8-34

MPEG Coder/Decoder

The MPEG video encoder uses predictive coding in the DCT domain and is shown in Figure 8-38a. A brief description of the predictors and quantizers is as follows.

Coding I Pictures

Because I pictures are compressed without reference to other pictures, the compression of I pictures uses the DCT-based coding as discussed earlier. MPEG specifies default quantization matrices for the luminance and chrominance components. The DC coefficients are compressed using the DPCM scheme. The DC differentials are represented in magnitude range and size category form, as explained previously. Huffman codes are generated for the size category of both luminance and chrominance components. Then a DC differential is encoded by first using the corresponding Huffman code for its size category followed by its position in the range. The quantized AC coefficients are zigzag scanned, run length coded, and then the size/run length pair is Huffman coded.

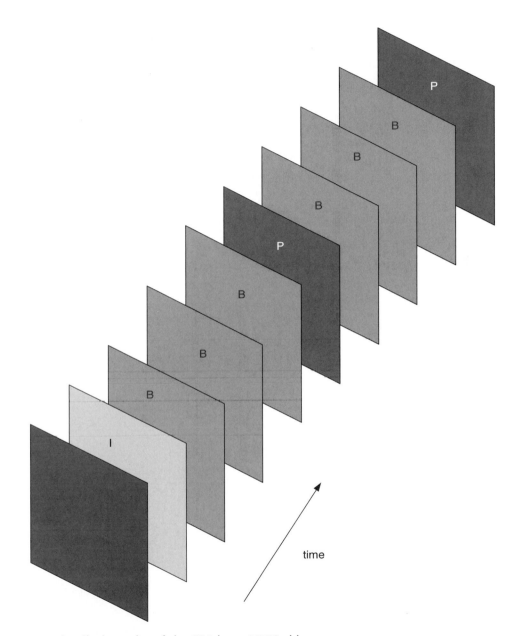

FIGURE

8-35

The display order of the GOP in an MPEG video sequence.

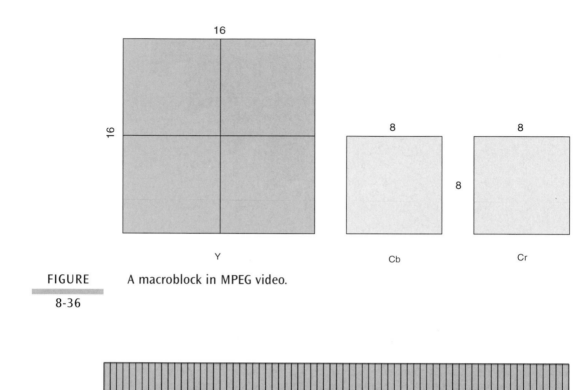

FIGURE   A macroblock in MPEG video.

8-36

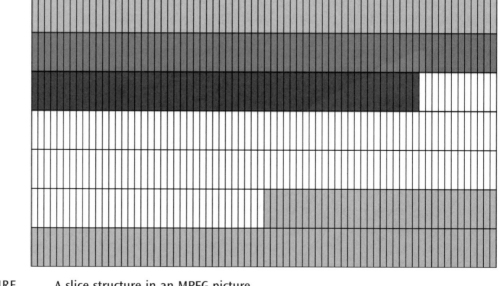

FIGURE   A slice structure in an MPEG picture.

8-37

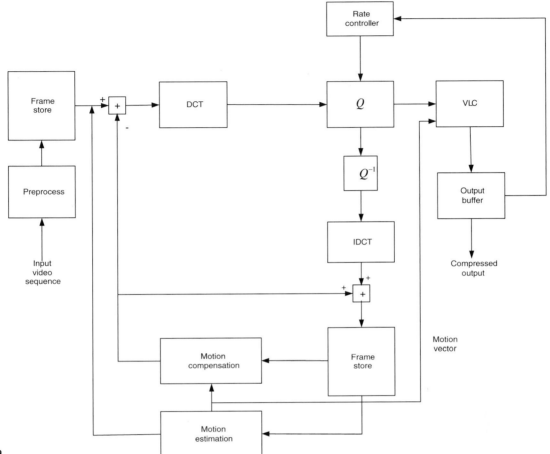

a

FIGURE   A simplified block diagram of an MPEG coder: (a) encoder and (b) decoder.

8-38

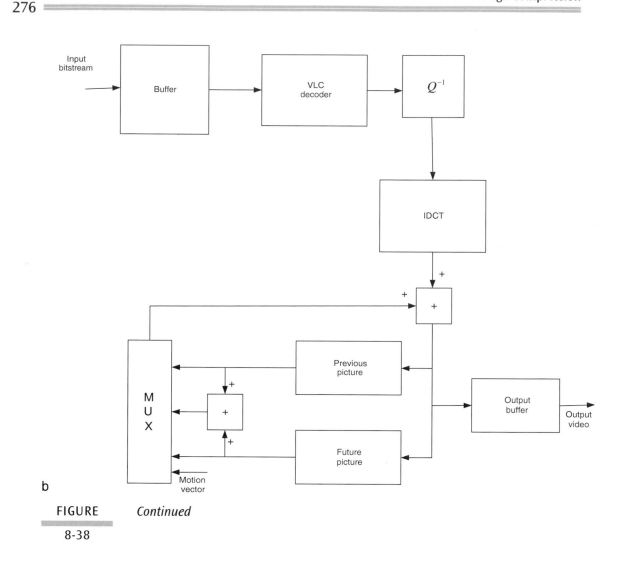

b

FIGURE   *Continued*

8-38

Coding of P and B Pictures

Motion compensated prediction is used to code P pictures. Motion is estimated for each macroblock in the current picture using a previously coded I or P picture in the sequence. As explained previously, motion estimation can be achieved using a suitable block- matching criterion. Because the decoder rules are fixed, the encoder has the burden of accomplishing motion estimation as best as possible. Therefore, it has the flexibility of choosing a suitable block-matching algorithm.

Coding of B pictures requires both preceding and future I or P pictures in the sequence. A block diagram of B picture prediction is shown in Figure 8-39.

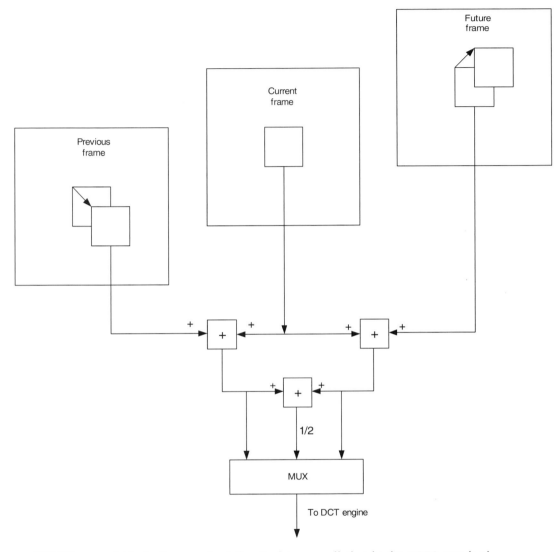

A block diagram depicting B picture prediction in the MPEG standard.

As shown from Figure 8-39, B picture prediction uses both forward and backward pictures, which are either I or P pictures.

The predicted P or B pictures are DCT transformed, and the DCT coefficients are quantized and entropy coded. A different set of quantization matrices is used for the predictive pictures. No DPCM coding is used on the DC coefficients of the P or B pictures, as they are already in differential form.

The rate controller on the encoding side is required, as the transmission rate is assumed to be constant. Depending on the buffer size, the rate controller adjusts the quantization scale factor to compress more aggressively or lightly. For instance, if the buffer is more than half full, the rate controller chooses a larger scale factor so that the DCT coefficients are quantized more heavily. This results in a lower bit rate and so the buffer starts to fill more slowly.

8.7   SUMMARY

This chapter has covered a number of techniques used in compressing image and video data. We started off with criteria to evaluate the quality of compressed/decompressed images both subjectively and objectively. We then described a few popular methods to compress images in a lossless manner. Huffman coding and arithmetic coding are the most popular lossless compression techniques in use. These two methods are used in JPEG and MPEG standards. However, in compressing integer differentials, as in predictive coding, the Golomb–Rice coding technique is very attractive. Run length coding, which is a precursor to coding in the transform domain, is an efficient method of generating symbols to represent DCT coefficients where a large number of them is zero most of the time.

Under the lossy compression category, we encounter various methods of reducing redundancies among pixels in a frame of image. The foremost among them is the DPCM. In image coding, both row-by-row (1-D) and 2-D DPCM techniques are used, although the advantage of using 2-D DPCM over the 1-D counterpart is not significant. The choice depends on available hardware system. Due to nonstationarity of images, some sort of adaptation is called for in coping with local variations in mean and standard deviation. One can use a number of quantizers, one for each class of the pixel, or one can use a single quantizer with an adaptive estimator of pixel variance.

We observed that transform domain coding is superior to the DPCM. The reason for this is the fact that the unitary transform compacts most of the pixel energy into a few transform coefficients and only significant coefficients are used in the reconstruction of the pixels. Although the KL transform is optimal, it is image dependent. As a result, 2-D DCT, which is the closest to the KL transform, is the preferred transform for the compression standards such as JPEG and MPEG. In using transform domain compression methods, an important task is to allocate bits to the transform coefficients so that the average bit rate complies with a bit budget. This problem arises because not all coefficients have equal variance. This problem is solved by the optimal bit allocation rule, wherein each coefficient gets a number of bits proportional to the logarithm of the ratio of the coefficient variance and the geometric variance. However, this optimal rule does not guarantee integer values for the number of bits. We, therefore, described an iterative procedure that allocates integer number of bits to the quantizers.

Wavelet transform has proven to be an efficient tool for the analysis of transient signals. It is another method of compacting pixel energy into few scales and orientations in the wavelet domain. A significant feature of the discrete wavelet transform is the manner in which it is implemented, i.e., subband coding. The same task of allocating bits to the wavelet coefficients to meet a given bit budget also exists in the wavelet domain. We found that the same optimal rule in the transform domain can be used in the wavelet domain as well. We described an elegant algorithm called embedded zero-tree wavelet coding, wherein the property of wavelet coefficients forming a tree of zeros in the various scales and orientations is exploited. This algorithm is called embedded because all the bits are included in the compressed bit stream so that one can stop encoding (or decoding) at any specified bit rate.

Video and motion pictures form an integral part of present-day society. Hence video coding needs greater attention. We described a method of removing temporal redundancy, wherein pixel motion between two consecutive frames is estimated and then the differential between pixels and motion compensated pixels is obtained before further processing. This type of predictive coding is termed interframe coding. The most demanding part of interframe coding is motion estimation, wherein an exhaustive search is made to find the block that best matches the current block of pixels. In practice, however, one uses a more efficient search algorithm, which may be suboptimal. In addition to temporal prediction, transform domain techniques exist to reduce temporal redundancy. In particular, we described a 3-D DCT technique of interframe coding, which has the potential to yield high compression ratios at good quality.

No matter what, one cannot ignore the human being in any image and video compression system, as the end user is the human being. Therefore, incorporating human visual characteristics in the design of a compression system is significant. To this end we described a model that accurately predicts the spatial and temporal masking phenomena in video signals. This model enables us to determine which part of the image is perceptually irrelevant and to incorporate this information in the compression process.

The material provided in this chapter will help us understand the factors that influence the technology behind delivering very high-quality movies digitally. The next chapter describes the requirements of digital cinema and considers two viable candidates in terms of their compression qualities.

REFERENCES

For general principles on compression, refer to texts by Jain (1989), Netravali and Haskell (1988), Jayant and Noll (1990), and Gersho and Gray (1992).

Details on lossless compression methods can be found in Huffman (1951), Gallagher (1978), Capon (1959), Pasco (1976), Rissanen and Langdon (1979), Golomb (1966), Rice (1979), Howard and Vitter (1993), Weinberger et al. (1996), and Thyagarajan (2004).

For further information on predictive coding, refer to O'Neal (1976), Algazi and DeWitte (1982), Netravali (1977), and Zetterberg et al. (1984).

Further details can be found for topics on transform domain compression in Habibi and Wintz (1971), Wintz (1972), Pratt et al. (1974), Rao et al. (1975), Jain (1976), Podilchuk et al. (1995), and Thyagarajan (2000).

Refer to the following for topics in wavelet domain compression: Burt and Adelson (1983), Ramachandran et al. (1994), Vetterli (1984), Adelson et al. (1987), Gharavi and Tabatabai (1988), Woods (1991), Antonini et al. (1992), Devore et al. (1992), Froment and Mallat (1992), Lewis and Knowles (1992), Shapiro (1993), Said and Pearlman (1996), and Lee et al. (1997).

To obtain more information relating to the role of human visual perception in image and video coding, refer to Ahumada and Peterson (1992), Peterson et al. (1993), Watson et al. (1997), Girod (1989), and Chou and Li (1995).

Materials related to JPEG and MPEG standards are found in Bhaskaran and Konstantinides (1997), Mitchel et al. (1996), Watkinson (2001), JPEG (2000), Skodras et al. (2001), and Varma and Bell (2004).

A.K. Jain, *Fundamentals of Digital Image Processing*, Prentice Hall, Englewood Cliffs, NJ, 1989.

A.N. Netravali and B.G. Haskell, *Digital Pictures*, Plenum Press, New York, 1988.

N.S. Jayant and P. Noll, *Digital Coding of Waveforms*, Prentice Hall, Englewood Cliffs, NJ, 1984.

A. Gersho and R.M. Gray, *Vector Quantization and Signal Compression*, Kluwer Academic Publishers, Boston, MA, 1992.

D.A. Huffman, "A method for the construction of minimum redundancy codes," Proceedings of the IRE, 40:1098–1101, 1951.

R.G. Gallagher, "Variations on a theme by Huffman," IEEE Trans. On Information Theory, IT-24(6):668–674, November 1978.

J. Capon, "A probabilistic model for run-length coding of pictures," IRE Trans. On Information Theory, pp. 157–163, 1959.

R. Pasco, *Source Coding Algorithms for Fast Data Compression*, Ph.D. thesis, Stanford University, 1976.

J.J. Rissanen and G.G. Langdon, "Arithmetic coding," IBM Journal of Research and Development, 23(2):149–162, March 1979.

S.W. Golomb, "Run-length encodings," IEEE Trans. Inform. Theory, IT-12:399–401, July 1966.

R.F. Rice, "Some practical universal noiseless coding techniques," Jet Propulsion Laboratory, JPL Publication 79–22, Pasadena, CA, March 1979.

P.G. Howard and J.S. Vitter, "Fast and efficient lossless image compression," Proceedings of the 1993 *Data Compression Conference*, pp. 351–360, Snowbird, Utah, March 1993.

M.J. Weinberger, G. Seroussi, and G. Sapiro, "LOCO-I: A low complexity, context-based, lossless image compression algorithm," Proceedings of the 1993 *Data Compression Conference*, Snowbird, Utah, March 1996.

K.S. Thyagarajan, "DCT compression using Golomb-Rice coding," U.S. Patent No. 6,735,254.

J.B. O'Neal Jr., "Differential pulse code modulation (DPCM) with entropy coding," IEEE. Trans. Inform. Theory IT-21(2):169–174, March 1976.

V.R. Algazi and J.T. DeWitte, "Theoretical performance of entropy coded DPCM," IEEE Trans. Commun. COM-30(5):1088–1095, May 1982.

A.N. Netravali, "On quantizers for DPCM coding of pictures," IEEE Trans. Inform. Theory IT-23: 360–370, May 1977.

L.H. Zetterberg, S. Ericsson, and C. Couturier, "DPCM Coding with two-dimensional control of adaptive quantization," IEEE Trans. Commun., COM-32(4):457–462, April 1984.

A. Habibi and P.A. Wintz, "Image coding by linear transformation and block quantization," IEEE Trans. Commun. Tech., COM-19(1):50–63, February 1971.

P.A. Wintz, "Transform picture coding," Proc. IEEE, Vol. 60, No.7, pp. 809–823, July 1972.

W.K. Pratt, W.H. Chen, and L.R. Welch, "Slant transform image coding," IEEE Trans. Commun., COM22(8), pp. 1075–1093, August 1974.

K.R. Rao, M.A. Narasimhan, and K. Revuluri, "Image data processing by Hadamard-Haar transform," IEEE Trans. Computers, C23(9), pp. 888–896, September 1975.

A.K. Jain, "A fast Karhunen-Loeve transform for a class of random processes," IEEE Trans. Commun. COM-24, pp. 1023–129, September 1976.

C.I. Podilchuk, N.S. Jayant, and N. Farvardin, "Three-dimensional subband coding of video," IEEE Trans. Image Process., Vol. 4, No.2, pp. 125–139, February 1995.

K.S. Thyagarajan, *Digital Cinema System: Encoder/decoder algorithm specifications*, Document No.80, Qualcomm, Inc., June 2000.

P.J. Burt and E.H. Adelson, "The Laplacian pyramid as a compact image code," IEEE Trans. Commun., 31(4):532–540, April 1983.

K. Ramachandran, A. Ortega, and M. Vetterli, "Bit allocation for dependent quantization with applications to multiresolution and MPEG video coders," IEEE Trans. Image Process., Vol. 3, No.5, pp. 533–545, September 1994.

M. Vetterli, "Multidimensional subband coding: Some theory and algorithms," Signal Process., 6(2):97–112, April 1984.

E.H. Adelson, E. Simoncelli, and R. Hingorani, "Orthogonal pyramid transforms for image coding," Proc. SPIE, Vol. 845, pp. 50–58, October 1987.

H. Gharavi and A. Tabatabai, "Subband coding of monochrome and color images," IEEE Trans. Circ. Syst., 35(2):207–214, February 1988.

J.W. Woods, editor, *Subband Image Coding*, Kluwer Academic Publishers, Boston, MA, 1991.

M. Antonini, M. Barlaud, P. Mathieu, and I. Daubechies, "Image coding using wavelet transform," IEEE Trans. Image Process., 1(2):205–220, April 1992.

R.A. DeVore, B. Jawerth, and B.J. Lucier, "Image compression through wavelet transform coding," IEEE Trans. Inform. Theory, Special issue on wavelet transforms and multiresolution signal analysis, 38(20):719–746, March 1992.

J. Froment and S. Mallat, "Second generation compact image coding with wavelets," in C.K. Chui, editor, *Wavelets: A Tutorial in Theory and Applications*, Academic Press, New York, 1992.

A.S. Lewis and G. Knowles, "Image compression using 2-D wavelet transform," IEEE Trans. Image Process., 1(2):244–250, April 1992.

J.M. Shapiro, "Embedded image coding using zerotrees of wavelet coefficients," IEEE Transactions on Signal Processing, Special Issue on Wavelets and Signal Processing, 41(12):3445–3462, December 1993.

A. Said and W.A. Pearlman, "A new, fast, and efficient image codec based on set partitioning in hierarchical trees," IEEE Trans. Circuits and Systems for Video Technology, Vol. 6, No. 3, pp. 243–250, June 1996.

K. Lee, S. Park, and W. Suh, "Wavelet-based image and video compression."

A.J. Ahumada Jr. and H.A. Peterson, "Luminance-model-based DCT quantization for color image compression," in B.E. Rogowitz, ed., *Human Vision, Visual Processing, and Digital Display III*, Proc. SPIE, Vol. 1666, pp. 365–374, 1992.

P.A. Heidi, A.J. Ahumada Jr., and A.B. Watson, "An improved detection model for DCT coefficient quantization," SPIE, Vol. 1913, pp. 191–201, 1993.

A.B. Watson et al., "Visibility of wavelet quantization noise," IEEE Trans. Image Process., Vol. 6, No. 8, pp. 1164–1175, 1997.

B. Girod, "The information theoretical significance of spatial and temporal masking in video signals," in B.E. Rogowitz, ed., *Human Vision, Visual Processing and Digital Display*, Proc. SPIE, Vol. 1077, pp. 178–187, 1989.

C. Chou and Y. Li, "A perceptually tuned subband image coder based on the measure of just-noticeable-distortion profile," IEEE Trans. On Circ. And Syst. For Video Tech., Vol. 5, No. 6, pp. 467–476, December 1995.

V. Bhaskaran and K. Konstantinides, *Image and Video Compression Standards: Algorithms and Applications*, 2nd Ed., Kluwer, MA, 1997.

J.L. Mitchell et al., *MPEG Video Compression Standard*, Kluwer Academic Publishers, MA, 1996.

J. Watkinson, *The MPEG Handbook*, Elsevier/Focal Press, 2001.

JPEG 2000 *Part I: Final Draft International Standard* (ISO/IEC FDIS15444–1), ISO/IEC JTC1/SC29/WG1 N1855, August 2000.

A. Skodras, C. Christopuolos, and T. Ebrahimi, "The JPEG 2000 still image compression standard," IEEE Signal Processing Magazine, pp. 36–58, September 2001.

K. Varma and A. Bell, "JPEG2000: Choices and tradeoff for encoders," IEEE Signal Processing Magazine, pp. 70–75, November 2004.

9 Application of Image Compression to Digital Cinema

9.1   INTRODUCTION

So far we have described various image processing algorithms and techniques as stand-alone systems. This chapter puts all of them together to meet the requirements of a *digital cinema system*. We are used to experiencing movies using film and film projectors. By digital cinema we mean delivery and projection of movies using digital data stored in a computer hard disk and digital projectors. Hence, we can consider digital cinema as a *filmless movie*. The Internet age has set the stage for presenting movies entirely in digital form. There will always be objection and lack of acceptance to any new ideas that replace age-old habits. This is very true in the movie industry, too. However, with the passage of time, digital cinema will become a common technology so why resist the inevitable to begin with?

This chapter addresses the issues behind the special requirements of digital cinema and discusses two approaches to image compression that meet these requirements. To this end we describe two case studies, namely QUALCOMM's system and the system based on the JPEG2000 standard.

9.2   DIGITAL CINEMA TECHNOLOGY REQUIREMENTS

9.2.1   Image Resolution and Format

Because digitally rendered images should be indistinguishable from their film counterparts, one would expect a large image size and pixel depth for digital cinema. The image size can range from 1980×1080 to as large as 4096×3112 pixels. Of course, we would like to have the highest resolution at the digital mastering or production with perhaps lower resolution for the projection.

The color space should be RGB for the production, otherwise some amount of color loss might occur, which is objectionable at the production side. However, for the projection a suitable color space is YCbCr. Chroma subsampling can be allowed for the digital projection. However, it should be such that no color degradation should be visible when digital pictures are projected. A chromatic subsampling format of 4:2:2 is acceptable at the projection side, whereas a sampling format of 4:4:4 (no chroma subsampling) should be used at the production end.

Because the dynamic range of a movie film image is very high, enough room should be allowed in the digital image representation for the wide signal excursion. This calls for a depth of 12 to 16 bits per component for the production and at least 10 bits per component for the projection. Film-based movies are captured and projected at a rate of 24 FPS. Hence we should use at least 24 FPS in a progressive fashion for digital cinema. These requirements are summarized in Table 9.1.

9.2.2   Digital Projector

Projection of movies in digital format requires a digital projector, i.e., a projector that accepts digital or computer data and projects optical images on a big screen. Cinema quality requirements call for special demands for high-quality, very bright images and highly reliable operation from digital projectors. There are a few digital imaging technologies used in digital projectors, including (1) digital light processing (DLP) using digital micromirror device (DMD) chips, (2) digital image light amplifier (D-ILA) chips, and (3) grating light valve (GLV) chips.

The DMD chip consists of a rectangular array of up to 2 million hinge-mounted micromirrors. This hinge mounting enables the mirrors to tilt either toward the light source in the DLP projection system (ON) or away from it

Table 9-1. Picture Resolution and Format of Digital Cinema

Parameter	Production	Projection
Image size in pixel	1920 × 1080 to 4096 × 3112	1920 × 1080 to 4096 × 3112
Color space	RGB or YCbCr	RGB or YCbCr
Bit depth	12 to 16 bit/ component	10 bit/component
Sampling format	4:4:4	4:2:2
Frame rate	24 FPS	24 FPS fixed

(OFF), creating a light or dark pixel on the screen. Each mirror can be switched on and off up to several thousand times per second. When a mirror is switched on more often than off, it reflects a light gray pixel. Similarly a mirror that is switched off more frequently reflects a darker gray pixel. In this manner a grayscale image is projected on a screen. In order to project a color image, three DMD chips are used, one for each of the R, G, and B lights. For low-end applications, a single DMD chip is used in conjunction with a color wheel to project color images.

In an ILA-based projection system the image to be projected is first written on to a liquid crystal at a low intensity by means of an electron beam, which modulates the refractive characteristics of the crystal. The liquid crystal is placed on top of a stationary mirror. High-intensity, polarized light is focused on to the mirror, which reflects the image on the crystal. As the design of an ILA projector system is complex and tedious, a pixilated IC version of this technology known as D-ILA is used. A D-ILA consists of an array of liquid crystals, built on a highly reflective surface.

The GLV projector also has an IC for its projection. However, GLV ICs consist of microscopic ribbons of reflective aluminum, which can be bent by electrostatic forces. A linear array of these ribbons reflects off light from a laser source and the reflected light is collected and projected as a vertical column of image, which is scanned across the scene to render a full image.

The DLP using DMD chips is the most widely used projector technology in today's digital cinema systems. One such digital projector from Christie is shown in Figure 9-1. It has a light output of about 3850 lumens. Other characteristics of this projector are as follows: full-field contrast ratio greater than 2000:1, brightness uniformity greater than 90% when displaying a full white screen, pixel depth of 45 bits (15 bit/component), and three-chip DMD technology with 2048 × 1080 resolution.

9.2.3 Image Compression System

Ideally, lossless compression should be used for digital cinema applications. However, the rate at which digital image data originates is enormous: $1920 \times 1080 \times 3 \times 10 \times 24 = 1,492,992,000$ bits/s. This is beyond the bandwidth capability of any practical present-day electronic system. Thus, we are fully convinced that some form of data compression is a must. As discussed in a previous chapter, lossless compression only yields about 2:1 compression savings. Thus, we still have to deal with about a 93-GB/s rate should we adopt a lossless compression. It is, therefore, clear that we must adopt a lossy compression scheme in such a way that the resultant data rate can be handled easily by off-the-shelf hardware

FIGURE
9-1

A digital projector based on three-chip DLP technology for digital cinema application, courtesy of Christie Digital Systems, Inc.

systems while maintaining the resulting image quality as visually lossless. Assuming a compressed data rate of about 60 Mb/s, we will then require a compression ratio of about 25:1.

The required compression could be easily achieved via interframe coding, as in MPEG standard. The problem with interframe coding is that it creates motion artifacts, especially when there are scenes with fast motion. One would expect fast motion from frame to frame in *action* and *adventure* movies and such artifacts are clearly unacceptable. This requirement, therefore, shifts the burden on the encoder, which should use only intraframe coding. At the same time the encoder should have built-in flexibility to accommodate various formats for projection. Additionally, if the compression system could seamlessly convert the movie data from one format to another for *repurposing* without having to decompress and compress multiple times, image quality would be preserved.

Finally, compressed movie data must be encrypted to deter piracy. In fact, the compressed data should be in encrypted form up until the projector. This will achieve the maximum possible protection against piracy. Intellectual property and copyright information needs to be inserted in the images as a means of authenticating the property owner. This is known as watermarking. The chosen compression scheme should accept *digital watermarking* data without being visible and without introducing any noticeable degradation in the projected pictures. Thus, we see that very stringent requirements are placed on the compression system fit for digital cinema application.

9.3   CASE STUDY

Having spelled out the unique requirements of a digital cinema system, let us consider two candidate systems. The first is QUALCOMM's digital cinema system utilizing DCT-based compression and the second based on Motion JPEG2000 utilizing DWT. Each one of the systems has its merits and demerits. Because Motion JPEG2000 is an international standard, it is being considered a digital cinema standard by the SMPTE standards organization.

9.3.1   QUALCOMM's Digital Cinema System

A unique feature of QUALCOMM's digital cinema system is that it combines both custom design and off-the-shelf components. Key considerations such as system economics, interoperability, ease of use, end-to-end consistent quality, reliability, and security require that the overall digital cinema solution be obtained from a system level approach rather than piecing together independent technologies. This was QUALCOMM's philosophy to a digital cinema system. An end-to-end digital cinema system envisioned by QUALCOMM is shown in Figure 9-2. Movies originating in film are first converted into digital format at the telecine suite, which is outside of the system. Digital image data are

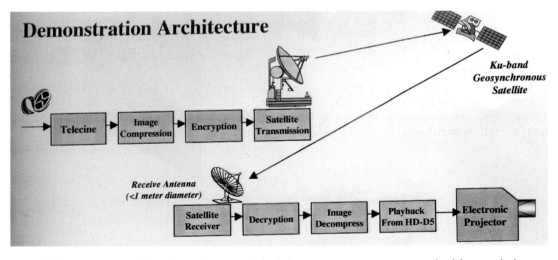

FIGURE
9-2

QUALCOMM's end-to-end digital cinema system, courtesy and with permission of QUALCOMM.

compressed, encrypted, and transmitted via a satellite transmission system. At the user end, the satellite receiver receives transmitted data. Received data are stored in hard disk arrays. At the appointed time, data are retrieved from the hard disks and fed to the projector. The real-time decompression system housed inside the projector first decrypts data, decompresses, and then outputs images to the projector system, which then projects the movie on to a large screen.

Let us describe a few specific subsystems of QUALCOMM's digital cinema system.

9.3.1.1   *Adaptive Block-Size DCT Encoder*

QUALCOMM's image compression system uses adaptive (variable) block-size discrete cosine transform (ABSDCT) and intraframe coding to meet the stringent quality requirements of a digital cinema as mentioned earlier. A block diagram of the ABSDCT encoder is shown in Figure 9-3. The input to the system is YCbCr with 8 or 10 bits per component. The encoder accepts both 4:4:4 and 4:2:2 chroma sampling formats.

The input image to be compressed is first divided into nonoverlapping rectangular blocks of size 16×16 pixels. An adaptive quad-tree decomposition procedure is used to subdivide each 16×16 block into subblocks down to size 2×2 pixels. The criterion used for decomposing a block is the local contrast. Thus, a block situated in a locally high contrast area will be subdivided into smaller blocks than a block in a relatively flat area. This adaptive block decomposition results in a high-quality image at a reasonable bit rate. An example of QUAL-

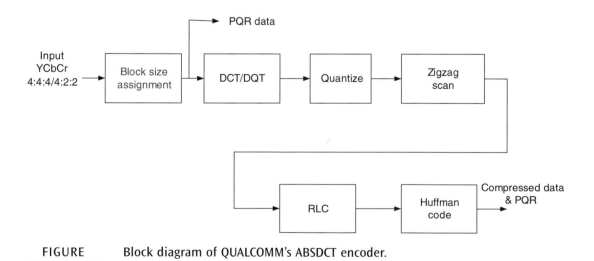

FIGURE   Block diagram of QUALCOMM's ABSDCT encoder.

9-3

FIGURE

9-4

Image showing adaptive block size assignment, courtesy and with permission of QUALCOMM.

COMM's adaptive block decomposition is shown in Figure 9-4. The quad-tree subdivision information called PQR data, which is variable in size, is sent to the decoder along with compressed data for each block. PQR data can vary between 1 and 21 bits.

Once the quad-tree decomposition is done, the 2-D DCT of each subblock is computed. In a DCT block the DC coefficient has the largest magnitude. When a 16×16 block has many smaller subblocks, there are as many DC coefficients as there are subblocks. These large DC values will lower the run length coding efficiency. In order to reduce these intermittent high DC values, QUALCOMM uses 2×2 DCT on the DC coefficients. This is called the *differential quad-tree transform* (DQT).

The DCT coefficients are quantized using perceptually adapted weights or *frequency-weighted masks* (FWM). For each size subblock there is an FWM. These weights are calculated by taking into account the projector characteristics, viewing distance, and the DCT frequency. The DC and DQT coefficients are quantized differently from the rest of the coefficients as these coefficients are perceptually more significant. The quantized coefficients are zigzag scanned, run length encoded, and then entropy coded using Huffman codes.

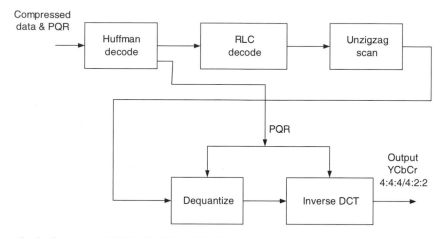

Block diagram of QUALCOMM's ABSDCT decoder.

9.3.1.2   ABSDCT Decoder

At the decoder the operations are reversed. The decoded PQR information is used to decode and dequantize the DCT coefficients and assemble the 16×16 blocks. Figure 9-5 illustrates the decoder functions.

9.3.1.3   QUALCOMM's Decoder ASIC

At the data rate used in digital cinema, which is around 40 Mb/s, a special purpose decoder was needed for real-time operation. QUALCOMM designed an ASIC chip using a standard CMOS process for this purpose, and Figure 9-6 shows the various functions it executes. In addition to decompressing data, the ASIC performs triple-DES (data encryption system) decryption of audio and video data. The chip is programmable via a general-purpose PCI bus. An external controller can download through the PCI bus specific configuration parameters such as horizontal and vertical pixel resolutions and chroma subsampling modes. Figure 9-7 shows the decoder module hardware incorporating the QUALCOMM ASIC chip.

The following provides a brief description of some of the functions the ASIC performs.

Security Functions

At the specified playback time, the compressed audio and video data are passed through the triple-DES decryption hardware. Audio data are sent off-chip because there is no audio compression in the QUALCOMM digital cinema

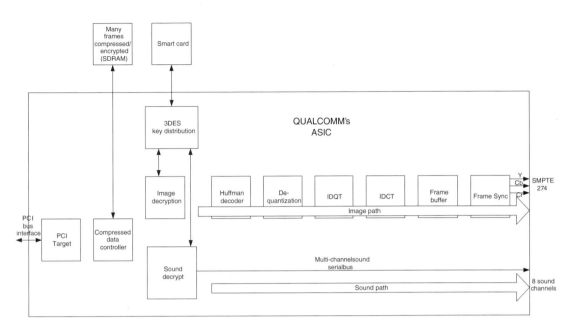

FIGURE

9-6

QUALCOMM's real-time ABSDCT image decoder.

FIGURE

9-7

QUALCOMM's real-time image decoder module, courtesy and with permission of QUALCOMM.

system. Image data are decompressed and then output to the projector. The triple-DES decryption hardware is under the control of an external *smart card* or other security module. Key scheduling and management are programmable within the ASIC.

Image Decompression

Compressed digital image information is decompressed by a number of engines. These are the Huffman decoder, dequantization of DCT coefficients, inverse DQT, and inverse DCT. All engines are controllable via an external CPU. Items that are configurable include Huffman code tables, quantization steps, frequency weighting masks, frame formats (4:4:4 or 4:2:2, interlaced or progressive, active picture area), decryption enable/disable, random access of frames, and playback black frame.

Audio Processing

Digitized audio information is received from the PCI bus along with image data, stored in the *compressed data RAM buffer*, decrypted, and then sent out serially. If audio was compressed (e.g., with Dolby or DTS coding), its decompression is performed external to the ASIC.

The serial sound interface accommodates both compressed and uncompressed 24-bit data sampled at a 48-kHz rate. The audio interface limits the rate to eight programs, which consist of a maximum of 12 channels per audio slice time. This limits the maximum rate the audio interface can support to about 13.92 Mbps.

Playback Output

The *image start of frame* (ISOF) can be slaved to an external strobe device or generated internally based on the configurable registers. Internal ISOF is configurable in various aspect ratios and up to 2.76 million pixels per frame.

Decompressed image data are output from the chip to an attached frame buffer memory in blocks of 16×16 pixels. The *pixel interface processor* (PIP)—an independent internal display engine block—reads scan lines from frame buffer memory to be output in SMPTE 274 and modified SMPTE 274 formats as streams of 30-bit pixels in the YCbCr component form.

The PIP is responsible for interfacing the frame buffer to the projector. This interface is unidirectional and supports playback only. Image devices connected to this interface are compatible with SMPTE274M. The frame buffer stores only the active pixels.

In addition to handling image data, PIP is also capable of displaying slides that are encoded in any of the supported formats. Slide playback is triggered when the software instructs the PIP to display the same frame a multiple of frame intervals. The ASIC is also capable of redisplaying the current frame or a black frame.

9.3.2 Digital Cinema Using Motion JPEG2000 Standard

The Motion JPEG2000 (MJ2K) image compression algorithm is based on part 1 codec of the JPEG2000 standard and uses discrete wavelet transform as the image compression vehicle. In particular, its general features are (1) intraframe coding, (2) MPEG-4-based file format, (3) audio–video synchronization, (4) embedding of metadata, and (5) multiple image sampling formats (4:4:4, 4:2:2) and color components. MJ2K also allows for lossless compression.

9.3.2.1 MJ2K Image Resolution and Format

For digital mastering, the 35-mm film scan size is up to 4096×3112 pixels per frame. The color space is RGB with 16 bits per component. An additional alpha channel is also present. Digital video cameras, if used, should have approximately the same resolution as the film scanner.

The formats for digital projection include aspect ratios of 1.85:1, 2:1, and 2.39:1 and corresponding image sizes of 3790×2048, 4096×2048, and 4096×1714, respectively. However, pixel grayscale resolution is an 8- to 10-bit/component with YUV and 4:2:2 chromatid subsampling format.

9.3.2.2 Compression in the Wavelet Domain

As mentioned earlier, MJ2K allows 9/7 wavelets for irreversible and 5/3 wavelets for reversible DWT. It can support up to five levels of wavelet transform. The compression is intraframe, which allows for random access and easy editing of frames.

9.3.2.3 MJ2K File Format

MJ2K uses a file format based on the MPEG4 file format, which is based on the QuickTime® file format from Apple Computer, Inc. It is platform independent, flexible, and allows for easy synchronization of audio and other metadata with compressed image data.

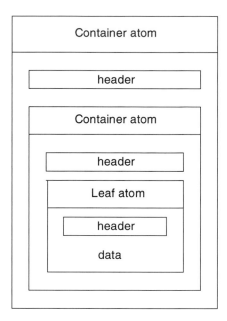

FIGURE
9-8
An example of an atom.

The MPEG4 file format is based on a hierarchical ordering of *objects* or *atoms*. Atoms can be of different types. This hierarchical structure (or tree structure) allows atoms to be nested with varying types. For instance, an atom of the type *movie* contains a *track* atom for each track in the movie. In turn, the track atoms can include one or more *media* atoms that describe other movie characteristics. Atoms, in general, describe a hierarchy of metadata containing information such as index points, duration, and pointers to media data. Actual media data such as audio/video itself may reside in the MPEG4 file or a separate file with a reference URL. Figure 9-8 illustrates the structure of an atom. Atoms include a header, followed by data. The header contains two fields, namely the atom type and size, which are 4-byte integers.

A movie atom is of type "*moov*" and is a container for metadata that describe a movie's data. These metadata, in turn, are stored in a number of atoms of different types. Movie atoms contain track atoms at the highest level. Track atoms contain media atoms and so on. The lowest level atoms are called *leaf* atoms and contain data in the form of tables or sets of data elements. A movie atom with subatoms is shown in Figure 9-9.

9.3.2.4   *Error Resilience*

Digital errors can occur when a data stream is transmitted through error-prone channels such as the wireless transmission system. In receiving compressed dig-

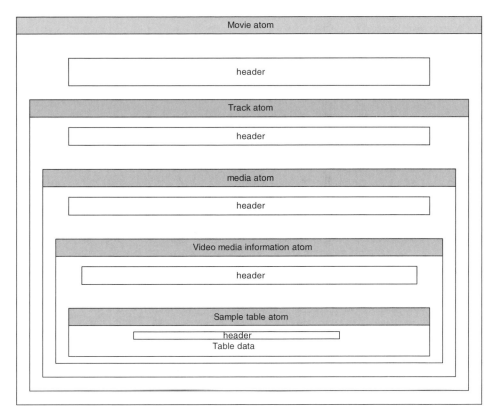

FIGURE   An example of a movie atom.

9-9

itized images, a system resilient to such burst errors is desirable. MJ2K uses pack-etized bit streams for the transmission or storage of compressed data. Packets are segmented and synchronization markers are inserted, which prevents errors from propagating to the whole frame or even beyond a frame.

9.4   CONCLUDING REMARKS

We have described two candidates, one based on block transform compression and the other on discrete wavelet transform, as competing systems for the distribution of movies in digital format. Both systems have been tested by the ETC, a nonprofit organization of the USC, and certified to be visually lossless at rates of about 100 Mb/s. However, the SMPTE organization is leaning toward the MJ2K as the recommended practice. A system based on a standard is likely to be interoperable with the result that it will be universal. It will create healthy competition so that the price of digital cinema equipment will be reduced dramatically in due course.

Even though a digital cinema standard is established, it does not imply that all movies will be shown in digital format. Economy is a crucial element in this game. First, there should be a large number of screens fitted with digital projectors. Second, satellite transmission should be deployed to distribute movies to reduce the cost of shipping the digital movies. Third, digital projectors should be inexpensive. Unfortunately, all three factors are linked and hence the inertia. It is hoped that digital projectors become much less expensive with much higher pixel resolution so that digital cinema becomes popular.

REFERENCES

The following articles and patents pertain to QUALCOMM's digital cinema system: Morley (2000), Thyagarajan (2000), Swartz (2005), Lee, Lee and Pian, Thyagarajan and Morley (2003), Thyagarajan (2003, 2004), Thyagarajan and Merritt (2003), QUALCOMM (1998), Thyagarajan and Irvine, Thyagarajan, Ratzel, Morley, and Raveendran, Thyagarajan and Irvine, Thyagarajan, Fudge, and Rosen, Thyagarajan, Levin, and Senthil. For the MJ2K-based system, one should refer to Foessel, Chiariglione, and QuickTime.

S.A. Morley, K.S. Thyagarajan, and A.C. Irvine, "Balancing technology in digital cinema systems," in Proceedings of the SMPTE Technical Conference and Exhibition, pp. 102–121, October 2000.

K.S. Thyagarajan, "Digital cinema system encoder/decoder algorithm specifications," Internal Document, Qualcomm, Inc., June 2000.

C.S. Swartz, editor, *Understanding Digital Cinema: A Professional Handbook*, Focal Press (an imprint of Elsevier), 2005.

C.U. Lee, "Adaptive block-size image compression method and system," U.S. patent No. 5452104.

C.U. Lee and D. Pian, "Interframe video coding and decoding system," U.S. patent No. 5576767.

K.S. Thyagarajan and S.A. Morley, "Quality-based image compression," U.S. patent No. 6600836.

K.S. Thyagarajan, "DCT compression using Golomb-Rice coding," U.S. patent No. 6735254.

K.S. Thyagarajan, "Lossless intraframe encoding using Golomb-Rice," U.S. patent No. 6650784.

K.S. Thyagarajan and M.J. Merritt, "Contrast sensitive variance-based adaptive block-size DCT image compression," U.S. patent pending.

Qualcomm Digital Cinema System Design, Internal Report, Qualcomm, Inc., 1998.

K.S. Thyagarajan and A.C. Irvine, "Hybrid lossy and lossless compression method and apparatus," U.S. patent pending.

K.S. Thyagarajan, J. Ratzel, S.A. Morley, and V.Raveendran, "Apparatus and method for encoding digital image data in a lossless manner," U.S. patent pending.

K.S. Thyagarajan and A.C. Irvine, "System and method for encoding digital image and audio data in a lossless manner," U.S. patent pending.

K.S. Thyagarajan, B. Fudge, and E. Rosen, "Apparatus and method for watermarking a digital image," U.S. patent pending.

K.S. Thyagarajan, J.A. Levin, and G. Senthil, "Configurable pattern optimizer," U.S. Patent No. 6,870,963.

S. Foessel, "Motion JPEG2000 and digital cinema." The Web site for this article: http://www.jpeg.org/public/DCINEMA-JPEG2000.ppt

ISO/IEC JTC1/SC29/WG11, http://www.chiariglione.org/mpeg/standards/mpeg-4/mpeg-4.htm

QuickTime® File Format Specification: http://developer.apple.com/documentation/QuickTime/QTFF/qtff.pdf

A
APPENDIX

Continuous and Discrete Fourier Transforms

A.1   CONTINUOUS FOURIER TRANSFORM

Fourier transform is of fundamental importance in the analysis and design of linear systems. They express time or spatial-domain signals in the respective frequency domains. The continuous Fourier transform or simply the Fourier transform of a signal $f(x)$ is defined as

$$F(u) = \int_{-\infty}^{\infty} f(x)e^{-j2\pi ux}dx, \tag{A-1}$$

where u is the frequency variable. If x is a spatial variable, then u is in cycles per unit distance. The inverse Fourier transform recovers the signal. Thus,

$$f(x) = \int_{-\infty}^{\infty} F(u)e^{j2\pi ux}du. \tag{A-2}$$

The extension of the 1-D Fourier transform to two dimensions is straight-forward. The forward and inverse 2-D Fourier transforms are given by

$$F(u,v) = \int_{-\infty}^{\infty} \int_{-\infty}^{\infty} f(x,y)e^{-j2\pi(ux+vy)}dxdy \tag{A-3}$$

$$f(x,y) = \int_{-\infty}^{\infty} \int_{-\infty}^{\infty} F(u,v)e^{j2\pi(ux+vy)}dudv \tag{A-4}$$

Because this book is about 2-D spatial signals, we only deal with 2-D Fourier transform in the rest of this Appendix.

A.1.1 Properties of Continuous Fourier Transform

Linearity

Fourier transform is linear with respect to the signals. Because the Fourier transform is an integral, it is easy to see that the Fourier transform of the sum of scaled signals equals the scaled sum of the individual Fourier transforms.

Separability

By separability we mean that the 2-D Fourier transform can be computed as a sequence of two 1-D transforms. To see this, we rewrite Eq. (A-3) as

$$F(u,v) = \int_{-\infty}^{\infty} \left[\int_{-\infty}^{\infty} f(x,y)e^{-j2\pi v y}dy \right] e^{-j2\pi u x}dx. \tag{A-5}$$

The inner integral is the Fourier transform along the y direction and the rest along the x direction.

Frequency Response

The frequency response of a 2-D space-invariant linear system is the 2-D Fourier transform of its point spread function h(x,y). Thus,

$$H(u,v) = \int_{-\infty}^{\infty} \int_{-\infty}^{\infty} h(x,y)e^{-j2\pi(ux+vy)}dxdy. \tag{A-6}$$

Because H is complex, it has magnitude and phase.

Convolution Theorem

The Fourier transform of the output of a 2-D linear space-invariant system is the product of the Fourier transforms of its input and the point spread function. If f(x,y) and h(x,y) are, respectively, the input and point spread function, then the output Fourier transform, G(u,v), of the linear space-invariant system is given by

$$G(u,v) = F(u,v)H(u,v). \tag{A-7}$$

This follows from the use of the convolution and Fourier transform.

A.2   DISCRETE FOURIER TRANSFORM

The discrete Fourier transform (DFT) of a discrete 2-D array $x(m,n)$ is defined as

$$X(k,l) = \sum_{m=0}^{M-1} \sum_{n=0}^{N-1} x(m,n) e^{-j2\pi\left(\frac{mk}{M}+\frac{nl}{N}\right)}. \tag{A-8}$$

The inverse DFT is given by

$$x(m,n) = \frac{1}{MN} \sum_{k=0}^{M-1} \sum_{l=0}^{N-1} X(k,l) e^{j2\pi\left(\frac{mk}{M}+\frac{nl}{N}\right)}. \tag{A-9}$$

Because the 2-D DFT is separable it can be realized as a sequence of two 1-D DFTs, first along the columns and then along the rows. The 2-D DFT can be computed efficiently using the fast Fourier transform (FFT) algorithm.

B
APPENDIX

Radiometric and Photometric Quantities

B.1 RADIOMETRIC QUANTITIES

Radiometry deals with the measurement of energy in an electromagnetic field. We shall define a few radiometric quantities that are of interest to image processing.

B.1.1 Radiant Energy

Radiant energy, Q, is the energy contained in an electromagnetic field or the energy delivered to a given receptor by such a field and its unit is joules (J).

B.1.2 Radiant Flux

Radiant flux, Φ, or power is the time rate of change of radiant energy, Q. It is the rate at which radiant energy is transferred between two regions. It is measured in watts, which is joules per second.

B.1.3 Radiant Exitance

Radiant exitance M is the flux density, i.e., it is the flux per unit area leaving a point on the surface of a source of radiation and has the unit of W/m^2.

B.1.4 Irradiance

Irradiance E refers to that which is incident on a surface. It refers to the flux per unit area incident on a surface. It has the same unit as radiance, which is W/m^2.

B.1.5   Radiant Intensity

Since a source is assumed to be isotropic, we need to quantify the flux emitted in a given direction over a unit solid angle. Thus, radiant intensity I is the flux per unit solid angle of a source in a given direction. It is measured in watts per steradian, W/sr. The solid angle is expressed in units of steradian. It is the ratio of the surface area, A, intercepted by a cone on the surface of a sphere of radius R centered on the cone vertex.

B.1.6   Radiance

Radiance, L, is the radiant flux per unit projected, area per unit solid angle exiting a point in a given direction or incident on a point in a given direction. It has the unit of W/m^2sr.

When each of these quantities is expressed as a function of wavelength, we explicitly use the wavelength, λ, to denote the functional relationship. For instance, the spectral radiant flux is denoted $\Phi(\lambda)$, which represents the flux centered at wavelength λ over an infinitesimal bandwidth $\Delta\lambda$. In terms of $\Phi(\lambda)$, the total flux, Φ, over the entire electromagnetic spectrum is expressed as

$$\Phi = \int_0^\infty \Phi(\lambda)d\lambda. \qquad \text{(B-1)}$$

B.2   PHOTOMETRIC QUANTITIES

The term photometry is used when dealing with human vision. It is essentially the same as radiometry.

B.2.1   Luminous Flux

Because the human vision is sensitive to the wavelength of the incident light, the total luminous flux, Φ_v in watts, is obtained from the spectral radiant flux by weighting it by the relative luminous efficiency, $Y(\lambda)$ and integrating over the visible spectrum. Thus,

$$\Phi_v = \int_{380}^{780} \Phi(\lambda)Y(\lambda)d\lambda. \tag{B-2}$$

Note that the luminous efficiency function is dimensionless. When the radiant flux creates a visual sensation, we call it the luminous flux. The visible spectrum extends from about 380 to 780 nm.

B.2.2   Lumens

Luminous flux is also expressed in a photometric unit called lumen (lm). Lumen is, therefore, the photometric analog of watts. The conversion between the two quantities is affected through

$$\Phi_v = k_m \int_{380}^{780} \Phi(\lambda)Y(\lambda)d\lambda \text{ lumens,} \tag{B-3}$$

where $k_m = 680$ lumens/watt.

B.2.3   Luminous Intensity

Luminous intensity, I_v, is the analog of radiant intensity and the two are expressed through

$$I_v = k_m \int_{380}^{780} I(\lambda)Y(\lambda)d\lambda \text{ candelas.} \tag{B-4}$$

Because the luminous intensity is the density of luminous flux per unit solid angle, we can also write

$$\Phi_v(\text{in lumens}) = I_v(\text{in candelas}) \times \Omega(\text{in steradians}). \tag{B-5}$$

B.2.4   Luminance

Luminance, L_v, or brightness is the scaled spectral radiance weighted by the luminous efficiency and integrated over the visible spectrum:

$$L_v = k_m \int\limits_{380}^{780} L(\lambda)Y(\lambda)d\lambda \text{ candelas}/\text{m}^2 . \qquad (\text{B-6})$$

B.2.5   Illumination

Spectral illumination, $E(\lambda)$, is the density of luminous flux incident upon a surface. Therefore, we can write

$$E(\lambda)_{\text{in lux}} = \frac{\Phi(\lambda)_{\text{in lumens}}}{\text{Area}(\text{m}^2)} \qquad (\text{B-7})$$

and

$$E(\lambda)_{\text{in foot candles}} = \frac{\Phi(\lambda)_{\text{in lumens}}}{\text{Area}(\text{ft}^2)} . \qquad (\text{B-8})$$

The conversion factor between foot candle and lux is expressed by

$$1 \text{ foot candle} = 10.76 \text{ lux}. \qquad (\text{B-9})$$

C | MATLAB M Files for Selected Chapters

In this appendix you will find M files (MATLAB files) to generate the figures in selected chapters. In order to run these programs you need to install MATLAB with image processing and wavelet toolboxes at a minimum. Make sure that these files are in the MATLAB path before running the programs. You should also make sure that the images specified in the M files are in the MATLAB path. If not, you can substitute them with other images, provided they are of the type that MATLAB can read. These files are simple to follow and you can modify them easily. The M files listed in this appendix are for your personal use. However, you can include them in your work, provided you give due credit to the author.

C.1   M FILES FROM CHAPTER 2

```
%     Example2_3.m
%     Calculation of 2-D DFT of camaraman
%     and displaying its magnitude spectrum
%     Author: K.S. Thyagarajan
%
%     Read input image
inImage = imread('cameraman.tif');
imshow(inImage)
inImage = im2double(inImage);
%     Calculate the 2-D DFT of the input image
%
fftImage = fft2(inImage);
%
%     Display the log magnitude of the 2-D DFT
figure,imshow(log(abs(fftImage)),[-1 5]);
colormap(jet);colorbar
%
%     Shift the origin of the frequency plane from
top-left corner
```

```
%    to the center
shiftFFTimage = fftshift(fftImage);
figure,imshow(log(abs(shiftFFTimage)),[-1 5]);
colormap(jet);colorbar




%    Example2_4.m
%    Calculation of the frequency response of a 2-D
%    discrete
%     LSI system and displaying the magnitude and phase
%    responses
%    Author: K.S. Thyagarajan
%
%    Define the transfer function
%    Real part, C =
%    cos(X)+cos(Y)+cos(2X)+cos(2Y)+cos(X+Y)
%    Imaginary part, S =
%    sin(X)+sin(Y)+sin(2X)+sin(2Y)+sin(X+Y)
%    |H| = sqrt(C^2 + S^2)
%    Theta = arctan(S/C), where X = normalized horizontal
%    frequency (rad)
%    and Y = normalized vertical frequency (rad)

%    Create a mesh grid plane covering -PI to +PI
[X,Y] = meshgrid(-pi:2*pi/64:pi);
%
%    Compute the cosine a
C10 = cos(X);
C20 = cos(2*X);
S10 = sin(X);
S20 = sin(2*X);
%
C01 = cos(Y);
C02 = cos(2*Y);
S01 = sin(Y);
S02 = sin(2*Y);
C11 = cos(X+Y);
S11 = sin(X+Y);
%
```

```
C = C10+C20+C01+C02+C11;
S = S10+S20+S01+S02+S11;
H = sqrt(C.^2+S.^2);
Hmax = max(H(:));
H = H/Hmax;
theta = atan2(S,C);
mesh(X,Y,H); view([-45 45])
xlabel('Omega1'); ylabel('Omega2'); zlabel('Magnitude')
figure, mesh(X,Y,theta); view([-45 45])
xlabel('Omega1'); ylabel('Omega2'); zlabel('Phase')
```

```
%    Fig2_5.m
% Mfile for figure Fig2_5
%    Ideal brick wall characteristic of a low-pass filter
%    Author: K.S. Thyagarajan
%
n = -100:100;   % No. of points
Omega = n/100 *pi;  % discrete freq. variable
Wc = pi/2;  % cutoff frequency
%
H = zeros(size(n));
ind1 = find(Omega == -Wc);
ind2 = find(Omega == Wc);
H(ind1:ind2) = 1;
%
plot(Omega,H),xlabel('Normalized frequency'),
ylabel('Magnitude')
```

```
%    Example2_5.m
%    1-D linear phase FIR filter approximating an ideal
%    filter
%    with a normalized cutoff frequency of PI/4.
%    A rectangular window of length 9 is used.
%    Author: K.S. Thyagarajan
%
```

```
n = -4:4;
hd = 0.25*sinc(n/4);
stem(n,hd,'filled'); xlabel('sample #');ylabel('h[n]')
%
A = zeros(size(hd));
A(5) = 1;
%
[H,W] = freqz(hd,A,256);
figure,plot(W,10*log10(abs(H)))
xlabel('Normalized frequency'); ylabel('Magnitude in dB')
%
figure,plot(W,angle(H))
xlabel('Normalized frequency'); ylabel('Phase in Rad')
%
%    Use Hanning, Hamming and Blackman windows
wh = hanning(9);
wham = hamming(9);
wb = blackman(9);
%
%    stemplot the windows
stem(n,wh,'filled','r'); hold on
stem(n,wham,'filled','b')
stem(n,wb,'filled','g')
xlabel('sample #');ylabel('w[n]');
legend('Hanning','Hamming','Blackman',0); hold off
%
%    generate the frequency responses of the windows
[Hh,W] = freqz(wh,A,256);
[Hham,W] = freqz(wham,A,256);
[Hb,W] = freqz(wb,A,256);
%
%    Plot the magnitude responses on the same plot
figure,plot(W,10*log10(abs(Hh)),'r'); hold on
plot(W,10*log10(abs(Hham)),'b')
plot(W,10*log10(abs(Hb)),'g')
xlabel('Normalized frequency');ylabel('Magnitude in dB')
legend('Hanning','Hamming','Blackman',0)
hold off
```

C.2   M FILES FROM CHAPTER 3

```
%    contrast.m
%    Contrast vs luminance
%    Author: K.S. Thyagarajan
%
f = 1:5:255;% intensity values
c1 = 50*log10(f);% contrast using log function
c2 = 21.9*f.^(1/3);% contrast using 1/3 power law
c3 = 10*f.^0.5;% contrast using square root law
plot(f,c1,f,c2,'g:',f,c3,'r--')
xlabel('luminance, f'),ylabel('contrast, c')
legend('50log10(f)','21.9f^1^/^3','10f^1^/^2',0)



%    machBand1.m
%    Mach Bands
%    Author: K.S. Thyagarajan
%
%
%    Create an image w/ a gradation of intensity
p = ones(256,256);
%
bL = 20;% background low
bH = 100;% background high
eL = 64;
eH = 80;
p(:,1:eL) = bL;
p(:,eH+1:256) = bH;
m = (bH-bL)/(eH-eL+1);
for n = 1:256
    if n <= eL
        p(:,n) = bL;
    elseif n > eH
        p(:,n) = bH;
    else
        p(:,n) = bL + m*(n-eL+1);
    end
end
%
%    Display banded image
```

```
%figure,imshow(uint8(p))
%
%    Create MTF filter impulse response
h = ones(1,7);
h(1) = -0.2; h(7) = h(1);
h(2) = -0.4; h(6) = h(2);
h(3) = 0.75; h(5) = h(3);
h(4) = 1;
h = h/sum(h);
%
%    Filter a row through the MTF filter
p1 = zeros(1,256);
p1 = p(64,:);
p2 = conv(p1,h);
p1 = p2(4:259);
%
%    Display profile
figure,plot((eL-8:eH+8),p(64,eL-8:eH+8),'r'); hold on
plot((eL-8:eL+8),p1(eL-8:eL+8),'k')
plot((eH-8:eH+8),p1(eH-8:eH+8),'k'); hold off
xlabel('pixel position along row 64')
ylabel('pixel value')
legend('Brightness','Luminance',0)




%    mtf.m
%    HVS impulse and frequency responses
%    Author: K.S. Thyagarajan
%    Reference:
%    J.L. Mannos & D.J. Sakrison, "The Effects of a
%    Visual Fidelity
%    Criterion on the Encoding of Images," IEEE Trans.
%    Info. Theory,
%    IT-20, No.4, July 1974.
%    HVS MTF
%    H(f1) = A(a+f1)exp(-f1^b)
%    f1 = f/f0
```

```
%     f is the frequency in cycles/degree
%
%     The corresponding impulse response when a = 0 &
%     b = 1 is
%     h(x) = 2Af0(1-(2.pi.f0.x)^2)/((1+(2.pi.f0.x)^2)^2)
A = 2.6;
a = 0.0192;
b = 1.1;
f0 = 8.772;
f = 0:0.1:60;
f1 = f/f0;
H = A*(a+f1).*exp(-f1.^b);
Hmax = max(H(:));
figure,loglog(f,H/Hmax)
xlabel('spatial frequency, cycles/degree')
ylabel('contrast sensitivity')
%
%
x = -1:0.005:1;
k = (2*pi*f0)^2;
h0 = 2*A*f0;
N1 = 1 - k*x.^2;
D1 = 1+k*x.^2;
D2 = D1.^2;
h = h0*N1./D2;
hmax = max(h(:));
figure,plot(x,h/hmax)
xlabel('x from the fovea, min of arc')
ylabel('h(x)')
axis([-0.25 0.25 -0.15 1.1])



%     sineGrating.m
%     Sinusoidal gratings for the MTF
%     Author: K.S. Thyagarajan
%
%
p = ones(256,256);
B = 140;                % background
Am = 50;                % amplitude of the sinusoid
```

```matlab
fMax = 100;                  % Maximum sinusoidal frequency
%
%    Contrast sensitivity parameters
A = 2.6;
a = 0.0192;
b = 1.1;
f0 = 8.772;
f = 0:fMax/256:fMax*255/256;
f1 = f/f0;
H = A*(a+f1).*exp(-f1.^b);
Hmax = max(H(:));
H = H/Hmax;
for i = 0:255
    f = i*fMax/256;    % spatial frequency varies
linearly
    t = B + Am*sin(2*pi*f*i/512);
    p(:,i+1)=t;
end
for i = 0:255
    %p(i+1,:)=p(i+1,:)*H(i+1);
    p(256-i,:)=p(256-i,:)*H(i+1);
end
%
%    Display banded image
figure,imshow(uint8(p))




%    weber.m
%    Simultaneous contrast Effect in the HVS
%    Author: K.S. Thyagarajan
%
f0 = 180;
fs1 = 80;
fs2 = 110;
fs3 = 140;
%
%    Background intensity
p1 = fs1*ones(129,129);
p2 = fs2*ones(129,129);
```

```
p3 = fs3*ones(129,129);
%
%    Object intensity
p1(65-16:65+16,65-16:65+16)=f0;
p2(65-16:65+16,65-16:65+16)=f0;
p3(65-16:65+16,65-16:65+16)=f0;
%
%
subplot(131),imshow(uint8(p1))
subplot(132),imshow(uint8(p2))
subplot(133),imshow(uint8(p3))
```

C.3   M FILES FROM CHAPTER 4

```
%    Fig4_12.m
%    M file to illustrate the effect of sampling
%    an image below Nyquist rate
%    Author: K.S. Thyagarajan
%
%    Read an imahe file
I = imread('lena.ras');     % 512x512 RGB image
Y = rgb2gray(I);     % convert RGB to intensity image
J = imresize(Y,[128 128]);  % subsample I without
%    lowpass filtering first
figure,imshow(J,[]) % display J
title('Subsampled image without lowpass prefiltering')
K = imresize(Y,[128 128],'bicubic');     % subsample I
%    with lowpass
%    filtering first and then subsample.
figure,imshow(K,[]) % display K
title('Subsampled image with lowpass prefiltering')
```

C.4   M FILES FROM CHAPTER 5

```
%     Fig5_1.m
%     Enhancement using log transformation
%     applied to the display of 2D spectrum
%     Author: K.S. Thyagarajan
%
%     Read input image
inImage = imread('cameraman.tif');
%imshow(inImage)
inImage = im2double(inImage);
%     Calculate the 2-D DFT of the input image
fftImage = fft2(inImage);
%
%     Display the magnitude of the 2-D DFT centered
figure,imshow(abs(fftshift(fftImage)))

%     Display the log magnitude of the 2-D DFT centered
k = 0.25;
figure,imshow(k*log10(1+abs(fftshift(fftImage))))
%
%     Plot y = kxlog10(1+x)
x = 0:255;
for j = 1:3
    k = j*0.25;
    y(j,:) = k * log10(1 + x);
end
figure,plot(x,y(1,:),'k',x,y(2,:),'k-.',x,y(3,:),'k:')
legend('k = 0.25','k = 0.50', 'k = 0.75')



%     Fig5_2.m
%     Piecewise linear tranformation for contrast
stretching
%     Author: K.S. Thyagarajan
%
```

```
%     Define the regions
x1 = 70;
x2 = 170;
xMax = 255;
%
%     Select slopes in the three regions:
%     [0,49], [50,119], [120,255]
a = 0.25; b = 1.55; c = 0.5;
y(1:x1) = a*(0:x1-1);
y(x1+1:x2) = y(x1) + b*(0:x2-x1-1);
y(x2+1:xMax+1) = y(x2) + c*(0:xMax-x2);
figure,plot(0:255,y,'k')



%     Fig5_3.m
%     Example of contrast stretching an image
%     Author: K.S. Thyagarajan
%

I = imread('couple.ras');
Ycbcr = rgb2ycbcr(I);
Y = Ycbcr(:,:,1);
imhist(Y,256)
%     We find that 35% of the pixels are between [0,70]
a = 1.75;
b = 0.75;
c = 0.5;
%
x1 = 50;
x2 = 170;
xMax = 255;
y(1:x1) = a*(0:x1-1);
y(x1+1:x2) = y(x1) + b*(0:x2-x1-1);
y(x2+1:xMax+1) = y(x2) + c*(0:xMax-x2);
%
Z = Y;
[indX,indY] = find(Y < x1);
for j = 1:length(indX)
    Z(indX(j),indY(j)) = y(Y(indX(j),indY(j)));
end
```

```
clear indX indY
[indX,indY] = find(Y>=x1 & Y<x2);
for j = 1:length(indX)
    Z(indX(j),indY(j)) = y(Y(indX(j),indY(j)));
end
clear indX indY
[indX,indY] = find(Y>=x2 & Y<=xMax);
for j = 1:length(indX)
    Z(indX(j),indY(j)) = y(Y(indX(j),indY(j)));
end
figure,imshow(Y,[])
figure,imshow(Z,[])




%    Fig5_4.m
%    Example of Histogram equalization
%    Author: K.S. Thyagarajan
%

I = imread('tiffany.ras');  % a color image
Ycbcr = rgb2ycbcr(I);    % convert rgb to ycbcr
Y = Ycbcr(:,:,1);    % extract Y component
imhist(Y,256)    % display histogram of the original
image
%
Z = histeq(Y,256);   % histogram equalize Y
figure,imhist(Z,256)    % display the histogram of the
equalized image
figure,imshow(Y,[]) % display the original intensity
image
figure,imshow(Z,[]) % display the equalized intensity
image




%    Fig5_5.m
%    Example of adaptive histogram equalization
%    Author: K.S. Thyagarajan
%
```

```
I = imread('couple.ras');   % a color image
Ycbcr = rgb2ycbcr(I);    % convert rgb to ycbcr
Y = Ycbcr(:,:,1);    % extract Y component
figure,imhist(Y,256)    % display histogram of the
%    original image
%
Z = adapthisteq(Y,'NumTiles',[8 8],'ClipLimit',0.01);   %
%    histogram equalize Y
figure,imhist(Z,256)    % display the histogram of the
%    equalized image
figure,imshow(Y,[]) % display the original intensity
%    image
figure,imshow(Z,[]) % display the equalized intensity
%    image




%    Fig5_7.m
%    Example of spatial mask operations for smoothing
%    Author: K.S. Thyagarajan
%

I = imread('baboon.ras');   % a color image
Ycbcr = rgb2ycbcr(I);    % convert rgb to ycbcr
Y = Ycbcr(:,:,1);    % extract Y component
%
H1 = [1/4 1/4; 1/4 1/4];      % 2x2 averaging mask
H2 = [1/9 1/9 1/9; 1/9 1/9 1/9; 1/9 1/9 1/9];
H3 = [0 1/8 0; 1/8 1/2 1/8; 0 1/8 0];
H4 = fspecial('gaussian',7,1.5);
Z1 = imfilter(Y,H1,'symmetric','same');
Z2 = imfilter(Y,H2,'symmetric','same');
Z3 = imfilter(Y,H3,'symmetric','same');
Z4 = imfilter(Y,H4,'symmetric','same');
figure,imshow(Y,[]) % display the original intensity
image
figure,imshow(Z1,[]) %
figure,imshow(Z2,[])
figure,imshow(Z3,[])
figure,imshow(Z4,[])
```

```
%     Fig5_8.m
%     Example of spatial mask operations for edge
%     sharpening
%     Author: K.S.  Thyagarajan
%

I = imread('barbara.ras');   % a B/W image
%
H1 = [0 -1 0; -1 5 -1; 0 -1 0];
H2 = [-1 -1 -1; -1 9 -1; -1 -1 -1];
H3 = [1 -2 1; -2 5 -2; 1 -2 1];
Z1 = imfilter(I,H1,'symmetric','same');
Z2 = imfilter(I,H2,'symmetric','same');
Z3 = imfilter(I,H3,'symmetric','same');
Z4 = imlincomb(1,double(I),0.75,double(Z3));
Max = max(Z4(:));
Min = min(Z4(:));
Z4 = (Z4-Min)/(Max-Min)*(255 - Min) + Min;
%
figure,imshow(I) % display the original intensity image
figure,imshow(Z1) %
figure,imshow(Z2)
figure,imshow(Z3)
figure,imshow(Z4,[])
```

```
%     Fig5_10.m
%     Example of spatial mask operations for edge
%     sharpening
%     Author: K.S.  Thyagarajan
%

I = imread('barbara.ras');   % a B/W image
%
H1 = [0 -1 0; -1 5 -1; 0 -1 0];
H2 = [-1 -1 -1; -1 9 -1; -1 -1 -1];
H3 = [1 -2 1; -2 5 -2; 1 -2 1];
Z1 = imfilter(I,H1,'symmetric','same');
Z2 = imfilter(I,H2,'symmetric','same');
```

```
Z3 = imfilter(I,H3,'symmetric','same');
Z4 = imlincomb(1,double(I),0.75,double(Z3));
Max = max(Z4(:));
Min = min(Z4(:));
Z4 = (Z4-Min)/(Max-Min)*(255 - Min) + Min;
%
figure,imshow(I) % display the original intensity image
figure,imshow(Z1) %
figure,imshow(Z2)
figure,imshow(Z3)
figure,imshow(Z4,[])




%    Fig5_11.m
%    Example of spatial filtering for image enhancement
%    Author: K.S. Thyagarajan
%

I = imread('barbara.ras');   % a B/W image
%
[f1,f2] = freqspace(13,'meshgrid'); % 13x13 grid of
% freq. points
H1 = ones(13);
H2 = ones(13);
f = sqrt(f1 .^2 + f2 .^2);   % 2D circularly symmetric
% freq.
H1((f>0.5)) = 0; % H is a lowpass filter
h1 = fwind1(H1,hamming(13));     % Design 2D hamming
%    windowed fir filter
freqz2(h1); % plot the lowpass filter freq. response
%
H2((f>0.5) & (f<0.75)) = 0.0;    % bandstop filter spec
h2 = fwind1(H2,hamming(13));
figure,freqz2(h2);
%
Z1 = imfilter(I,h1,'symmetric','same'); % lowpass filtered
%    image
Z2 = imfilter(I,h2,'symmetric','same'); % bandstop filtered
%    image
```

```
%
figure,imshow(I) % display the original intensity image
figure,imshow(Z1) %
figure,imshow(Z2) %




%    Fig5_12.m
%    Example of median filtering an image for noise
%    cleaning
%    Author: K.S. Thyagarajan
%

I = imread('girl.ras');  % a color image
Ycbcr = rgb2ycbcr(I);    % convert RGB to YCbCr
Y = Ycbcr(:,:,1);    % extract the intensity image
%
Y1 = imnoise(Y,'salt & pepper',0.05);
Y2 = imnoise(Y,'gaussian',0,0.01);
figure,imshow(Y)
%
figure,imshow(Y1)    % display salt & pepper image
figure,imshow(medfilt2(Y1,[3 3]))% display medfilt 3 x 3
figure,imshow(medfilt2(Y1,[5 5]))% display medfilt 5x5
%
figure,imshow(Y2)    % display gaussian noisy image
figure,imshow(medfilt2(Y2,[3 3]))
figure,imshow(medfilt2(Y1,[5 5]))




%    Fig5_14.m
%    Example of image enhancement by homomorphic filtering
%    Author: K.S. Thyagarajan

I = imread('girl.ras');  % a color image
Ycbcr = rgb2ycbcr(I);    % convert RGB to YCbCr
Y = Ycbcr(:,:,1);    % extract the intensity image
```

```
%
[f1,f2] = freqspace(13,'meshgrid'); % 13x13 grid of
%     freq. points
H = ones(13);
f = sqrt(f1 .^2 + f2 .^2);   % 2D circularly symmetric
%     freq.
H((f<=0.5)) = 0.5;   % H has lowpass response of 0.5
H((f>0.5)) = 1.0;    % and highpass response of 1
h = fwind1(H,hamming(13));      % Design 2D hamming
%     windowed fir filter
freqz2(h); % plot the lowpass filter freq. response
Z = imfilter(log(double(Y)+1.0),h,'symmetric','same'); %
%     filter
% the log image through H; 1 is added to map 0 to 0
%     value
figure,imshow(Y)
figure,imshow(exp(Z)-1,[])% Exponentiate, subtract 1 and
%     display




%    Fig5_15.m
%    Example of color image enhancement
%    Author: K.S. Thyagarajan

I = imread('couple.ras');   % a color image
ColorSpace = 'HSI'; % YUV or HSI or RGB
ProcType = 'I+H+S';
switch ColorSpace
    case 'HSI'
        J = rgb2hsv(I);    % convert RGB to HSV; each
        of HSV is in (0,1)
        %
        switch ProcType
            case 'I'
                Y = J(:,:,3);    % extract the
                intensity image
                Y1 = adapthisteq(Y,'NumTiles',[8 8]);
                J(:,:,3) = Y1;
                J1 = hsv2rgb(J);
```

```
                    figure,imshow(I);    % original image
                    figure,imshow(J1)    % processed image
            case 'I+S'
                    Y = J(:,:,3);    % extract the
                    % intensity image
                    Y1 = adapthisteq(Y,'NumTiles',[8 8]);%
                    % Hist equalize I
                    J(:,:,3) = Y1;
                    S = J(:,:,2);
                    S = 0.65*S; % scale down saturation
                    % value
                    J(:,:,2) = S;
                    J1 = hsv2rgb(J);
                    figure,imshow(I);    % original image
                    figure,imshow(J1)    % processed image
            case 'S'
                    S = J(:,:,2);
                    S = 0.7*S;
                    J(:,:,2) = S;
                    J1 = hsv2rgb(J);
                    figure,imshow(I);
                    figure,imshow(J1)
            case 'H'
                    Hu = J(:,:,1);
                    Hu = Hu - 0.01;
                    J(:,:,1) = Hu;
                    J1 = hsv2rgb(J);
                    figure,imshow(I);
                    figure,imshow(J1)
            case 'I+H+S'
                    Hu = J(:,:,1);
                    Hu = Hu - 0.01; % scale down
                    % saturation value
                    J(:,:,1) = Hu;
                    %
                    S = J(:,:,2);
                    S = 0.7*S;
                    J(:,:,2) = S;
                    %
                    Y = J(:,:,3);    % extract the
                    % intensity image
```

```
                        Y1 = adapthisteq(Y,'NumTiles',[8 8]);%
                        % Hist equalize I
                        J(:,:,3) = Y1;
                        %
                        J1 = hsv2rgb(J);
                        figure,imshow(I);    % original image
                        figure,imshow(J1)    % processed image
                end
        case 'YUV'
                J = rgb2ycbcr(I);
                Y = J(:,:,1);    % extract the intensity image
                Y1 = adapthisteq(Y,'NumTiles',[8
                8],'Range','full');
                J(:,:,1) = Y1;
                J1 = ycbcr2rgb(J);
                figure,imshow(I);    % original image
                figure,imshow(J1)    % processed image
                [f1,f2] = freqspace(13,'meshgrid');
                H = ones(13);
                f = sqrt(f1 .^2 + f2 .^2);   % 2D circularly
                % symmetric freq.
                H((f>0.75)) = 0.0;   % H has lowpass response
                % of 0.5
                h = fwind1(H,hamming(13));
                Z = imfilter(Y1,h,'symmetric','same');
                J(:,:,1) = Z;
                J1 = ycbcr2rgb(J);
                figure,imshow(J1)
        case 'RGB'
                R = adapthisteq(I(:,:,1),'NumTiles',[8 8]);
                G = adapthisteq(I(:,:,2),'NumTiles',[8 8]);
                B = adapthisteq(I(:,:,3),'NumTiles',[8 8]);
                I1(:,:,1) = R;
                I1(:,:,2) = G;
                I1(:,:,3) = B;
                figure,imshow(I)
                figure,imshow(I1)
end
```

```
%     AdaptHistogramEq.m
%     Enhances a luminance image by adaptive histogram
%     equalization
%     Author: K.S. Thyagarajan


I = imread('couple.ras');     % A color image
Ycbcr = rgb2ycbcr(I);     % convert rgb into YCbCr
Y = Ycbcr(:,:,1);     % extract the luminance component;
% it is type uint8

% adaptively equalize the histogram of the luminance
% component
Z = adapthisteq(Y,'NumTiles',[16 16]);
%     Display both images
figure,imshow(Y)
figure,imshow(Z)
%
% Display histograms before and after equalization w/
% 128 bins
figure,imhist(Y,128), ylabel('No. of pixels')
figure,imhist(Z,128), ylabel('No. of pixels')




%     NoiseClean.m
%     Removes noise using adaptive filtering
%     Author: K.S. Thyagarajan

I = imread('couple.ras');     % A color image
D = size(I);
if length(D) < 3
     Y = I;
else
     Ycbcr = rgb2ycbcr(I);     % convert rgb into YCbCr
     Y = Ycbcr(:,:,1);     % extract the luminance
     % component; it is type uint8
end
%
snr = 5;     % Signal-toNoise ratio of snr dB
```

```
varN = std2(double(Y))^2 * ((10 ^ (-0.1*snr))); % Noise
% variance
Y1 = sqrt(sigN) * randn(size(Y)) + double(Y); % add
% Gaussian noise to image
h1 = fspecial('average',[3 3]); % design a 5x5 averaging
% filter
h2 = fspecial('gaussian',[3 3],2.5); % design a Gaussian
% lpf w/ sigma=2.5
%
Z1 = imfilter(double(Y1),h1,'symmetric','same');    %
% filter Y through h
Z2 = imfilter(double(Y1),h2,'symmetric','same');
Z3 = wiener2(double(Y1),[3 3]); % filter through adaptive
% Wiener filter

figure,imshow(Y1,[])     % Display noisy brightness image
figure,imshow(Z1,[])     % smoothing filtered image
figure,imshow(Z2,[])     % lowpass gaussian filtered
figure,imshow(Z3,[])     % adaptively filtered




%    HistogramEq.m
%    Enhances a luminance image by histogram equalization
%    Author: K.S. Thyagarajan


I = imread('couple.ras');    % A color image
Ycbcr = rgb2ycbcr(I);   % convert rgb into YCbCr
Y = Ycbcr(:,:,1);    % extract the luminance component;
% it is type uint8

Z = histeq(Y);  % histogram equalize the luminance
% component
%    Display both images
figure,imshow(Y)
figure,imshow(Z)
%
% Display histograms before and after equalization w/
% 128 bins
```

```
figure,imhist(Y,128), ylabel('No. of pixels')
figure,imhist(Z,128), ylabel('No. of pixels')




%     NoiseClean.m
%     Removes noise using neighborhood smoothing,
%     median filtering, and adaptive filtering
%     Author: K.S. Thyagarajan

I = imread('couple.ras');    % A color image
D = size(I);
if length(D) < 3
    Y = I;
else
    Ycbcr = rgb2ycbcr(I);    % convert rgb into YCbCr
    Y = Ycbcr(:,:,1);    % extract the luminance
    % component; it is type uint8
end
%
Y1 = imnoise(Y,'salt & pepper',0.05); % add impulse
% noise w/ density 0.05
h1 = fspecial('average',[3 3]); % design a 5x5 averaging
% filter
h2 = fspecial('gaussian',[3 3],2.5); % design a Gaussian
% lpf w/ sigma=1.5
%
Z1 = imfilter(Y1,h1,'symmetric','same');    % filter Y
% through h
Z2 = imfilter(Y1,h2,'symmetric','same');
Z3 = medfilt2(Y1,[3 3], 'symmetric');

figure,imshow(Y1)    % Display brightness image
figure,imshow(Z1)
figure,imshow(Z2)
figure,imshow(Z3)
```

```
%     unsharp.m
%     Increases the sharpness of an image using
%     unsharp masking: y(m,n) = f(m,n) + a*g(m,n)
%     f is the input image
%     y is the sharpened image
%     g is the gradient image
%     a > 0
%     Author: K.S. Thyagarajan

%I = imread('couple.ras');   % A color image
I = imread('xray1_sml','jpg');
%I = imread('Aral1997','tiff');
%I = imread('mri','tiff');
D = size(I);
if length(D) < 3
    Y = I;
else
    Ycbcr = rgb2ycbcr(I);   % convert rgb into YCbCr
    Y = Ycbcr(:,:,1);   % extract the luminance
    % component; it is type uint8
end

%
h = fspecial('unsharp',0.4);    % design a 2D unsharp
% filter
%h = fspecial('log',[5 5]);
%
Z = imfilter(Y,h,'symmetric','same');   % filter Y through
% h
figure,imshow(Y)
figure,imshow(Z)
```

C.5   M FILES FROM CHAPTER 6

```
% BasisImages.m
% Generates Basis images for DCT, DST, Hadamard, Hartley
% 2D discrete image transforms
```

```matlab
% TransformType = 'dct' for DCT; 'dst' for discrete sine
% transform;
%    'hadamard', 'hartley'
%    Author: K.S. Thyagarajan

N = 8;   % transform size N x N
TransformType = 'slant';
switch TransformType
    case 'dct'
        % generate y(k,m) =
        a(k)sum(cos((2n+1)pi*k/(2N)))
        %    a(0) = 1/sqrt(N); a(k) = sqrt(2/N), 1<= k
        %  <= N-1
        for k = 0:N-1
            y(k+1,:) = cos((2*(0:N-1)+1)*pi*k/(2*N));
        end
        y(1,:) = y(1,:)/sqrt(N);
        y(2:N,:) = y(2:N,:) * sqrt(2/N);
    case 'hadamard'
        y = [1 1; 1 -1];
        y = y/sqrt(2);
        n = 2;
        while n < N
            n = 2*n;
            y = [y y; y -y];
            y = y/sqrt(2);
        end
    case 'haar'
        sq2 = sqrt(2);
        h1 = [1 1 1 1 1 1 1 1];
        h2 = [1 1 1 1 -1 -1 -1 -1];
        h3 = [sq2 sq2 -sq2 -sq2 0 0 0 0];
        h4 = [0 0 0 0 sq2 sq2 -sq2 -sq2];
        h5 = [2 -2 0 0 0 0 0 0];
        h6 = [0 0 2 -2 0 0 0 0];
        h7 = [0 0 0 0 2 -2 0 0];
        h8 = [0 0 0 0 0 0 2 -2];
        y = [h1;h2;h3;h4;h5;h6;h7;h8]/sqrt(8);
    case 'dst'
        for k = 0:N-1
            y(k+1,:) = sin(((0:N-1)+1)*pi*(k+1)/(N+1));
        end
        y = y*sqrt(2/(N+1));
```

```
        case 'slant'
            a8 = sqrt(16/21);
            b8 = sqrt(5/21);
            s4 = [1 1 1 1; 3/sqrt(5) 1/sqrt(5) -1/sqrt(5)
            -3/sqrt(5);...
                1 -1 -1 1; 1/sqrt(5) -3/sqrt(5) 3/sqrt(5)
                -1/sqrt(5)];
            s4 = s4/2;
            h1 = [1 0 0 0 1 0 0 0];
            h2 = [a8 b8 0 0 -a8 b8 0 0];
            h3 = [0 0 1 0 0 0 1 0];
            h4 = [0 0 0 1 0 0 0 1];
            h5 = [0 1 0 0 0 -1 0 0];
            h6 = [-b8 a8 0 0 b8 a8 0 0];
            h7 = [0 0 1 0 0 0 -1 0];
            h8 = [0 0 0 1 0 0 0 -1];
            y = [h1;h2;h3;h4;h5;h6;h7;h8]*[s4 zeros(4,4);..
.
                zeros(4,4) s4]/sqrt(2);
end
%
y = y'; % Transpose the transform matrix
%
X = ones(192,192) * 16; % inscribe each N x N submatrix
% into X
for k = 0:N-1
    rIndx = k*24 + 1;
    for l = 0:N-1
        cIndx = l*24 +1;
        T = y(:,k+1) * y(:,l+1)';
        if k == 0
            T = T/max(T(:))*255;
        else
            T = (T-min(T(:)))/(max(T(:))-
min(T(:)))*255;
        end
        T1 = imresize(T,[16 16],'bicubic'); % exapnd
% matrix to 2N x 2N
        X(rIndx+3:rIndx+18,cIndx+3:cIndx+18) = T1;
        %subplot(N,N,k*N+l+1),imshow(T,[])
    end
end
figure,imshow(X,[])
```

```
% genHistTransform.m.m
% Generates histograms of coefficients of DCT, DST,
% Hadamard, Hartley
% 2D discrete image transforms
% TransformType = 'dct' for DCT; 'dst' for discrete sine
% transform;
%    'hadamard', 'hartley'
%    Author: K.S. Thyagarajan

N = 8;   % transform size N x N
TransformType = 'haar';
switch TransformType
    case 'dct'
        % generate y(k,m) =
        % a(k)sum(cos((2n+1)pi*k/(2N)))
        %    a(0) = 1/sqrt(N); a(k) = sqrt(2/N), 1<= k
        % <= N-1
        for k = 0:N-1
            y(k+1,:) = cos((2*(0:N-1)+1)*pi*k/(2*N));
        end
        y(1,:) = y(1,:)/sqrt(N);
        y(2:N,:) = y(2:N,:) * sqrt(2/N);
    case 'hadamard'
        y = [1 1; 1 -1];
        y = y/sqrt(2);
        n = 2;
        while n < N
            n = 2*n;
            y = [y y; y -y];
            y = y/sqrt(2);
        end
    case 'haar'
        sq2 = sqrt(2);
        h1 = [1 1 1 1 1 1 1 1];
        h2 = [1 1 1 1 -1 -1 -1 -1];
        h3 = [sq2 sq2 -sq2 -sq2 0 0 0 0];
        h4 = [0 0 0 0 sq2 sq2 -sq2 -sq2];
        h5 = [2 -2 0 0 0 0 0 0];
        h6 = [0 0 2 -2 0 0 0 0];
        h7 = [0 0 0 0 2 -2 0 0];
        h8 = [0 0 0 0 0 0 2 -2];
```

```
        y = [h1;h2;h3;h4;h5;h6;h7;h8]/sqrt(8);
    case 'dst'
        for k = 0:N-1
            y(k+1,:) = sin(((0:N-1)+1)*pi*(k+1)/(N+1));
        end
        y = y*sqrt(2/(N+1));
    case 'slant'
        a8 = sqrt(16/21);
        b8 = sqrt(5/21);
        s4 = [1 1 1 1; 3/sqrt(5) 1/sqrt(5) -1/sqrt(5)
        -3/sqrt(5);...
            1 -1 -1 1; 1/sqrt(5) -3/sqrt(5) 3/sqrt(5)
            -1/sqrt(5)];
        s4 = s4/2;
        h1 = [1 0 0 0 1 0 0 0];
        h2 = [a8 b8 0 0 -a8 b8 0 0];
        h3 = [0 0 1 0 0 0 1 0];
        h4 = [0 0 0 1 0 0 0 1];
        h5 = [0 1 0 0 0 -1 0 0];
        h6 = [-b8 a8 0 0 b8 a8 0 0];
        h7 = [0 0 1 0 0 0 -1 0];
        h8 = [0 0 0 1 0 0 0 -1];
        y = [h1;h2;h3;h4;h5;h6;h7;h8]*[s4 zeros(4,4);..
.
            zeros(4,4) s4]/sqrt(2);
end
%
%    for 8 bpp, maximum DC coef. value = 2040;
%    range of AC coef. values is -1019 to +1020
coefHist = zeros(N,N,2040); % assign an array to store
% histogram counts
%
for j = 1:5
    switch num2str(j)
        case '1'
            I = imread('cameraman.tif');
        case '2'
            I = imread('cornfield.ras');
        case '3'
            I = imread('image3.ras');
```

```
        case '4'
            I = imread('lighthouse.ras');
        case '5'
            I = imread('yacht.ras');
    end
    % perform NxN transform on each image
    for r = 1:N:size(I,1)
        for c = 1:N:size(I,2)
            I1(r:r+N-1,c:c+N-1) = y*double( I(r:r+N-
            1,c:c+N-1))*y';
            %   do histogram count for each of NxN
            % coefficients
            for m = 1:N
                for n = 1:N
                    if m==1 & n==1
                        Indx = round(I1(r+m-1,c+n-
                        1));
                    else
                        Indx = round(I1(r+m-1,c+n-
                        1)) + 1020;
                    end
                    coefHist(m,n,Indx) =
                    coefHist(m,n,Indx) + 1;
                end
            end

        end
    end
end
%
HistCoef = zeros(1,2040);   % store histogram counts of
% each coef. in
%   a 1D array for plotting
for m = 1:3
    for n = 1:3
        HistCoef(1,:) = coefHist(m,n,:);
        figure,plot(HistCoef,'k'), axis tight
        xlabel('amplitude of coefficient')
        ylabel('count')

    end
end
```

```
% UseBasisImage.m
% Generates Basis images for DCT, DST, Hadamard, Hartley
% 2D discrete image transforms and builds an image using
%    basis images
% TransformType = 'dct' for DCT; 'dst' for discrete sine
% transform;
%    'hadamard', 'hartley'
%    Author: K.S. Thyagarajan

N = 8;   % transform size N x N
TransformType = 'dst';
switch TransformType
    case 'dct'
        % generate y(k,m) =
        % a(k)sum(cos((2n+1)pi*k/(2N)))
        %    a(0) = 1/sqrt(N); a(k) = sqrt(2/N), 1<= k
        % <= N-1
        for k = 0:N-1
            y(k+1,:) = cos((2*(0:N-1)+1)*pi*k/(2*N));
        end
        y(1,:) = y(1,:)/sqrt(N);
        y(2:N,:) = y(2:N,:) * sqrt(2/N);
    case 'hadamard'
        y = [1 1; 1 -1];
        y = y/sqrt(2);
        n = 2;
        while n < N
            n = 2*n;
            y = [y y; y -y];
            y = y/sqrt(2);
        end
    case 'haar'
        sq2 = sqrt(2);
        h1 = [1 1 1 1 1 1 1 1];
        h2 = [1 1 1 1 -1 -1 -1 -1];
        h3 = [sq2 sq2 -sq2 -sq2 0 0 0 0];
        h4 = [0 0 0 0 sq2 sq2 -sq2 -sq2];
        h5 = [2 -2 0 0 0 0 0 0];
        h6 = [0 0 2 -2 0 0 0 0];
        h7 = [0 0 0 0 2 -2 0 0];
        h8 = [0 0 0 0 0 0 2 -2];
```

```
                        y = [h1;h2;h3;h4;h5;h6;h7;h8]/sqrt(8);
            case 'dst'
                for k = 0:N-1
                    y(k+1,:) = sin(((0:N-1)+1)*pi*(k+1)/(N+1));
                end
                y = y*sqrt(2/(N+1));
            case 'slant'
                a8 = sqrt(16/21);
                b8 = sqrt(5/21);
                s4 = [1 1 1 1; 3/sqrt(5) 1/sqrt(5) -1/sqrt(5)
                -3/sqrt(5);...
                    1 -1 -1 1; 1/sqrt(5) -3/sqrt(5) 3/sqrt(5)
                    -1/sqrt(5)];
                s4 = s4/2;
                h1 = [1 0 0 0 1 0 0 0];
                h2 = [a8 b8 0 0 -a8 b8 0 0];
                h3 = [0 0 1 0 0 0 1 0];
                h4 = [0 0 0 1 0 0 0 1];
                h5 = [0 1 0 0 0 -1 0 0];
                h6 = [-b8 a8 0 0 b8 a8 0 0];
                h7 = [0 0 1 0 0 0 -1 0];
                h8 = [0 0 0 1 0 0 0 -1];
                y = [h1;h2;h3;h4;h5;h6;h7;h8]*[s4 zeros(4,4);...
                    zeros(4,4) s4]/sqrt(2);
        end
        %
        y = y'; % Transpose the transform matrix
        T = zeros(N*N,N*N);
        % Determine the N^2 x N^2 basis images
        for k = 0:N-1
            rInd = k*N + 1;
            for l = 0:N-1
                cInd = l*N + 1;
                T(rInd:rInd+N-1,cInd:cInd+N-1) = y(:,k+1) *
        y(:,l+1)';
            end
        end
        %
        I = imread('cameraman.tif');
        I1 = blkproc(I,[N N],@dct2);        % compute 2D DCT for
        % every N x N block
```

```
I2 = zeros(size(I));
mse = zeros(N,N);
%
for m = 0:N-1    % take each basis image along rows
    mInd = m*N + 1;
    for n = 0:N-1    % take each basis image along
    % columns
        nInd = n*N + 1;
        for r = 1:N:size(I,1) % take N rows at a time
            for c = 1:N:size(I,2)    % take N columns
            % at a time
                I1(r:r+N-1,c:c+N-1) = y'*double(
                I(r:r+N-1,c:c+N-1))*y;
                sum1 = I2(r:r+N-1,c:c+N-1);
                I2(r:r+N-1,c:c+N-1) = sum1 +...
                    I1(r+m,c+n)*T(mInd:mInd+N-
                    1,nInd:nInd+N-1);
            end
        end
        subplot(N,N,m*N+1+n),imshow(I2,[])
        mse(m+1,n+1) = (std2(double(I) - I2)) ^2;
    end
end
%
switch TransformType
    case 'dct'
        xTitle = 'DCT coefficient #';
    case 'hadamard'
        xTitle = 'Hadamard coefficient #';
    case 'dst'
        xTitle = 'DST coefficient #';
    case 'haar'
        xTitle = 'Haar coefficient #';
    case 'slant'
        xTitle = 'Slant coefficient #';
end
figure,plot(0:N^2-1,[mse(1,:) mse(2,:) mse(3,:) mse(4,:)
mse(5,:) mse(6,:)...
    mse(7,:) mse(8,:)],'k')
xlabel(xTitle)
ylabel('MSE')
```

C.6   M FILES FROM CHAPTER 7

```
%      WaveletSeriesEx.m
%      An example to compute the wavelet series
%      Author: K.S. Thyagarajan
%

%      f(t) = 2(1-t),  0<=t<=1
%      Consider Haar scaling functions and wavelets
t = linspace(0,1);

f = 2*(1-t);
%f = t .* t;
%      Haar scaling functions
phi00(1:100) = 1;
figure,plot(t,phi00,'k')
xlabel('Time'),ylabel('Amplitude'),legend('phi(0,0)',0)
%
%      Haar wavelets
% j = 0
psi00(1:50) = 1;
psi00(51:100) = -1;
%
% j = 1
psi10(1:25) = sqrt(2);
psi10(26:50) = -sqrt(2);
psi10(51:100) = 0;
psi11(1:50) = 0;
psi11(51:75) = sqrt(2);
psi11(76:100) = -sqrt(2);
% j = 2
psi20(1:12) = 2;psi20(13:25) = -2;psi20(26:100) = 0;
psi21(1:25) = 0;psi21(26:38) = 2;psi21(39:50) = -
2;psi21(51:100) = 0;
psi22(1:50) = 0;psi22(51:62) = 2;psi22(63:75) = -
2;psi22(76:100) = 0;
psi23(1:75) = 0;psi23(76:87) = 2;psi23(88:100) = -2;
figure,subplot(311)
stem(t,psi00,'k'),ylabel('Amplitude'),
legend('psi(0,0)',0)
subplot(312),stem(t,psi10,'k')
```

```
ylabel('Amplitude'), legend('psi(1,0)',0)
subplot(313),stem(t,psi11,'k')
xlabel('Time'),ylabel('Amplitude'), legend('psi(1,1)',0)
%
figure,subplot(411)
stem(t,psi20,'k'),ylabel('Amplitude'),
legend('psi(2,0)',0)
subplot(412),stem(t,psi21,'k')
ylabel('Amplitude'), legend('psi(2,1)',0)
subplot(413),stem(t,psi22,'k')
xlabel('Time'),ylabel('Amplitude'), legend('psi(2,2)',0)
subplot(414),stem(t,psi23,'k')
xlabel('Time'),ylabel('Amplitude'), legend('psi(2,3)',0)
%
%    approximation of f(t) using scaling functions
N = length(t);
c00 = sum(f .* phi00)/N;
%
f1 = c00*phi00;

%    compute wavelet coefficients and the details upto j
= 2
d00 = sum(f .* psi00)/N;
d10 = sum(f .* psi10)/N;
d11 = sum(f .* psi11)/N;
d20 = sum(f .* psi20)/N;
d21 = sum(f .* psi21)/N;
d22 = sum(f .* psi22)/N;
d23 = sum(f .* psi23)/N;
f2 = d00*psi00;
%
figure,plot(t,f1,'k')
xlabel('Time'), ylabel('Amplitude'),legend('level 0
approx.',0)
%
figure,plot(t,f2,'k')
xlabel('Time'), ylabel('Amplitude'),legend('level 0
detail',0)
%
%    Add the details to the approximation
```

```
figure,plot(t,f,'k',t,f1+f2,'--k')
xlabel('Time'), ylabel('Amplitude'),legend('f(t)','level
0 approx. + detail',0)
%%
f2 = f2 + d10*psi10 + d11 * psi11;
figure,plot(t,f2,'k')
xlabel('Time'), ylabel('Amplitude'),legend('level 1
detail',0)
%
figure,plot(t,f,'k',t,f1+f2,'--k')
xlabel('Time'), ylabel('Amplitude'),legend('f(t)','level
1 approx. + detail',0)
%
f2 = f2 + d20*psi20 + d21 * psi21 + d22 * psi22 + d23 *
psi23;
figure,plot(t,f2,'k')
xlabel('Time'), ylabel('Amplitude'),legend('level 2
detail',0)
%
figure,plot(t,f,'k',t,f1+f2,'--k')
xlabel('Time'), ylabel('Amplitude'),legend('f(t)','level
2 approx. + detail',0)




%     TestBiortho.m
%     Test biorthogonality of the analysis and
%     synthesis filters of a 2-channel filter bank subband
%     coding
%     Author: K.S. Thyagarajan

[Ld,Hd] = wfilters('rbio5.5','d');  % LPF & HPF of
% analysis
[Lr,Hr] = wfilters('rbio5.5','r');  % LPF & HPF of
% synthesis
%
n1 = length(Ld);      % length of Ld FIR filter
n2 = 2*n1 -1;          % length of conv(Lr,Ld)
%
figure,stem(0:n2-1,conv(Lr,Ld).*((-1) .^(1:n2)) +
conv(Lr,Ld),'k','filled')
```

```
%
figure,stem(0:n2-1,conv(Hr,Hd).*((-1) .^(1:n2)) +
conv(Hr,Hd),'k','filled')
%
figure,stem(0:n2-1,conv(Lr,Hd).*((-1) .^(1:n2)) +
conv(Lr,Hd),'k','filled')
%
figure,stem(0:n2-1,conv(Hr,Ld).*((-1) .^(1:n2)) +
conv(Hr,Ld),'k','filled')



function [Low,High] = BuildWavelet(WaveletName,Iter)
%    [Low,High] = BuildWavelet(WaveletName,Iter)
%    Builds the wavelet and scaling function for the
%    wavelet
%    WaveletName using Iter number of
%    iterations.
%    WaveletName can be one of 'db2','db4','db6',
%    'bior5.5', etc.
%    Author: K.S. Thyagarajan


if ~exist('WaveletName')
    Wtype = 'rbio5.5';
end
if ~exist('Iter')
    Iter = 1;
end
if nargin < 1
    error('at least one argument is required');
end
%    loop through twice to design analysis and synthesis
%    scaling function
%    and wavelets
for n = 1:2
    %   Get the lowpass (L) and highpass (H) filters
    %   for the specified wavelet
    if n == 1
        [L,H] = wfilters(WaveletName,'d');
    else
        [L,H] = wfilters(WaveletName,'r');
    end
```

```matlab
    H = ((-1) .^ (0:length(L)-1)) .* wrev(L);
    %    upsample H and convolve it with L repeatedly
%    Iter # times to
    %    obtain the wavelet function
    for i = 1:Iter
        Hu = dyadup(H,2);
        h = conv(Hu,L);
        H = h;
    end
    High(n,:) = h;
    %    upsample L and convolve it with L repeatedly
%    Iter # times to
    %    obtain the wavelet function
    L1 = L;
    for i = 1:Iter
        Lu = dyadup(L1,2);
        L2 = conv(Lu,L);
        L1 = L2;
    end
    Low(n,:) = L2/sum(L2);    % normalize the
% coefficients so the sum = 1
end
%
N = length(Low);    % length of wavelet
figure,subplot(4,1,1),plot(0:N-1,High(1,:),'k')
ylabel('Amplitude')
title([WaveletName ' :' 'Analysis' ' Wavelet
function'])
subplot(4,1,2),plot(0:N-1,Low(1,:),'k')
ylabel('Amplitude')
title([WaveletName ' :' 'Analysis' ' Scaling function'])
subplot(4,1,3),plot(0:N-1,High(2,:),'k')
ylabel('Amplitude')
title([WaveletName ' :' 'Synthesis' ' Wavelet
function'])
subplot(4,1,4),plot(0:N-1,Low(2,:),'k')
ylabel('Amplitude')
title([WaveletName ' :' 'Synthesis' ' Scaling
function'])
xlabel('Sample #')
```

```
function [Bin,H] = showHistogram(inImage,N)
%    [Bin,H] = showHistogram(inImage,N)
%    calculates the histogram of the inImage with N bins
%    Author: K.S. Thyagarajan


if class(inImage) ~= 'double'
    inImage = double(inImage);
end
%
%    Calculate the histogram of inImage
ImageSize = size(inImage,1)*size(inImage,2);
if nargin == 1
    N = 128;
    imageName = 'input image';
end
%N = 512;      % # bins
H = zeros(1,N); % Histogram of inImage
MinImage = min(inImage(:));
MaxImage = max(inImage(:));
BinWidth = (MaxImage - MinImage)/N;
BinBy2 = BinWidth/2;
Bin(1) = min(inImage(:)) + BinWidth/2;
Bin(2:N) = (1:N-1)* BinWidth + Bin(1);

for i = 1:N
    if i == 1
        [x,y] = find((inImage(:,:) >= MinImage) &
(inImage(:,:) < Bin(i)+BinBy2));
        H(i) = H(i) + size(x,1);
    elseif i == N
        [x,y] = find((inImage(:,:)>=Bin(i)-BinBy2) &
(inImage(:,:)<= MaxImage));
        H(i) = H(i) + size(x,1);
    else
        [x,y] = find((inImage(:,:)>=Bin(i)-BinBy2) &
(inImage(:,:)<Bin(i)+BinBy2));
        H(i) = H(i) + size(x,1);
    end
end
```

C.7   M FILES FROM CHAPTER 8

```
%    Ch8Fig1.m
%    Plots the profile of an image
%    Author: K.S. Thyagarajan

A = imread('barbara.ras');
figure,imshow(A),title('Original Image')
%
rowNo = 128;
x = double(A(rowNo,:));
Cols = size(A,2);
%
MaxNum = 128;
for k = 1:MaxNum
    l = length(k:Cols);
    Cor(k) = sum(x(k:Cols) .* x(1:Cols-k+1))/l;
end
MaxCor = max(Cor);
Cor = Cor/MaxCor;
subplot(2,1,1),plot(1:Cols,x,'k')
xlabel('Pixel number'), ylabel('Amplitude')
legend(['Row' ' ' num2str(rowNo)],0)
subplot(2,1,2),plot(0:MaxNum-1,Cor,'k')
xlabel('Pixel displacement'), ylabel('Normalized corr.')


%    Ch8Fig2.m
%    Plots the DCT of a row of an image
%    Author: K.S. Thyagarajan

A = imread('barbara.ras');
figure,imshow(A),title('Original Image')
%
rowNo = 128;
x = double(A(128,128:135));
y = dct2(x);
subplot(3,1,1),plot(1:size(A,2),A(rowNo,:),'k')
title(['Row' ' ' num2str(rowNo)]),ylabel('Amplitude')
subplot(3,1,2), stem(x,'k','filled')
title('image pixel'), ylabel('Amplitude')
%
```

```
subplot(3,1,3), stem(y,'k','filled')
title('DCT'),xlabel('Pixel number'), ylabel('Amplitude')




%    CodingGainOfDWT.m
%    Computes the coding gain of 2D DWT
%    for a given level.
%    Specify the wavelet name "wname" and
%    number of levels "NumLevel"
%    Author: K.S. Thyagarajan



A = imread('barbara.ras');   % read an image
%
NumLevel = 3;    % # levels of DWT
TotalBands = 3*NumLevel +1;
%
wname = 'db4';
[C,S] = wavedec2(double(A),NumLevel,wname);     %
NumLevel DWT2
%    find the variances of the different scales
for l = 1:NumLevel
    if l == NumLevel
        cA = appcoef2(C,S,wname,l);
        VarOfCoef(l,1) = std2(cA)^2;
        [H,V,D] = detcoef2('all',C,S,l);
        VarOfCoef(l,2) = std2(H)^2;
        VarOfCoef(l,3) = std2(V)^2;
        VarOfCoef(l,4) = std2(D)^2;
    else
        [H,V,D] = detcoef2('all',C,S,l);
        VarOfCoef(l,2) = std2(H)^2;
        VarOfCoef(l,3) = std2(V)^2;
        VarOfCoef(l,4) = std2(D)^2;
    end
end
MeanOfVar = 0;
GeoMeanOfVar = 1;
for l = 1:NumLevel
    if l == NumLevel
```

```
                startBand = 1;
        else
                startBand = 2;
        end
        for  k = startBand:4
                P1 = VarOfCoef(1,k)  ^  (1/(TotalBands));
                GeoMeanOfVar = GeoMeanOfVar*P1;
                MeanOfVar = MeanOfVar + VarOfCoef(1,k);
        end
end
MeanOfVar = MeanOfVar/TotalBands;
CG = 10*log10(MeanOfVar/GeoMeanOfVar)




%    CodingGainOfTC.m
%    computes the coding gain for the 2D DCT coder
%    Specify block size "N"
%    Author: K.S. Thyagarajan


N = 32;   % N x N block
A = imread('cameraman.tif');   % read an image
[Rows,Cols] = size(A);
fun = @dct2;
T = blkproc(A,[N N],fun);     % do N x N 2D DCT
%    compute the DCT coefficient variance
for  k = 1:N
    for  l = 1:N
        V = std2(T(k:N:Rows,l:N:Cols));
        VarOfCoef(k,l) = V * V;
    end
end

%
MeanOfVar = mean(VarOfCoef(:));
P1 = VarOfCoef .^  (1/(N^2));
GeoMeanOfVar = prod(P1(:)); % geometric mean of the
% coef. variances
CG = 10*log10(MeanOfVar/GeoMeanOfVar)
```

```
%    CompressDWT.m
%    Assigns quantizer bits optimally using
%    recursive integer bit allocation rule for the DWT
%    coefficients
%    and then quantizes the DWT coefficients and
%    dequantize the coefficients and reconstructs the
%    image.
%    Author: K.S. Thyagarajan

%    Choose average overall bit rate for R


R = 0.5;    % overall average bit rate is 1 bpp
A = imread('barbara.ras');  % read an image
[Rows,Cols] = size(A);
NumLevel = 4;   % # levels of DWT
TotalBands = 3*NumLevel + 1;
%RT = R*TotalBands;  % Total number of bits
RT = R*13;  % Total number of bits
typeOfBit = 'noninteger';
wname = 'coif2';
[C,S] = wavedec2(double(A),NumLevel,wname);    % 3-level
DWT2
%    find the variances of the different scales
for l = 1:NumLevel
    if l == NumLevel
        cA = appcoef2(C,S,wname,l);
        VarOfCoef(l,1) = std2(cA)^2;
        [H,V,D] = detcoef2('all',C,S,l);
        VarOfCoef(l,2) = std2(H)^2;
        VarOfCoef(l,3) = std2(V)^2;
        VarOfCoef(l,4) = std2(D)^2;
    else
        [H,V,D] = detcoef2('all',C,S,l);
        VarOfCoef(l,2) = std2(H)^2;
        VarOfCoef(l,3) = std2(V)^2;
        VarOfCoef(l,4) = std2(D)^2;
    end
end
%
R1 = zeros(NumLevel,4);
```

```
switch typeOfBit
    case 'noninteger'
        GeoMeanOfVar = 1;
        for l = 1:NumLevel
            if l == NumLevel
                startBand = 1;
            else
                startBand = 2;
            end
            for k = startBand:4
                P1 = VarOfCoef(l,k) ^
                (1/(TotalBands));
                GeoMeanOfVar = GeoMeanOfVar*P1;
            end
        end
        % find the optimal quantzer bits
        for k = 1:NumLevel
            if k == NumLevel
                startBand = 1;
            else
                startBand = 2;
            end
            for l = startBand:4
                b = R +
0.5*log10(VarOfCoef(k,l)/GeoMeanOfVar)/log10(2);
                if b < 0
                    R1(k,l) = 0;
                else
                    R1(k,l) = floor(b);
                end
            end
        end
    case 'integer'
        Var = VarOfCoef;
        while RT > 0
            Max = -9999;
            for k = 1:NumLevel
                for l = 1:4
                    if Max < Var(k,l)
                        Max = Var(k,l);
                        Indx = [k l];
```

```
                              end
                          end
                      end
                      R1(Indx(1),Indx(2)) = R1(Indx(1),Indx(2)) +
1;
                      Var(Indx(1),Indx(2)) =
Var(Indx(1),Indx(2))/2;
                      RT = RT - 1;
              end
end
%
%     convert the bits to Q step
R1 = (2 .^ R1); % convert bits to # levels
%for l = 1:4
%     R1(l,:) = R1(l,:)/(4^l);
%end
for k = 1:NumLevel
      for l = 1:4
            if R1(k,l) == 1
                  Qstep(k,l) = 35;
            else
                  %Qstep(k,l) =
round(2*sqrt(VarOfCoef(k,l))/R1(k,l));
                  Qstep(k,l) =
round(sqrt(VarOfCoef(k,l))/R1(k,l));
            end
      end
end
%     Quantize the coefficients
%l1 = NumLevel;
l1 = 3;
for l = NumLevel:-1:1
    if l == NumLevel
            cA = appcoef2(C,S,wname,l);
            cA1 = round(cA / Qstep(l,1))*Qstep(l,1);
            [H,V,D] = detcoef2('all',C,S,l);
            H1 = round(H / Qstep(l,2))*Qstep(l,2);
            V1 = round(V / Qstep(l,3))*Qstep(l,3);
            D1 = round(D / Qstep(l,4))*Qstep(l,4);
            y = idwt2(cA1,H1,V1,D1,wname,S(l1,:));
      else
```

```
            l1 = l1 +1;
            [H,V,D] = detcoef2('all',C,S,1);
            H1 = round(H / Qstep(1,2))*Qstep(1,2);
            V1 = round(V / Qstep(1,3))*Qstep(1,3);
            D1 = round(D / Qstep(1,4))*Qstep(1,4);
            y = idwt2(y,H1,V1,D1,wname,S(l1,:));
        end
end
figure,imshow(A),title('Original image')
figure,imshow(y,[]),title('DWT compressed/decompressed
image')
%
PSNR = 20*log10(255/std2(double(A)-y))   % find the PSNR




%    dwtTile.m
%    performs dwt2 on tiles of an image
%    Tile size can be changed by assigning values to
%    TileRows and TileCols.
%    Typically TileRows = image height/2 and
%    TileCols = image width/2
%    Author: K.S. Thyagarajan

A = imread('barbara.ras');  % read an image
[Height,Width] = size(A);
%TileRows = size(A,1)/2;  % tile size
%TileCols = size(A,2)/2;
TileRows = Height/8;  % tile size
TileCols = Width/8;
NumLevel = 4;    % # levels of DWT
wname = 'coif2'; % wavelet name
%    perform 2D DWT on each tile of NumLevel
for m = 1:TileRows:Height
    row = floor(m/TileRows)+1;
    for n = 1:TileCols:Width
        col = floor(n/TileCols)+1;
        temp = double(A(m:m+TileRows-1,n:n+TileCols-1));
        [C,S] = wavedec2(temp,NumLevel,wname);       %
% NumLevel DWT2
        C1(row,col,:) = C;
    end
end
```

```
%     reconstruct the image from the 2D DWT coefficients
for m = 1:Height/TileRows
    rowBegin = (m-1)*TileRows + 1;
    rowEnd = rowBegin + TileRows - 1;
    for n = 1:Width/TileCols
        colBegin = (n-1)*TileCols + 1;
        colEnd = colBegin + TileCols - 1;
        ll = 3;
        for l = NumLevel:-1:1
            if l == NumLevel
                    cA = appcoef2(C1(m,n,:),S,wname,l); %
% extract approx. coefficients
                    [H,V,D] =
detcoef2('all',C1(m,n,:),S,l);
                    y = idwt2(cA,H,V,D,wname,S(ll,:));
              else
                    ll = ll + 1;
                    [H,V,D] =
detcoef2('all',C1(m,n,:),S,l);
                    y = idwt2(y,H,V,D,wname,S(ll,:));
              end
          end
          OutImg(rowBegin:rowEnd,colBegin:colEnd) = y;
      end
end
std2(double(A)-OutImg)
figure,imshow(A),title('Original image')
figure,imshow(OutImg,[]),title('Tiled dwt/idwt image')



%     DWTvarOfCoef.m
%     Computes the variance of the 2D DWT coefficients
%     at different scales.
%     The output is a matrix with number of rows = number
%     of DWT level,
%     and the number of columns = 4.
%     The first row corresponds to the lowest level and
%     the last
%     row to the highest level coefficient variances.
%     Note that the highest level consists of
```

```
%     approximation and
%     detail coefficients while other levels have only the
%     details.
%     The details are Horizontal, Vertical, and Diagonal.
%     Author: K.S. Thyagarajan


A = imread('barbara.ras');   % read an image
%
NumLevel = 4;    % # levels of DWT
%
wname = 'coif2';
[C,S] = wavedec2(double(A),NumLevel,wname);        %
% NumLevel DWT2
%     find the variances of the different scales
for l = 1:NumLevel
    if l == NumLevel
        cA = appcoef2(C,S,wname,l);
        VarOfCoef(l,1) = std2(cA)^2;
        MagSq(l,1) = sum(sum(cA .* cA));
        [H,V,D] = detcoef2('all',C,S,l);
        VarOfCoef(l,2) = std2(H)^2;
        VarOfCoef(l,3) = std2(V)^2;
        VarOfCoef(l,4) = std2(D)^2;
        MagSq(l,2) = sum(sum(H .* H));
        MagSq(l,3) = sum(sum(V .* V));
        MagSq(l,4) = sum(sum(D .* D));
    else
        [H,V,D] = detcoef2('all',C,S,l);
        VarOfCoef(l,2) = std2(H)^2;
        VarOfCoef(l,3) = std2(V)^2;
        VarOfCoef(l,4) = std2(D)^2;
        MagSq(l,2) = sum(sum(H .* H));
        MagSq(l,3) = sum(sum(V .* V));
        MagSq(l,4) = sum(sum(D .* D));
    end
end
MagSq
sum(MagSq(:))
sum(sum(double(A) .* double(A)))
```

```
%       Entropy.m
%       Plots the histogram of the image and computes its
%       entropy
%       H in bits
%       Author: K.S. Thyagarajan

%A = imread('barbara.ras');
A = imread('cornfield.ras');
figure,imshow(A),title('Original Image')
%
imSize = size(A,1) * size(A,2);
[p,x] = imhist(A);
%
p = p/imSize;
%
figure,plot(x,p,'k'),title('Histogram of the image')
xlabel('Pixel value'), ylabel('relative count')
H = sum(-p .* log10(p+1e-06))/log10(2)
```

```
function AvgCodeLn = GRcode(E)
%       Determine the average length of Golomb-Rice code
%       for the residual image E
%       Author: K.S. Thyagarajan

E1 = E;
[y,x] = find(E<0);
% map all negative values to odd positive integers
for i = 1:size(x,1)
    E1(y(i),x(i)) = 2*abs(E(y(i),x(i)))-1;
end
clear x y;
[y,x] = find(E>=0);
% map all positive values to even positive integers
for i = 1:size(x,1)
    E1(y(i),x(i)) = 2*E(y(i),x(i));
end
% determine m = 2^k
k = ceil(log10(mean(E1(:)))/log10(2));
m = 2^k;
```

```
N = max(E1(:)) + 1;
[Bin,H] = showHistogram(E1,N);
Total = sum(H);
H = H/Total;
%figure, plot(Bin,H)
% compute the average length of GR code = k+floor(n/m)+1
AvgCodeLn = sum((floor(Bin/m)) .* H)+k+1;




%     OptBitAssign.m
%     Assigns quantizer bits optimally using
%     isotropic covariance model r(m,n) = sig^2 exp(-
%     |a|sqrt(m^2+n^2))
%     Author: K.S. Thyagarajan

N = 16;   % 8 x 8 block
A = imread('barbara.ras');   % read an image
[Rows,Cols] = size(A);
fun = @dct2;
T = blkproc(A,[N N],fun);    % do N x N 2D DCT
%     compute the DCT coefficient variance
for k = 1:N
    for l = 1:N
        V = std2(T(k:N:Rows,l:N:Cols));
        VarOfCoef(k,l) = V * V;
    end
end

%
R = 1.0;     % overall average bit rate is 1 bpp
P1 = VarOfCoef .^ (1/(N^2));
GeoMeanOfVar = prod(P1(:)); % geometric mean of the
%     coef. variances
for k = 1:N
    for l = 1:N
        b = R + 0.5*log10(VarOfCoef(k,l)/GeoMeanOfVar)/
        log10(2);
        if b < 0
            R1(k,l) = 0;
```

```
            else
                  R1(k,l) = floor(b);
            end
      end
end



%     OptIntgrBitAssign.m
%     Assigns quantizer bits optimally using
%     recursive integer bit allocation rule.
%     Author: K.S. Thyagarajan

N = 8;   % N x N block
M = N*N;
R = 1.0;     % overall average bit rate is 1 bpp
RT = M*R;    % total bits for the N x N block
A = imread('barbara.ras');   % read an image
[Rows,Cols] = size(A);
fun = @dct2;
T = blkproc(A,[N N],fun);    % do N x N 2D DCT
%    compute the DCT coefficient variances
for k = 1:N
    for l = 1:N
          V = std2(T(k:N:Rows,l:N:Cols));
          VarOfCoef(k,l) = V * V;
    end
end
%    assign integer bits recursively
R1 = zeros(N,N);
Var = VarOfCoef;
while RT > 0
    Max = -9999;
    for k = 1:N
        for l = 1:N
              if Max < Var(k,l)
                    Max = Var(k,l);
                    Indx = [k l];
              end
        end
    end
```

```
        R1(Indx(1),Indx(2))  =  R1(Indx(1),Indx(2))  +  1;
        Var(Indx(1),Indx(2))  =  Var(Indx(1),Indx(2))/2;
        RT  =  RT  -  1;
end




%    OptIntgrBitDWT.m
%    Assigns quantizer bits optimally using
%    recursive integer bit allocation rule for the DWT
%    coefficients.
%    Author: K.S. Thyagarajan


R = 1.0;      % overall average bit rate is 1 bpp
A = imread('barbara.ras');   % read an image
[Rows,Cols] = size(A);
RT = R*4;
[Ta,Th,Tv,Td] = dwt2(double(A),'db4');   % 1-level DWT2
%    compute the DWT coefficient variances
VarOfCoef(1,1) = (std2(Ta))^2;
VarOfCoef(1,2) = (std2(Th))^2;
VarOfCoef(2,1) = (std2(Tv))^2;
VarOfCoef(2,2) = (std2(Td))^2;
%    assign integer bits recursively
R1 = zeros(2,2);
Var = VarOfCoef;
while RT > 0
    Max = -9999;
    for k = 1:2
        for l = 1:2
            if Max < Var(k,l)
                Max = Var(k,l);
                Indx = [k l];
            end
        end
    end
    R1(Indx(1),Indx(2))  =  R1(Indx(1),Indx(2))  +  1;
    Var(Indx(1),Indx(2))  =  Var(Indx(1),Indx(2))/2;
    RT  =  RT  -  1;
end
```

```
%     PredError.m
%     Computes optimal & suboptimal predictor coefficients
%     and finds the residual variance and prediction gain.
%     Author: K.S. Thyagarajan

A = imread('yacht.ras');
[Rows,Cols] = size(A);
%
A = double(A);
R(1) = sum(sum(A .* A));   % autocorrelation for lag 0
R(2) = sum(sum(A(:,2:Cols) .* A(:,1:Cols-1))); % auto.
% corr. for lag 1
R(3) = sum(sum(A(:,3:Cols) .* A(:,1:Cols-2))); % auto.
% corr. for lag 2
%
%     1st-order optimal predictor
a1 = R(2)/R(1);   % optimal 1st-order coefficient
e = A;
for m = 1:Rows
    for n = 2:Cols
            e(m,n) = A(m,n) - a1*A(m,n-1);
    end
end
figure,imshow(e,[]), title('1st-order prediction error')
VarE1 = mean(mean(e .* e));
VarA = (std2(A))^2;
G1 = 10*log10(VarA/VarE1)
N1 = floor(max(e(:)) - min(e(:)) + 1);
[Bin1,H1] = showHistogram(e,N1);
%
%     2nd-order optimal predictor
alfa = inv([R(1) R(2); R(2) R(1)]) * [R(2) R(3)]';
e = A;
for m = 1:Rows
    for n = 2:Cols
            if n > 2
                e(m,n) = A(m,n) - alfa(1)*A(m,n-1) -
alfa(2)*A(m,n-2);
            else
                e(m,n) = A(m,n) - alfa(1)*A(m,n-1);
            end
     end
end
```

```
figure,imshow(e,[]), title('2nd-order prediction error')
VarE2 = mean(mean(e .* e));
G2 = 10*log10(VarA/VarE2)
N2 = floor(max(e(:)) - min(e(:)) + 1);
[Bin2,H2] = showHistogram(e,N2);
%
figure,subplot(2,1,1),plot(Bin1,H1,'k')
title('1st-order prediction'),ylabel('count')
subplot(2,1,2),plot(Bin2,H2,'k')
title('2nd-order prediction'),xlabel('pixel
error'),ylabel('count')




%    Residue.m
%    Computes the difference of two image frames
%    and computes the histogram of the residue
%    Author: K.S. Thyagarajan

%Frm1 = imread('tt005.ras');
%Frm2 = imread('tt006.ras');
Frm1 = imread('twy014.ras');
Frm2 = imread('twy015.ras');
e = double(Frm1) - double(Frm2);    % obtain the
% residual
figure,imshow(e,[])
N = max(e(:)) - min(e(:)) + 1;  % number of bins in the
% histogram
[Bin,H] = showHistogram(e,N);   % compute the histogram
Total = sum(H); % total count
H = H/Total;    % normalize the hisyogram by the total
% count
figure,plot(Bin,H,'k')
xlabel('pixel difference'), ylabel('Normalized count')




%    TCquantize.m
%    Assigns quantizer bits using optimal bit allocation
%    rule and
%    quantizes the coefficients using uniform quantizers
```

```
%     Author: K.S. Thyagarajan
%

N = 8;   % 8 x 8 block
Type = 'optimalInt';
Qtype = 'uniform';
Scale = 1.0;
R = 0.5;     % overall average bit rate is 1 bpp
jpgMat = [16  11  10  16  24  40  51  61;
          12  12  14  19  26  58  60  55;
          14  13  16  24  40  57  69  56;
          14  17  22  29  51  87  80  62;
          18  22  37  56  68  109 103 77;
          24  35  55  64  81  194 113 92;
          49  64  78  87  103 121 120 101;
          72  92  95  98  121 100 103 99];
A = imread('barbara.ras');   % read an image
[Rows,Cols] = size(A);
fun = @dct2;
T = blkproc(A,[N N],fun);    % do N x N 2D DCT
%for k = 1:N
%    for l = 1:N
%           acMax(k,l) =
%    max(max(max(T(k:N:Rows,l:N:Cols))),
%    abs(min(min(T(k:N:Rows,l:N:Cols)))));
%    end
%end
%
switch Type
    case 'optimal'
          %    compute the DCT coefficient variances
          for k = 1:N
              for l = 1:N
                    V = std2(T(k:N:Rows,l:N:Cols));
                    VarOfCoef(k,l) = V * V;
              end
          end
          StdOfCoef = sqrt(VarOfCoef);
          % compute geometric mean of the coef. variances
          P1 = VarOfCoef .^ (1/(N^2));
          GeoMeanOfVar = prod(P1(:));
```

```
% find the optimal quantzer bits
for k = 1:N
    for l = 1:N
        b = R +
0.5*log10(VarOfCoef(k,l)/GeoMeanOfVar)/log10(2);
        if b < 0
            R1(k,l) = 0;
        else
            R1(k,l) = floor(b);
        end
    end
end

R1(1,1) = 8; %    Assign different bit length
to the DC
R1 = (2 .^ R1); % convert bits to # levels
%
case 'optimalInt'
    %    compute the DCT coefficient variances
    for k = 1:N
        for l = 1:N
            V = std2(T(k:N:Rows,l:N:Cols));
            VarOfCoef(k,l) = V * V;
        end
    end
    %    assign integer bits recursively
    R1 = zeros(N,N);
    Var = VarOfCoef;
    RT = R*N*N;
    while RT > 0
        Max = -9999;
        for k = 1:N
            for l = 1:N
                if Max < Var(k,l)
                    Max = Var(k,l);
                    Indx = [k l];
                end
            end
        end
        R1(Indx(1),Indx(2)) = R1(Indx(1),Indx(2)) + 1;
```

```
                              Var(Indx(1),Indx(2)) =
Var(Indx(1),Indx(2))/2;
                  RT = RT - 1;
            end
         R1 = (2 .^ R1); % convert bits to # levels
         switch Qtype
              case 'uniform'
                   %    convert the bits to Q step
                   for k = 1:N
                        for l = 1:N
                             if R1(k,l) == 1
                                  Qstep(k,l) = 50;
                             else
                                  %Qstep(k,l) =
round(sqrt(VarOfCoef(k,l))/R1(k,l));
                                  Qstep(k,l) =
round(2*sqrt(VarOfCoef(k,l))/R1(k,l));
                             end
                        end
                   end
                   %    Quantize the rest of the
                   %    coefficients
                   for k = 1:N:Rows
                        for l = 1:N:Cols
                             T1(k:k+N-1,l:l+N-1) =
round(T(k:k+N-1,l:l+N-1)./ Qstep).*Qstep;
                        end
                   end
              case 'nonuniform'
                   % tables of decision & reconstruction
                   % levels
                   d(1,1) = 0; r(1,1) = 0;
                   d(2,1) = 0; r(2,1) = .7071;
                   d(2,2) = inf; r(2,2) = r(2,1);
                   %
                   d(4,1) = 0; r(4,1) = 0.4198;
                   d(4,2) = 1.1269; r(4,2) = 1.8340;
                   d(4,3) = inf; r(4,3) = r(4,2);
                   %
                   d(8,1) = 0; r(8,1) = 0.2334;
                   d(8,2) = 0.5332; r(8,2) = 0.8330;
```

```matlab
                              d(8,3) = 1.2528; r(8,3) = 1.6725;
                              d(8,4) = 2.3797; r(8,4) = 3.0868;
                              d(8,5) = inf; r(8,5) = r(8,4);
                              %    Quantize the rest of the
% coefficients

                              for k = 1:N:Rows
                                  for l = 1:N:Cols
                                      for m = k:k+N-1
                                          m1 = mod(m,N);
                                          if m1 == 0
                                              m1 = N;
                                          end;
                                          for n = 1:l+N-1
                                              n1 = mod(n,N);
                                              if n1 == 0
                                                  n1 = N;
                                              end
                                              L = R1(m1,n1);
                                              if m1 == 1 & n1 ==
1
                                                  T1(m,n) =
round(T(m,n)/8)*8;

                                              elseif L == 1
                                                  T1(m,n) = 0;
                                              else
                                                  flag = 1;
                                                  if T(m,n) < 0
                                                      flag = -1;
                                                  end
                                                  t =
abs(T(m,n))/StdOfCoef(m1,n1);

                                                  for s = 1:L/2
                                                      if
t>=d(L,s) & t<d(L,s+1)

T1(m,n) = StdOfCoef(m1,n1)*r(s)* flag;

break;

                                                      end
                                                  end
                                              end
```

```
                                    end
                            end
                        end
                    end
            end
        case 'jpg'
            Qstep = jpgMat * Scale;
            %    Quantize the rest of the coefficients
            for k = 1:N:Rows
                for l = 1:N:Cols
                    T1(k:k+N-1,l:l+N-1) = round(T(k:k+N-
1,l:l+N-1)./ Qstep).*Qstep;
                end
            end
end
%
%    obtain the IDCT
fun = @idct2;
y = blkproc(T1,[N N],fun);
figure,imshow(A),title('Original image')
figure,imshow(y,[]),title('Compressed/decompressed image')
%
MSE = std2(double(A)-y)^2;
PSNR = 10*log10(255^2/MSE)
```

D | Suggested MATLAB-Oriented Projects

APPENDIX

For all the suggested projects you can use the MATLAB tool to implement them. You will need image processing and wavelet toolboxes for these projects.

D.1 PROJECTS IN CHAPTER 2

D.1.1 Effect of Filtering an Image

Study the effects of filtering an intensity image through different filters. Read an intensity image, e.g., Barbara image. This image has some fine structures and so the effect of filtering will be clear. Design low-pass and high-pass filters of suitable size and filter the image through them and display the filtered images. You can design either 1-D filters or true 2-D filters for this project. If the filter size is large, the filter will have a tendency to introduce ringing along the edges. Try and observe such a phenomenon. Would you prefer FIR or IIR filters?

D.1.2 Nonlinear Filtering

Read an intensity image that has very poor contrast but a fairly high intensity range. Design a suitable filter for processing the image homomorphically. The homomorphic filter you design is supposed to cut down the illumination and boost the high-frequency details to produce an improved, overall contrast.

D.1.3 Phase Distortion

Filters with nonlinear phase response tend to introduce *phase* distortion in the processed image. This may be objectionable in some applications. For this project, design a low-pass filter with a nonlinear phase. Generally, IIR filters exhibit nonlinear phase characteristics as well as the optimally designed

(Chebyshev) FIR filters. Pick any one of the types and pass an intensity image through this filter and compare it with the original image.

D.2   PROJECTS IN CHAPTER 3

D.2.1   Contrast Sensitivity

Generate a sinusoidal grating intensity image and modify it by the contrast sensitivity of the human visual system. When you view the image from a normal viewing distance, you should be able to see the shape of the contrast sensitivity (roughly an inverted parabola) function.

D.2.2   Spatial Masking Effect

Use Girod's linearized HVS model to generate the spatial masking curve. Generate an intensity image that has a sharp vertical line of high intensity in the middle, lower uniform intensity on to the left, and somewhat higher intensity to the right of the vertical line. Repeat the experiment with varying thickness of the vertical line and observe the difference, if any.

D.2.3   Color Sensitivity

The aim of this project is to determine how sensitive your vision is to small color differences. You should create an RGB image of a certain brightness and saturation and vary the hue around a nominal value. For this purpose, it is better to create an HSI image first and then convert to RGB for displaying. Vary the hue slightly around the nominal value and compute the color distance between the two images.

D.3   PROJECTS IN CHAPTER 5

D.3.1   Adaptive Histogram Equalization

Consider an intensity image with very poor contrast and low intensity. Process the image using adaptive histogram equalization such that the processed image has a histogram following a power law in each region.

D.3.2   Noise Cleaning

Add noise to an intensity image. You may consider two types of noise, namely Gaussian noise with a specified SNR value and salt and pepper noise with a specified density. Try different order statistics filters, such as the median filter to remove noise from the image. If you have noticed that the median filter does a better job on salt and pepper noise, explain why. Study the effect of median filtering on the size of the filter. You may try 3×3, 5×5, and 7×7 for this purpose. Gaussian noise can be reduced more effectively using the so-called *Wiener* filtering. MATLAB has the function to design Wiener filters. Use the built-in function to clean the image with Gaussian noise.

D.3.3   Color Image Enhancement

Apply the aforementioned two projects to a color image. Start with an RGB image and convert it to a suitable color space and then apply the techniques. Consider one project at a time. You may want to try these two projects using more than one color space, e.g., RGB and HSI.

D.4   PROJECTS IN CHAPTER 8

D.4.1   DPCM

Design an optimal, second-order, line-by-line DPCM to compress an intensity image. Assume that you have the budget for a 2-bit/pixel encoding rate. You must design the optimal quantizer and Huffman codebook to encode the differential image. Your program should then read the compressed image file and decompress it. Calculate the PSNR of the decompressed image.

D.4.2   DPCM Using GR Coding

Repeat Section D.4.1 using Golomb–Rice codes instead of Huffman codes.

D.4.3   Transform Coder

Design a DCT-based block encoder whose encoding rate is 0.5 bit/pixel. Choose a block size of 8×8 pixels and a uniform quantizer for the coefficients. You can use the optimal bit allocation rule to assign bits to the quantizers. In order to generate a compressed bit stream, you may have to generate Huffman codes for the RLC. Calculate the resulting PSNR of the decompressed image. Use an intensity image for this project.

D.4.4   Transform Coder for Color Images

Repeat Section D.4.3 to encode a color image. Work with the YCbCr color space. If you really want to write the compressed bit stream to a file, you have to generate Huffman codes for the RLC on all three components. After decompression, convert decompressed data to RGB space for visualizing.

D.4.5   Encoder Using Discrete Wavelet Transform

Consider the design of a DWT-based encoder for an intensity image. Choose a suitable wavelet and the number of levels of DWT. The average encoder bit rate should be 0.5 bit/pixel. Use the optimal bit assignment rule to determine the number of bits for the uniform quantizers. Optionally, you can design the Huffman codes for the quantized coefficients, generate the bit streams, decode, and decompress the image.

D.4.6   DWT Encoder for Color Image Compression

Repeat Section D.4.5 to compress a color image. Use a suitable color space to work with.

D.4.7   Motion Estimation

Consider a sequence image and estimate the motion between two consecutive frames. Because motion estimation is computationally intensive, especially the brute force method, use a small image (256×256 pixels or less) for this project. Use a block size of 16×16 pixels and MAD as the matching criterion. It would be interesting to plot the motion vectors as a quiver plot. MATLAB has a built-in quiver function that is suitable for this purpose.

Index

A

ABSCT, *see* Adaptive block-size discrete
    cosine transform
Adaptive block-size discrete cosine
    transform, QUALCOMM digital
    cinema system
  decoder, 292
  encoder, 290–291
Adaptive histogram equalization
  image enhancement, 104, 320–321
  MATLAB exercises, 368
Arithmetic coding, lossless compression,
    206–208
ASIC chip, QUALCOMM digital cinema
    system
  audio processing, 294
  decompression, 294
  playback output, 294–295
  security functions, 292, 294
Atom, Motion JPEG2000, 296

B

Biorthogonal discrete wavelet transform, *see*
    Wavelet transform
Blackman window, function, 32
Brightness, perception, 47–49

C

CCD, *see* Charge-coupled device
CFA, *see* Color filter array

Charge-coupled device
  architecture
    frame-transfer, 77, 79
    full-frame, 76
    interline, 76
  color sensors, 79
  image quantization, *see* Quantization
  parameters, 75
  principles, 74–75
  self-scanning, 90
Chebyshev criterion, 40
Chromacity, 63
CMF, *see* Color matching function
CMOS sensor
  color sensors, 79
  principles, 79
Color filter array, color sensing, 79–80, 82
Color image enhancement, 117, 119–120,
    325–328, 369
Color matching function, 61–63
Color perception
  attributes, 60
  color coordinate systems
    chromacities, 63
    CIE XYZ primary system, 64–66
    National Television Systems Committee
      receiver and transmission
      primaries, 66–68
  color matching functions, 61–63
  MATLAB exercises for color sensitivity,
    368
  models, 69–70
  tristimulus theory, 60–61
Compression
  bandwidth versus data compression,
    193–194

Compression *(continued)*
  digital cinema, 287–288
  discrete image transforms, *see*
      Karhunen–Loeve transform;
      Unitary transforms
  human visual system considerations in
      image and video coding
    masking models, 266–270
    quantization matrix
      discrete cosine transform domain
          coding, 263–265
      wavelet domain coding, 265–266
  image fidelity criteria
    quantitative measures, 197–198
    subjective measures, 198–199
  intraframe images, 197
  JPEG2000, *see* JPEG2000
  loss of data, 194
  lossless compression
    arithmetic coding, 206–208
    Golomb–Rice coding, 208, 210,
        355–356, 369
    Huffman coding, 202–205
    information theory, 199–200
    run-length coding, 205–206
  overview, 4–5
  predictive coding, *see* Predictive coding
  ratio, 193
  redundant data removal, 194–196, 346
  transform coding, *see* Transform coding
  video, *see* Video coding
  wavelet domain
    MATLAB encoders, 370
    overview, 231–232
    quantization, 234
    wavelet selection
      coding gain, 233
      filter length, 232
      linear or nonlinear phase, 232
      orthogonality, 233
      smoothness of filter, 233
    zero-tree wavelet coding
      coding significance map, 237
      embedded zero-tree wavelet coding,
          236
      example, 240–243
      overview, 234, 236
      successive approximation, 238–240
Computed tomography, 8
Cone, eye, 49
Contrast
  just noticeable difference, 51
  MATLAB files

luminance comparison, 313
  simultaneous contrast effect in human
      visual system, 316–317
  ratio, 50
  sensitivity, 50, 368
  sensitivity function, 54–55
  simultaneous contrast ratio, 50
Contrast stretching, image enhancement,
    98, 100, 318–320
CT, *see* Computed tomography

D

Data rates, television standards, 193–194
DCPM, *see* Differential pulse code
    modulation
Differential pulse code modulation
  adaptive differential pulse code
      modulation, 215–216
  MATLAB exercises, 369
  one-dimensional differential pulse code
      modulation, 212–215
  two-dimensional differential pulse code
      modulation, 218
Digital cinema system
  compression, 287–288
  frame rate, 286
  image resolution, 285–286
  Motion JPEG2000 standard
    error resilience, 296–297
    file format, 295–296
    format, 295
    overview, 295
    resolution, 295
    wavelet domain compression, 295
  projectors, 286–287
  prospects, 297–298
  QUALCOMM system
    adaptive block-size discrete cosine
        transform
      decoder, 292
      encoder, 290–291
    architecture, 289–290
    ASIC chip
      audio processing, 294
      decompression, 294
      playback output, 294–295
      security functions, 292, 294
Digital image light amplifier chip, digital
    cinema system projection,
    286–287
Digital image processing, scope, 1

Digital micromirror device chip, digital
cinema system projection,
286–287
D-ILA chip, *see* Digital image light amplifier
chip
Discrete image transforms, *see*
Karhunen–Loeve transform;
Unitary transforms
Discrete wavelet transform, *see* Wavelet
transform
DMD chip, *see* Digital micromirror device
chip

E

Edge sharpening, image enhancement,
107, 109, 322–323
Embedded zero-tree wavelet coding
coding significance map, 237
example, 240–243
overview, 236
successive approximation, 238–240
Enhancement
color image enhancement, 117, 119–120,
325–328
medical images, 2
neighborhood operations
homomorphic filtering, 116–117,
324–325
median filtering, 111, 113–114, 116, 324
simple mask operations
edge sharpening, 107, 109, 322–323
smoothing, 106–107, 321–322
two-dimensional finite impulse
response filter, 109, 111, 323–324
noise cleaning, 3–4
overview, 1–2, 97
point processing
adaptive histogram equalization, 104,
320–321, 368
contrast stretching, 98, 100, 318–320
histogram equalization, 101–102, 104,
329–330
logarithmic transformation, 98, 318
Entropy coding
coder, 226–230
JPEG2000, 253
three-dimensional discrete cosine
transform interframe coding,
261–263
EZW coding, *see* Embedded zero-tree
wavelet coding

F

Filmless movie, *see* Digital cinema system
Film-to-digital conversion, 93–94
Filtering, *see* Finite impulse response filter;
Homomorphic filtering; Median
filtering; Two-dimensional infinite
impulse response filter
Finite impulse response filter
nonseparable filter design, 40–42
separable filter design
frequency sampling, 36, 39
low-pass filter, 27, 311
MATLAB files, 311–312
optimization, 40
window-based methods, 27–29, 31–32,
34–36
two-dimensional finite impulse response
filter
advantages, 25–26
definition, 25
image enhancement, 109, 111,
323–324
nonseparable filter, 26
separable filter, 26
FIR filter, *see* Finite impulse response
filter
Fourier transform, *see* Two-dimensional
discrete Fourier transform
continuous transform
convolution theorem, 302
forward transform, 301
frequency response, 302
inverse transform, 301
linearity, 302
separability, 302
one-dimensional discrete Fourier
transform, 124–125
sampled image, 83, 317
short-time Fourier transform, 147
wavelet transform comparison, 147, 149
Frequency response, two-dimensional
discrete systems, 19–23
Frequency sampling, finite impulse
response filter design, 36, 39

G

GLV chip, *see* Grated light valve chip
Golomb–Rice coding, lossless compression,
208, 210, 355–356, 369
GOP, *see* Group of pictures

GR coding, *see* Golomb–Rice coding
Grated light valve chip, digital cinema
    system projection, 286–287
Group of pictures, MPEG, 271

H

Haar scaling functions, wavelet series
    calculation, 153, 155–156
Haar transform, 131
Hadamard transform, 128–130
Hamming window, function, 32
Hanning window, function, 31
Histogram equalization, image
    enhancement, 101–102, 104,
    329–330
Homomorphic filtering, image
    enhancement, 116–117,
    324–325
Hotelling transform, *see* Karhunen–Loeve
    transform
Huffman coding, lossless compression,
    202–205
Human visual system
  brightness perception, 47–49
  color perception
    attributes, 60
    color coordinate systems
      chromacities, 63
      CIE XYZ primary system, 64–66
      National Television Systems
        Committee receiver and
        transmission primaries, 66–68
    color matching functions, 61–63
    models, 69–70
    tristimulus theory, 60–61
  contrast
    just noticeable difference, 51
    ratio, 50
    sensitivity, 50
    sensitivity function, 54–55
    simultaneous contrast ratio, 50
  eye anatomy, 48–49
  image and video coding
    considerations
    masking models, 266–270
    quantization matrix
      discrete cosine transform domain
        coding, 263–265
      wavelet domain coding, 265–266
  impulse and frequency responses,
    314–315

Mach band effect, 52, 313–314
monochrome vision model, 55, 57
visual masking model of vision, 57–59
HVS, *see* Human visual system

I

Illumination, definition, 308
Image analysis, overview, 8, 11
Image sampling
  Fourier transform of sampled image, 83,
    317
  Nyquist frequencies, 85, 87
  sensor arrays, 82–83
  theorem, 85, 87
Image scanning
  color encoding subsampling schemes
    4:2:0, 92
    4:2:2, 92
    4:4:4, 91
  color image scanning, 91
  frame standards, 90
  interlaced scanning, 90–91
  progressive scanning, 91
  self-scanning, 90
Information theory, lossless compression,
    199–200
Interlaced scanning, 90–91
Irradiance, definition, 305

J

JPEG, compression standard, 223
JPEG2000
  component transformation, 245–246
  DC level shifting, 245
  encoding procedure, 244
  entropy coding, 253
  quantization, 252–253
  tiling, 244–245
  video standards, *see* Motion JPEG2000
  wavelet transform, 246–247

K

Kaiser window, finite impulse response
    filter design, 32, 34–35, 41
Karhunen–Loeve transform, 140,
    143–144
Key frames, MPEG, 271

■■■■ L

Lloyd–Max algorithm, 222
Lloyd–Max quantizer, 89
Logarithmic transformation, image
    enhancement, 98, 318
Lumen, definition, 307
Luminance
    definition, 307–308
    intensity relationship, 49
    MATLAB file for contrast comparison,
        313
Luminous flux, definition, 306–307
Luminous intensity, definition, 307

■■■■ M

Mach band effect, 52, 313–314
Macroblock, MPEG, 271
MAD, *see* Mean absolute difference
MATLAB
    biorthogonal discrete wavelet transform,
        168, 171, 342–343
    coding gain calculation, 348–352
    color image enhancement, 369
    contrast sensitivity exercise, 368
    discrete transform basis image
        generation, 331–333
    discrete wavelet transform, 353–355
    filtering exercises, 367
    frequency response for two-dimensional
        discrete system, 22–23, 310–311
    histogram of coefficients generation,
        334–339
    image enhancement
        adaptive histogram equalization, 104,
            320–321, 368
        color image enhancement, 117,
            119–120, 325–328
        contrast stretching, 98, 100,
            318–320
        edge sharpening, 107, 109,
            322–323
        histogram equalization, 101–102, 104,
            329–330
        homomorphic filtering, 116–117,
            324–325
        logarithmic transformation, 98, 318
        median filtering, 111, 113–114, 116,
            324
        noise removal programs
            adaptive filtering, 328–329

        neighborhood smoothing, median
            filtering, and adaptive filtering,
            330–331
        smoothing, 106–107, 321–322
    image sampling, 317
    installation, 309
    low-pass finite impulse response filters,
        27, 40, 311–312
    one-dimensional discrete cosine
        transform, 346–347
    quantizer bit assignment
        isotropic covariance model,
            356–357
        optimal bit allocation rule, 360–365
        recursive integer bit allocation rule,
            357–360
    two-dimensional discrete Fourier
        transform solution, 19,
        309–310
    wavelet compression encoders, 370
    wavelet construction, 171, 343–344
    wavelet series computation, 340–342
Mean absolute difference, motion
        estimation in video compression,
        258–259
Mean opinion score, image fidelity criteria,
        199
Median filtering, image enhancement, 111,
        113–114, 116, 324
Minimax criterion, 40
MJ2K, *see* Motion JPEG2000
Monochrome vision model, 55, 57
MOS, *see* Mean opinion score
Motion compensated prediction, video
        compression, 255
Motion JPEG2000
    error resilience, 296–297
    file format, 295–296
    format, 295
    overview, 295
    resolution, 295
    wavelet domain compression, 295
MPEG
    coder/decoder, 272
    coding
        B pictures, 276, 278
        I pictures, 272
        P pictures, 276, 278
    historical perspective of standards,
        270–271
    MPEG4, *see* Motion JPEG2000
    picture types, 271
    terminology, 271

N

National Television Systems Committee, receiver and transmission primaries, 66–68
Noise
  cleaning, 3–4, 369
  probability density functions
    Gaussian distribution, 113
    impulse noise, 114, 116
    Rayleigh distribution, 114
    uniform distribution, 113
NTSC, *see* National Television Systems Committee
Nyquist frequency, image sampling considerations, 85, 87

O

One-dimensional discrete cosine transform
  data compression, 195–196, 346–347
  overview, 125–126
One-dimensional discrete Fourier transform, 124–125
One-dimensional discrete Harley transform, 127–128
One-dimensional discrete sine transform, 126–127
Opponent color vision model, 70
Optimal bit allocation, overview, 220–222
Orthogonal discrete wavelet transform, *see* Wavelet transform

P

Phase distortion, MATLAB exercises, 367–368
Predictive coding
  adaptive differential pulse code modulation, 215–216
  one-dimensional differential pulse code modulation, 212–215
  overview, 195, 212
  two-dimensional differential pulse code modulation, 218
Probability density function, *see* Noise
Progressive scanning, 91

Q

QUALCOMM digital cinema system, *see* Digital cinema system
Quantization
  JPEG2000, 252–253
  Lloyd–Max quantizer, 89
  matrices for image and video coding
    discrete cosine transform domain coding, 263–265
    wavelet domain coding, 265–266
  optimal quantization, 88–89
  quantizer design
    coding gain, 224–226, 348–352
    discrete cosine transform, 222–223
    JPEG compression standard, 223
    three-dimensional discrete cosine transform interframe coding, 262
  uniform quantization, 87–88
  wavelet domain compression, 234

R

Radiance, definition, 306
Radiant energy, definition, 305
Radiant excitance, definition, 305
Radiant flux, definition, 305
Radiant intensity, definition, 306
Restoration, overview, 6–7
Rod, eye, 49
Run-length coding, lossless compression, 205–206

S

Scanning, *see* Image scanning
Signal-to-noise ratio
  equation, 197
  image fidelity criteria, 197–198
  peak signal-to-noise ratio, 198
  signal variance, 197–198
  uniform quantization, 88
Slant transform, 131–133
Smoothing, image enhancement, 106–107, 321–322
SNR, *see* Signal-to-noise ratio
Spatial masking, MATLAB exercise, 368
Subband coding scheme, two-dimensional discrete wavelet transform, 177, 180

T

Telecine, film-to-digital conversion, 93–94
Three-dimensional discrete cosine transform interframe coding
  entropy coding, 263
  equations, 261–262
  principles, 260
  quantization, 262
  temporal depth, 261
  zigzag scanning, 263
Transform coding
  components, 219
  entropy coder, 226–230
  MATLAB
    exercises, 369–370
    quantizer bit assignment, 360–365
  optimal bit allocation, 220–222
  overview, 218–219
  quantizer design
    coding gain, 224–226, 348–352
    discrete cosine transform, 222–223
    JPEG compression standard, 223
  unitary transform selection, 220
  variable block size discrete cosine transform coder, 230–231
Two-dimensional discrete cosine transform, coding gain calculation, 224–226, 348–352
Two-dimensional discrete Fourier transform
  array transform, 23
  derivation, 17–18, 303
  inverse discrete Fourier transform, 19
  inverse transform, 303
  MATLAB files, 309–310, 347–348
Two-dimensional discrete signals
  complex exponential, 13, 15
  impulse function, 13
  step function, 13
  sunusoidal signals, 15
Two-dimensional discrete systems
  causal systems, 17
  frequency response, 19–23
  linear systems, 15–16
  space invariant systems, 16
  stable systems, 17
  system response via two-dimensional convolution, 16–17
Two-dimensional infinite impulse response filter, definition, 25

U

Unitary transforms
  discrete transform properties
    conservation of energy, 137, 139
    energy compaction, 139
    fast transforms, 140
    transform coefficient amplitude distributions, 140
  one-dimensional unitary transforms
    Haar transform, 131
    Hadamard transform, 128–130
    linear transforms, 123–124
    one-dimensional discrete cosine transform, 125–126
    one-dimensional discrete Fourier transform, 124–125
    one-dimensional discrete Harley transform, 127–128
    one-dimensional discrete sine transform, 126–127
    orthogonal transform, 124
    slant transform, 131–133
    unitary transform, 124
  selection for application, 144
  transform coding, 220
  two-dimensional discrete transforms
    basis image, 134, 136–137, 331–333
    separable transforms, 133

V

Video coding
  human visual system considerations in image and video coding
    masking models, 266–270
    quantization matrix
      discrete cosine transform domain coding, 263–265
      wavelet domain coding, 265–266
  motion compensated prediction, 255
  motion estimation with MATLAB, 370
  MPEG, *see* MPEG
  overview, 5–6
  redundancy between frames, 255
  temporal prediction in pixel domain
    interframe predictive coder scheme, 256
    motion estimation, 256, 258–259
    three-dimensional discrete cosine transform interframe coding
      entropy coding, 263

Video coding *(continued)*
  equations, 261–362
  principles, 260
  quantization, 262
  temporal depth, 261
  zigzag scanning, 263
  wavelet-based interframe coding, 259
Video frame rate, 73, 286
Vision, *see* Human visual system

W

Wavelet transform
  compression, *see* Compression; Video
      coding
  continuous wavelet transform, 149–151
  discrete wavelet transform
    expression, 160
    implementation, 160–164
  Fourier transform comparison, 147, 149
  two-dimensional discrete wavelet
      transform
    four-level transform of orthogonal and
        biorthogonal wavelets, 180–181,
        188–189
    histogram calculations, 345
    overview, 171, 177
    subband coding scheme for
        calculation, 177, 180
  wavelet relationship to scaling and
      wavelet filters

biorthogonal discrete wavelet
    transform, 168, 171, 342–343
orthogonal discrete wavelet transform,
    166, 168
overview, 164, 166
wavelet construction, 171, 343–344
wavelet series
  computation with MATLAB,
      340–342
  expansion, 152
  Haar scaling functions in calculation,
      153, 155–156
Weber's law, 51–52

X

XYZ primary system, 64–66

Z

Zero-tree wavelet coding
  coding significance map, 237
  embedded zero-tree wavelet coding,
      236
  example, 240–243
  overview, 234, 236
  successive approximation, 238–240
Zigzag scanning, three-dimensional discrete
    cosine transform interframe
    coding, 263